All-Suite  Hotel Guide

Pamela Lanier

John Muir Publications

Other books by Pamela Lanier:

22 Days in Alaska (John Muir Publications)

The Complete Guide to Bed & Breakfasts, Inns and Guesthouses
(John Muir Publications)

Elegant Small Hotels: A Connoisseur's Guide (John Muir Publications)

The Bed & Breakfast Cookbook (Running Press)

To contact the Guide, please write to:

All-Suite Hotel Guide
P.O. Box 20429
Oakland, CA 94620-0429

Production and design by John Stick
Cover production & design by Mary Shapiro
Cover photograph: Embassy Suites Hotel at Oxnard-Mandalay Beach, CA

Published by: John Muir Publications
P.O. Box 613
Santa Fe, NM 87504

Library of Congress Catalog Card No. 88-42982

ISBN 0-945465-08-4

First Edition September 1987
Second Edition September 1988

Distributed to the booktrade by:
W.W. Norton & Company, Inc.
New York, NY

Printed in the United States of America

Contents

ACKNOWLEDGEMENTS

I would like to express my gratitude to the following people for their enthusiasm and support for this project, for their tremendous contribution to all-suite hotel development, and for their hospitality to the traveler:

Gus Boss, James Bradley, Robert Brock, John Burlingame, Curt Carlson, Joseph Cotter, Michael Dickens, Joe Faulk, Hervey Feldman, John Q. Hammons, Mark Harris, Michael Littler, John Norlander, Robert Palmer, Bob Pearce, Jim Pickett, Jack Rogers, Michael Rose, Mike Ruffer, Andre Tatibouet, and Robert Woolley.

I would also like to acknowledge the assistance rendered and information provided to me by the following individuals and organizations:

Beacon Hospitality/Guest Quarters: Bob Bettner, Lisa Fruitt and Dana Woods. *Best Western Bradbury Suites:* Suzanne Kunz and Cheryl Korenic. *Embassy Suites:* Patricia Cox, Ken Hamlet, Judy Heinrich, Joan Herman, Monica Hildebrand and Sean Keough, as well as Sara Lerner at Stern & Monroe. *Hawthorn Suites:* Joe McInerney. *Hilton Suites:* John Weeman and Mike Radell. *Laventhol & Horwath:* Elizabeth Rifkin and the research staff. *Lexington Companies:* J. Patrick Neeley. *Manhattan East Suite Hotels:* Priscilla Hurley. *Marriott Corporation:* Joel Eisemann and Julie Moll. *Michigan State School of Hotel and Restaurant Management:* Dr. Bonnie Knutson. *Pannell, Kerr & Forster:* Charles Kaiser, Jr., Ted Mandigo, Patrick Quek, Bonnie Blomarz, Peter Griffith, Maryellen Hogan and the research staff. *Park Suite Hotels:* Robin Cogdill and also Rebecca Binno of Sohigian and LaChiusa. *Pickett Hotel Company:* Francis Kercheval and Vendo Toming. *Quality International:* Ruth Ormsby and John Jorgenson. *Radisson Hotel Corporation:* Jaryon Bartells, Jay Witzel, Tom Polski, Alice Anderson and Jack Bunett. *Residence Inns by Marriott:* Martha Ballard, Lorraine Epperly, B. Anthony Isaac, Lisa Jabarra and Pat Sanders. *Sheraton Corporation:* Rick Kasch. *The Management Group, Inc.:* C.A. (Bud) Cataldo. *The Warmington Group:* Harold Parker. *Hardage Management:* Ray Hendon. *Doubletree Inns, Inc.:* Joe Salembier, and also Marian Eckstrom of The Fontayne Group. *Bleichner, Bonta, Martinez & Brown:* Ann S. Watson. *Aaron Cushman & Associates:* Megan Bueschel. *AmeriSuites:* Robin Goacher. *InnSuites:* Joel Burns. *Amberley Hotel Corporation:* Donald Redford.

For their assistance and devotion to this project I wish to especially thank the following people:

Marianne Barth, Laura Keenan, Mary Callahan, Bill Kane, Maggie Kane, Leslie Chan, Mary Shapiro, John Stick, and the staff of John Muir Publications.

Special thanks to Mort, Martha and especially Aaron Liebman of Copygraphics, Inc. in Santa Fe, New Mexico, for their dedication and care in bringing this book to type.

This book is dedicated to Mariposa and Juan.

Introduction

All-Suite Hotels provide travelers with a better alternative to traditional hotels and motels.

What Is An All-Suite Hotel?

An all-suite hotel is a lodging which features suites rather than single rooms. By suites we mean, generally, at least two distinct rooms, separated by a door which can be closed. Other than that primary criterion, the all-suite hotels we feature run the gamut from inexpensive (i.e., $30 per night) to the top of the line, and from city center locations to getaway resorts.

Who Stays in All-Suite Hotels?

A vast array of people from all walks of life utilize all-suite hotels: salespeople, engineers, accountants, lawyers and, especially on weekends, families.

The word "suite" conjures up images of entertainers, celebrities, and chairpersons of the board. Actually, nowadays anyone who appreciates the added value of staying in a suite can do so for little more than the price of an ordinary room in most hotels.

Why Stay In An All-Suite Hotel?

There are many reasons:

Business people love the convenience of having a real work place—almost all are equipped with a large desk with the phone right on it, and many have computer hookups.

A comfortable, well-appointed space with room to move around in, and for two people traveling together, the opportunity to have some separate space.

Families appreciate having a room for the kids and a room for Mom and Dad, usually each with its own TV.

The home-like atmosphere so important for relaxing after a hard day's work, and in addition, most suites provide a small kitchen to do a little cooking for yourself.

The flexibility of having a separate room in which to conduct business and do your work out of sight of the bedroom.

The convenience and time saved of waking up in the morning to a breakfast and not having to go out to a restaurant. In most cases the breakfast is complimentary, ready and waiting for you.

The pleasure of coming home to a warm and convivial atmosphere and perhaps relaxing with your fellow guests at the manager's complimentary cocktail party, a regular feature in many all-suite hotels.

We believe that American travelers want better accommodations, and all-suite hotels represent an excellent value for your money.

We hope this Guide will help you find the best hotel for your needs among the ever-increasing number of all-suite hotels available.

Have a good stay,
Pamela Lanier, August 1988

How To Use This Guide

How It Is Organized

This book is organized alphabetically by state, and within a state alphabetically by cities or towns. At the back of the guide is a cross reference index by name of hotel, listed alphabetically for your convenience.

Location

This section of each listing offers information on the distance from the airport, distance from downtown, and other major areas, and proximity to shopping, restaurants, and other important services and attractions.

Prices

Where available, we give the full range of each hotel's suite offering. All rates are for the lowest quoted price and are the most current available. However, we recommend that you call beforehand to verify rates and other amenities. The price code is as follows:

$ = up to 50 dollars $$ = 51-80 dollars $$$ = 81-110 dollars

$$$$ = 111-200 dollars $$$$+ = 201 dollars and up

All prices are expressed in U.S. dollars.

Many hotels offer discount rates to senior citizens and off-season guests, as well as discounts for long-term guests. Children are usually accommodated free when accompanied by their parents; however, be sure to check this at each hotel when you book your suite. We also make note under the price section which credit cards are accepted (Amex = American Express; MC = Master Card; Visa; and Other CC = other major credit cards) and whether a travel agent commission (TAC) is paid to travel professionals when they book a room.

Hotel Amenities

This section describes the hotel amenities available to guests, such as laundry, parking, car hire, TV lounge. In this section we also make special note of the availability of suites for the handicapped and the number of such suites, if known. (Make your reservation well in advance if a hotel has only a small number of suites for the handicapped.) Also noted is whether pets are permitted. As children are welcome in nearly all hotels listed, we only note those that do not allow children.

Business Facilities

We know that many of the people who stay in all-suite hotels are traveling business people. We have made a special point to find out about the services available in each hotel for business people, such as: secretarial services, copiers, a message center, computer hookups, teleconferencing, audio-visual equipment, conference room facilites and banquet facilities. We note if the hotel has a complete business service center on the premises.

Recreational Facilities

In this section of each listing we indicate what recreational facilities are available to guests, such as: swimming pools, whirlpools, saunas, fitness centers, tennis courts as well as nearby golf courses, fishing, hiking, boating, etc. And for the indoor sports we make note if there is a game room available.

Restaurants

Under food facilities, we make note of the name of the restaurant and indicate if there is entertainment available in the public areas.

Complimentary Features

Here we discuss whether the establishment provides a complimentary breakfast, and if so, what type of breakfast. "Continental" we define as juice, coffee, bread or pastry. "Continental plus" includes juice, coffee, a choice of several breads and pastries, and possibly more. We define a "Full Breakfast" as one that includes eggs or meat with the usual breads, toast, juice and coffee.

We also make note of whether the establishment offers complimentary refreshments such as cocktails and possibly hors d'oeuvres. One of the things many people enjoy most about all-suite hotels is the convivial evening refreshment hour. Where it is available we note it.

Room Amenities

In this section we note those amenities that pertain particularly to the rooms themselves, such as a complimentary newspaper, TV, whether there is cable TV or a video cassette machine, telephones and how many, radio, wet bar, kitchen, individual air and heat control, whatever special features the hotel offers.

We include a description of some of the special features of the property.

Reservations

Reservations are advised at all times. We include toll-free reservation numbers where available. Please be sure to confirm all of the features offered by the hotel as well as the price.

Every attempt has been made to provide current information. Most of the information in this Guide has been provided by the hotel's management, and management policies may change. If you feel that anything in this book is inaccurate, please inform us so that we can correct it in future editions. We appreciate readers' comments.

We have made every attempt to locate all of the all-suite hotels that are currently open; however, there may be some that we are not aware of. If you know of an all-suite hotel which is not listed here, please drop us a line at All-Suite Hotel Guide, P.O. Box 20429, Oakland, CA 94620.

 Alabama

BIRMINGHAM

Embassy Suites Hotel
2300 Woodcrest Place
Birmingham, AL 35209

243 Suites
205-879-7400 800-362-2779

Location: Homewood; Downtown
Airport: 15 min.
Near: Rolling Hills, Palisades Shops, Health Club
Walking Distance To: Downtown
Area Attractions: Zoo, Museum, Botanical Gardens, Univ. of Alabama

Price Range & Credit Cards: 1 Bedroom Suite $$, 2 Bedrooms $$$$, AmEx/MC/Visa/Other CC, Children Free, TAC 7%

Hotel Amenities: Laundry, Car Hire, TV Lounge, Pets Allowed, Handicap (12)

Business Facilities: Conf. Rm. Cap. 250, Banquet Fac., Copier, Aud/Vis.

Recreational Facilities: Pool, Sauna, Whirlpool; Steam room

Restaurant/Bar: Entertainment

Comps: Full Breakfast, Refreshments, Hors d'oeuvres

Room Amenities: Room Service, Free Paper, TV, Phones in Rm. (2), Cable TV, Radio, Wet Bar, Kitchen, Ind. Heat Ctl., Ind. AC Ctl.

Close to the airport and downtown this 2-acre property is enhanced by lush tropical plants surrounding gazebo waterfalls and an open atrium. Every suite features a balcony overlooking the memorable rolling hills of Alabama. The surrounding area offers many attractions including: Botanical Gardens, the Palisades Shopping Center, and a Zoo.

━━━━━━━━━━━━━━ BIRMINGHAM ━━━━━━━━━━━━━━

The Residence Inn by Marriott
3 Greenhill Parkway & Rt. 280
Birmingham, AL 35242

128 Suites
205-991-8686 800-331-3131

Location: Southside; Downtown: 10 mi.
Airport: 14 miles
Near: Inverness Area, Galleria Shops
Walking Distance To: Lake
Area Attractions: Lake, Oak Mountain State
Park, Fishing, Zoo

Price Range & Credit Cards: 1 Bedroom Suite $$$, 2 Bedrooms $$$, AmEx/MC/
Visa/Other CC, Children Free, TAC 10%

Hotel Amenities: Laundry, Library, Parking, TV Lounge, Pets Allowed, Handicap (12)

Business Facilities: Conf. Rm. Cap. 15, Copier, Aud/Vis.

Recreational Facilities: Pool, Sauna, Fitn. Ctr., Golf, Fishing, Hiking, Recreation Pass,
Game Area; Health Club privileges

Comps: Continental Breakfast, Hospitality Hour

Room Amenities: TV, Phone in Rm., Cable TV, Kitchen, Ind. Heat Ctl., Ind. AC Ctl.

Situated on a private lake The Residence Inn by Marriott offers you a pleasant and tranquil setting. Golf, fishing and hiking are all nearby. The Riverchase Galleria is a shopper's delight with over 200 shops to entice you. Experience the beauty of Birmingham (THE MAGIC CITY). Rates discounted for extended stay. A real value for your money.

━━━━━━━━━━━━━━ DECATUR ━━━━━━━━━━━━━━

Amberley Suite Hotel
807 Bank St., N.E.
Decatur, AL 35601

110 Suites
205-355-6800 800-228-5151

Location: Historic; Downtown
Airport: Hway. 20 W.
Near: Old State Bk.Museum, Point Mallard Pool
Walking Distance To: Wave Pool
Area Attractions: Alabama Space & Rocket
Center

Price Range & Credit Cards: 1 Bedroom Suite $$, 2 Bedrooms $$$, Junior $, AmEx/
MC/Visa/Other CC, Children Free, TAC 10%

Hotel Amenities: Laundry, TV Lounge, Pets Allowed, Handicap (1)

Business Facilities: Conf. Rm. Cap. 85, Banquet Fac., Copier, Aud/Vis.

Recreational Facilities: Pool, Sauna, Whirlpool, Fitn. Ctr., Tennis, Golf, Skiing, Game
Area, Ice skating

Restaurant/Bar: Watson's Cafe

Comps: Hors d'oeuvres

Room Amenities: TV, Phones in Rm. (2), Cable TV, Radio, Wet Bar, Kitchen, Ind. Heat
Ctl., Ind. AC Ctl.

Located in Old Decatur, Amberley Suites is adjacent to the Old Bank which was built in 1833. Historic homes from a bygone time are within walking distance. For business there are 3 Banquet/Conference rooms, copiers and an audio-visual room. And leisure activities abound nearby with an 18-hole golf course, tennis and the wave pool.

---------------------- HUNTSVILLE ----------------------

Amberley Suite Hotel
4880 University Dr.
Huntsville, AL 35816

140 Suites
205-837-4070 800-228-5151

Location: Northside; Downtown: 5 miles
Airport: 1 mile west
Near: Research Park, Health Club, Restaurant Row
Walking Distance To: Space and Rocket Center
Area Attractions: North Alabama's Largest Mall

Price Range & Credit Cards: 1 Bedroom Suite $$, 2 Bedrooms $$$, Junior $$, AmEx/ MC/Visa/Other CC, Children Free, TAC 10%

Hotel Amenities: Laundry, TV Lounge, Pets Allowed, Handicap (8)

Business Facilities: Conf. Rm. Cap. 125, Banquet Fac., Mess. Ctr., Sec. Serv., Copier, Aud/Vis., Comp. Hook-up

Recreational Facilities: Pool, Sauna, Whirlpool, Fitn. Ctr., Golf, Game Area

Restaurant/Bar: Watson's Cafe

Comps: Hors d'oeuvres

Room Amenities: TV, Phone in Rm., Cable TV, Radio, Wet Bar, Kitchen, Ind. Heat Ctl., Ind. AC Ctl.

The comfort of home with the full service of a luxury hotel is what Amberley supplies. Here you'll be frequently surprised by the little things provided like kitchens with built-in microwaves and coffee makers. You will also appreciate the fully appointed 24-hour health facility, and a contemporary delicatessen.

---------------------- HUNTSVILLE ----------------------

The Residence Inn by Marriott
4020 Independence Dr.
Huntsville, AL 35816

112 Suites
205-837-8907 800-331-3131

Location: ; Downtown: 5 miles
Airport: 12 miles
Near: 6 Theatre Complex
Walking Distance To: Restaurants
Area Attractions: Space Museum, Theatres

Price Range & Credit Cards: 1 Bedroom Suite $$, 2 Bedrooms $$$, AmEx/MC/ Visa/Other CC, Children Free, TAC 10%

Hotel Amenities: Laundry, Parking, Pets Allowed

Business Facilities: Copier, FAX

Recreational Facilities: Pool, Whirlpool, Sportcourt; Health Club privileges

Restaurant/Bar: Gatehouse Lodge

Comps: Continental Breakfast, Hors d'oeuvres

Room Amenities: Free Paper, Phone in Rm., Cable TV, Radio, Kitchen, Ind. Heat Ctl., Ind. AC Ctl.

The Residence Inn lives up to the status of a suite hotel, one reason so many guests return. The hotel is located 12 miles from the airport and 5 miles from downtown. Relax in the comfortable pine furniture and queensize bed, or get some exercise by using the complimentary daily pass to a local health club. Rates discounted for extended stay.

⚜ Alaska

ANCHORAGE

McKinley Chalet Resort
825 W. 8th Ave. #240
Anchorage, AK 99501

219 Suites
907-279-2653 907-276-7234

Location: Wilderness
Airport: 1.5 miles
Near: Denali National Park, Restaurants
Walking Distance To: Nenana River, Nature walks
Area Attractions: Wildlife Bus Tours, Mount McKinley

Price Range & Credit Cards: 1 Bedroom Suite $$$$, 2 Bedrooms $$$$, AmEx/MC/Visa, Children Free, TAC 10%

Hotel Amenities: Parking, TV Lounge, Handicap (1)

Business Facilities: Conf. Rm. Cap. 300, Banquet Fac., Copier, Aud/Vis.

Recreational Facilities: Pool, Sauna, Whirlpool, Fitn. Ctr., Fishing, Hiking, Game Area; River rafting, Flying

Restaurant/Bar: The Chalet Dining Room, Cocktail Lounge, Entertainment

Room Amenities: Phone in Rm., Ind. Heat Ctl.

The rustic elegance of this resort hotel offers a tranquil retreat in the midst of Alaska's wilderness with a spectacular view of Nenana River and surrounding mountains. After a day of touring, relax in a hot tub at the Chalet Club. Enjoy fine dining in the Chalet Dining Room and afterwards, join other guests in the Lounge for live entertainment.

--------------------------------- FAIRBANKS ---------------------------------

Regency Fairbanks Hotel
95 10th Ave.
Fairbanks, AK 99701

129 Suites
907-452-3200

Location: Eastside; Downtown: Nearby
Airport: Near
Near: Central Business
Walking Distance To: Central Business Area
Area Attractions: River Boat Discovery, Univ. of Alaska Museum

Price Range & Credit Cards: 1 Bedroom Suite $$$$, 2 Bedrooms $$$$+, Junior $$, AmEx/MC/Visa/Other CC, Children Free, TAC 10%

Hotel Amenities: Laundry, TV Lounge, Pets Allowed, Handicap (2)

Business Facilities: Conf. Rm. Cap. 230, Banquet Fac., Mess. Ctr., Copier, Aud/Vis., Comp. Hook-up

Recreational Facilities: Whirlpool, Golf, Skiing; Ice skating, Bowling

Restaurant/Bar: Regency Dining Room, Regency Lounge, Entertainment

Comps: Hors d'oeuvres

Room Amenities: Room Service, TV, Phone in Rm., Cable TV, Kitchen, Ind. Heat Ctl., Ind. AC Ctl.

"Affordably luxurious" is an apt description of the Regency Fairbanks. Conveniently located close to the downtown area, this hotel provides many extras that make your trip a treat. All suites come with walk-in closets. Many suites include oversized jacuzzis, full kitchens, and microwave ovens. After a busy day stop by the lounge for live entertainment.

--------------------------------- KETCHIKAN ---------------------------------

Royal Executive Suites
1471 Tongass Ave.
Ketchikan, AK 99901

9 Suites
907-225-1900

Location: W.End Bus.; Downtown: 0.5 mi.
Airport: 1 mile
Near: Major Highway, Athletic Club
Walking Distance To: Mall Shopping
Area Attractions: Alaska's Busiest Ports

Price Range & Credit Cards: 1 Bedroom Suite $$$, 2 Bedrooms $$$$, Junior $$, AmEx/MC/Visa/Other CC, Children Free, TAC 10%

Hotel Amenities: Laundry, Handicap (3)

Business Facilities: Conf. Rm. Cap. 10, Sec. Serv., Copier, Aud/Vis.

Recreational Facilities: Sauna, Whirlpool, Fitn. Ctr., Fishing

Restaurant/Bar: The Galley

Room Amenities: TV, Phone in Rm., Cable TV, VCR, Radio, Kitchen, Ind. Heat Ctl.

Centrally located between downtown and the Airport, the Royal Executive Suites boast of their view and business facilities and justifiably so. The spectacular view is of the Tongass Narrows, one of Alaska's busiest ports bustling with seaplanes, cruiseships, and fishing vessels. The hotel was designed with the executive in mind, business needs are met.

 **Arizona**

Prescott •   • Sedona

• Carefree
Scottsdale
Phoenix •• Mesa
Surprise • • Tempe
Yuma
• Tucson

• Nogales

MESA

Lexington Hotel Suites
1410 So. Country Club Dr.
Mesa, AZ 85210

120 Suites
602-964-2897 800-527-1877

Location: ; Downtown: 10 mi.
Airport: 8 Miles
Near: Fiesta Mall
Area Attractions: University, L.D.S. (Mormon)

Price Range & Credit Cards: 1 Bedroom Suite $$, 2 Bedrooms $$$, Junior $$, AmEx/MC/Visa/Other CC, Children Free, TAC 15%

Hotel Amenities: Laundry, Pets Allowed, Handicap (2)

Business Facilities: Conf. Rm. Cap. 75, Aud/Vis.

Recreational Facilities: Pool, Whirlpool, Tennis, Golf, Skiing

Comps: Continental Breakfast

Room Amenities: TV, Phone in Rm., Radio, Kitchen, Ind. Heat Ctl., Ind. AC Ctl.

With a traditional environment that can easily accommodate the business traveler or vacationer, Lexington offers a good value. Three sizes of suites are available along with 3 different conference rooms and a 670 square foot atrium. Sightseers will want to visit the neighboring Botanical Gardens or the Phoenix Zoo. Shopping is also close by.

12   Arizona

Embassy Suites Camelhead Hotel   *Location:* Eastside; Downtown: 8 miles
1515 No. 44th St.   *Airport:* 2.5 miles
Phoenix, AZ 85008   *Near:* Camelback Mountain, Central district
                                                                  Walking Distance To: Financial Institutions
227 Suites   *Area Attractions:* Sports Arenas, Zoo, Histor-
602-244-8800 800-447-8483   ical Sites

Price Range & Credit Cards: 1 Bedroom Suite $$, AmEx/MC/Visa/Other CC, Children Free, TAC 7.6%

Hotel Amenities: Laundry, TV Lounge, Handicap (4)

Business Facilities: Conf. Rm. Cap. 400, Banquet Fac., Sec. Serv., Copier, Aud/Vis., FAX, Telex, Comp. Hook-up

Recreational Facilities: Pool, Sauna, Whirlpool, Game Area; Golf and Tennis nearby

Restaurant/Bar: Two Roses Restaurant, Pub, Entertainment

Comps: Full Breakfast, Refreshments

Room Amenities: Room Service, Free Paper, Phones in Rm. (2), Cable TV, Radio, Wet Bar, Kitchen, Ind. Heat Ctl., Ind. AC Ctl.

A resort hotel designed with the Southwestern flair of Spanish tile and stained glass the Camelhead features a lush, tropical courtyard. A full complimentary breakfast is served daily at the Gazebo, and in the evening, dine in the relaxed, comfortable environment of the Two Roses Restaurant or enjoy live entertainment provided at the Pub.

Embassy Suites Hotel   *Location:* Heart of Biltmore
2630 E. Camelback Rd.   *Airport:* Near
Phoenix, AZ 85016   *Near:* Biltmore Fashion Park, Many Fine
                                                          Restaurants
232 Suites   *Walking Distance To:* Finest Shops
602-955-3992 800-362-2779   *Area Attractions:* Camelback Business
                                                         Corridor

Price Range & Credit Cards: 1 Bedroom Suite $$$, AmEx/MC/Visa/Other CC, Children Free, TAC 10%

Hotel Amenities: Laundry, Parking, Car Hire, Handicap (4)

Business Facilities: Conf. Rm. Cap. 300, Banquet Fac., Mess. Ctr., Copier, Aud/Vis., Comp. Hook-up

Recreational Facilities: Pool, Whirlpool, Championship Golf nearby

Restaurant/Bar: The Other Place

Comps: Full Breakfast, Airport Van, Refreshments, Hors d'oeuvres

Room Amenities: Room Service, TV, Phone in Rm., Cable TV, Wet Bar, Kitchen

Embassy Suites-Biltmore conveniently accommodates both the business and vacation traveler. Adjacent to the hotel are the exclusive Biltmore Shopping Park and the Biltmore championship golf course; minutes away are "Old Scottsdale" and the famed "5th Avenue Shops". Art Deco in design, suites open into the sunny atrium courtyard with tropical plants.

Embassy Suites Camelhead Hotel, Phoenix, AZ

PHOENIX

Embassy Suites Hotel-Westside
3210 Northwest Grand Ave.
Phoenix, AZ 85017

167 Suites
602-279-3211 800-362-2779

Location: Westside; Downtown: 5 miles
Airport: 12 miles
Near: Suburban Area, Arizona Coliseum
Walking Distance To: Restaurants & Discount Shops
Area Attractions: Metro Center Shops, Phoenix International Raceway

Price Range & Credit Cards: 1 Bedroom Suite $$, AmEx/MC/Visa/Other CC, Children Free, TAC 10%

Hotel Amenities: Laundry, Parking, Car Hire, TV Lounge, Pets Allowed

Business Facilities: Conf. Rm. Cap. 350, Banquet Fac., Mess. Ctr., Sec. Serv., Copier, Aud/Vis., Teleconf., FAX, Comp. Hook-up

Recreational Facilities: Pool, Sauna, Whirlpool, Game Area; Golf and Tennis nearby

Restaurant/Bar: Gregory's Restaurant

Comps: Full Breakfast, Cocktail Reception

Room Amenities: Room Service, Free Paper, Phones in Rm. (2), Cable TV, Radio, Wet Bar, Kitchen, Ind. Heat Ctl., Ind. AC Ctl.

Lush greenery and pastel decor in the lobby are the special touches that warm your welcome to this contemporary Southwestern-styled hotel. Every suite has a view towards the plant-filled atrium courtyard, where informal sitting areas, guest barbeques, and a large heated swimming pool provide pleasant places to relax. Golf & tennis only 3 miles away.

PHOENIX

The Residence Inn by Marriott
8242 North Black Canyon Frway.
Phoenix, AZ 85051

128 Suites
602-864-1900 800-331-3131

Location: Hi-Tech; Downtown: 18 mi.
Airport: 20 miles
Near: Scottsdale-20 miles
Walking Distance To: Metrocenter
Area Attractions: 250 Shops, 18 Theatres, 51 Restaurants

Price Range & Credit Cards: 1 Bedroom Suite $$, 2 Bedrooms $$$, AmEx/MC/Visa/Other CC, Children Free, TAC 10%

Hotel Amenities: Laundry, Library, Parking, TV Lounge, Pets Allowed, Handicap (4)

Business Facilities: Conf. Rm. Cap. 20, Mess. Ctr., Copier, Aud/Vis.

Recreational Facilities: Pool, Whirlpool, Tennis, Basketball, Volleyball, Putting Green; Lakes nearby

Comps: Full Breakfast, Refreshments, Hors d'oeuvres

Room Amenities: Free Paper, TV, Phones in Rm. (2), Cable TV, Radio, Wet Bar, Kitchen, Ind. Heat Ctl., Ind. AC Ctl.

The Residence Inn by Marriott by its excellent friendly service and complimentary hospitality is dedicated to making each traveler a resident who feels at home. The Inn provides spacious, tastefully decorated suites (King & Double/Double available) with full kitchens, some fireplaces, and even popcorn auto-poppers. Rates discounted for extended stays.

SCOTTSDALE

Embassy Suites Hotel
5001 N. Scottsdale Rd.
Scottsdale, AZ 85253

311 Suites
602-949-1414 800-528-1456

Location: Resort area; Downtown: 1 mile
Airport: 11 miles
Near: Championship Golfing, Major Shopping Center
Walking Distance To: Fifth Ave. Shops
Area Attractions: Racquet Club Resort, Mountains, Financial District

Price Range & Credit Cards: 1 Bedroom Suite $$$$, 2 Bedrooms $$$$+, AmEx/MC/Visa/Other CC, Children Free, TAC 10%

Hotel Amenities: Laundry, Gift Shop, Parking, Car Hire, TV Lounge, Pets Allowed, Handicap (4)

Business Facilities: Conf. Rm. Cap. 450, Banquet Fac., Copier, Aud/Vis., Teleconf., Comp. Hook-up

Recreational Facilities: Pool, Whirlpool, Fitn. Ctr., Tennis, Boating, Air Ballooning, River tubing, Golf privileges

Restaurant/Bar: Gregory's, Entertainment

Comps: Full Breakfast, Refreshments

Room Amenities: Room Service, TV, Phone in Rm., Cable TV, Radio, Wet Bar, Kitchen, Ind. Heat Ctl., Ind. AC Ctl.

Scottsdale's largest all-suite resort, Embassy conveniently accommodates business and pleasure travelers. 13 meeting rooms make business pleasurable for large and small groups, while the indoor fitness center, Tennis Center, and the nearby Championship Camelback Golf Club are perfect for the athletic enthusiasts. Gregory's offer elegant dining.

———————————— SCOTTSDALE ————————————

Hospitality Suites Resort
409 N. Scottsdale Rd.
Scottsdale, AZ 85257

210 Suites
602-949-5115 800-522-5115

Location: Eastside; Phoenix-0.5 mi.
Airport: 10 minutes
Near: Scottsdale Trolley, Shopping, Dining, Gardens
Walking Distance To: Large Mall
Area Attractions: Zoo, 5th. Ave. Shops

Price Range & Credit Cards: 1 Bedroom Suite $$, Junior $$, AmEx/MC/Visa/Other CC, Children Free, TAC 10%

Hotel Amenities: Laundry, Parking, Car Hire, Handicap (6)

Business Facilities: Conf. Rm. Cap. 100, Banquet Fac., Copier

Recreational Facilities: Pool, Whirlpool, Tennis, Golf, Horseshoes, Pool tables

Restaurant/Bar: Pewter Mug

Comps: Full Breakfast, Refreshments

Room Amenities: Room Service, TV, Phone in Rm., Cable TV, Radio, Wet Bar, Full Kitchen, Ind. Heat Ctl., Ind. AC Ctl.

This is a moderately priced resort, set in a landscape of plants indigenous to Arizona, with spacious and comfortable suites. Enjoy the Arizona sun in one of 3 pools by day, and the daily complimentary cocktail party at poolside—the "specialty" of the hotel with managers and guests gathering to relax by night.

———————————— SCOTTSDALE ————————————

Marriott Suites Scottsdale
7325 E. 3rd Ave.
Scottsdale, AZ 85251

251 Suites
602-945-1550 800-228-9290

Location: ; Downtown
Airport: Phoenix: 20 min.
Near: Shopping Plazas
Area Attractions: Fine Restaurants, Boutiques, Galleries

Price Range & Credit Cards: 1 Bedroom Suite $$$, AmEx/MC/Visa/Other CC, Children Free, TAC 10%

Hotel Amenities: Laundry, Parking, Gift Shop, Handicap (10)

Business Facilities: Conf. Rm. Cap. 144, Mess. Ctr., Copier, Aud/Vis., FAX, Telex, Comp. Hook-up

Recreational Facilities: Pool, Sauna, Whirlpool, Fitn. Ctr.; Golf & Tennis nearby

Restaurant/Bar: Windows Restaurant/Windows Lounge

Comps: Full Breakfast, Refreshments, Beverages & Snacks

Room Amenities: Room Service, Free Paper, TV, Phones in Rm. (2), Cable TV, Radio, Wet Bar, Ind. Heat Ctl., Ind. AC Ctl.

Located in Scottsdale's business and cultural center, Marriott Suites Scottsdale serves the lodging and meeting needs of business travelers, families and small groups. After a day of work, touring, sport or shopping, relax in the pool, sauna, or in the privacy of your elegant, yet home-like, suite. Then enjoy fine American cuisine at Windows Restaurant.

--------------------------------- SEDONA ---------------------------------

Los Abrigados Resort   **Location:** Southeast; Downtown: Nearby
160 Portal Lane   **Airport:** 20 minutes
Sedona, AZ 86336   **Near:** Hushed Fountains, Crafts Village
                                  Walking Distance To: Tlaquepaque Art,
183 Suites   Shopping
602-282-1777 800-521-3131   **Area Attractions:** Jazz on the Rocks, Red
                                  Rocks, Sedona Arts Center

Price Range & Credit Cards: 1 Bedroom Suite $$$, 2 Bedrooms $$$$, AmEx/MC/ Visa/Other CC, Children Free, TAC 10%

Hotel Amenities: Laundry, Parking, TV Lounge, Handicap (4)

Business Facilities: Conf. Rm. Cap. 100, Banquet Fac., Copier, Aud/Vis.

Recreational Facilities: Pool, Sauna, Whirlpool, Fitn. Ctr., Golf, Jeep Tours, Surrey rides, Hiking, Game Area, Horses

Restaurant/Bar: Canyon Rose

Room Amenities: Room Service, TV, Phones in Rm. (2), Cable TV, VCR, Radio, Wet Bar, Ind. Heat Ctl., Ind. AC Ctl.

Winding walkways and quaint bridges connect individual casitas, elegant dining, and the Paragon fitness club to Sedona's famous Tlaquepaque arts and crafts village. Many of the private casitas offer the charm of your own fireplace and whirlpool, as well as a stunning view of red rock country. Hushed fountains and Spanish style plazas add to the theme.

--------------------------------- TEMPE ---------------------------------

Embassy Suites Hotel   **Location:** Suburban; Phoenix: 8 miles
4400 South Rural Rd.   **Airport:** 6 miles
Tempe, AZ 85282   **Near:** Superstition Freeway, Arizona State
                                  Research Park
224 Suites   **Walking Distance To:** Tech Central Park
602-897-7444 800-362-2779   **Area Attractions:** Arizona State Univ. and
                                  Phoenix Cardinals Stadium

Price Range & Credit Cards: 1 Bedroom Suite $$, AmEx/MC/Visa/Other CC, Children Free, TAC 7.4%

Hotel Amenities: Laundry, Car Hire, Airport Limo, No-smoke suites, Handicap (2)

Business Facilities: Conf. Rm. Cap. 350, Banquet Fac., Mess. Ctr., Sec. Serv., Copier, Aud/Vis., Teleconf., FAX, Computers

Recreational Facilities: Pool, Sauna, Whirlpool, Fitn. Ctr., Tennis, Golf, Racquetball, Hiking, Game Area; NCAA Athletics 3 miles

Restaurant/Bar: City Grill, Firefly Lounge, Entertainment

Comps: Full Breakfast, Refreshments, Hors d'oeuvres

Room Amenities: Room Service, Free Paper, TV, Phones in Rm. (2), Wet Bar, Kitchen, Ind. Heat Ctl., Ind. AC Ctl.

You'll enjoy your stay at Embassy Suites Hotel, which is both beautifully secluded and conveniently located in the center of the Valley-of-the-Sun. The soothing desert landscape is repeated inside in warm blues and mauves. Gardens and walkways enhance the interior courtyards, and the hotel offers a fine view of Superstition Mountains.

──────────────── TEMPE ────────────────

Lexington Hotel Suites
1660 W. Elliott Rd.
Tempe, AZ 85283

139 Suites
602-345-8585 800-537-8483

Location: East Valley; Downtown: 8 miles
Airport: 7 miles
Near: Downtown Phoenix 8 miles
Area Attractions: Arizona State Univ.-4 miles

Price Range & Credit Cards: 1 Bedroom Suite $, 2 Bedrooms $$, Junior $, AmEx/MC/Visa/Other CC, Children Free, TAC 15%

Hotel Amenities: Laundry, Handicap (2)

Business Facilities: Conf. Rm. Cap. 60, Banquet Fac., Copier, Aud/Vis., Telex

Recreational Facilities: Pool, Whirlpool; Golf & Fitn. Ctr.-1 mi

Comps: Continental Plus Breakfast

Room Amenities: TV, Phone in Rm., Cable TV, Radio, Kitchen, Ind. Heat Ctl., Ind. AC Ctl.

Lexington Hotel Suites offers you more—A Suite For The Price Of A Room—providing you with the comfort and conveniences of home. Each Lexington Suite has a complete kitchen with a full-sized refrigerator, stove, and sink; and a color TV and AM-FM radio. Our suites are designed to give you plenty of room to relax and make yourself comfortable.

──────────────── TUCSON ────────────────

Embassy Suites Hotel
5335 E. Broadway
Tucson, AZ 85711

142 Suites
602-745-2700 800-362-2779

Location: Eastside; Downtown: 5 miles
Airport: 9.5 miles
Near: Catalina Mountains, Restaurant Row
Walking Distance To: Major Bus Route
Area Attractions: Davis Monthan AFB, Univ. of Arizona

Price Range & Credit Cards: 1 Bedroom Suite $$, AmEx/MC/Visa/Other CC, Children Free, TAC 10%

Hotel Amenities: Laundry, Pets Allowed, Handicap (1)

Business Facilities: Conf. Rm. Cap. 150, Banquet Fac., Mess. Ctr., Sec. Serv., Copier, Aud/Vis., FAX

Recreational Facilities: Pool, Sauna, Whirlpool, Fitn. Ctr., Tennis, Golf, Racquetball, Hiking, Game Area

Restaurant/Bar: Black Angus, Entertainment

Comps: Full Breakfast, Refreshments, Airport Shuttle

Room Amenities: Room Service, Free Paper, Phones in Rm. (2), Cable TV, Radio, Wet Bar, Kitchen

Located in central Tucson, Embassy Suites is close to "Restaurant Row" and to 2 major shopping malls. The University of Arizona & Davis Monthan Air Force Base are also within easy reach. Guests have health club privileges with golf, tennis and hiking nearby. The lush tropical courtyard and large fireplace in the lounge provide a "homey" atmosphere.

18   Arizona

Embassy Suites Hotel
7051 S. Tucson Blvd.
Tucson, AZ 85706

204 Suites
602-573-0700 800-362-2779

Location: Southwest; Old Tucson: 12 mi
Airport: At Door
Near: Airport-Tucson, Convenient to Restaurants
Area Attractions: Desert Museum, Shopping Mall

Price Range & Credit Cards: 1 Bedroom Suite $$, Junior $$, AmEx/MC/Visa/Other CC, Children Free

Hotel Amenities: Laundry, Car Hire, TV Lounge, Handicap (3)

Business Facilities: Conf. Rm. Cap. 500, Banquet Fac., Copier, Aud/Vis., Teleconf., FAX

Recreational Facilities: Pool, Whirlpool, Fitn. Ctr.; Golf and Tennis 5 miles

Restaurant/Bar: Finnegan's

Comps: Full Breakfast, Refreshments

Room Amenities: Room Service, Free Paper, TV, Phone in Rm., Cable TV, Radio, Wet Bar, Kitchen, Ind. Heat Ctl.

Conveniently located at the Tucson International Airport gate, Embassy's Spanish style hotel will meet the needs of the traveling businessperson or vacationer. A popular gathering place is Finnegan's with their unique menu which blends Mexican delicacies, fine steaks and seafood. Everyone enjoys the landscaped courtyard and pool.

Lexington Hotel Suites
7411 N. Oracle Rd.
Tucson, AZ 85704

157 Suites
602-575-9255 800-527-1877

Location: Northwest; Downtown: 8 miles
Airport: 19 miles
Near: Desert Areas
Area Attractions: Saquaro National Monument, Kitt Peak

Price Range & Credit Cards: 1 Bedroom Suite $$, 2 Bedrooms $$$$, Junior $, AmEx/MC/Visa/Other CC, Children Free, TAC 15%

Hotel Amenities: Laundry, Handicap (2)

Business Facilities: Conf. Rm. Cap. 35

Recreational Facilities: Pool, Whirlpool, Skiing; Golf and Tennis nearby

Comps: Continental Breakfast, Airport courtesy van

Room Amenities: TV, Phone in Rm., Radio, Kitchen, Ind. Heat Ctl., Ind. AC Ctl.

A traditional environment is offered by Lexington, and one of the three types of suites is sure to fit your needs. During leisure time bask in the sun by the pool and spa or enjoy all the privileges of a beautiful new country club nearby. And if that's not enough, a drive to Old Tucson Theme Park or the Arizona Sonora Desert Museum takes under 30 minutes.

―――――――――――― TUCSON ――――――――――――

The Residence Inn by Marriott
6477 E. Speedway Blvd.
Tucson, AZ 85710

128 Suites
602-721-0991 800-331-3131

Location: Eastside; Downtown: 10 mi.
Airport: 12 miles
Near: Residential Area, 64 Restaurants
Area Attractions: Sabino Canyon, Saguaro
National Park

Price Range & Credit Cards: 1 Bedroom Suite $$, 2 Bedrooms $$$, AmEx/MC/ Visa/Other CC, Children Free, TAC 10%

Hotel Amenities: Laundry, Library, Parking, Car Hire, TV Lounge, Pets Allowed, Handicap (5)

Business Facilities: Conf. Rm. Cap. 80, Mess. Ctr., Sec. Serv., Copier, Aud/Vis., Comp. Hook-up

Recreational Facilities: Pool, Whirlpool, Fitn. Ctr., Tennis, Golf, Basketball, Game Area, Volleyball

Comps: Continental Plus Breakfast, Refreshments, Hors d'oeuvres

Room Amenities: Room Service, Free Paper, TV, Phone in Rm., Cable TV, VCR, Radio, Wet Bar, Kitchen, Ind. Heat Ctl., Ind. AC Ctl.

From the flame in your fireplace to the warm welcome at the Gatehouse, The Residence Inn by Marriott has created a comfortable neighborhood environment. Located in the eastside business district with fine restaurants and shopping, the 16 low-rise buildings offer a view of the Catalina Mountains and many activities. Discounted rates for extended stays.

―――――――――――― TUCSON ――――――――――――

Tucson National Resort & Spa
2727 West Club Dr.
Tucson, AZ 85741

24 Suites
602-297-2271 800-528-4856

Location: North; Downtown: 10 min.
Airport: I-19 North
Near: Exclusive 650 Acres, Business District, Mission San Xavier del Bac
Walking Distance To: Countryside, Tucson Valley
Area Attractions: Mexico, Kitt Peak Observatory, Arizona-Sonora Desert Museum

Price Range & Credit Cards: 1 Bedroom Suite $$$, Junior $$, AmEx/MC/Visa/ Other CC, Children Free, TAC 10%

Hotel Amenities: Laundry, Parking, TV Lounge, Handicap (1)

Business Facilities: Conf. Rm. Cap. 100, Banquet Fac., Mess. Ctr., Sec. Serv., Copier, Aud/Vis., Telex

Recreational Facilities: Pool, Sauna, Whirlpool, Fitn. Ctr., Tennis, Championship Golf Course

Restaurant/Bar: Fiesta Room, Catalina Room., Entertainment

Room Amenities: Room Service, Free Paper, TV, Phone in Rm., Cable TV, Radio, Wet Bar, Kitchen, Ind. Heat Ctl., Ind. AC Ctl.

This exclusive 650 acre resort combines natural high chaparral desert beauty with a blend of architectural distinction and gracious hospitality. But with 27 holes of USGA Championship golf, tennis courts, pools and a world class spa, you might never leave this piece of paradise on earth. Truly an outstanding retreat for relaxing.

TUCSON

Ventana Canyon Golf Club
6200 No. Clubhouse Lane
Tucson, AZ 85715

46 Suites
602-577-1400 800-447-4787

Location: Country; Downtown: 15 min.
Airport: Half mile
Near: Mountain Foothills, Restaurant Row
Walking Distance To: Wildlife habitat
Area Attractions: Mission San Xavier del
Bac, Museums, Mexico

Price Range & Credit Cards: 1 Bedroom Suite $$$$, 2 Bedrooms $$$$+, AmEx/MC/Visa, Children Free, TAC 10%

Hotel Amenities: Laundry, Parking, TV Lounge

Business Facilities: Conf. Rm. Cap. 30, Banquet Fac., Mess. Ctr., Copier, Aud/Vis., Comp. Hook-up

Recreational Facilities: Pool, Sauna, Whirlpool, Fitn. Ctr., Golf, Skiing, Balloon rides, Hiking, Game Area, Horses

Restaurant/Bar: Clubhouse Room

Comps: Continental Breakfast, Hors d'oeuvres

Room Amenities: Room Service, Free Paper, TV, Phone in Rm., Cable TV, Radio, Wet Bar, Kitchen, Ind. Heat Ctl., Ind. AC Ctl.

Ventana Golf and Racquet Club is designed to impress the discerning guest. A day there might include 27 holes on the Fazio designed course, tennis, or a balloon ride! Dine while viewing a legendary Arizona sunset. The suites are luxuriously appointed in a contemporary style with a beige, mauve, and blue color scheme, and each has a mountain view.

YUMA

Days Inn Suite Hotel
2600 4th Ave.
Yuma, AZ 85364

164 Suites
602-726-4830 800-325-2525

Location: Central City; Downtown: 10 min.
Airport: Nearby
Near: Northside, 3 Major Golf Courses, Civic Center
Walking Distance To: Yuma Malls
Area Attractions: Museum, Sonora, Mexico, Sand Dunes, Convention Center

Price Range & Credit Cards: 1 Bedroom Suite $$, AmEx/MC/Visa/Other CC, Children Free, TAC 10%

Hotel Amenities: Laundry, Car Hire, Handicap (2)

Business Facilities: Conf. Rm. Cap. 180, Sec. Serv., Copier, Aud/Vis., Teleconf.

Recreational Facilities: Pool, Whirlpool, Fitn. Ctr., Tennis, Golf, Soccer, Racquetball, Baseball Fields

Restaurant/Bar: Gas barbeque grills for guest's use

Comps: Continental Breakfast, Refreshments, Airport Limousine

Room Amenities: Free Paper, TV, Phones in Rm. (2), Cable TV, Radio, Wet Bar, Kitchen, Ind. Heat Ctl., Ind. AC Ctl.

Days Inn is the first and only all-suite hotel in the Yuma area. All suites are two rooms, equipped with wet bar, refrigerator, and microwaves. Management hosts a complimentary breakfast every morning and complimentary happy hour every evening. Suites are equipped with amenities including: blow dryers & weight scales. Heated pool and jacuzzi on property.

⚜ Arkansas

● Little Rock

──────── LITTLE ROCK ────────

Governor's Inn of Little Rock
1501 Merrill Dr.
Little Rock, AR 72211

50 Suites
901-224-8051 800-443-9350

Location: Westside; Downtown: 10 min.
Airport: Nearby
Near: Central City, Convenient Shopping
Walking Distance To: Shopping Malls
Area Attractions: Hills, Creeks, Trees

Price Range & Credit Cards: 1 Bedroom Suite $$, 2 Bedrooms $$, Junior $$, AmEx/ MC/Visa/Other CC, Children Free, TAC 10%

Hotel Amenities: Laundry, Parking, Car Hire, Pets Allowed, Handicap (3)

Business Facilities: Conf. Rm. Cap. 65, Banquet Fac., Mess. Ctr., Sec. Serv., Copier, Aud/Vis.

Recreational Facilities: Pool, Sauna, Whirlpool

Restaurant/Bar: Governors Club and Lounge, Entertainment

Comps: Full Breakfast, Hors d'oeuvres

Room Amenities: Room Service, Free Paper, TV, Phone in Rm., Cable TV, Radio, Wet Bar, Ind. Heat Ctl., Ind. AC Ctl.

Governor's Inn offers exceptional accommodations for the discriminating traveler. The skylit atrium and landscaped gardens reflect your appreciation of style and insistance on quality. Thoughtful extras include complimentary overnight shoe-shine, Perrier, and coffee in each suite. The warm atmosphere is certain to make you feel right at home.

⚜ California

Squaw Valley
Olympic Valley •

• South Lake Tahoe
• Napa   • Sacramento

So. San Francisco
San Francisco   San Mateo   Newark
Foster City Burlingame   • Fremont
Mountain View   • Milpitas   Sunnyvale
Santa Clara   • Silicon Valley   San Jose
                Campbell

Pacific Grove • Monterey
                • Carmel

                        • Fresno

Big Bear Lake
                        Inglewood
West Hollywood — Hollywood   • Arcadia
        Beverly Hills   • Buena Park
        El Segundo   • Anaheim   • Placentia
Manhattan Beach   • Santa Ana Huntington Beach
Marina Del Rey Torrance   • Newport Beach
Playa Del Rey   Long Beach   • Irvine
                Cypress Costa Mesa   • South Laguna

                • San Luis Obispo
                • Pismo Beach
        Lompoc — Santa Maria
                • Los Olivos
Solvang   • Oxnard   • San Dimas
Santa Barbara /   • Ontario
Ventura   Santa Monica   • Covina
        West Los Angeles   • Downey   Palm Springs
        Los Angeles • Orange   • Cathedral City
                Brea   Oceanside   • Palm Desert
                                • Indio
                                • Borrego Springs
                        • Carlsbad
                        • La Jolla
        Imperial Beach   • San Diego

---------------------- ANAHEIM ----------------------

The Residence Inn by Marriott
1700 South Clementine St.
Anaheim, CA 92802

200 Suites
714-533-3555 800-331-3131

Location: Disneyland; Downtown: 3 miles
Airport: John Wayne: 9 miles
Near: Anaheim Convention Center, Anaheim Stadium, Disneyland
Walking Distance To: Disneyland
Area Attractions: Knott's Berry Farm, Wax Museum, Universal Studios

Price Range & Credit Cards: 1 Bedroom Suite $$, 2 Bedrooms $$$, AmEx/MC/Visa/Other CC, Children Free, TAC 10%

Hotel Amenities: Laundry, Library, Gift Shop, TV Lounge, Handicap (7)

Business Facilities: Conf. Rm. Cap. 50, Copier, Aud/Vis.

Recreational Facilities: Pool, Sauna, Sport Court, Volleyball, Basketball, Badminton, Game Area; Tennis nearby

Restaurant/Bar: TGI Fridays (room service only)

Comps: Continental Plus Breakfast, Refreshments, Hors d'oeuvres

Room Amenities: Room Service, Free Paper, TV, Phones in Rm. (2), Cable TV, VCR, Radio, Kitchen, Ind. Heat Ctl., Ind. AC Ctl.

This Residence Inn is within walking distance to Disneyland, a mile from Anaheim Convention Center, and 2 miles from Anaheim Stadium. Six different types of luxurious suites all have full kitchens, fireplaces, and large livingrooms. Facilities include two jacuzzis and large swimming pool. Many attractions nearby. Rates discounted for extended stays.

---------------------- ARCADIA ----------------------

Embassy Suites Hotel
211 E. Huntington Dr.
Arcadia, CA 91006

194 Suites
818-445-8525 800-362-2779

Location: Central; Pasadena: 5 miles
Airport: LAX 40 miles
Near: Movie Theatres, Many Restaurants, LA City Arboretum, Burbank Airport-30 mi.
Walking Distance To: Shopping Malls
Area Attractions: Rosebowl & Convention Center, Santa Anita Park, Golf Course

Price Range & Credit Cards: 1 Bedroom Suite $$$, AmEx/MC/Visa/Other CC, Children Free, TAC 10%

Hotel Amenities: Laundry, Pets Allowed, Handicap (7)

Business Facilities: Conf. Rm. Cap. 250, Banquet Fac., Copier, Aud/Vis.

Recreational Facilities: Pool, Sauna, Whirlpool, Tennis, Golf, Game Area; Santa Anita Race Track

Restaurant/Bar: Velvet Turtle and Lounge, Entertainment

Comps: Full Breakfast, Refreshments

Room Amenities: Room Service, Free Paper, TV, Phone in Rm., Cable TV, Radio, Wet Bar, Kitchen, Ind. AC Ctl.

With a view to the north of the San Gabriel Mountains Embassy Suites Arcadia has a convenient suburban location, yet is only eight miles from the Pasadena Rose Bowl and Convention Center. Shopping, restaurants, and recreation, such as golf, racquetball, and tennis are nearby. Suites open onto the interior atrium, with plants and rock waterfalls.

Embassy Suites Hotel-Westside, Phoenix, AZ

———————————————— BEVERLY HILLS ————————————————

L'Ermitage Hotel
9291 Burton Way
Beverly Hills, CA 90210

114 Suites
213-278-3344   800-424-4443

Location: Central; Downtown
Airport: LAX
Near: Rodeo Drive Shops, Convenient to everything L.A.
Walking Distance To: Century City, Shopping Malls
Area Attractions: West Hollywood Shopping, Rosebowl, Convention Center

Price Range & Credit Cards: 1 Bedroom Suite $$$$+, 2 Bedrooms $$$$+, Junior $$$$+, AmEx/MC/Visa/Other CC, Children Free, TAC 10%

Hotel Amenities: Parking, Car Hire

Business Facilities: Conf. Rm. Cap. 100, Banquet Fac.

Recreational Facilities: Pool, Whirlpool; Sports: see Concierge

Restaurant/Bar: Cafe Russe, Entertainment

Comps: Continental Breakfast, Hors d'oeuvres

Room Amenities: Room Service, Free Paper, TV, Phone in Rm., Cable TV, Radio, Wet Bar, Kitchen, Ind. Heat Ctl., Ind. AC Ctl.

Here, old world grace and charm are faultlessly married to contemporary comfort and service. Located on a tree-lined residential boulevard, L'Ermitage is a short stroll from Rodeo Drive, while a chauffeured limousine is yours for longer Beverly Hills jaunts. Original artwork is displayed throughout the hotel and within the spacious, luxurious suites.

━━━━━━━━━━━━━━━━━━━━ BUENA PARK ━━━━━━━━━━━━━━━━━━━━

Embassy Suites Hotel
7762 Beach Blvd.
Buena Park, CA 90620

203 Suites
714-739-5600 800-362-2779

Location: Central; L.A.: 30 minutes
Airport: 3 miles
Near: Knott's Berry Farm, Many Exclusive Shops
Walking Distance To: Entertainment
Area Attractions: Disneyland, Movieland Wax Museum, Medieval Times

Price Range & Credit Cards: 1 Bedroom Suite $$$, AmEx/MC/Visa/Other CC, TAC 10%

Hotel Amenities: Laundry, Car Hire, TV Lounge, Handicap (1)

Business Facilities: Conf. Rm. Cap. 225, Banquet Fac., Copier, Aud/Vis.

Recreational Facilities: Pool, Whirlpool, Golf, Game Area; Fitness Center nearby

Restaurant/Bar: Le Bistro

Comps: Full Breakfast, Refreshments

Room Amenities: Room Service, TV, Phones in Rm. (2), Cable TV, Radio, Wet Bar, Kitchen

The Embassy Suites Hotel Buena Park is located close to many attractions. It is only a half block from Knott's Berry Farm, across from Movieland Wax Museum, and 30 minutes away from Los Angeles and Hollywood. Free shuttle service is provided to Disneyland. Suites face a Mexican courtyard decorated with fountains and lush tropical foliage.

━━━━━━━━━━━━━━━━━━━━ BURLINGAME ━━━━━━━━━━━━━━━━━━━━

Embassy Suites Hotel
150 Anza Blvd.
Burlingame, CA 94010

344 Suites
415-342-4600 800-362-2779

Location: Central; San Fran.:15 mi.
Airport: 3 miles
Near: "The Strip"
Walking Distance To: Quaint Shops
Area Attractions: Bay cruises, Bay Meadows Track

Price Range & Credit Cards: 1 Bedroom Suite $$$$, AmEx/MC/Visa/Other CC, Children Free, TAC 10%

Hotel Amenities: Laundry, Car Hire, Free Parking, Handicap (10)

Business Facilities: Conf. Rm. Cap. 400, Banquet Fac., Copier, Aud/Vis., FAX

Recreational Facilities: Pool, Sauna, Whirlpool, Golf, Fishing, Wind Surfing, Jogging path; Health Center nearby

Restaurant/Bar: Bobby McGee's, Entertainment

Comps: Full breakfast, Refreshments, Airport shuttle

Room Amenities: Room Service, Free Paper, TV, Phones in Rm. (2), Cable TV, Radio, Wet Bar, Kitchen, Ind. Heat Ctl., Ind. AC Ctl.

The lush foliage and bird cages of the central atrium suggest a vacation on an exotic island. The Embassy Suites Hotel is near many attractions of the San Francisco peninsula. Fisherman's Wharf, Moscone Convention Center, and the Golden Gate Bridge are all within a 20-minute drive. Overlooking the bay; 3 miles to the San Francisco International airport.

─────────────── CARLSBAD ───────────────

Beach Terrace Inn
2775 Ocean St.
Carlsbad, CA 92008

34 Suites
619-729-5951 800-433-5415

Location: Oceanside; Downtown: 1 mile
Airport: 30 miles
Near: Gold Coast, San Diego Oceanside Beaches
Walking Distance To: Village Stores and Restaurants
Area Attractions: Sea World, Zoo, Disneyland, Mexico

Price Range & Credit Cards: 1 Bedroom Suite $$$$, AmEx/MC/Visa/Other CC, TAC 10%

Hotel Amenities: Laundry, Car Hire

Business Facilities: Conf. Rm. Cap. 50, Aud/Vis.

Recreational Facilities: Pool, Sauna, Whirlpool, Beach sports; Golf Courses nearby

Comps: Continental Breakfast

Room Amenities: TV, Phone in Rm., Cable TV, Radio, Wet Bar, Kitchen, Ind. Heat Ctl., Ind. AC Ctl.

Swim, surf, or fish on the adjacent beach, or enjoy one of the many nearby golf courses. Carlsbad village stores and restaurants are an easy quarter mile walk. Only thirty minutes to San Diego attractions, 60 minutes to Disneyland and Knott's Berry Farm. Enjoy a complimentary continental breakfast in the spacious guest lounge.

─────────────── CARLSBAD ───────────────

Lexington Hotel Suites
751 Macadamia Drive
Carlsbad, CA 92009

120 Suites
619-438-2285 800-537-8483

Location: Oceanside; Downtown: Nearby
Airport: 4 miles
Near: Flower Fields, Many Shops, Carlsbad State Park
Walking Distance To: Pacific Ocean Beaches
Area Attractions: Zoo, La Jolla, Camp Pendleton

Price Range & Credit Cards: 1 Bedroom Suite $$, 2 Bedrooms $$$, Junior $$, AmEx/MC/Visa/Other CC, Children Free, TAC 15%

Hotel Amenities: Laundry, Parking, Handicap (5)

Business Facilities: Conf. Rm. Cap. 50, Banquet Fac., Telecopier, Sec. Serv., Copier

Recreational Facilities: Pool, Whirlpool, Boating, Water Skiing; Golf and Tennis nearby

Comps: Continental breakfast

Room Amenities: TV, Phones in Rm. (2), Cable TV, HBO, Radio, Kitchen, Ind. Heat Ctl., Ind. AC Ctl.

The many nearby attractions include Sea World, the Wild Animal Park, and the San Diego Zoo, all within 30 miles. Or, take a short stroll to the Pacific Ocean and beaches. Also nearby are water skiing, golf, and tennis. Suites include a complete livingroom, one or two bedrooms, and a complete kitchen with dining area.

──────────────── CARMEL ────────────────

Carmel Valley Ranch Resort
One Old Ranch Rd.
Carmel, CA 93923

100 Suites
408-625-9500 800-422-7635

Location: Country; Downtown: 6 miles
Airport: 20 miles
Near: Exclusive private gardens, Restaurants
Walking Distance To: Countryside
Area Attractions: Monterey Bay, Wildlife
Reserve, Quaint Shops

Price Range & Credit Cards: 1 Bedroom Suite $$$$, 2 Bedrooms $$$$+, AmEx/MC/ Visa/Other CC, Children Free, TAC 10%

Hotel Amenities: Laundry, Parking, Car Hire, Handicap (2)

Business Facilities: Conf. Rm. Cap. 400, Banquet Fac., Mess. Ctr., Sec. Serv., Copier, Aud/Vis., Teleconf., Telex

Recreational Facilities: Pool, Sauna, Whirlpool; Pete Dye Golf Course

Room Amenities: Room Service, Free Paper, TV, Phones in Rm. (3), Cable TV, Radio, Wet Bar, Ind. Heat Ctl., Ind. AC Ctl.

Situated on 1700 lush acres, the Carmel Valley Ranch Resort is your private retreat. An 18-hole Pete Dye championship golf course, 12 tennis courts, and many beautiful pools and spas await you. Enjoy colorful sunsets from the lodge or private dining room. The warmly appointed suites with wood-burning fireplaces give you the feeling of home.

──────────────── CARMEL ────────────────

Highlands Inn
Box 1700
Carmel, CA 93921

144 Suites
408-624-3801 800-538-9525

Location: Country; Downtown: 5 miles
Airport: 8 miles
Near: Pine-covered hillside, Big Sur Coast
Walking Distance To: Nature Reserve
Area Attractions: Monterey Jazz Festival, Car Races

Price Range & Credit Cards: 1 Bedroom Suite $$$$, 2 Bedrooms $$$$+, Junior $$$$, AmEx/MC/Visa/Other CC, Children Free, TAC 10%

Hotel Amenities: Laundry, Parking, TV Lounge, Handicap (5)

Business Facilities: Conf. Rm. Cap. 120, Banquet Fac., Mess. Ctr., Sec. Serv., Copier, Aud/Vis., Telex

Recreational Facilities: Pool, Golf, Bicycling, Ballooning, Scuba diving, Game Area

Restaurant/Bar: Pacific's Edge

Room Amenities: Room Service, Free Paper, TV, Phone in Rm., VCR, Radio, Wet Bar, Kitchen, Ind. Heat Ctl.

A fully restored romantic hideaway resort in the world famous Carmel coast. 17 golf courses, tennis, boating, fishing, and hiking are some of the many nearby activities. Back at the inn, a skylighted promenade leads to glass-walled restaurants and lounges. Each suite is complete with spa bath, woodburning fireplace, and deck views of the Big Sur coast.

COSTA MESA

The Residence Inn by Marriott
881 Baker Street
Costa Mesa, CA 92626

144 Suites
714-241-8800 800-331-3131

Location: Metropolitan; Downtown: 1 mile
Airport: John Wayne-2 miles
Near: Orange County Fairgrounds, Pacific Amphitheatre, South Coast Mall
Area Attractions: Newport Beach-20 min., Disneyland-30 min., Shops, Harbor

Price Range & Credit Cards: 1 Bedroom Suite $$$, 2 Bedrooms $$$, AmEx/MC/Visa/Other CC, Children Free, TAC 10%

Hotel Amenities: Laundry, Library, Parking, Car Hire, TV Lounge, Pets Allowed, Handicap (3)

Business Facilities: Conf. Rm. Cap. 60, Banquet Fac., Mess. Ctr., Copier, Aud/Vis.

Recreational Facilities: Pool, Whirlpool, Sport Court, Game Area; Golf and Tennis nearby

Comps: Continental Plus Breakfast, Refreshments, Hors d'oeuvres

Room Amenities: Free Paper, TV, Phone in Room, Cable TV, VCR, Radio, Full Kitchen, Ind. Heat Ctl., Ind. AC Ctl.

The Residence Inn, located close to shopping, suburbs and downtown, offers all the amenities of home. A complimentary breakfast buffet is served daily and an evening social hour with refreshments (Mon.-Fri.). Our warm, friendly staff offer thoughtful service—even do grocery shopping or the dishes! Discounted rates for extended stays.

COVINA

Embassy Suites Hotel
1211 E. Garvey St.
Covina, CA 91724

264 Suites
818-915-3441 800-362-2779

Location: Suburban; Downtown: 2 miles
Airport: LAX: 40 miles
Near: Rose Bowl, Huntington Library; Ontario Airport-20 miles
Walking Distance To: Residential neighborhood
Area Attractions: Santa Anita Track, Disneyland

Price Range & Credit Cards: 1 Bedroom Suite $$$, AmEx/MC/Visa/Other CC, Children Free, TAC 10%

Hotel Amenities: Laundry, Parking, Car Hire, TV Lounge, Pets Allowed, Handicap (3)

Business Facilities: Conf. Rm. Cap. 35, Banquet Fac., Copier

Recreational Facilities: Pool, Whirlpool, Game Area

Restaurant/Bar: Velvet Turtle, Entertainment

Comps: Full Breakfast, Refreshments

Room Amenities: Room Service, TV, Phones in Rm. (2), Cable TV, Radio, Wet Bar, Kitchen

Escape to the world of Spanish-styled buildings & tiled walkways. Set in lush, tropical surroundings, Embassy Suites is located conveniently for everyone. The Rose Bowl, Knott's Berry Farm, Anaheim Stadium, Disneyland, Brookside Winery & Raging Water Swim Park are all 45 min. or less away. When you return, enjoy cocktails in the Velvet Turtle Piano Bar.

━━━━━━━━━━━━━━ DOWNEY ━━━━━━━━━━━━━━

Embassy Suites Hotel
8425 Firestone Blvd.
Downey, CA 90241

220 Suites
213-861-1900 800-362-2779

Location: Downtown
Airport: 1 Hour
Near: Downey Civic Center, Many Freeways
Walking Distance To: Industrial Area, Downtown
Area Attractions: Disneyland, Shoreline Village, Beverly Hills

Price Range & Credit Cards: 1 Bedroom Suite $$$, AmEx/MC/Visa/Other CC, Children Free, TAC 10%

Hotel Amenities: Laundry, Parking, Pets Allowed, Handicap (9)

Business Facilities: Conf. Rm. Cap. 400, Banquet Fac., Mess. Ctr., Copier, Aud/Vis., Teleconf.

Recreational Facilities: Pool, Sauna, Whirlpool, Golf, Game Area; YMCA 1 mile

Restaurant/Bar: Gregory's

Comps: Full Breakfast, Refreshments

Room Amenities: Room Service, Free Paper, TV, Phones in Rm. (2), VCR, Radio, Wet Bar, Kitchen, Ind. Heat Ctl., Ind. AC Ctl.

Embassy Suites is adjacent to the Downey Civic Center; Disneyland and Knott's Berry Farm are within 20 miles. The sunny courtyard atrium of the hotel is filled with plants, fountains, charm & elegance. Suites are highlighted with distinctive furniture, and striking graphics, remote-control TV in the bedroom, and a roomy work area in the living room.

━━━━━━━━━━━━━━ EL SEGUNDO ━━━━━━━━━━━━━━

Embassy Suites Hotel
1440 East Imperial Ave.
El Segundo, CA 90245

350 Suites
213-640-3600 800-362-2779

Location: Metropolitan; Downtown: 40 min.
Airport: 0.5 miles
Near: Residential Area, Del Amo Mall, El Segundo Aerospace Facilities, LAX
Area Attractions: Beaches, Knott's Berry Farm, Hollywood Park Racetrack

Price Range & Credit Cards: 1 Bedroom Suite $$$$, AmEx/MC/Visa/Other CC, Children Free, TAC 10%

Hotel Amenities: Laundry, Gift Shop, Parking, Car Hire, TV Lounge, Pets Allowed, Handicap (3)

Business Facilities: Conf. Rm. Cap. 325, Banquet Fac., Copier, Aud/Vis.

Recreational Facilities: Pool, Sauna, Whirlpool; Golf and Tennis nearby

Restaurant/Bar: Capistrano, Courtyard, Entertainment

Comps: Full Breakfast, Refreshments, Hors d'oeuvres

Room Amenities: Room Service, Free Paper, TV, Phone in Rm., Radio, Wet Bar, Ind. Heat Ctl., Ind. AC Ctl.

Besides its proximity to Los Angeles International Airport, the Embassy Suites is near many corporate headquarters, including Hughes Aircraft, Rockwell, Northrop, McDonnell-Douglas, TRW, and Xerox. Manhattan Beach, Marina Del Rey, and downtown Los Angeles are also nearby. The hotel is decorated in warm yet comfortable sophistication.

─────────────── IMPERIAL BEACH ───────────────

Hawaiian Gardens Suite Hotel
1031 Imperial Beach Blvd.
Imperial Beach, CA 92032

64 Suites
619-429-5303 800-222-1232

Location: Beach; San Diego: 10 mi.
Airport: 12 miles
Near: Civic Center, Public Beaches
Walking Distance To: Civic Center, Pier
Fishing
Area Attractions: Minutes to Old Mexico, Zoo, Shops

Price Range & Credit Cards: 1 Bedroom Suite $$, 2 Bedrooms $$, Junior $, AmEx/ MC/Visa/Other CC

Hotel Amenities: Laundry, Library, Parking, TV Lounge, Pets Allowed

Business Facilities: Conf. Rm. Cap. 20, Mess. Ctr., Copier

Recreational Facilities: Pool, Sauna, Movies, Game Area; Fishing & Boating near

Room Amenities: TV, Phone in Rm., Cable TV, Kitchen, Ind. Heat Ctl.

Hawaiian Gardens is for those who love beauty and privacy. The setting is in exotic Oriental Gardens with running fountains and flaming tiki torches. The recreation room is copied from an ancient Shintu Shrine, and contains ancient Polynesian artifacts. Discount admission coupons are available for Sea World, San Diego Zoo, Harbor excursions, & more!

─────────────── INDIAN WELLS ───────────────

The Sands of Indian Wells
75-188 Highway 111
Indian Wells, CA 92210

48 Suites
619-340-4364

Location: Resort Area; Downtown: 5 min.
Airport: 20 minutes
Near: Bob Hope Cultural Center, PGA West, Over 90 Golf Courses nearby
Area Attractions: El Paseo Shops, Joshua Tree National Monument

Price Range & Credit Cards: 1 Bedroom Suite $$$$, Junior $$, /MC/Visa, Children Free, TAC 10%

Hotel Amenities: Laundry, Library, TV Lounge, Handicap (2)

Business Facilities: Conf. Rm. Cap. 20, Banquet Fac., Copier

Recreational Facilities: Pool, Whirlpool, Barbeque, Volleyball, Putting Green, Child Play Area, Game Area; Tennis & Parks nearby

Restaurant/Bar: The Nest Restaurant and Bar, Dancing & Piano Bar

Comps: Sunday Brunch

Room Amenities: TV, Phones in Rm. (2), Cable TV, Radio, Kitchen, Ind. Heat Ctl., Ind. AC Ctl.

Sands guests return year after year to be pampered by our personal service. . . to relax in beautifully decorated junior and one-bedroom suites, all with kitchens. Sands is famous for their private-club atmosphere, pool area and the "one day" tan! In the center of the world's most splendid golf community, Sands is also close to shopping and dining.

──────────────── INDIO ────────────────

Grand Champions Resort
44-600 Indian Wells Lane
Indio, CA 92210

340 Suites
619-341-1000   800-828-1112

Location: Country; Downtown: 2 miles
Airport: Half Hour
Near: Mountains, Lakes, Town & Country
Walking Distance To: Tennis Stadium
Area Attractions: Country, Desert, Palm Springs

Price Range & Credit Cards: 1 Bedroom Suite $$$$+, 2 Bedrooms $$$$+, Junior $$$$, AmEx/MC/Visa/Other CC, Children Free, TAC 10%

Hotel Amenities: Laundry, Parking, Car Hire, Handicap (20)

Business Facilities: Conf. Rm. Cap. 500, Banquet Fac., Mess. Ctr., Sec. Serv., Copier, Aud/Vis., Teleconf., Telex, Comp. Hook-up

Recreational Facilities: Pool, Sauna, Whirlpool, Fitn. Ctr., Tennis, Golf

Restaurant/Bar: Trattoria, Jasmine. Charlie's, Entertainment

Room Amenities: Room Service, Free Paper, TV, Phone in Rm., Cable TV, Radio, Wet Bar, Ind. Heat Ctl., Ind. AC Ctl.

A Hotel in the grand European tradition where excellence is the assumed standard. 340 exquisite suites are only a part of their breath-taking 34 acres. Tempted to view world class tennis or golf? It is there! Along with 3 restaurants (formal and informal). Exceptional style is the status quo from antiques and original art to butler service.

Embassy Suites Hotel, Covina, CA

─────────────── IRVINE ───────────────

Embassy Suites Hotel
2120 Main St.
Irvine, CA 92714

293 Suites
714-553-8332 800-362-2779

Location: Koll Center; Business Area.
Airport: 1 mile
Near: Airport District, Major Shopping Area
Walking Distance To: Koll Center North
Area Attractions: Fine Dining, Music, Disneyland, Knott's Berry Farm

Price Range & Credit Cards: 1 Bedroom Suite $$$, 2 Bedrooms $$$$+, AmEx/MC/Visa/Other CC, Children Free, TAC 10%

Hotel Amenities: Laundry, Parking, Car Hire, TV Lounge, Pets Allowed, Handicap (9)

Business Facilities: Conf. Rm. Cap. 60, Banquet Fac., Mess. Ctr., Copier, Aud/Vis., Teleconf., FAX, Comp. Hook-up

Recreational Facilities: Pool, Sauna, Whirlpool, Tennis, Golf, Game Area; Newport Beach

Restaurant/Bar: Main Street Grille

Comps: Full Breakfast, Refreshments

Room Amenities: Room Service, Coffee Maker, TV, Phones in Rm. (2), Free Paper, Radio, Cable TV, Wet Bar, Refrigerator, Ind. Heat Ctl., Ind. AC Ctl.

Located near the Orange County Airport, Irvine Embassy Suites is surrounded by attractions. It is 15 minutes from Disneyland, and 20 miles from Knott's Berry Farm. Shopping in Newport Beach is 3 miles away, and boat charters are available. Golf, tennis, and health clubs are also nearby. Contemporarily decorated suites open onto the atrium courtyard.

─────────────── LA JOLLA ───────────────

The Residence Inn by Marriott
8901 Gilman Dr.
La Jolla, CA 92037

287 Suites
619-587-1770 800-331-3131

Location: Residential; Downtown: 2 miles
Airport: 12 miles
Near: Suburbs, I-5, Scripps Pier, Balboa Park
Walking Distance To: Pacific Ocean Beaches
Area Attractions: Seaworld, Zoo, Old Town, Mexico, San Diego Harbor

Price Range & Credit Cards: 1 Bedroom Suite $$$, 2 Bedrooms $$$$, AmEx/MC/Visa/Other CC, Children Free, TAC 10%

Hotel Amenities: Laundry, Parking, TV Lounge, Pets Allowed

Business Facilities: Conf. Rm. Cap. 60, Mess. Ctr., Copier, Aud/Vis.

Recreational Facilities: Pool, Whirlpool, Fitn. Ctr., Golf, Surfing; Public Beaches

Restaurant/Bar: T.G.I.Fridays

Comps: Continental Plus Breakfast, Refreshments, Hors d'oeuvres

Room Amenities: Room Service, Free Paper, TV, Phone in Rm., Cable TV, Radio, Kitchen, Ind. Heat Ctl., Ind. AC Ctl.

Special service is given to each guest of The Residence Inn. Facilities include five jacuzzis, and two pools. Its ten acres are beautifully landscaped and surrounded by exceptional Southern California homes. Other nearby attractions include La Jolla beaches, San Diego Harbor, Sea World, San Diego Zoo, Balboa Park, Old Town and San Diego Wild Animal Park

--- LOMPOC ---

Embassy Suites Hotel
1117 N. "H" St.
Lompoc, CA 93436

156 Suites
805-735-8311 800-362-2779

Location: Central; Downtown: 1 mile
Airport: 1 mile
Near: Convention Center, Beach
Walking Distance To: Flower fields, La Purisima
Area Attractions: Missions, Wineries, Solvang, Golf Courses

Price Range & Credit Cards: 1 Bedroom Suite $$, AmEx/MC/Visa/Other CC, Children Free, TAC 10%

Hotel Amenities: Laundry, TV Lounge, Handicap (6)

Business Facilities: Conf. Rm. Cap. 50, Banquet Fac., Mess. Ctr., Sec. Serv., Copier, Aud/Vis., Teleconf.

Recreational Facilities: Pool, Whirlpool, Fitn. Ctr.; Golf Course-3.5 miles

Comps: Full Breakfast, Beverages, Hors d'oeuvres

Room Amenities: Free Paper, TV, Phones in Rm. (2), Radio, Wet Bar, Ind. Heat Ctl., Ind. AC Ctl.

The Embassy Suites-Lompoc lies in the heart of the beautiful central California coast. Lompoc experiences great all-year around weather, little rain and clean air. Only 8 miles from an uncrowded beach, visitors are conveniently located to explore historic missions, wineries, flower fields (May-Sept), shops, and Solvang. So why not Lompoc this year!

--- LOS ANGELES ---

Clark Plaza
141 S. Clark Dr.
Los Angeles, CA 90048

105 Suites
800-252-0268 800-421-0745

Location: Metropolitan; L.A.
Airport: LAX 5 miles
Near: Major Shopping Areas, Many Restaurants
Walking Distance To: Boutiques
Area Attractions: UCLA Campus , Theatres, Beach

Price Range & Credit Cards: 1 Bedroom Suite $$$, 2 Bedrooms $$$$, Junior $$, AmEx/MC/Visa/Other CC, TAC 10%

Hotel Amenities: Laundry, Library, Parking, Pets Allowed

Business Facilities: Conf. Rm. Cap. 20, Mess. Ctr., Copier, Telex

Recreational Facilities: Pool, Sauna, Fitn. Ctr.

Comps: Continental Breakfast

Room Amenities: Room Service, TV, Phones in Rm. (2), Cable TV, Kitchen, Ind. Heat Ctl., Ind. AC Ctl.

Plaza Suites are beautifully decorated to give you the feeling of an elegant hotel. Each includes a large living room, two color televisions, and a woodburning fireplace. The fully-equipped kitchen gives you the flexibility of dining in your own suite. The comforts will make you feel you're coming home at night.

34 California

Franklin Plaza
7230 Franklin Ave
Los Angeles, CA 90046

80 Suites
213-874-7450 800-421-0745

Location: Metropolitan; L.A.
Airport: LAX 5 miles
Near: Major Shopping Areas, Many Restaurants
Walking Distance To: Boutiques
Area Attractions: UCLA Campus, Theatres, Beach

Price Range & Credit Cards: 1 Bedroom Suite $$$, 2 Bedrooms $$$$, Junior $$, AmEx/MC/Visa/Other CC, TAC 10%

Hotel Amenities: Laundry, Library, Parking, Pets Allowed

Business Facilities: Conf. Rm. Cap. 20, Mess. Ctr., Copier, Telex

Recreational Facilities: Pool, Sauna

Comps: Continental Breakfast

Room Amenities: Room Service, TV, Phones in Rm. (2), Cable TV, Kitchen, Ind. Heat Ctl., Ind. AC Ctl.

Plaza suites are beautifully decorated to give you the feeling of an elegant hotel. Each suite includes a large living room, two color televisions, and a woodburning fireplace. The fully-equipped kitchen gives you the flexibility of dining in your own suite. The comforts will make you feel you are coming home at night.

Regency
7940 Hollywood Blvd.
Los Angeles, CA 90046

70 Suites
800-252-0268 800-421-0745

Location: Metropolitan; L.A.
Airport: LAX 5 miles
Near: Sunset Boulevard, Hollywood Bowl
Walking Distance To: Various Elegant Shops
Area Attractions: Film Studios, Theatres, Rodeo Drive

Price Range & Credit Cards: 1 Bedroom Suite $$$, 2 Bedrooms $$$$, Junior $$, AmEx/MC/Visa/Other CC, TAC 10%

Hotel Amenities: Laundry, Library, Parking, Pets Allowed

Business Facilities: Conf. Rm. Cap. 10, Mess. Ctr., Copier, Telex

Recreational Facilities: Pool, Sauna, Swimming

Comps: Continental Breakfast

Room Amenities: Room Service, TV, Phones in Rm. (2), Cable TV, Kitchen, Ind. Heat Ctl., Ind. AC Ctl.

These suites are beautifully decorated to give you the feeling of an elegant hotel. Each suite includes a large living room, two color televisions, and a woodburning fireplace. The fully-equipped kitchen gives you the flexibility of dining in your own suite, day or night. The comforts will make you feel you are coming home at night.

---------------------------- LOS ANGELES ----------------------------

Westwood Marquis Hotel
930 Hilgard Ave.
Los Angeles, CA 90024

257 Suites
213-208-8765 800-421-2317

Location: Metropolitan; L.A.
Airport: LAX 5 miles
Near: Major Shopping Areas, Many Restaurants
Walking Distance To: Boutiques
Area Attractions: UCLA Campus, Theatres, Beach

Price Range & Credit Cards: 1 Bedroom Suite $$$$, 2 Bedrooms $$$$, AmEx/MC/ Visa/Other CC, TAC 10%

Hotel Amenities: Laundry, Parking, Car Hire, Handicap (20)

Business Facilities: Conf. Rm. Cap. 150, Banquet Fac., Mess. Ctr., Sec. Serv., Copier, Aud/Vis., Telex

Recreational Facilities: Pool, Sauna, Fitn. Ctr., Universal Equipment

Restaurant/Bar: Dynasty Room

Comps: Hors d'oeuvres

Room Amenities: TV, Phones in Rm. (2), Cable TV, Radio, Wet Bar, Ind. Heat Ctl., Ind. AC Ctl.

Created with the philosophy that the traveler deserves to be pampered, your stay begins with a greeting from a liveried doorman. Exquisite dining is only steps away in the critically acclaimed Dynasty Room and Garden Terrace Room, where service is attentive but not intrusive. California style with European flair, the Westwood Marquis is a grand hotel.

---------------------------- MANHATTAN BEACH ----------------------------

The Residence Inn by Marriott
1700 N.Sepulveda Blvd.
Manhattan Beach, CA 90266

175 Suites
213-546-7627 800-331-3131

Location: Metropolitan; Downtown: 10 mi.
Airport: LAX 5 miles
Near: Beach community, Convenient to Restaurants and Shops
Walking Distance To: Gardens, Beach
Area Attractions: Hometown Fair, Malls

Price Range & Credit Cards: 1 Bedroom Suite $$$, 2 Bedrooms $$$$, AmEx/MC/ Visa/Other CC, Children Free, TAC 10%

Hotel Amenities: Laundry, Parking, TV Lounge, Pets Allowed, Handicap (4)

Business Facilities: Conf. Rm. Cap. 40, Mess. Ctr., Sec. Serv., Copier, Aud/Vis., Teleconf.

Recreational Facilities: Pool, Whirlpool, Tennis, Golf; Fitness Center nearby

Comps: Continental Plus Breakfast, Refreshments, Airport Van

Room Amenities: Free Paper, TV, Phones in Rm., Cable TV, Radio, Kitchen, Ind. Heat Ctl., Ind. AC Ctl.

The Manhattan Beach Residence Inn is situated near LAX and a mile and a half from the beach, yet rests away from the downtown traffic and airport congestion. Well-kept gardens make the area colorful and peaceful. Comfortable suites include fully equipped kitchens, private sundecks, and woodburning fireplaces, giving each guest a taste of home.

---------------------------- MILPITAS ----------------------------

Embassy Suites Hotel
901 Calaberas Blvd.
Milpitas, CA 95035

267 Suites
408-942-0400 800-362-2779

Location: I-680 & 237; Downtown: 1 mile
Airport: 7 miles
Near: Downtown San Jose-6 miles
Walking Distance To: Town Center Shopping
& Theatre
Area Attractions: Great America Amusement
Park-5 miles

Price Range & Credit Cards: 1 Bedroom Suite $$$, AmEx/MC/Visa/Other CC, Children Free, TAC 10%

Hotel Amenities: Laundry, Gift Shop, Parking, TV Lounge, Pets Allowed, Handicap (9)

Business Facilities: Conf. Rm. Cap. 10-450, Banquet Fac., Copier, Aud/Vis., Teleconf., FAX

Recreational Facilities: Pool, Sauna, Whirlpool; Golf, Fitness Center nearby

Restaurant/Bar: Swan Court Cafe/Swan Court Lounge, Comedy, Dancing, Jazz

Comps: Full Breakfast, Refreshments, Hors d'oeuvres

Room Amenities: Room Service, Free Paper, TV, Phones in Rm. (2), Cable TV, Radio, Wet Bar, Refrigerator, Microwave

The Embassy Suites Hotel in Milpitas can be reached conveniently by freeway or hotel limousine from the airport. Great America Amusement Park is just five miles. The Embassy Suites offers on-site entertainment in the Swan Court Lounge. Additional recreation is available with golf and a fitness center nearby.

---------------------------- NAPA ----------------------------

Embassy Suites Hotel
1075 California Blvd.
Napa, CA 94558

205 Suites
707-253-9540 800-362-2779

Location: Central; Downtown: 3 min.
Airport: 1 Hour
Near: Wine Country, Convenient to Restaurants
Walking Distance To: Downtown, Residential Area
Area Attractions: Marineworld Africa U.S.A., Vineyards

Price Range & Credit Cards: 1 Bedroom Suite $$$, AmEx/MC/Visa/Other CC, Children Free, TAC 10%

Hotel Amenities: Laundry, TV Lounge, Handicap (7)

Business Facilities: Conf. Rm. Cap. 250, Banquet Fac., Aud/Vis., FAX

Recreational Facilities: Pool, Sauna, Whirlpool; Golf and Tennis nearby

Restaurant/Bar: Swan Court Cafe

Comps: Full Breakfast, Refreshments

Room Amenities: Room Service, Free Paper, TV, Phone in Rm., Cable TV, Wet Bar, Microwave, Refrigerator

Situated in the heart of the Napa Valley, Embassy Suites offers access to some of California's finest vintages and exquisite cuisine. Explore the quaint village specialty shops, then relax in the intimate comfort of park-like garden courtyards. Each suite has a wet bar, microwave, refrigerator, two speaker phones with separate lines, and a coffee-maker.

NAPA

Silverado Country Club
1600 Atlas Peak Rd.
Napa, CA 94558

280 Suites
707-257-0200 800-532-0500

Location: Country; Downtown: 5 min.
Airport: Napa 5 miles
Near: Country Enviroment, Many Restaurants
Walking Distance To: Countryside, Golf, Tennis
Area Attractions: Century-Old Winery Complex

Price Range & Credit Cards: 1 Bedroom Suite $$$$, 2 Bedrooms $$$$+, Junior $$$$, AmEx/MC/Visa/Other CC, TAC 10%

Hotel Amenities: Laundry, Parking, Car Hire, TV Lounge

Business Facilities: Conf. Rm. Cap. 500, Banquet Fac., Mess. Ctr., Sec. Serv., Copier, Aud/Vis.

Recreational Facilities: Pool, Whirlpool, Tennis, Golf, Fishing, Hot Air Balloon

Restaurant/Bar: Royal Oak

Room Amenities: Room Service, TV, Phone in Rm., Cable TV, Radio, Wet Bar, Kitchen, Ind. Heat Ctl., Ind. AC Ctl.

Experience Silverado, a 1200 acre resort tucked in amongst hills, ancient groves, and a generous choice of Napa Vineyards. Two 18-hole championship golf courses, the largest tennis complex in Northern California, jogging trails, and eight swimming pools. Although suites are each equipped like a luxurious residence, no two units are exactly alike.

NEWARK

Woodfin Suites Hotel & Bus.Ctr
39150 Cedar Blvd.
Newark, CA 94560

Location: E. Bay I-880;
Airport: Oakland: 20 minutes
Walking Distance To: Newpark Mall
Area Attractions: 45 min. to San Francisco

415-795-1200 800-237-8811

Price Range & Credit Cards: 1 Bedroom Suite $$$, 2 Bedrooms $$$$, AmEx/MC/Visa/Other CC, Children Free, TAC 10%

Hotel Amenities: Laundry, Library, Handicap (8)

Business Facilities: Conf. Rm. Cap. 75, Banquet Fac., Sec. Serv., Copier, Aud/Vis., Telex, Comp. Hook-up, Bus. Ctr.

Recreational Facilities: Pool, Sauna, Boating near; Golf & Fishing nearby

Restaurant/Bar: Bar

Comps: Full Breakfast, Refreshments, Hors d'oeuvres

Room Amenities: Room Service, Free Paper, TV, Phones in Rm. (2), VCR, Radio, Kitchen, Ind. Heat Ctl., Ind. AC Ctl.

The Woodfin Suites Hotel, Newark, is just minutes from Fremont, the San Jose and Oakland airports. Elegant 1 and 2 bedroom suites have full kitchens, VCR's, and wood-burning fireplaces. A complimentary business center provides computer, typewriter, copier. Groups, or extended stay travellers, will find the Woodfin especially comfortable. Free movies.

──────────────── NEWPORT BEACH ────────────────

Marriott Suites-Newport Beach   **Location:** Bayside;
500 Bayview Circle   **Airport:** John Wayne: 5 min.
Newport Beach, CA 92660   **Near:** Newport Beach's Back Bay
                                       Walking Distance To: Beaches, Tennis, Golf
250 Suites   **Area Attractions:** Disneyland, Knott's Berry
714-854-4500 800-228-9290   Farm, Boating & Fishing Charters

Price Range & Credit Cards: 1 Bedroom Suite $$$, AmEx/MC/Visa/Other CC, Children Free, TAC 10%

Hotel Amenities: Laundry, Parking, Pets Allowed, Handicap (1)

Business Facilities: Conf. Rm. Cap. 180, Mess. Ctr., Copier, Aud/Vis., FAX, Comp. Hook-up

Recreational Facilities: Pool, Sauna, Whirlpool, Health Club; Golf & Tennis nearby

Comps: Full Breakfast, Beverages & Snacks, Airport Shuttle

Room Amenities: Room Service, Free Paper, TV, Phones in Rm. (2), Cable TV, Radio, Wet Bar, Refrigerator, Ind. Heat Ctl., Ind. AC Ctl.

The new Marriott Suites-Newport Beach will make your stay in Orange County something special. Breathtaking hotel overlooks the picturesque waters of Newport Beach's Back Bay. Experience the luxury, comfort, and convenience of the elegant yet home-like suites. Relax in the pool or enjoy nearby tennis, golf, or beaches. An exceptional value.

──────────────── ORANGE ────────────────

The Residence Inn by Marriott   **Location:** Orange; Downtown: 2-4 mi.
201 N. State College Blvd.   **Airport:** LAX: 45 minutes
Orange, CA 92668   **Near:** John Wayne Airport-20 min., Anaheim
                                       Convention Center & Stadium
105 Suites   **Area Attractions:** Disneyland, Crystal Cathe-
714-978-7700 800-331-3131   dral, Knott's Berry Farm-7 miles

Price Range & Credit Cards: 1 Bedroom Suite $$$, 2 Bedrooms $$$$, AmEx/MC/Visa/Other CC, Children Free, TAC 10%

Hotel Amenities: Laundry, Library, Parking, TV Lounge, Small Pets Fee, Handicap (2)

Business Facilities: Conf. Rm. Cap. 12-14, Banquet Fac., Mess. Ctr., Sec. Serv., Copier, Aud/Vis., Teleconf., Telex

Recreational Facilities: Pool, Jacuzzi, Sport Court, Golf-3 miles, Game Area; Sports Gallery nearby

Restaurant/Bar: TGI Friday's (room service only)

Comps: Continental Plus Breakfast, Refreshments, Hors d'oeuvres

Room Amenities: Room Service, Free Paper, TV, Phone in Rm., Cable TV, Radio, Kitchen, Ind. Heat Ctl., Ind. AC Ctl.

The Residence Inn by Marriott/Orange is a charming, tudor-style hotel with a European inn flavor and homelike service, set in magnificently landscaped grounds. Convenient to Disneyland and Convention Center, with easy freeway access. Cozy fireplaces, elegant surroundings, and complimentary hospitality hour. Discounted rates for extended stay.

─────────────── ORANGE ───────────────

Woodfin Suites Hotel & Bus.Ctr
720 The City Drive South
Orange, CA 92668

124 Suites
714-740-2700 800-237-8811

Location: City Square; Orange County-Ctr
Airport: LAX-35 min.
Near: Orange County Airport-15 min., Disneyland-3 mi., Anaheim Stadium-1 mi.
Area Attractions: Knotts Berry Farm, City Shopping Mall, Crystal Cathedral

Price Range & Credit Cards: 1 Bedroom Suite $$$, 2 Bedrooms $$$$, Junior $$$, AmEx/MC/Visa/Other CC, Child Free, TAC 10%

Hotel Amenities: Laundry, Library, Car Hire, TV Lounge, Small Pets Fee, Handicap (4)

Business Facilities: Conf. Rm. Cap. 125, Banquet Fac., Mess. Ctr., Sec. Serv., Copier, Aud/Vis., FAX, Comp. Hook-up, Bus. Ctr.

Recreational Facilities: Pool, Whirlpool, Massage, Beaches, Horses, Water Skiing, Gift Shop, Golf and Tennis nearby

Restaurant/Bar: Clubhouse, Automatic Piano

Comps: Continental Plus Breakfast, Refreshments, Van within 5 miles

Room Amenities: Room Service, Free Paper, TV, Phones in Rm. (2), VCR, Radio, Wet Bar, Kitchen, Ind. Heat Ctl., Ind. AC Ctl.

Woodfin Suites is an elegant little hotel! Guest feel comfortable whether staying a day, a week or a month in the beautiful spacious suites. No guest request is too great or too small for their accomodating and friendly staff to carry out. Woodfin Suites makes the perfect home and office while on the road. There is another Woodfin in the city of Brea.

─────────────── OXNARD ───────────────

Embassy Suites Hotel
2101 Mandalay Beach Rd.
Oxnard, CA 93035

250 Suites
805-984-2500 800-362-2779

Location: Beach; Downtown: 3 miles
Airport: LAX One hour
Near: Pacific Ocean, Oxnard Airport-2 miles
Walking Distance To: Harbor, Beach
Area Attractions: Ventura Marina, Golf, Museums

Price Range & Credit Cards: 1 Bedroom Suite $$$$, 2 Bedrooms $$$$+, Junior $$$, AmEx/MC/Visa/Other CC, Children Free, TAC 10%

Hotel Amenities: Laundry, Parking, TV Lounge

Business Facilities: Conf. Rm. Cap. 500, Banquet Fac., Mess. Ctr., Sec. Serv., Copier, Aud/Vis., Teleconf., Telex, Comp. Hook-up

Recreational Facilities: Pool, Whirlpool, Tennis, Golf, Fishing, Sailing; Windsurfing nearby

Restaurant/Bar: Mandalay Beach Opus One Restaurant and Lounge, Entertainment

Comps: Full Breakfast, Refreshments

Room Amenities: Room Service, Free Paper, TV, Phones in Rm. (2), Cable TV, VCR, Radio, Wet Bar, Kitchen, Ind. Heat Ctl., Ind. AC Ctl.

Mandalay Beach Resort is truly a great ocean hotel. The Mediterranean courtyards of marble and stone are complemented by streams, waterfalls, anad fountains. Beautifully appointed suites are spacious and equipped with wet bar, refrigerator, and microwave oven. Lighted tennis courts, golf, and a jogging trail are available.

Embassy Suites Hotel, Oxnard, CA

OXNARD

Radisson Suite Hotel
2101 W. Vineyard Ave.
Oxnard, CA 93030

253 Suites
805-988-0130 800-333-3333

Location: Residential; Downtown: 10 min.
Airport: 5 minutes
Near: Financial Plaza, Beaches-15 min. away
Area Attractions: Fisherman's Wharf-10 min.,
Santa Barbara-30 minutes

Price Range & Credit Cards: 1 Bedroom Suite $$$, 2 Bedrooms $$$, Junior $$,
AmEx/MC/Visa/Other CC, Children Free, TAC 10%

Hotel Amenities: Laundry, Gift Shop, TV Lounge, Handicap (8)

Business Facilities: Conf. Rm. Cap. 900, Banquet Fac., Copier, Aud/Vis.

Recreational Facilities: Pool, Whirlpool, Fitn. Ctr., Tennis; Golf & Sailing nearby

Restaurant/Bar: Fairway's/Club 30-Love, DJ, Live Band, etc.

Comps: Full Breakfast, Hors d'oeuvres

Room Amenities: Room Service, Free Paper, TV, Phone in Rm., Cable TV, Radio,
Kitchen, Ind. Heat Ctl., Ind. AC Ctl.

Radisson Suites overlooks an 18-hole championship golf course and is the summer home of the LA Raiders. Thirty-two buildings surround the conference center. Many suites have wood-burning fireplaces; all have full kitchens with refrigerator, stove and other amenities; contemporary furnishings in mauve with contrasting trim.

─────────────── PALM DESERT ───────────────

Embassy Suites Hotel
74-700 Hiway 111
Palm Desert, CA 92260

199 Suites
619-340-6600 800-362-2779

Location: Eastside; Downtown: 15 min.
Airport: 20 miles
Near: Date groves, Mountains, Town Center Mall, Golf
Area Attractions: El Paseo Shops, Living Desert, Aerial Tramway

Price Range & Credit Cards: 1 Bedroom Suite $$$$, AmEx/MC/Visa/Other CC, Children Free, TAC 10%

Hotel Amenities: Laundry, Parking, Handicap (3)

Business Facilities: Conf. Rm. Cap. 675, Banquet Fac., Mess. Ctr., Copier, Aud/Vis., Teleconf., Comp. Hook-up

Recreational Facilities: Pool, Whirlpool, Fitn. Ctr., Tennis; 12 Golf Courses nearby

Restaurant/Bar: Sonoma Grill, Entertainment

Comps: Full Breakfast, Refreshments, Airport Shuttle

Room Amenities: Room Service, Free Paper, TV, Phones in Rm. (2), Cable TV, Radio, Wet Bar, Kitchen, Ind. Heat Ctl., Ind. AC Ctl.

Three Spanish fountains rise amidst lush foliage in the landscaped gardens of the inner courtyard. Enjoy the warm sun at the pool, or relax in the spa. There are also a jogging track, lighted tennis courts, an exercise room with equipment, and chipping/putting greens. Complimentary full American breakfast, and cocktails each evening are included.

─────────────── PALM DESERT ───────────────

Palm Desert Resort Hotel
77-333 Country Club Dr.
Palm Desert, CA 92260

300 Suites
619-345-2781 800-662-4387

Location: Suburban; Downtown: 5 min.
Airport: 20 Minutes
Near: Living Desert, El Paseo Shops
Walking Distance To: Shopping Center
Area Attractions: Aerial Tramway, Oasis Water Park, Palm Springs

Price Range & Credit Cards: 1 Bedroom Suite $$$$, 2 Bedrooms $$$$+, AmEx/MC/Visa/Other CC, TAC 10%

Hotel Amenities: Laundry, Parking, Car Hire, TV Lounge

Business Facilities: Conf. Rm. Cap. 100, Banquet Fac., Copier, Aud/Vis.

Recreational Facilities: Pool, Whirlpool, Tennis, Racquetball; Golfer's Delight

Restaurant/Bar: Papagayo Room, Conquistador, Entertainment

Room Amenities: TV, Phone in Rm., Cable TV, Wet Bar, Kitchen, Ind. Heat Ctl., Ind. AC Ctl.

An oasis of pleasure, Palm Desert Resort provides a homey and spacious atmosphere. Private resort villas overlook mountains, sun-dappled lakes or country club fairways. Try the 18-hole championship golf course, or one of 16 lighted tennis courts. Understated elegance, Western informality and friendliness make you feel welcome as you enter the resort.

PALM SPRINGS

Cathedral Canyon Resort Hotel
34567 Cathedral Canyon Dr.
Palm Springs, CA 92264

162 Suites
619-321-9000 800-237-6923

Location: Suburban; Downtown: 10 min.
Airport: 8 minutes
Near: Theatres, Department Stores, Restaurants, Cathedral Canyon Golf Course
Walking Distance To: 450 Acre Club, 22 Lakes
Area Attractions: Finer Shops, Desert Museum, Sightseeing, Bob Hope Center

Price Range & Credit Cards: 1 Bedroom Suite $$$$, AmEx/MC/Visa/Other CC, Children Free, TAC 10%

Hotel Amenities: Laundry, Handicap (5)

Business Facilities: Conf. Rm. Cap. 250, Banquet Fac., Copier, Aud/Vis.

Recreational Facilities: Pool, Sauna, Bicycles, 10 Tennis Courts; Golf Course nearby

Comps: Newspaper, Hors d'oeuvres

Room Amenities: Room Service, TV, Phone in Rm., Cable TV, Radio, Wet Bar, Kitchen, Ind. Heat Ctl., Ind. AC Ctl.

The luxurious Cathedral Canyon Resort Hotel at the foot of the snow-capped San Jacinto Mountains, offers you a P.G.A. rated 18-hole championship golf course and 10 tennis courts. The 3,300 sq. ft. meeting room is ideal for conferences. The in-house restaurant features panoramic views and an excellent cuisine certain to please the most exacting guest.

PALM SPRINGS

Maxim's de Paris Suite Hotel
285 No. Palm Canyon Dr.
Palm Springs, CA 92262

194 Suites
619-322-9000 800-562-9467

Location: Central; Downtown
Airport: 20 Minutes
Near: Theatres, Department Stores, Restaurants
Walking Distance To: City Center
Area Attractions: Finest Shops, Desert Museum

Price Range & Credit Cards: 1 Bedroom Suite $$$$, 2 Bedrooms $$$$+, AmEx/MC/Visa/Other CC, Children Free, TAC 10%

Hotel Amenities: Laundry, Parking, Car Hire, Handicap (7)

Business Facilities: Conf. Rm. Cap. 150, Banquet Fac., Mess. Ctr., Sec. Serv., Copier, Aud/Vis., Telex, Comp. Hook-up

Recreational Facilities: Pool, Sauna, Whirlpool, Fitn. Ctr., Tennis, Game Area; Member, Palm Springs Tennis Club

Restaurant/Bar: Le Jardin, Palm Court, Entertainment

Comps: Rolls Royce to & from airport, Hors d'oeuvres

Room Amenities: Room Service, Free Paper, TV, Phones in Rm. (3), Cable TV, Radio, Wet Bar, Ind. Heat Ctl., Ind. AC Ctl.

Overlooking the "Rodeo Drive" of Palm Springs to the east and the lush fairways of an exclusive country club to the west, Maxim's De Paris is a posh hotel that can truly boast of having a world-class reputation. Superb, state-of-the-art business facilities create an ideal environment for your meetings or private gatherings. Maxim's is unique!

─────────────── PISMO BEACH ───────────────

Quality Suites Pismo Beach
651 Five Cities Drive
Pismo Beach, CA 93449

133 Suites
805-773-3773 800-228-5151

Location: Highway 101; Downtown: 5 min.
Airport: 15 minutes
Near: Suburbs, Pismo State Beach
Walking Distance To: Public Beach, Golf, Horses
Area Attractions: Pismo State Beach

Price Range & Credit Cards: 1 Bedroom Suite $$, AmEx/MC/Visa/Other CC, Children Free, TAC 10%

Hotel Amenities: Laundry, Library, Gift Shop, Handicap (5)

Business Facilities: Conf. Rm. Cap. 20, Sec. Serv., Copier

Recreational Facilities: Pool, Whirlpool, Putting Green; Golf & Boating nearby

Comps: Full Breakfast, Refreshments, Airport Transit

Room Amenities: Free Paper, TV, Phones in Rm. (1), Cable TV, VCR, Radio, Wet Bar, Ind. Heat Ctl., Ind. AC Ctl.

The 2-story Quality Suites structure spreads out over 3 acres of land with 3 individual court-yards, all beautifully landscaped. In the lobby, where complimentary beer and wine are served, is a delightful fountain surrounded by peach and soft pastel colors. Nearby sights to see include: Wineries, Pismo State Beach, and the legendary Hearst Castle-60 mi.

─────────────── PLACENTIA ───────────────

The Residence Inn by Marriott
700 W. Kimberly
Placentia, CA 92670

112 Suites
714-996-0555 800-331-3131

Location: Indust. Park; Downtown: 45 min.
Airport: LAX: 40 miles
Near: Long Beach Airport-22 miles, Ontario Airport-18 miles
Area Attractions: Disneyland-8 mi., Knott's Berry Farm-10 mi., Anaheim Stadium

Price Range & Credit Cards: 1 Bedroom Suite $$$, 2 Bedrooms $$$$, AmEx/MC/Visa/Other CC, Children Free, TAC 10%

Hotel Amenities: Pets Allowed, Handicap (5)

Business Facilities: Conf. Rm. Cap. 25, Mess. Ctr., Copier, Aud/Vis., FAX

Recreational Facilities: Pool, Whirlpool, Golf, Fishing, Boating, Fitness Center

Comps: Continental Plus Breakfast, Refreshments, Hors d'oeuvres

Room Amenities: Room Service, Free Paper, TV, Phones in Rm. (2), Cable TV, Radio, Ind. Heat Ctl., Ind. AC Ctl.

Residence Inn, Placentia, located on the 57 Freeway north of 91, is convenient for business travellers to Anaheim, Brea, Fullerton, and Placentia. The Inn has spacious bedroom suites, ideal for families, with full kitchens and cheery fireplaces. The staff is dedicated to making you feel at home by thoughtful service. Rates discounted for extended stays.

---------------------------- SAN DIEGO ----------------------------

Balboa Park Inn
3402 Park Blvd.
San Diego, CA 92103

25 Suites
619-298-0823

Location: Balboa Park; Downtown: 2 min.
Airport: 5 minutes
Near: Museums, 1300-acre Balboa Park
Walking Distance To: World's Largest Zoo
Area Attractions: Old Globe, Starlight, Space Theatres

Price Range & Credit Cards: 1 Bedroom Suite $$, 2 Bedrooms $$$, Junior $$, AmEx/ MC/Visa, Children Free, TAC 10%

Hotel Amenities: Laundry, Car Hire, TV Lounge, Pets Allowed

Business Facilities: Conf. Rm. Cap. 25-100, Banquet Fac., Mess. Ctr., Sec. Serv.

Recreational Facilities: Sunning Terrace, Game Area; Tennis, Golf, Swimming nearby

Comps: Continental Breakfast, Toiletries

Room Amenities: Room Service, Free Paper, TV, Cable TV, Radio, Kitchen, Ind. Heat Ctl., Ind. AC Ctl.

Balboa Park Inn, built in 1915 for the World's Fair, is adjacent to beautiful Balboa Park and San Diego Zoo. The 25 over-sized suites ensure guests great comfort. Each suite has a different theme, (e.g. Paris in the 30's, Marianne's Southwest), and returning guests often select a new one each time to suit their mood.

---------------------------- SAN DIEGO ----------------------------

Crown Point View Suite Hotel
4088 Crown Point Dr.
San Diego, CA 92109

19 Suites
619-272-0676 800-572-5767

Location: Northside; Downtown: 10 min.
Airport: 15 minutes
Near: Pacific Beach, Mission Bay Park
Walking Distance To: Public Beach
Area Attractions: Sea World, Balboa Park, Zoo

Price Range & Credit Cards: 1 Bedroom Suite $$, 2 Bedrooms $$$, Junior $$, AmEx/ MC/Visa, Children Free, TAC 10%

Hotel Amenities: Laundry, Parking, Pets Allowed

Recreational Facilities: Tennis, Golf; Water activities nearby

Comps: Continental Breakfast

Room Amenities: TV, Phones in Rm. (2), Cable TV, Movies, Kitchen, Ind. Heat Ctl.

The intimate size of Crown Point View enables the friendly staff to add that special extra touch. The sun-deck on the roof affords a spectacular view of Mission Bay, and bring your binoculars so you can spy on the water birds that nest directly across the street. Each suite (495-1,000 sq. ft.) is individually decorated with tasteful furnishings.

―――――――――――――― SAN DIEGO ――――――――――――――

Embassy Suites Hotel
4550 La Jolla Village Drive
San Diego, CA 92122

335 Suites
619-453-0400 800-362-2779

Location: High Tech; Downtown: 15 min.
Airport: 15 minutes
Near: University Towne Center Shopping Mall
Area Attractions: 10-15 minutes from all
Local Beaches

Price Range & Credit Cards: 1 Bedroom Suite $$$$, 2 Bedrooms $$$$+, AmEx/MC/ Visa/Other CC, Children Free, TAC 10%

Hotel Amenities: Laundry, Gift Shop, Parking, Car Hire, TV Lounge, Handicap (11)

Business Facilities: Conf. Rm. Cap. 16-18, Banquet Fac., Mess. Ctr., Copier, Aud/Vis., Teleconf., Telex

Recreational Facilities: Pool, Sauna, Whirlpool, Fitn. Ctr., Tennis, Golf, Scuba Diving, Jogging Track nearby

Restaurant/Bar: "The Other Place"/"The Other Place Lounge"; Live Jazz Band (Mon)

Comps: Full Breakfast, Refreshments, Hors d'oeuvres

Room Amenities: Room Service, Free Paper, TV, Phones in Rm. (2), Cable TV, Radio, Wet Bar, Microwave, Ind. Heat Ctl., Ind. AC Ctl.

The Embassy Suites Hotel in La Jolla provides the comforts of home for the price of a single room. Each suite offers a spacious living room, dining area, color TV, telephone, wet bar, microwave, & refrigerator. Included in the rate is a full breakfast and beverages in the evening. Enjoy a courtyard atrium filled with plants, ponds, charm and elegance.

―――――――――――――― SAN FRANCISCO ――――――――――――――

The Elles'mere
655 Powell St.
San Francisco, CA 94108

48 Suites
415-477-4600 800-426-6161

Location: Nob Hill; Downtown: 5 min.
Airport: 45 minutes
Near: Union Square (3 blocks), All Major Shops
Walking Distance To: San Francisco's Finest Shops
Area Attractions: Financial District, Theatres, Civic Center

Price Range & Credit Cards: 1 Bedroom Suite $$$$, Junior $$$, AmEx/MC/Visa/ Other CC, Children Free, TAC 10%

Hotel Amenities: Laundry, Library, Parking, Car Hire

Business Facilities: Mess. Ctr., Copier, Teleconf., Comp. Hook-up, Bus. Ctr.

Recreational Facilities: Game Area; Health Club nearby

Comps: Breakfast, Refreshments

Room Amenities: Free Paper, TV, Phones in Rm. (2), VCR, Radio, Wet Bar, Kitchen, Ind. Heat Ctl., Ind. AC Ctl.

The elegantly designed, refurnished, 1923 building is conveniently located five minutes from Union Square's famous stores and repertory theatres, with the financial district within walking distance! Suites are lavishly equipped with oversized desk, posture chair, loveseat, live plants, answering machine, TV-VCR, and more. This is a no-tipping hotel.

─────────────── SAN FRANCISCO ───────────────

Hyde Park Suites
2655 Hyde Street
San Francisco, CA 94109

24 Suites
415-771-0200 800-227-3608

Location: Metropolitan; Downtown: 20 min.
Airport: 30 minutes
Near: Fisherman's Wharf, Ghirardelli Square, Cannery, Alcatraz, Angel Island
Walking Distance To: North Beach, China Town
Area Attractions: Theatres, Nob Hill, Fort Mason, Civic Center, Union Square

Price Range & Credit Cards: 1 Bedroom Suite $$$$, 2 Bedrooms $$$$, AmEx/MC/Visa/Other CC, Children Free, TAC 10%

Hotel Amenities: Laundry, Parking, Car Hire

Business Facilities: FAX, Mess. Ctr., Sec. Serv., Copier, Aud/Vis., Telex

Recreational Facilities: Parcourse; Jogging Trails

Restaurant/Bar: Hospitality Hour

Comps: Downtown Limousine, Wine Nightly, Hors d'oeuvres

Room Amenities: Free Paper, TV, Phones in Rm. (2), Cable TV, VCR, Radio, Wet Bar, Full Kitchen, Ind. Heat Ctl.

At Hyde Park, a stone's throw from Fisherman's Wharf, luxury and location combine to create the potential for a perfect travel experience. Equipped with many business services and amenities, Hyde Park can please everyone. Take in the panoramic view of Alcatraz Island and the world famous Golden Gate Bridge from the secluded sundeck. Charming atrium.

─────────────── SAN LUIS OBISPO ───────────────

Embassy Suites Hotel
333 Madonna Road
San Luis Obispo, CA 93401

196 Suites
805-549-0800 800-422-9495

Location: Central Coast Plaza
Airport: 30 minutes
Near: 63-store Mall, Fair, Music Festival
Walking Distance To: Golf
Area Attractions: Hearst Castle, Wine Festival

Price Range & Credit Cards: 1 Bedroom Suite $$, AmEx/MC/Visa/Other CC, Children Free, TAC 10%

Hotel Amenities: Laundry, Handicap (6)

Business Facilities: Conf. Rm. Cap. 700, Banquet Fac., Mess. Ctr., Sec. Serv., Copier, Aud/Vis., Teleconf., Comp. Hook-up

Recreational Facilities: Pool, Sauna, Whirlpool, Fitn. Ctr., Tennis, Golf, Beach; Jogging Trail

Restaurant/Bar: Park Cafe, Atrium Bar, Entertainment

Comps: Full Breakfast, Manager's Reception

Room Amenities: Room Service, Free Paper, TV, Phones in Rm. (2), Cable TV, VCR, Radio, Wet Bar, Ind. Heat Ctl., Ind. AC Ctl.

Adjacent to a 63-store enclosed shopping mall, the Embassy Suites Hotel is a superb site to meet all your business and leisure needs. Functional meeting rooms able to seat up to 700 and many services make for productive business. The on-site pool, sauna, and fitness center are all guest favorites. This relaxed park-like hotel is near many attractions.

─────────────────────── SAN LUIS OBISPO ───────────────────────

Quality Suites
1631 Monterey Street
San Luis Obispo, CA 93103

138 Suites
805-541-5001 800-228-5151

Location: ; Downtown: 0.5 mi.
Airport: 5 miles
Area Attractions: San Luis Mission, Wine Country, & Hearst Castle-1 hour

Price Range & Credit Cards: 1 Bedroom Suite $$$, AmEx/MC/Visa, Children Free, TAC 10%

Hotel Amenities: Handicap (5)

Business Facilities: Conf. Rm. Cap. 25, Sec. Serv., Copier

Recreational Facilities: Pool, Whirlpool, Tennis, Golf, Fishing, Boating nearby

Comps: Full Breakfast, Refreshments

Room Amenities: Free Paper, TV, Phones in Rm. (2), Cable TV, VCR, Radio, Wet Bar

Located convenient to San Luis Obispo business, wine country and Cal Poly, Quality Suites is situated to provide every guest a relaxed, quiet retreat. The design award-winning lobby provides every guest with a feeling of comfort and a great place to gather. The staff offers the finest in personal service. This is an excellent hotel.

─────────────────────── SANTA ANA ───────────────────────

Comfort Suites
2620 Hotel Terrace Drive
Santa Ana, CA 92705

130 Suites
714-966-5200 800-228-5150

Location: Metropolitan; Downtown: 5 min.
Airport: 5 minutes
Near: Disneyland, Newport Beaches, Knott's Berry Farm
Walking Distance To: Civic Center
Area Attractions: Universal Studios, L.A. Beaches, Sea World

Price Range & Credit Cards: Junior $$, AmEx/MC/Visa/Other CC, Children Free, TAC 10%

Hotel Amenities: Laundry, Handicap (5)

Business Facilities: Conf. Rm. Cap. 15, Sec. Serv., Copier

Recreational Facilities: Pool, Whirlpool, Tennis, Golf, Fishing, Boating, Fitness Center nearby

Comps: Continental Breakfast

Room Amenities: Free Paper, TV, Phone in Rm., Cable TV

Situated on 2 acres, the fine buildings of Comfort Suites are connected by covered walkways. Right outside your door is a swimming pool and spa surrounded by beautiful landscaping. The handsome tiled lobby features a hacienda-like decor including a fireplace. Also in the lobby is the breakfast alcove where guests are served complimentary breakfast.

48 California

Embassy Suites Hotel
1325 E. Dyer Rd.
Santa Ana, CA 92705

308 Suites
714-241-3800 800-362-2779

Location: Metropolitan; Downtown: Nearby
Airport: 10 minutes
Near: Performing Arts Center, South Coast Plaza
Walking Distance To: Civic Center
Area Attractions: Disneyland, Orange Coast College, Beaches

Price Range & Credit Cards: 1 Bedroom Suite $$$, AmEx/MC/Visa/Other CC, Children Free, TAC 10%

Hotel Amenities: Valet Laundry, Handicap (9)

Business Facilities: Conf. Rm. Cap. 50, Banquet Fac., Mess. Ctr., Aud/Vis., Teleconf., FAX

Recreational Facilities: Pool, Sauna, Whirlpool, Steamroom; Golf nearby

Restaurant/Bar: Woolley's Restaurant & Lounge, Entertainment

Comps: Full Breakfast, Refreshments, Popcorn

Room Amenities: Room Service, Clock Radio, TV, Phones in Rm. (2), Wet Bar, Kitchen, Ind. Heat Ctl., Ind. AC Ctl.

Featuring Mediterranean decor with waterfalls, fish, and lush tropical foliage inside an enclosed atrium that creates a soothing environment for business or pleasure. Located 2 miles from John Wayne Airport, this 308-suite structure has 6 meeting rooms (or ballroom) that accommodate 250 people banquet-style. Pool, spa, sauna & steamroom are all available.

Quality Suites
2701 Hotel Terrace Drive
Santa Ana, CA 92705

177 Suites
714-957-9200 800-228-5151

Location: Metropolitan; Downtown: 5 min.
Airport: 5 minutes
Near: Suburbs, Airport, Disneyland, Knott's Berry Farm
Walking Distance To: Civic Center
Area Attractions: Universal Studios, L.A., Newport Beaches

Price Range & Credit Cards: 1 Bedroom Suite $$, AmEx/MC/Visa/Other CC, Children Free, TAC 10%

Hotel Amenities: Laundry, Library, Gift Shop, Handicap (5)

Business Facilities: Sec. Serv., Copier

Recreational Facilities: Pool, Whirlpool, Tennis, Golf, Fishing, Boating, Fitness Center; all sports nearby

Comps: Full Breakfast, Refreshments, Airport Shuttle

Room Amenities: Free Paper, TV, Phones in Rm. (2), Cable TV, VCR, Radio, Wet Bar, Ind. Heat Ctl., Ind. AC Ctl.

In the quiet, suave environment of Quality Suites you'll be free to accomplish business goals or take part in recreational activities. The 177 suites have built-in furniture and offer a selection of 3 color schemes. The three-story buildings are connected by covered walkways bordered by lush landscaping and flowers in terracotta pots.

Maxim's de Paris Suite Hotel, Palm Springs, CA

──────────── SANTA ANA ────────────

Woolley's Petite Suites Hotel
2721 Hotel Terrace Drive
Santa Ana, CA 92734

184 Suites
714-540-1111

Location: Industrial; Downtown: 1 mile
Airport: 4 miles
Near: South Coast Plaza-3 miles
Area Attractions: Disneyland-20 minutes

Price Range & Credit Cards: 1 Bedroom Suite $$, AmEx/MC/Visa/Other CC, Children Free, TAC 10%

Hotel Amenities: Laundry, Parking, Gift Shop, Pets Allowed, Handicap (6)

Business Facilities: Conf. Rm. Cap. 230, Mess. Ctr., Copier, Aud/Vis.

Recreational Facilities: Pool, Whirlpool; Golf Newport Beach

Comps: Full Breakfast, Refreshments & Popcorn, Airport Shuttle

Room Amenities: Free Paper, TV, Phones in Rm. (2), Cable TV, Radio, Wet Bar, Kitchen, Ind. Heat Ctl., Ind. AC Ctl.

The comforts of home are important while on the road. . . but all too often you pay dearly for those little extras. Now at Woolley's Petite Suites you can enjoy the comfort of a suite at an uncommon value. The motto at Woolley's Petite Suite Hotel is "We Care About Your Comfort."

―――――――――――― SANTA CLARA ――――――――――――

Embassy Suites Hotel
2885 Lakeside Dr.
Santa Clara, CA 95051

257 Suites
408-496-6400 800-362-2779

Location: Central; San Jose: 5 miles
Airport: 5 miles
Near: Heart of Silicon Valley, Santa Clara Convention Center, Techmart
Walking Distance To: Many Restaurants
Area Attractions: Winchester Mystery House, Great America, Stanford Univ.

Price Range & Credit Cards: 1 Bedroom Suite $$$$, Junior $$$, AmEx/MC/Visa/Other CC, Children Free, TAC 10%

Hotel Amenities: Parking, TV Lounge, Handicap (32)

Business Facilities: Conf. Rm. Cap. 65, Banquet Fac., Copier, Aud/Vis., Teleconf., FAX, Comp. Hook-up

Recreational Facilities: Pool, Sauna, Whirlpool; Golf and Tennis nearby

Restaurant/Bar: Cafe Bon Appetit, Entertainment

Comps: Full breakfast, Refreshments, Airport ride, Hors d'oeuvres

Room Amenities: Room Service, Free Paper, TV, Phones in Rm. (2), Cable TV, Radio, Wet Bar, Coffee maker, Ind. Heat Ctl., Ind. AC Ctl.

With a well-balanced offering of recreational facilities as well as business services and meeting rooms, Embassy has developed an excellent place to stay and more! Located near many local attractions and only 5 miles from the San Jose International Airport, the 257 suites are well-appointed with a mauve color scheme. Golf and tennis are nearby.

―――――――――――― SO. SAN FRANCISCO ――――――――――――

Comfort Suites
121 East Grand Ave.
So. San Francisco, CA 94080

165 Suites
415-589-7766 800-228-5151

Location: 101 Frwy.; Downtown: 12 mi.
Airport: 2 miles
Area Attractions: 12 mi. to Fishermans's Wharf, Chinatown & Financial District

Price Range & Credit Cards: 1 Bedroom Suite $$, AmEx/MC/Visa/Other CC, Children Free, TAC 10%

Hotel Amenities: Laundry, Handicap (5)

Business Facilities: Conf. Rm. Cap. 20, Sec. Serv., Copier

Recreational Facilities: Whirlpool, Tennis, Golf, Fishing, Boating; all sports nearby

Comps: Continental Breakfast, Refreshments

Room Amenities: Free Paper, TV, Phone in Rm., Cable TV

The 5 buildings of Comfort Suites are connected by covered walkways. Right outside your door is an oversized spa surrounded by beautiful landscaping. Handsome tiled lobby features a hacienda-like decor including a fireplace. Also in the lobby is a breakfast alcove where a complimentary breakfast is served each morning and soup and chili each evening.

---------------------------- SUNNYVALE ----------------------------

The Residence Inn by Marriott
750 Lakeway
Sunnyvale, CA 94086

232 Suites
408-720-1000   800-331-3131

Location: Business; Downtown: 10 min.
Airport: 4 miles
Near: Central Area Shops, Heart of Silicon Valley
Walking Distance To: Business Area
Area Attractions: Great America Theme Park, Restaurants

Price Range & Credit Cards: 1 Bedroom Suite $$$, 2 Bedrooms $$$$, AmEx/MC/Visa/Other CC, Children Free, TAC 10%

Hotel Amenities: Laundry, Parking, TV Lounge, Pets Allowed

Business Facilities: Conf. Rm. Cap. 12, Mess. Ctr., Copier, Aud/Vis.

Recreational Facilities: Pool, Whirlpool, Fitn. Ctr., Decathlon Club

Restaurant/Bar: Rusty Scupper

Comps: Continental Breakfast, Happy Hour

Room Amenities: Room Service, Free Paper, TV, Phone in Rm., Cable TV, Radio, Kitchen, Microwave, Ind. Heat Ctl., Ind. AC Ctl.

Business travellers enjoy the convenience and comforts of home while staying at this Residence Inn-Silicon Valley 1. Complimentary breakfast in the Gatehouse starts the day pleasantly. Enjoy the Happy Hour, or relax in the pool when business is completed. Discounted rates for extended stay.

---------------------------- SUNNYVALE ----------------------------

The Residence Inn by Marriott
1080 Stewart Dr.
Sunnyvale, CA 94086

247 Suites
408-720-8893   800-331-3131

Location: Business; Downtown: 10 min.
Airport: 4 miles
Near: Central Area Shops, Heart of Silicon Valley
Walking Distance To: Business Area, Restaurants
Area Attractions: Great America Theme Park

Price Range & Credit Cards: 1 Bedroom Suite $$$, 2 Bedrooms $$$$, AmEx/MC/Visa/Other CC, Children Free, TAC 10%

Hotel Amenities: Laundry, Parking, TV Lounge, Pets Allowed

Business Facilities: Conf. Rm. Cap. 60, Mess. Ctr., Copier, Aud/Vis.

Recreational Facilities: Pool, Whirlpool, Fitn. Ctr., Decathlon Club

Restaurant/Bar: Rusty Scupper

Comps: Continental Breakfast, Happy Hour

Room Amenities: Room Service, Free Paper, TV, Phones in Rm. (2), Cable TV, Radio, Kitchen, Microwave, Ind. Heat Ctl., Ind. AC Ctl.

The Residence Inn is situated in the heart of Silicon Valley surrounded by sleek high tech buildings, small restaurants and shops. Each suite is homelike with traditional furnishings, spacious living area, full kitchen with breakfast bar. Three conference rooms. Discounted rates for extended stays.

SUNNYVALE

Woodfin Suites Hotel
635 East El Camino Real
Sunnyvale, CA 94086

88 Suites
408-738-1700 800-237-8811

Location: Downtown-2m.; Silicon Valley
Airport: 10 minutes
Near: Center of Silicon Valley, ½ mile to Sunny-vale Shopping Ctr.; Amphitheatre
Walking Distance To: Community Center
Area Attractions: Great America Amusement Park: 5 mi.

Price Range & Credit Cards: 1 Bedroom Suite $$$, 2 Bedrooms $$$$, AmEx/MC/Visa/Other CC, Children Free, TAC 10%

Hotel Amenities: Parking, Pets Allowed, Handicap (4)

Business Facilities: Conf. Rm. Cap. 50, Mess. Ctr., Sec. Serv., Copier, Aud/Vis., Comp. Hook-up, Bus. Ctr.

Recreational Facilities: Pool, Whirlpool, Tennis, Golf, Water Skiing, Beaches-40 min.; Para Sailing: 10 mi.

Comps: Breakfast, Airport Shuttle

Room Amenities: Room Service, Free Paper, TV, Phones in Rm. (2), VCR, Radio, Kitchen, Ind. Heat Ctl., Ind. AC Ctl.

Experience us and you will never stay in an ordinary hotel again! We offer the luxury and spaciousness of a townhouse at the price of an ordinary hotel room. Each suite has a living room with a TV, VCR, and cozy fireplace, a kitchen with full size appliances and separate bedroom with its own TV, radio, and mirrored dressing and vanity area.

WEST HOLLYWOOD

Le Bel Age
1020 N. San Vicente Blvd.
West Hollywood, CA 90069

198 Suites
213-854-1111 800-424-4443

Location: Theatre Dist; Downtown: 15 min.
Airport: 8 miles
Near: Design Center of World, All Fine Shops
Walking Distance To: Galleries, Boutiques
Area Attractions: Sunset Plaza District

Price Range & Credit Cards: 1 Bedroom Suite $$$$, 2 Bedrooms $$$$+, Junior $$$$, AmEx/MC/Visa/Other CC, Children Free, TAC 10%

Hotel Amenities: Laundry, Parking, Car Hire, Handicap (99)

Business Facilities: Conf. Rm. Cap. 350, Banquet Fac., Mess. Ctr., Sec. Serv., Copier, Aud/Vis., Teleconf., Telex

Recreational Facilities: Pool, Sauna, Tennis, Golf; Fitn. Ctr. @ Mondrian

Restaurant/Bar: Bel Age, Entertainment

Comps: Hors d'oeuvres

Room Amenities: Room Service, Free Paper, TV, Phones in Rm. (2), Cable TV, Wet Bar, Kitchen, Ind. Heat Ctl., Ind. AC Ctl.

Elegant Bel Age, radiant with the mood of a French Country Manor, is a 198-suite grand luxury hotel located near Beverly Hills. The distinguished characteristics of the Bel Age all point toward attention to detail, from the state-of-the-art business facilities to the stunning rooftop garden and pool with its spectacular panoramic view of vibrant L.A.

────────────── WEST HOLLYWOOD ──────────────

Le Mondrian
8440 Sunset Blvd.
West Hollywood, CA 90069

188 Suites
213-650-8999 800-424-4443

Location: Westside; Downtown: 15 min.
Airport: 8 miles
Near: Fancy Shops, Century City
Walking Distance To: Pacific Design Center
Area Attractions: Beverly Hills, Melrose
Shops

Price Range & Credit Cards: 1 Bedroom Suite $$$$+, 2 Bedrooms $$$$+, Junior $$$$, AmEx/MC/Visa/Other CC, Children Free, TAC 10%

Hotel Amenities: Parking, Car Hire

Business Facilities: Conf. Rm. Cap. 120, Banquet Fac.

Recreational Facilities: Pool, Sauna, Whirlpool, Fitn. Ctr., Tennis; Golf nearby

Restaurant/Bar: Cafe Mondrian

Comps: Hors d'oeuvres

Room Amenities: Room Service, Free Paper, TV, Phone in Rm., Cable TV, Radio, Kitchen, Ind. Heat Ctl., Ind. AC Ctl.

This award winning hotel is conveniently located close to Beverly Center, Beverly Hills, the unique shops of Melrose Avenue, and the fine restaurants on La Cienega. Suites have ultra modern decor, multi-line phones, and spectacular views of dynamic L.A. Golf and tennis are nearby with a fitness center, pool, sauna, and whirlpool all in-house.

────────────── WEST HOLLYWOOD ──────────────

Sunset Marquis Hotel & Villas
1200 N. Alta Loma Rd.
West Hollywood, CA 90069

120 Suites
213-657-1333 800-692-2140

Location: Westside; Downtown: 15 min.
Airport: 8 miles
Near: Trendy Boutiques, Rodeo Drive
Walking Distance To: Century City
Area Attractions: Westwood, Sunset Strip, Melrose shops

Price Range & Credit Cards: 1 Bedroom Suite $$$$, 2 Bedrooms $$$$+, Junior $$$$, AmEx/MC/Visa/Other CC, Children Free, TAC 10%

Hotel Amenities: Laundry, Parking, Car Hire, Handicap (2)

Business Facilities: Conf. Rm. Cap. 65, Banquet Fac., Mess. Ctr., Sec. Serv., Copier, Aud/Vis., Teleconf., Telex, Bus. Ctr.

Recreational Facilities: Pool, Sauna, Whirlpool, Fitn. Ctr., Tennis, Golf, Sportfishing; Yachting nearby

Restaurant/Bar: Notes, Entertainment

Room Amenities: Room Service, Free Paper, TV, Phones in Rm. (2), Cable TV, VCR, Radio, Wet Bar, Kitchen, Ind. Heat Ctl., Ind. AC Ctl.

A remarkable array of business and recreational facilities is the hallmark of Sunset Marquis. Beautifully located amidst lush greenery with private gardens featuring acres of rolling hills, all 120 suites provide soft, subtle, relaxing pastels with comfortable stylish furnishings, artwork, and sculptures, exquisite use of colors, textures, and patterns.

 **Colorado**

Steamboat Springs • Silver Creek
• Boulder •• Longmont
Winter Park • •
Vail • Avon • Englewood
•• Apsen Denver
Snowmass Village •
Colorado Springs

• Durango

──────────────── ASPEN ────────────────

The Inn @ Aspen   **Location:** Downtown-1m.; Buttermilk Mtn.
21646 W. Highway 82   **Airport:** 1 mile
Aspen, CO 81611   **Near:** Summer and Winter Sports, Shops, Bal-
                             looning
124 Suites   **Walking Distance To:** Snow (seasonal)
303-925-1500 800-952-1515   **Area Attractions:** Aspen Music Festival,
                             Ballet

Price Range & Credit Cards: 1 Bedroom Suite $$$$, Junior $$$, AmEx/MC/Visa/
Other CC, Children Free, TAC 10%

Hotel Amenities: Laundry, Car Hire, TV Lounge, Handicap (2)

Business Facilities: Conf. Rm. Cap. 150, Banquet Fac., Mess. Ctr., Sec. Serv., Copier,
Aud/Vis.

Recreational Facilities: Pool, Sauna, Whirlpool, Fitn. Ctr., Golf, Skiing, Fishing, Hik-
ing, Game Area; Swim up to Bar

Restaurant/Bar: Barringtons

Comps: Hors d'oeuvres

Room Amenities: Room Service, Free Paper, TV, Phone in Rm., Cable TV, Radio,
Kitchen, Ind. Heat Ctl., Ind. AC Ctl.

*Any time of the year The Inn at Aspen makes business a pleasure and pleasure an art. All
the glory of each season can be fully appreciated at this 2-story, 10-acre landscaped resort.
But those with an affection for skiing will be in paradise. Only 35 paces from the lifts to the
34 different slopes of Buttermilk Mountain.*

──────────────── BOULDER ────────────────

The Residence Inn by Marriott
3030 Center Green Dr.
Boulder, CO 80301

128 Suites
303-449-5545   800-331-3131

Location: Northside; Downtown: 3 miles
Airport: 40 minutes
Near: Residential Area, Univ. of Colorado, Pearl
Street Mall
Walking Distance To: Community Area
Area Attractions: Rocky Mountain Nat. Park

Price Range & Credit Cards: 1 Bedroom Suite $$$, 2 Bedrooms $$$$, AmEx/MC/Visa/Other CC, Children Free, TAC 10%

Hotel Amenities: Laundry, Library, Parking, TV Lounge, Pets Allowed, Handicap (3)

Business Facilities: Conf. Rm. Cap. 50, Mess. Ctr., Copier, Aud/Vis.

Recreational Facilities: Pool, Whirlpool, Golf, Skiing, Bicycle path, Hiking, Game Area, Sportcourt

Comps: Continental Plus Breakfast, Refreshments, Coffee, Popcorn

Room Amenities: Fireplaces, TV, Phone in Rm., Cable TV, Radio, Kitchen, Ind. Heat Ctl., Ind. AC Ctl.

Resembling a community of fine townhomes, Residence Inn suits travellers who are relocating or on extended business stays. Suites include modern furnishings, satellite T.V., kitchen and breakfast bar, maid service, and fireplaces in most units. Complimentary breakfast and cocktails also included. Rates discounted for extended stay.

──────────────── COLORADO SPRINGS ────────────────

Embassy Suites Hotel
7290 Commerce Center Dr.
Colorado Springs, CO 80919

207 Suites
719-599-9100   800-362-2779

Location: Northeast; Downtown
Airport: Colorado Springs
Near: Creek with Trout, Mountain Area
Walking Distance To: Countryside, Air Force
Academy
Area Attractions: Garden of the Gods, Pikes
Peak

Price Range & Credit Cards: 1 Bedroom Suite $$$, AmEx/MC/Visa/Other CC, Children Free, TAC 10%

Hotel Amenities: Laundry, Handicap (3)

Business Facilities: Conf. Rm. Cap. 250, Banquet Fac., Sec. Serv., Copier, Aud/Vis., Teleconf.

Recreational Facilities: Pool, Sauna, Whirlpool, Golf, Skiing, Sightseeing, Hiking; Mountain climbing nearby

Restaurant/Bar: The Polo Club A Bar and Grill, Entertainment

Comps: Full Breakfast, Refreshments, Airport Limousine

Room Amenities: Room Service, TV, Phones in Rm. (2), Cable TV, Radio, Wet Bar, Kitchen

Embassy's 4-story Mediterranean style structure contains an atrium with a charming creek flowing and splashing at the bottom of 2 waterfalls. Many recreational and business facilities are available. Enjoy quality cuisine at the in-house restaurant—Polo Club Grill. Golfing is nearby and complimentary limousine service to the airport is available.

COLORADO SPRINGS

The Residence Inn by Marriott
3880 N. Academy Blvd.
Colorado Springs, CO 80917

96 Suites
719-574-0370   800-331-3131

Location: Northeast; Downtown: 5 mi.
Airport: 7 miles
Near: Residential District, Several Restaurants
Walking Distance To: Garden of the Gods
Area Attractions: Air Force Academy, Pikes Peak

Price Range & Credit Cards: 1 Bedroom Suite $$$, 2 Bedrooms $$$, AmEx/MC/Visa/Other CC, Children Free, TAC 10%

Hotel Amenities: Laundry, Library, Parking, TV Lounge, Pets Allowed, Handicap (2)

Business Facilities: Conf. Rm. Cap. 80, Banquet Fac., Mess. Ctr., Copier

Recreational Facilities: Pool, Whirlpool, Sportcourt;Patty Jewett Golf Cr.

Comps: Continental Plus Breakfast, Refreshments, Summer Barbeques

Room Amenities: Free Paper, TV, Phone in Rm., Cable TV, Radio, Kitchen, Ind. Heat Ctl., Ind. AC Ctl.

The landscaped walks, courtyards and quiet suburban-like structures of Residence Inn have the feeling of home. Within walking distance of several restaurants and a new mall, some of the features you'll enjoy include full maid service, horseshoes, and a fully equipped kitchen with dishes and appliances. Rates discounted by length of stay.

Hyde Park Suites, San Francisco, CA

────────────── DENVER ──────────────

Cambridge Club Hotel
1660 Sherman St.
Denver, CO 80203

27 Suites
303-831-1252 800-752-1252

Location: ; Downtown
Airport: 12 miles
Near: Business District, Major Shops
Walking Distance To: Night Life
Area Attractions: Entertainment, State Capitol

Price Range & Credit Cards: 1 Bedroom Suite $$$$, 2 Bedrooms $$$$+, Junior $$$, AmEx/MC/Visa/Other CC, TAC 10%

Hotel Amenities: Parking, Car Hire

Business Facilities: Conf. Rm. Cap. 25, Mess. Ctr., Sec. Serv., Copier, Aud/Vis., Telex, Comp. Hook-up

Recreational Facilities: Pool, Sauna, Whirlpool, Fitn. Ctr.; Athletic Club/Fee

Comps: Continental Plus Breakfast, Refreshments, Hors d'oeuvres

Room Amenities: Room Service, Free Paper, TV, Phone in Rm., Cable TV, Radio, Wet Bar, Kitchen, Ind. Heat Ctl.

Cambridge Club is an elegant hotel that has all the advantages of being in downtown Denver but located on a quiet tree-lined street. This intimate hotel has an abundance of business services and facilities including computer hook-ups, teleconferencing capabilities, copy service and more. All suites are unique with large desks or tables.

────────────── DENVER ──────────────

Embassy Suites Hotel
4444 N. Havana St.
Denver, CO 80239

212 Suites
303-375-0400 800-362-2779

Location: Downtown: 6 mi.
Airport: Adjacent
Near: Aurora Shopping Mall
Area Attractions: State Capitol & US Mint-12 miles, Skiing

Price Range & Credit Cards: 1 Bedroom Suite $$$, AmEx/MC/Visa/Other CC, Children Free, TAC 10%

Hotel Amenities: Laundry, Parking, Car Hire, Handicap (14), Gift Shop

Business Facilities: Conf. Rm. Cap. 700, Banquet Fac., Copier, Aud/Vis., Telex

Recreational Facilities: Pool, Sauna, Whirlpool; Best ski area 1 hour

Restaurant/Bar: La Veranda, Entertainment

Comps: Breakfast, Refreshments, Airport Transport

Room Amenities: Room Service, Free Paper, TV, Phones in Rm. (2), Cable TV, Radio, Wet Bar, Kitchen, Ind. Heat Ctl., Ind. AC Ctl.

Business can be handled easily and efficiently at Embassy, located in the airport district. The in-house restaurant, La Veranda, has a comfortable open and airy ambiance accented with lush greenery, natural wood furnishings and cozy booths. After a satisfying meal, relax in the steamroom or whirlpool.

---------------------- DENVER ----------------------

Embassy Suites Hotel Southeast   ***Location:*** Southeast; Downtown: 12 min.
7525 E. Hampden Ave.   ***Airport:*** 15 minutes
Denver, CO 80231   ***Near:*** Business District, Entertainment
                                      Walking Distance To: Night Life
208 Suites   ***Area Attractions:*** Major Shopping Areas,
303-696-6644 800-825-3585   Theatres

Price Range & Credit Cards: 1 Bedroom Suite $$$, AmEx/MC/Visa/Other CC, Children Free, TAC 10%

Hotel Amenities: Laundry, Parking, Car Hire, Pets Allowed, Handicap (14)

Business Facilities: Conf. Rm. Cap. 200, Banquet Fac., Copier, Aud/Vis., Comp. Hook-up

Recreational Facilities: Pool, Sauna, Whirlpool, Tennis, Golf, Jogging nearby

Restaurant/Bar: Gregory's, Live Entertainment

Comps: Full Breakfast, Refreshments, Hors d'oeuvres

Room Amenities: Room Service, TV, Phones in Rm. (2), Cable TV, Radio, Wet Bar

Relaxation is easy at the Southeast Embassy. With a pool, sauna, and whirlpool this 208-suite building is within walking distance to 2 major shopping and entertainment areas. 4 meeting rooms with a 6000 square foot potential make large meetings easy to accommodate. After business, socialize in the atrium during the cocktail party from 5:30 to 7:30 p.m.

---------------------- DENVER ----------------------

Embassy Suites Hotel-Downtown   ***Location:*** Downtown
1881 Curtis St.   ***Airport:*** 12 miles
Denver, CO 80202   ***Near:*** Business District, One mile to Tivoli
                                      Walking Distance To: 16th Street Mall
335 Suites   ***Area Attractions:*** Art Museum, Historical
303-297-8888 800-362-2779   Center

Price Range & Credit Cards: 1 Bedroom Suite $$$, 2 Bedrooms $$$$, AmEx/MC/Visa/Other CC, Children Free, TAC 10%

Hotel Amenities: Parking, Handicap (54)

Business Facilities: Conf. Rm. Cap. 220, Banquet Fac., Sec. Serv., Copier, Aud/Vis., Teleconf., Telex, Comp. Hook-up

Recreational Facilities: Sauna, Whirlpool, Fitn. Ctr., Golf, Skiing nearby

Restaurant/Bar: Plaza Cafe, Burgundy's Restaurant, Piano Bar

Comps: Full Breakfast, Refreshments

Room Amenities: Room Service, Free Paper, TV, Phones in Rm. (2), Cable TV, Radio, Wet Bar, Ind. Heat Ctl., Ind. AC Ctl.

Gracious European-style personal service, and luxuriously appointed two-room suites with everything you need for business, entertainment or relaxation await you at the Downtown Embassy. There is a pleasing mountain view to the South, and of the Eastern plains to the North at this large highrise hotel, with golf and skiing under 60 miles away.

--------------------------------- DENVER ---------------------------------

The Burnsley Hotel
1000 Grant St.
Denver, CO 80203

82 Suites
303-830-1000 800-231-3915

Location: Central; Downtown:8 Blocks
Airport: 7.5 miles
Near: Capitol Bldg. (4 Blocks), Larimer Square
Walking Distance To: Cherry Creek Center
Area Attractions: Zoo, Botanical Gardens, Art Museum

Price Range & Credit Cards: 1 Bedroom Suite $$$, AmEx/MC/Visa/Other CC, TAC 10%

Hotel Amenities: Laundry, Parking, Car Hire, Pets Allowed, Handicap (38)

Business Facilities: Conf. Rm. Cap. 80, Banquet Fac., Mess. Ctr., Copier, Aud/Vis., Telex

Recreational Facilities: Pool, Fitn. Ctr., Tennis, Skiing, Fishing, Bowling, Game Area, Horses nearby

Restaurant/Bar: The Burnsley, Entertainment

Comps: Hors d'oeuvres

Room Amenities: Room Service, Free Paper, TV, Phone in Rm., Cable TV, Radio, Kitchen, Ind. Heat Ctl., Ind. AC Ctl.

An intimately luxurious all-suite hotel which has many pleasant surprises. The owner often greets guests as they arrive in the richly decorated lobby with its comfortable furnishings, polished brass, Italian marble and original oil paintings. Four blocks from the Capitol Building and close to other attractions. Many business services are available.

--------------------------------- DURANGO ---------------------------------

Jarvis Suite Hotel
125 W. 10th St.
Durango, CO 81301

22 Suites
303-259-6190 800-824-1024

Location: Historic Downtown
Airport: 12 miles
Near: Business District, Major Shops
Walking Distance To: Night Life
Area Attractions: Entertainment, State Capitol

Price Range & Credit Cards: 1 Bedroom Suite $$, 2 Bedrooms $$$, Junior $$, AmEx/MC/Visa, Children Free, TAC 10%

Hotel Amenities: Laundry, Parking, Handicap (1)

Business Facilities: Conf. Rm. Cap. 15, Banquet Fac., Mess. Ctr., Sec. Serv., Copier, Aud/Vis.

Recreational Facilities: Pool, Sauna, Whirlpool, Fitn. Ctr., Golf, Skiing, Fishing, Boating, Hunting, Horses

Restaurant/Bar: Hunter's

Room Amenities: Free Paper, TV, Phone in Rm., Cable TV, Radio, Kitchen, Ind. Heat Ctl., Ind. AC Ctl.

Jarvis Suite Hotel has succeeded in combining the old with the new to create the perfect enjoyment headquarters. Listed in the National Register of Historic Places, this luxurious 1889 building contains 22 unique suites with modern conveniences. Within walking distance of most activities and dining facilities. Shuttle service is offered.

60   Colorado

Embassy Suites Hotel
10250 East Costilla Ave.
Englewood, CO 80112

236 Suites
303-792-0433   800-654-4810

Location: SE Corridor; Downtown: 20 min.
Airport: 40 minutes
Near: Shopping Centers, Golf Courses, and Health Facilities
Walking Distance To: Movie Theatres, Restaurants
Area Attractions: Inverness & Rampart Business Parks

Price Range & Credit Cards: 1 Bedroom Suite $$$, 2 Bedrooms $$$$+, AmEx/MC/Visa/Other CC, Children Free, TAC 10%

Hotel Amenities: Laundry, Gift Shop, Parking, Car Hire, TV Lounge, Pets Allowed, Handicap (4)

Business Facilities: Mess. Ctr., Sec. Serv., Copier, Aud/Vis., Telex

Recreational Facilities: Pool, Sauna, Whirlpool, Golf, Skiing, Jogging nearby; Health Club Privileges

Restaurant/Bar: Dewberry's/Dewberry's Lounge, Piano Entertainment

Comps: Full Breakfast, Refreshments, Hors d'oeuvres

Room Amenities: Room Service, Free Paper, TV, Phones in Rm. (2), Cable TV, VCR, Radio, Wet Bar, Microwave, Refrigerator, Ind. Heat Ctl., Ind. AC Ctl.

Our exciting new hotel is conveniently located in Denver's rapidly growing South Metro Business Corridor. Our proximity to I-25 from both Araphoe Rd. & Dry Creek Rd. Interchanges is an ideal location for travelers driving or flying to Denver. Embassy Suites Tech Center is proud to offer the comfort and convenience of a suite at a reasonable price.

The Residence Inn by Marriott
6565 So. Yosemite
Englewood, CO 80111

128 Suites
303-740-7177   800-331-3131

Location: South Metro Denver
Airport: 12 miles
Near: Greenwood Plaza, Major Shops, Denver Tech Center and Inverness
Walking Distance To: Night Life, Tech. Center
Area Attractions: Amphitheatre, Park, Mountains

Price Range & Credit Cards: 1 Bedroom Suite $$$, 2 Bedrooms $$$, AmEx/MC/Visa/Other CC, Children Free, TAC 10%

Hotel Amenities: Laundry, Library, TV Lounge, Pets Allowed, Handicap (6)

Business Facilities: Mess. Ctr., Copier, Aud/Vis., Telex, Comp. Hook-up

Recreational Facilities: Pool, Sauna, Fitn. Ctr., Sportscourt, Game Area; Golf Courses nearby

Comps: Continental Plus Breakfast, Refreshments, Hors d'oeuvres

Room Amenities: Free Paper, TV, Phone in Rm., Cable TV, Radio, Kitchen, Ind. Heat Ctl., Ind. AC Ctl.

Surrounded by great restaurants, varied shopping malls, and theatres, the Residence Inn is designed to be your home-away-from-home. Business services and leisure facilities can be found on-site with major golf courses near by. Complimentary breakfast is served daily in the handsome lobby. Discounted rates for extended stay.

---------------------- LONGMONT ----------------------

Raintree Plaza Hotel
1900 Diagonal Hwy.
Longmont, CO 80501

150 Suites
303-776-2000 800-843-8240

Location: Industrial; Boulder: 12 min.
Airport: 40 miles
Near: Foothills of The Rockies
Walking Distance To: Twin Peaks
Area Attractions: Boulder County Fairgrounds,
Mountains

Price Range & Credit Cards: 1 Bedroom Suite $$$, 2 Bedrooms $$$$, Junior $$, AmEx/MC/Visa/Other CC, Children Free, TAC 10%

Hotel Amenities: Laundry, TV Lounge, Pets Allowed, Handicap (1)

Business Facilities: Conf. Rm. Cap. 350, Banquet Fac., Mess. Ctr., Copier, Aud/Vis., Teleconf., Comp. Hook-up, Bus. Ctr.

Recreational Facilities: Pool, Sauna, Whirlpool, Fitn. Ctr., Estes Park; Rocky Mtn. National Pk. nearby

Restaurant/Bar: Summit, Entertainment

Comps: Continental Plus Breakfast, Refreshments, Hors d'oeuvres

Room Amenities: Free Paper, TV, Phone in Rm., Cable TV, Radio, Wet Bar, Kitchen, Ind. AC Ctl.

In the quiet foothills of the Colorado Rockies, Raintree has the experience and facilities to meet your every business need. Its banquet room, multi-media presentation amphitheatre, and individual conference rooms are available to serve you. After business, or sight-seeing, enjoy a relaxing dip in the whirlpool or get a workout at the fitness center.

---------------------- SILVER CREEK ----------------------

Moutainside Silver Creek
P. O. Box 4104
Silver Creek, CO 80466

102 Suites
303-887-2571 800-223-7677

Location: Resort area; Denver: 78 Miles
Airport: 80 miles
Near: Base of Ski area, Grand County Mountains
Walking Distance To: Ski Area Base
Area Attractions: 21 Ski Runs with 3 Lifts

Price Range & Credit Cards: 1 Bedroom Suite $$, 2 Bedrooms $$, AmEx/MC/Visa/ Other CC, Children Free, TAC 10%

Business Facilities: Copier, Mess. Ctr., Aud/Vis.

Recreational Facilities: Pool, Whirlpool, Ballooning, All snow sports; Serious skiing country

Room Amenities: Phone in Rm., Cable TV, Radio, Kitchen, Ind. Heat Ctl., Fireplace

Located at the base of Silver Creek ski area, Mountainside affords endless recreational opportunities year round or "doing nothing" in a picturesque Colorado setting. Skiing slopes are plentiful for all skill levels and all suites have "ski-in, ski-out" capabilities. Each has a panoramic view of the Continental Divide, an in-room jacuzzi, and a full kitchen.

--- SNOWMASS VILLAGE ---

Crestwood Lodge
400 Wood Rd./P.O.Box 5460
Snowmass Village, CO 81615

142 Suites
303-923-2450

Location: Resort; Aspen: 8 Miles
Airport: 3 miles
Near: Village Center, Resort Area
Walking Distance To: Village Mall
Area Attractions: Fanny Hill, Assay Hill, Mount Daly

Price Range & Credit Cards: 1 Bedroom Suite $$$$, 2 Bedrooms $$$$+, Junior $$$$, AmEx/MC/Visa/Other CC, TAC 10%

Hotel Amenities: Laundry, Parking

Business Facilities: Conf. Rm. Cap. 230, Banquet Fac., Mess. Ctr., Sec. Serv., Copier, Aud/Vis.

Recreational Facilities: Pool, Sauna, Whirlpool, Golf, Skiing, Fishing, Gymnasium, Snowshoeing

Room Amenities: TV, Phone in Rm., Cable TV, Radio, Kitchen, Ind. Heat Ctl.

The Crestwood is situated right on the ski slopes, with "ski-in/ski-out" access to the base lifts. But winter here is much more than skiing. The dogsled ride is a thrill and the hot-air balloon and sleigh rides are other adventures. In the warmer months activities including fishing, golf, tennis, and white water rafting await you. Excellent facilities.

--- WINTER PARK ---

Silverado II
380 Alpine Vista
Winter Park, CO 80486

70 Suites
303-726-5753 800-654-7157

Location: Resort; Downtown:0.5 mile
Airport: 70 miles
Near: Ski Area with 22 Ski-lifts
Walking Distance To: Restaurants
Area Attractions: Renowned Ski Area

Price Range & Credit Cards: 1 Bedroom Suite $$, 2 Bedrooms $$, Junior $, AmEx/MC/Visa/Other CC, TAC 10%

Hotel Amenities: Laundry, Parking, Car Hire, Pets Allowed

Business Facilities: Conv. Ctr., Aud/Vis., Telex

Recreational Facilities: Pool, Sauna, Whirlpool, Fitn. Ctr., Skiing, Tubing, River rafting, Ice fishing, Game Area

Restaurant/Bar: Dougal's

Room Amenities: TV, Phone in Rm., Radio, Kitchen

Very conveniently located 1/5 mile from downtown Winter Park. Silverado II is a year round resort in the midst of one of the best known ski areas in the world. Other attractions and events include rafting down the Colorado River, jazz festivals, rodeos, Arapaho and Rocky Mountain National Parks. Your stay is sure to be active and varied at Silverado.

⚜ Connecticut

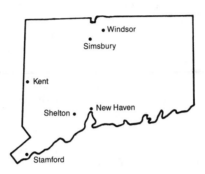

NEW HAVEN

The Residence Inn by Marriott
1 Long Wharf Dr.
New Haven, CT 06511

112 Suites
203-776-7666 800-331-3131

Location: Long Wharf; Downtown: 2 miles
Airport: 5 miles
Near: Highway I-95
Area Attractions: Yale Univ., Jai-Alai 5 miles, Shopping 2 miles

Price Range & Credit Cards: 1 Bedroom Suite $$, 2 Bedrooms $$$, AmEx/MC/ Visa/Other CC, Children Free, TAC 10%

Hotel Amenities: Laundry, Library, Parking, TV Lounge, Handicap (5)

Business Facilities: Conf. Rm. Cap. 40, Mess. Ctr., Copier, Aud/Vis., FAX, Comp. Hook-up

Recreational Facilities: Pool, Whirlpool, Basketball, Paddle Tennis, Volleyball, Game Area; Health Club privileges

Comps: Continental Plus Breakfast, Refreshments, Hors d'oeuvres

Room Amenities: Free Paper, TV, Phones in Rm. (2), Cable TV, Radio, Kitchen, Ind. Heat Ctl., Ind. AC Ctl.

The Marriott Residence Inn is truly a new kind of hotel. Suites with full kitchens and living areas and a warm friendly staff make your stay with us more like home than hotel. The Inn is located minutes from downtown New Haven, Yale University and the New Haven Airport. Rates discounted for extended stay.

—————————————— SHELTON ——————————————

The Residence Inn By Marriott
1001 Bridgeport Ave.
Shelton, CT 06484

96 Suites
203-926-9000 800-331-3131

Location: Fairfield Co; Downtown: 10 min.
Airport: Bradley: 60 minutes
Near: Beardsley Zoo , Bridgeport Jai-Alai-10 min., La Guardia Airprt-90 min
Area Attractions: American Shakespeare Theatre-7 mi., Captain's Cove Seaport

Price Range & Credit Cards: 1 Bedroom Suite $$$, 2 Bedrooms $$$, AmEx/MC/Visa/Other CC, Children Free, TAC 10%

Hotel Amenities: Laundry, Library, TV Lounge, Pets Allowed, Handicap (4)

Business Facilities: Conf. Rm. Cap. 20-25, Mess. Ctr., Copier

Recreational Facilities: Pool, Hot Tub, Sports Court, Basketball, Volleyball; Tennis & Golf nearby

Comps: Continental Plus Breakfast, Refreshments, Hors d'oeuvres

Room Amenities: Free Paper, TV, Phone in Rm., Cable TV, Radio, Kitchen, Ind. Heat Ctl., Ind. AC Ctl.

Residence Inn By Marriott offers home-away-from home-convenience in a townhouse ambience. Daily complimentary breakfast is served in the Gatehouse, with hospitality hour Mon-Thurs. Van service is available, or grocery shopping is provided from your list. Outdoor swimming pool, jacuzzi and sports court available. Discounted rates for extended stay.

—————————————— STAMFORD ——————————————

Le Pavillon Hotel Deluxe
60 Strawberry Hill Ave.
Stamford, CT 06902

165 Suites
203-357-8100 800-243-7660

Location: Northside; Downtown: 3 min.
Airport: Limousine Service
Near: Tranquil Residential, Theatres and Restaurants
Walking Distance To: Gigantic Mall
Area Attractions: Museum, Jai-Alai, N.Y.C.40 minutes

Price Range & Credit Cards: 1 Bedroom Suite $$, AmEx/MC/Visa/Other CC, Children Free, TAC 10%

Hotel Amenities: Laundry, Parking, Pets Allowed

Business Facilities: Conf. Rm. Cap. 50, Banquet Fac., Mess. Ctr., Sec. Serv., Copier, Aud/Vis., Teleconf., Telex, Comp. Hook-up

Recreational Facilities: Sauna, Whirlpool, Fitn. Ctr., Skiing-40 min., Hiking, Game Area; Golf Course 5 minutes

Restaurant/Bar: Aux Beaux Jardins

Comps: Refreshments

Room Amenities: Room Service, TV, Phone in Rm., Cable TV, VCR, Radio, Kitchen, Ind. Heat Ctl., Ind. AC Ctl.

A superb site to meet all your business and travel needs, Le Pavillon Hotel De Luxe rests on the highest ground in Stamford and offers a picturesque view of all Stamford and more! While there visit the world class restaurant—Aux Beaux Jardins. Its stunning dining room and exquisite Oriental antiques are sure to leave a lasting impression.

T.L.C. Suites, San Francisco, CA

--- WINDSOR ---

The Residence Inn by Marriott
100 Dumfey Lane
Windsor, CT 06095

96 Suites
203-688-7474 800-331-3131

Location: Northside; Downtown: 7 miles
Airport: 8 miles
Near: Residential & Business District, Interstate 91
Area Attractions: Historic Tobacco Valley

Price Range & Credit Cards: 1 Bedroom Suite $$$, 2 Bedrooms $$$, AmEx/MC/Visa/Other CC, Children Free, TAC 10%

Hotel Amenities: Laundry, Parking, TV Lounge, Pets Allowed, Handicap (4)

Business Facilities: Conf. Rm. Cap. 20, Mess. Ctr., Copier, Comp. Hook-up

Recreational Facilities: Pool, Whirlpool, Golf, Skiing, Jai-Alai, Game Area; Millbrook Golf Course

Comps: Continental Breakfast, Hors d'oeuvres

Room Amenities: Free Paper, TV, Phone in Rm., Cable TV, Kitchen, Ind. Heat Ctl., Ind. AC Ctl.

Close to the Airport the Inn can meet all your travel needs. Socialize in the Hearthroom, take advantage of the business facilities; enjoy a leisurely game of golf, or view the furious game of jai alai at the Hartford Center nearby. The suites are comfortable with a home-away-from-home feeling. Discounted rates for extended stay.

Florida

Pensacola
Destin
Middleburg
Jacksonville
St. Augustine
Gainsville
Daytona Beach
Wildwood • • Ocala
Altamonte Springs
Orlando
Tarpon Springs
Clearwater
Lake Buena Vista
Indialantic
Kissimmee
Vero Beach
St. Petersburg Beach
Tampa
Longboat Key • Sarasota
Hutchinson Island
Port St. Lucie
Punta Gorda
Jupiter West Palm Beach
Captiva Island
Naples
Delray Beach
Englewood Sanibel Island
Fort
Boca Raton
Fort Myers Fort Myers Beach Lauderdale
Deerfield Beach
Coral Springs
Marco Island •
Miami
Miami Beach
Coconut Grove
Miami Airport
Sunny Isles
Surfside
Treasure Island
Biscayne Bay
Key Largo
Plantation
Key West

ALTAMONTE SPRINGS

The Residence Inn by Marriott
270 Douglas Ave.
Altamonte Springs, FL 32714

128 Suites
407-788-7991 800-331-3131

Location: Northside; Orlando: 15 Miles
Airport: 25 miles
Near: Residential Area, Maitland Center
Walking Distance To: Fine Restaurants
Area Attractions: Disney World, Sea World, Daytona Beach

Price Range & Credit Cards: 1 Bedroom Suite $$, 2 Bedrooms $$$, AmEx/MC/ Visa/Other CC, Children Free, TAC 10%

Hotel Amenities: Laundry, Parking, TV Lounge, Pets Allowed, Handicap (4)

Business Facilities: Conf. Rm. Cap. 45, Mess. Ctr., Copier, Aud/Vis.

Recreational Facilities: Pool, Whirlpool, Fitn. Ctr., Golf, Game Area

Comps: Continental Plus Breakfast, Refreshments, Hors d'oeuvres

Room Amenities: Free Paper, TV, Phone in Rm., Cable TV, Radio, Kitchen, Ind. Heat Ctl., Ind. AC Ctl.

The Residence Inn has planned very carefully to make you feel you're still at home. You'll be impressed by the special little things that add to the comfort of your stay, like a complimentary log for your fireplace, passes to a nearby fitness center and a gazebo with heated jacuzzi in the courtyard of the complex. Discounted rates for extended stay.

──────────────── BOCA RATON ────────────────

Park Place Suite Hotel
661 N.W. 53rd St.
Boca Raton, FL 33431

263 Suites
305-994-8200   800-228-5250

Location: Outskirts; Downtown: Nearby
Airport: 5 minutes
Near: Arvida Park, Town Center
Walking Distance To: IBM, Siemens, NCCI
Area Attractions: Over 180 Fine Stores, Beach

Price Range & Credit Cards: 1 Bedroom Suite $$$$, 2 Bedrooms $$$$+, AmEx/ MC/Visa/Other CC, Children Free, TAC 10%

Hotel Amenities: Laundry, Parking, Car Hire, TV Lounge, Handicap (6)

Business Facilities: Conf. Rm. Cap. 500, Banquet Fac., Mess. Ctr., Copier, Aud/Vis.

Recreational Facilities: Pool, Sauna, Whirlpool, Fitn. Ctr., Tennis, Golf, Jogging, Hiking, Game Area, Water Sports

Restaurant/Bar: Cafe In The Park, Champs, Entertainment

Comps: Full Breakfast, Refreshments, Hors d'oeuvres

Room Amenities: Room Service, Free Paper, TV, Phones in Rm. (2), Cable TV, Radio, Ind. Heat Ctl., Ind. AC Ctl.

Park Place is sure to meet all your business and pleasure needs. The conference facilities are state-of-the-art. Recreational activities abound. While there, a meal at Cafe In The Park is something you won't want to miss. The atrium restaurant is surrounded by lush plants while decorative hot air balloons grace the air above.

──────────────── BOCA RATON ────────────────

Radisson Suite Hotel
7920 Glades Road
Boca Raton, FL 33434

201 Suites
407-483-3600   800-777-7800

Location: Arvida Parkway Center; Downtown: Nearby
Airport: Palm Beach: 35 min.
Near: Boca Raton Executive Airport, Fort Lauderdale Airport-35 minutes
Walking Distance To: Arvida Parkway Center
Area Attractions: Town Center Mall, Beaches, Tennis Courts, Golf Courses

Price Range & Credit Cards: 1 Bedroom Suite $$$, 2 Bedrooms $$$, AmEx/MC/ Visa/Other CC, Children Free, TAC 10%

Hotel Amenities: Gift Shop, Parking, Pets Deposit, Handicap (11)

Business Facilities: Conf. Rm. Cap. 50, Banquet Fac., Mess. Ctr.

Recreational Facilities: Pool, Whirlpool, Tennis, Golf, Fitness Ctr., Jogging Trail; all sports nearby

Restaurant/Bar: Glades Terrace Bar

Comps: Full Breakfast, Refreshments, Hors d'oeuvres

Room Amenities: Room Service, Free Paper, TV, Phones in Rm. (2), Cable TV, VCR, Radio, Wet Bar, Microwave, Ind. Heat Ctl., Ind. AC Ctl.

At the Radisson Suite Hotel Boca Raton, every guest enjoys the luxury of spacious accommodations with outstanding amenities. This fine hotel provides a standard of service that is distinctly Radisson. Each of the 201 suites offers a bedroom, separate sitting room, plus a private terrace. Guests enjoy complimentary breakfast & cocktail reception daily.

--------------------------------- BOCA RATON ---------------------------------

The Residence Inn by Marriott
525 N.W. 77th St.
Boca Raton, FL 33487

120 Suites
305-994-3222 800-331-3131

Location: Downtown; Boca Commerce Ct.
Airport: 15 miles
Near: Convenient to major companies (IBM, Siemens, and others)
Area Attractions: Fine Shops, Beach-2 miles

Price Range & Credit Cards: 1 Bedroom Suite $$, 2 Bedrooms $$$, AmEx/MC/Visa/Other CC

Hotel Amenities: No-smoke suites

Business Facilities: Conf. Rm. Cap. 70

Recreational Facilities: Pool, Whirlpool, Sport Court; Ocean Beaches nearby

Comps: Continental Plus Breakfast, Refreshments, Hors d'oeuvres

Room Amenities: Free Paper, TV, Phones in Rm. (2), Cable TV, Radio, Kitchen, Ind. Heat Ctl., Ind. AC Ctl.

The Residence Inn provides the comforts of home for business or vacation travellers. Each suite includes comfortable livingroom with woodburning fireplace and fully equipped kitchen—even free grocery shopping service. Enjoy a complimentary breakfast and newspaper at the Gatehouse. Free hospitality hour (Mon-Thur). Discounted rates for extended stays.

--------------------------------- CAPTIVA ISLAND ---------------------------------

South Seas Plantation Resort
P.O.Box 194
Captiva Island, FL 33924

300 Suites
813-472-5111 800-237-3102

Location: Island; Tampa: 3.5 hours
Airport: 30 miles
Near: 330 Acre Resort, Mainland, 13 Boutiques
Walking Distance To: Beach, Shops
Area Attractions: Lush Tropical Foliage, Wildlife Sanctuary

Price Range & Credit Cards: 1 Bedroom Suite $$$$, 2 Bedrooms $$$$, Junior $$$$, AmEx/MC/Visa/Other CC, Children Free, TAC 10%

Hotel Amenities: Laundry, Parking, Car Hire, Handicap (4)

Business Facilities: Conf. Rm. Cap. 950, Banquet Fac., Sec. Serv., Copier, Aud/Vis., Telex

Recreational Facilities: Pool, Whirlpool, Tennis, Golf, Skiing, Fishing, Jet Skis, Charter Boats, Game Area

Restaurant/Bar: King's Crown, Chadwick's, Ship's Lantern, Entertainment

Comps: Hors d'oeuvres

Room Amenities: Room Service, TV, Phone in Rm., Cable TV, Radio, Kitchen, Ind. Heat Ctl., Ind. AC Ctl.

A luxurious 330-acre island resort, South Seas Plantation offers the truly discerning guests a virtually endless variety of recreational activities, superb dining and full meeting facilities. Unique features include: an island style shopping plaza, jet skiing, game fishing, and windsurfing.

--------------------- DAYTONA BEACH ---------------------

Captain's Quarters Inn
3711 So. Atlantic Ave
Daytona Beach, FL 32019

25 Suites
904-767-3119

Location: Seaside; Downtown: 0.5 mi.
Airport: 7 miles
Near: Halifax River, Daytona Beach, International Speedway
Walking Distance To: Beach, Shops
Area Attractions: Disney World: 60 min., Sea World, Kennedy Space Center

Price Range & Credit Cards: 1 Bedroom Suite $$, AmEx/MC/Visa, Children Free, TAC 10%

Hotel Amenities: Laundry, Handicap (2)

Recreational Facilities: Pool, Tennis, Golf, Game Area; Deep Sea Fishing

Restaurant/Bar: The Galley

Comps: Full Breakfast, Refreshments

Room Amenities: Room Service, Free Paper, TV, Phones in Rm. (2), Cable TV, Radio, Kitchen, Ind. Heat Ctl., Ind. AC Ctl.

You'll find a delightful combination of New England charm and tropical Florida at Captain's Quarters Inn. Hospitality and homey touches are the main emphasis here—from individually decorated, oceanfront suites to a newspaper and complimentary breakfast delivered to your suite every morning. Spend an afternoon on your private patio.

--------------------- DEERFIELD BEACH ---------------------

Embassy Suites Hotel
950 SE 20th. Avenue
Deerfield Beach, FL 33441

244 Suites
305-426-0478 800-362-2779

Location: Beach
Airport: Ft. Lauderdale: 25 mi
Near: International Fishing Pier, Deerfield Island Park Nature Conservatory
Area Attractions: Loxahatchee Tropical Park- 14 miles

Price Range & Credit Cards: 1 Bedroom Suite $$$$, AmEx/MC/Visa/Other CC, Children Free, TAC 10%

Hotel Amenities: Laundry, Gift Shop, Parking, TV Lounge, Handicap (6)

Business Facilities: Conf. Rm. Cap. 300, Banquet Fac., Aud/Vis.

Recreational Facilities: Pool, Whirlpool, Tennis, Golf, Boating, Scuba Diving, Wind Surfing; all sports nearby

Restaurant/Bar: The Swan Court Cafe, Piano (Tues-Sat)

Comps: Refreshments & Popcorn, Airport Transit, Full Breakfast

Room Amenities: Room Service, TV, Phones in Rm. (2), Cable TV, Radio, Wet Bar, Kitchen, Ind. Heat Ctl., Ind. AC Ctl.

The suite idea goes to the beach—just 5 miles from the plush playgrounds and famous golf courses of Boca Raton; only 31 miles from the elegant shops and lifestyle of Palm Beach; and 9 miles from Fort Lauderdale. The location is a perfect stepping-off point for day trips to the many diversions of Florida's southeast coast.

———————————— FORT LAUDERDALE ————————————

Embassy Suites Hotel
555 N.W. 62nd St.
Fort Lauderdale, FL 33309

254 Suites
305-772-5400 800-362-2779

Location: Northside; Downtown: 4 miles
Airport: 7 miles
Near: Suburban & Busines Area, Cypress Creek and Boca Raton Corporate Parks
Walking Distance To: Busines Areas
Area Attractions: Port Everglades

Price Range & Credit Cards: 1 Bedroom Suite $$$, AmEx/MC/Visa/Other CC, Children Free, TAC 10%

Hotel Amenities: Laundry, Handicap (8)

Business Facilities: Conf. Rm. Cap. 400, Banquet Fac., Sec. Serv., Copier, Aud/Vis.

Recreational Facilities: Pool, Sauna, Whirlpool, Tennis, Golf, Windsurfing, Water Skiing nearby

Restaurant/Bar: Fergusons Gator Bar & Grill, Entertainment

Comps: Full Breakfast, Refreshments

Room Amenities: Room Service, Free Paper, TV, Phones in Rm. (2), Cable TV, Radio, Kitchen, Ind. Heat Ctl., Ind. AC Ctl.

This striking Spanish designed, 8 story hotel which houses 254 one-bedroom suites is sure to leave a lasting impression. Take advantage of the complimentary cooked-to-order breakfast and complimentary cocktails, evenings in the atrium. Leisure activities in the hotel include pool & sauna. Close by are tennis, golf, deep sea fishing & water skiing.

———————————— FORT LAUDERDALE ————————————

Embassy Suites Hotel
1100 S.E. 17th St.
Fort Lauderdale, FL 33316

359 Suites
305-527-2700 800-362-2779

Location: Southside; Downtown: 2 miles
Airport: 4 miles
Near: Port Everglades, Causeway Area, Beach
Walking Distance To: Busines Areas
Area Attractions: Port Everglades, Beach, Ocean World

Price Range & Credit Cards: 1 Bedroom Suite $$$$, AmEx/MC/Visa/Other CC, Children Free, TAC 10%

Hotel Amenities: Laundry, Parking, Car Hire, TV Lounge, Handicap (88)

Business Facilities: Conf. Rm. Cap. 500, Banquet Fac., Copier, Aud/Vis., Telex

Recreational Facilities: Pool, Jacuzzi, Steamroom, Sports Complex; Intracoastal Waterway

Restaurant/Bar: Salute, Entertainment

Comps: Airport & Beach Shuttle, Refreshments, Full Breakfast

Room Amenities: Room Service, Free Paper, TV, Phones in Rm. (2), Cable TV, Radio, Wet Bar, Kitchen, Ind. Heat Ctl., Ind. AC Ctl.

Enjoy a full cooked-to-order breakfast and a 2-hour cocktail party each day in our beautiful atrium surrounded by waterfalls and tropical landscaping. If you're planning a meeting, take advantage of our 16,000 ft. of convention space & 13 breakout rooms that, along with a convention service team, can make your next conference a successful experience.

─────────────── FORT LAUDERDALE ───────────────

Guest Quarters Suite Hotel
2670 East Sunrise Blvd.
Fort Lauderdale, FL 33304

234 Suites
305-565-3800 800-424-2900

Location: Waterfront; Downtown: 1 mile
Airport: 5 miles
Near: Public Dock, Boat Slips, I-95 and Florida Turnpike
Walking Distance To: Beaches
Area Attractions: Galleria, Intracoastal Waterway

Price Range & Credit Cards: AmEx/MC/Visa/Other CC, Children Free, TAC 10%

Hotel Amenities: Laundry, Gift Shop, Parking, Car Hire, Pets Allowed, Handicap (11)

Business Facilities: Conf. Rm. Cap. 350, Banquet Fac., Mess. Ctr., Sec. Serv., Copier, Aud/Vis., Comp. Hook-up

Recreational Facilities: Pool, Sauna, Whirlpool, Fitn. Ctr.; Scuba Diving nearby

Restaurant/Bar: Docksiders, Entertainment

Comps: Full Breakfast, Refreshments, Hors d'oeuvres, Airport Van

Room Amenities: Room Service, TV, Phones in Rm. (2), Cable TV, Radio, Kitchen, Ind. Heat Ctl., Ind. AC Ctl.

A handsome stucco building in a lush location, Guest Quarters-Ft. Lauderdale restates the meaning of tropical splendor. So near beautiful beaches and directly adjacent to a busy pleasure boat thoroughfare, this new Guest Quarters promises an exciting vacation. Spacious suites with every convenience are luxurious but homey.

─────────────── FORT LAUDERDALE ───────────────

The Breakers of Ft. Lauderdale
909 Breakers Ave.
Fort Lauderdale, FL 33304

181 Suites
305-566-8800 800-525-2535

Location: Seaside; Downtown: 2 miles
Airport: 6 miles
Near: Birch State Park, Elegant Shops
Walking Distance To: Galleria Mall
Area Attractions: Bartlett Estate, Museum

Price Range & Credit Cards: 1 Bedroom Suite $$$, 2 Bedrooms $$$$+, Junior $$, AmEx/MC/Visa/Other CC, Children Free, TAC 10%

Hotel Amenities: Laundry, Parking, Car Hire

Business Facilities: Conf. Rm. Cap. 300, Banquet Fac., Mess. Ctr., Sec. Serv., Copier, Aud/Vis., Telex, Comp. Hook-up

Recreational Facilities: Pool, Sauna, Whirlpool, Golf, Jogging, Bicycles; All water sports

Restaurant/Bar: Chatters, Brass Monkey, Entertainment

Comps: Hors d'oeuvres

Room Amenities: Room Service, TV, Phone in Rm., Cable TV, Kitchen, Ind. Heat Ctl., Ind. AC Ctl.

Located one short block from the beach and with each suite's private balcony offering a magnificent view, The Breakers will tailor their business facilities and services to your exact specifications. Some of the unique attractions you'll find are the health and beauty suite, where you can receive a first class massage, and the sundeck.

Embassy Suites Hotel, Englewood, CO

——————————— FT. MYERS ———————————

Comfort Suites Hotel
20091 Summerlin Rd.
Ft. Myers, FL 33908

160 Suites
813-466-1200

Location: Downtown: 20 min.
Airport: 40 minutes
Near: Sanibel Island-3 minutes
Area Attractions: Fort Myers Beach, Edison
Home and Mall Shopping

Price Range & Credit Cards: 1 Bedroom Suite $$$$, AmEx/MC/Visa/Other CC,
Child Free, TAC 10%

Hotel Amenities: Laundry, TV Lounge, Pets Allowed, Handicap (8)

Business Facilities: Conf. Rm. Cap. 25, Banquet Fac., Comp. Hook-up, FAX

Recreational Facilities: Pool, Sauna, Spa-2.5 miles, Game Area, Golf packages-15
miles

Restaurant/Bar: Rios Bar and Grill

Comps: Continental Breakfast

Room Amenities: Phone in Rm., Cable TV, Radio, Wet Bar, Ind. Heat Ctl., Ind. AC Ctl.

*This hotel is situated 2.5 miles from Sanibel Island. The 160 all-suite property is known
for its relaxed atmosphere and Rio's Bar and Grill's local favorite meals at reasonable
prices. The olympic size pool has the only underwater sound system in the area. Guests
can relax in the whirlpool while sipping a famous specialty drink and watch the sunset.*

──────────────── GAINSVILLE ────────────────

The Residence Inn by Marriott
4001 S.W. 13th St.
Gainesville, FL 32608

80 Suites
904-371-2101   800-331-3131

Location: Suburbs; Downtown: 5 min.
Airport: 15 minutes
Near: Residential Area
Area Attractions: Univ. of Florida, State Theatre, Florida State Museum

Price Range & Credit Cards: 1 Bedroom Suite $$, 2 Bedrooms $$$, AmEx/MC/Visa/Other CC, Children Free, TAC 10%

Hotel Amenities: Laundry, Library, Parking, TV Lounge, No smoke rooms, Handicap (2)

Business Facilities: Conf. Rm. Cap. 25, Mess. Ctr., Sec. Serv., Copier

Recreational Facilities: Pool, Jacuzzi, Sportcourt

Restaurant/Bar: Several within close proximity

Comps: Continental Breakfast, Hospitality Hour, Newspaper

Room Amenities: Fireplace, Phone in Rm., Cable TV, Radio, Wet Bar, Kitchen, Ind. Heat Ctl., Ind. AC Ctl.

The Residence Inn staff "welcomes you home" to your suite, including living area with fireplace, dining room, full electric kitchen, private bedroom and bath. Two-bedroom suites have a loft bedroom, with private bath, featuring an In-Tub Jacuzzi. Discounted rates for extended stay.

──────────────── INDIALANTIC ────────────────

Radisson Suite Hotel Oceanside
3101 North Highway AIA
Indialantic, FL 32903

168 Suites
305-773-9260   800-228-9822

Location: Oceanfront; Downtown: 15 min.
Airport: Melbourne 15 min.
Near: State Parks and Reserves, Orlando
Walking Distance To: Shopping Malls
Area Attractions: Kennedy Space Center, Disney World, Cruise Terminals-25 min.

Price Range & Credit Cards: 1 Bedroom Suite $$$, AmEx/MC/Visa/Other CC, Children Free, TAC 10%

Hotel Amenities: Laundry, Gift Shop, Parking, TV Lounge, Handicap (9)

Business Facilities: Conf. Rm. Cap. 25, Banquet Fac., Aud/Vis., Comp. Hook-up

Recreational Facilities: Pool, Whirlpool, Fitn. Ctr., jacuzzi (some); Golf, Boating nearby

Restaurant/Bar: Coco De Mer, Entertainment

Comps: Continental Breakfast, Refreshments, Hors d'oeuvres

Room Amenities: Room Service, Free Paper, TV, Phones in Rm. (2), Cable TV, Wet Bar, Kitchen, Ind. Heat Ctl., Ind. AC Ctl.

The Radisson Suite Hotel is located on the "Space Coast Beaches" known as the closest beaches to Orlando/Disney attractions. Each suite has its own balcony and panoramic oceanviews from both bedroom and livingroom. Some units have bunk beds for families; everyone will enjoy over 500 feet of sandy beach and deck.

———————————— JACKSONVILLE ————————————

Park Suite Hotel
9300 Baymeadows Rd.
Jacksonville, FL 32256

210 Suites
904-731-3555 800-432-7272

Location: Off I-95; Downtown: 12 mi.
Airport: 30 miles
Near: Baymeadows Area
Area Attractions: Beaches, Covention Center, Jacksonville Landing

Price Range & Credit Cards: 1 Bedroom Suite $$$, AmEx/MC/Visa/Other CC, Children Free, TAC 10%

Hotel Amenities: Laundry, Gift Shop, Handicap (14)

Business Facilities: Conf. Rm. Cap. 20, Banquet Fac.

Recreational Facilities: Pool, Sauna, Whirlpool, Steam room; Golf nearby

Restaurant/Bar: Plaza on the Green/The Reef @ Baymeadows/Park Cafe, Entertainment

Comps: Full breakfast, Refreshments, Hors d'oeuvres

Room Amenities: Room Service, TV, Phones in Rm. (2), Cable TV, Radio, Wet Bar, Microwave, Ind. Heat Ctl., Ind. AC Ctl.

The Park Suite Hotel provides the business or vacation traveller with two-room, luxurious suites and all the amenities of a full-service hotel. The lobby is attractively decorated in shades of peach and aqua, accented with Mexican tile. You will enjoy the relaxing tropical atmosphere of the Park Suite.

———————————— JACKSONVILLE ————————————

The Residence Inn by Marriott
8365 Dix Ellis Trail
Jacksonville, FL 32256

112 Suites
904-733-8088 800-331-3131

Location: Suburbs; Downtown: 15 min.
Airport: 40 minutes
Near: Deerwood, Beaches, Downtown
Walking Distance To: Dining, Theatres, Comedy Club
Area Attractions: Gator Bowl Festival, Shopping, Beaches

Price Range & Credit Cards: 1 Bedroom Suite $$, 2 Bedrooms $$$, AmEx/MC/Visa/Other CC, Children Free, TAC 10%

Hotel Amenities: Laundry, Handicap (4)

Business Facilities: Conf. Rm. Cap. 35, Mess. Ctr., Copier

Recreational Facilities: Pool, Whirlpool, B-B-Que Fac., Sportscourt

Comps: Cont'l Breakfast, Refreshments, Hors d'oeuvres, Newspaper

Room Amenities: Fireplaces, TV, Phone in Rm., Cable TV, Radio, Kitchen, Ind. Heat Ctl., Ind. AC Ctl.

Every detail at the Residence Inn, from the low-rise buildings to the finely manicured lawns, reminds you of a quiet residential neighborhood. Recreational facilities include tennis, basketball, volleyball, and a barbeque grill. Your comfortable suite is close to fine restaurants, and interesting theatres. Rates discounted for extended stay.

────────────────── JUPITER ──────────────────

Quality Royale Resort
350 South U.S. Highway One
Jupiter, FL 33477

165 Suites
305-744-0210 800-228-5152

Location: Resort; Downtown: 18 mi.
Airport: 25 miles
Near: Jupiter Mall, Suburbs, Beach
Walking Distance To: Banana Max Bar, Restaurants
Area Attractions: Burt Reynolds Dinner Theatre, Beaches

Price Range & Credit Cards: 1 Bedroom Suite $$$, 2 Bedrooms $$$$, Junior $$, AmEx/MC/Visa/Other CC, Children Free, TAC 10%

Business Facilities: Conf. Rm. Cap. 120, Banquet Fac., Copier

Recreational Facilities: Pool, Whirlpool, Tennis, Golf, Fishing, Jai-Alai, Dog Tracks

Restaurant/Bar: Jessica's

Comps: Hors d'oeuvres

Room Amenities: TV, Phone in Rm., Cable TV, Radio, Kitchen, Ind. Heat Ctl., Ind. AC Ctl.

At the Quality Royale Resort the sun never sets on relaxation and recreation. Nestled around a serene 6 acre lake and waterfall the 6 four story buildings are a short walk from the famous Florida coast. The suites are luxuriously furnished with every convenience and each has a screened terrace overlooking the lake and waterfall.

────────────────── KEY WEST ──────────────────

The Galleon Marina Resort
617 Front St.
Key West, FL 33040

64 Suites
305-296-7711 800-544-3030

Location: Old Town; Downtown: 2 min.
Airport: 2 miles
Near: Boardwalk, Gulf of Mexico
Walking Distance To: Beach, Entertainment, Theatres
Area Attractions: Fine Restaurants, Night Life, Many Shops

Price Range & Credit Cards: 2 Bedrooms $$$$+, AmEx/MC/Visa, Children Free, TAC 10%

Hotel Amenities: Laundry, Parking

Business Facilities: Mess. Ctr., Copier

Recreational Facilities: Pool, Sauna, Whirlpool, Fitn. Ctr., Mopeds, Golf, Skiing, Jet-Ski, Bicycles, Snorkeling

Restaurant/Bar: Entertainment

Comps: Refreshments, Hors d'oeuvres

Room Amenities: TV, Phone in Rm., Cable TV, VCR, Radio, Wet Bar, Kitchen, Ind. Heat Ctl., Ind. AC Ctl.

Located just 2 blocks north from downtown, the Galleon Marina is within walking distance to many fine restaurants, shopping centers, and theatres. But with all that's offered at the hotel you'll find it hard to leave. Join the Monday night sunset party and see why Florida sunsets are like no other sunsets.

--------------------------------- KISSIMMEE ---------------------------------

The Residence Inn by Marriott
4786 W.Irlo Bronson Mem. Hwy.
Kissimmee, FL 32741

160 Suites
407-296-2056   800-331-3131

Location: Lakeside; Orlando: 20 miles
Airport: 20 minutes
Near: Highway 192 (Irlo Bronson), Resort lake, Water Mania, Boardwalk & Baseball
Walking Distance To: Boating, Sailing, Water Skiing
Area Attractions: Walt Disney World/Epcot Ctr., Wet'n Wild Park, Sea World

Price Range & Credit Cards: 1 Bedroom Suite $$$, 2 Bedrooms $$$$, Junior $$, AmEx/MC/Visa/Other CC, Children Free, TAC 10%

Hotel Amenities: Laundry, Car Hire

Business Facilities: Conf. Rm. Cap. 35, Mess. Ctr., Copier, Aud/Vis., FAX, Comp. Hook-up

Recreational Facilities: Pool, Whirlpool, Playground, Sailing, Boating, 2 Fishing docks, Water Skiing, Picnic area

Comps: Continental Breakfast, Newspaper

Room Amenities: TV, Phones in Rm. (2), Cable TV, Radio, Full Kitchen, Ind. Heat Ctl., Ind. AC Ctl.

The nearness to attractions, beautiful decor, multitude of amenities and business capabilities will thoroughly satisfy the vacationing family or traveling business person. Located on tranquil Lake Cecile, the Residence Inn by Marriott has 2 docks for sunning, fishing, sailing, skiing and boating! Rates discounted for extended stay.

--------------------------- LAKE BUENA VISTA ---------------------------

Pickett Suite Resort
2305 Hotel Plaza Boulevard
Lake Buena Vista, FL 32830

229 Suites
407-934-1000   800-742-5388

Location: Disney Ct.; Downtown: 15 min.
Airport: 15 minutes
Near: Disney World, EPCOT Center
Area Attractions: 5 miles to Sea World

Price Range & Credit Cards: 1 Bedroom Suite $$$$, 2 Bedrooms $$$$+, AmEx/MC/Visa/Other CC, TAC 10%

Hotel Amenities: Laundry, Gift Shop, Parking, Car Hire, TV Lounge, Handicap (12)

Business Facilities: Conf. Rm. Cap. 12-50, Banquet Fac., Mess. Ctr., Sec. Serv., Copier, Aud/Vis., Telex

Recreational Facilities: Pool, Whirlpool, Fitn. Ctr., Tennis, Jogging, Water Skiing, Horseback Riding, Game Area; access to golf courses

Restaurant/Bar: Parrot Patch/Parrot Patch Lounge

Comps: Transportation to Disney World, Full Breakfast

Room Amenities: TV, Phones in Rm. (2), Radio, Wet Bar, Ind. Heat Ctl., Ind. AC Ctl.

Pickett Suite Resort is the only all-suite resort in Walt Disney World Village. We feature a large aviary in the lobby, Disney gift shop, heated pool, wading pool, whirlpool spa, exercise room, ice cream parlor, game room, lighted tennis courts, jogging trail, complimentary transportation to Disney World/EPCOT center and complimentary full breakfast.

──────────────── MARCO ISLAND ────────────────

Marco Bay Resort
1001 N. Barfield Dr.
Marco Island, FL 33937

320 Suites
813-394-8881 800-228-0661

Location: Bayside; Downtown: Nearby
Airport: 20 minutes
Near: Marina, Restaurants
Walking Distance To: 2 Shopping Areas
Area Attractions: 30 minutes to Everglades,
Golf

Price Range & Credit Cards: 1 Bedroom Suite $$$$, 2 Bedrooms $$$$, Junior $$$, AmEx/MC/Visa/Other CC, Children Free, TAC 10%

Hotel Amenities: Laundry, Parking, Car Hire

Business Facilities: Conf. Rm. Cap. 250, Banquet Fac., Mess. Ctr., Copier, Aud/Vis., Telex

Recreational Facilities: Pool, Sauna, Whirlpool, Fitn. Ctr., Golf, Bicycles, Aerobics, Paddleboats, Game Area, Aquacize Classes

Restaurant/Bar: Christine's, Entertainment

Comps: Continental Breakfast, Hors d'oeuvres

Room Amenities: TV, Phone in Rm., Cable TV, Kitchen, Ind. Heat Ctl., Ind. AC Ctl.

At Marco Bay Resort you are surrounded by a sea of tranquility or take full advantage of the recreational and business facilities. For that special business meeting use the 57-foot yacht to make a lasting impression; after that play some tennis or try out the putting greens. Vacationers will appreciate the organized programs for children.

──────────────── MARCO ISLAND ────────────────

Radisson Suite Beach Resort
600 S. Collier Blvd.
Marco Island, FL 33937

214 Suites
813-394-4100 800-333-3333

Location: Beach; Naples: 25 min.
Airport: Naples-25 min.
Near: Ft. Myers Airport-1 hour, Everglades-20 minutes
Area Attractions: Jungle Larry's African Safari, Audubon Bird Sanctuary

Price Range & Credit Cards: 1 Bedroom Suite $$$$, 2 Bedrooms $$$$+, AmEx, Children Free, TAC 10%

Hotel Amenities: Laundry, Parking

Business Facilities: Conf. Rm. Cap. 200, Banquet Fac., Telex

Recreational Facilities: Pool, Whirlpool, Fitn. Ctr., Game Area; Golf and Tennis nearby

Restaurant/Bar: Tradewinds/Bluebeard's Beach Club & Grill, Live Music

Comps: Hors d'oeuvres

Room Amenities: Room Service, TV, Phone in Rm., Cable TV, Kitchen, Ind. Heat Ctl., Ind. AC Ctl.

The Radisson Suite Beach Resort is the newest, and only all-suite, beachfront resort hotel on Marco Island. It overlooks the Gulf of Mexico from its beachfront location. All suites have Gulf views, fully equipped kitchens, and soft beige and cream with rattan decor. Besides the pool and whirlpool, additional water sports are available on the beach.

---------------------------------- MIAMI ----------------------------------

Mayfair House Hotel Grand Luxe **Location:** Coconut Grove; Downtown: 4 miles
3000 Florida Ave. **Airport:** 9 miles
Miami, FL 33133 **Near:** Artisans Heaven, World of Mayfair Shops
  Area Attractions: Boutiques, many Fine Res-
181 Suites taurants, Coconut Grove Playhouse
305-441-0000 800-433-4555

Price Range & Credit Cards: 1 Bedroom Suite $$$$, 2 Bedrooms $$$$+, Junior $$$$, AmEx/MC/Visa/Other CC, Children Free, TAC 10%

Hotel Amenities: Laundry, Parking

Business Facilities: Conf. Rm. Cap. 500, Banquet Fac., Mess. Ctr., Sec. Serv., Copier, Aud/Vis., Telex, Comp. Hook-up, Bus. Ctr.

Recreational Facilities: Pool, Sauna, Whirlpool, Fitn. Ctr., Tennis, Bicycling; Golf & Fishing nearby

Restaurant/Bar: Mayfair Grill, Ensign Bitters, Entertainment

Comps: Airport Limousine

Room Amenities: Room Service, Free Paper, TV, Phone in Rm., Cable TV, VCR, Radio, Wet Bar, Kitchen, Ind. Heat Ctl., Ind. AC Ctl.

From the moment you board the complimentary limousine at the airport, you'll know the Mayfair House is an extraordinary suite hotel. Located close to downtown, each suite features a private terrace with Japanese hot tub, imported furnishings, marble bathroom, and Laura Ashley bed linens. Fine restaurants and boutiques are steps away!

---------------------------------- MIAMI ----------------------------------

Riverparc Hotel **Location:** Downtown
100 SE 4th St. **Airport:** 30 minutes
Miami, FL 33131 **Near:** River Walk, Convention Center
  Walking Distance To: Many Shops
129 Suites **Area Attractions:** Cultural Center, City, River
305-374-5100 800-521-5100

Price Range & Credit Cards: 1 Bedroom Suite $$$$, 2 Bedrooms $$$$, Junior $$$, AmEx/MC/Visa/Other CC, Children Free, TAC 10%

Hotel Amenities: Laundry, Parking, Car Hire, Handicap (35)

Business Facilities: Conf. Rm. Cap. 100, Banquet Fac., Mess. Ctr., Sec. Serv., Copier, Aud/Vis., Telex, Comp. Hook-up, Bus. Ctr.

Recreational Facilities: Pool, Whirlpool, Tennis, Golf, Health Club

Restaurant/Bar: Parc Grill, P.J.'s, Entertainment

Comps: Continental Breakfast

Room Amenities: Room Service, Free Paper, TV, Phones in Rm. (3), Cable TV, Radio, Wet Bar, Ind. Heat Ctl., Ind. AC Ctl.

Riverparc is sure to please any traveling business person with their services and wide variety of facilities. Conference rooms, computer hook-ups and audio-visual capabilities are just some of the conveniences that await you. In the evening visit the Parc Grill (formal) or P.J.'s (casual) for a large variety of enticing fare.

─────────────── MIDDLEBURG ───────────────

The Inn at Ravines
2932 Ravines Rd.
Middleburg, FL 32068

50 Suites
904-282-1111 800-872-9980

Location: Country; Jacksonville: 30 mi.
Airport: 40 minutes
Near: Black Creek, Florida Highlands
Walking Distance To: Exquisite riverside
Area Attractions: Country Atmosphere, St.
Augustine

Price Range & Credit Cards: 1 Bedroom Suite $$, Junior $$, MC/Visa, Children Free

Hotel Amenities: Laundry

Business Facilities: Conf. Rm. Cap. 50

Recreational Facilities: Pool, Whirlpool, Tennis, Golf; Jogging/Fitness Trail

Restaurant/Bar: Trulock's, Groff's Scottish Pub

Room Amenities: TV, Phone in Rm., Cable TV, Radio, Kitchen, Ind. Heat Ctl., Ind. AC Ctl.

Located 45 minutes from downtown Jacksonville, St. Augustine, The Inn At Ravines offers luxuriously appointed suites, each with a spectacular view of the golf course (ranked 6th in the State)! Besides golf there is tennis, and some of the finest bass fishing in the country. You're sure to leave this secluded country atmosphere satisfied and relaxed.

─────────────── NAPLES ───────────────

Edgewater Beach Suite Hotel
1901 Gulfshore Blvd. North
Naples, FL 33940

124 Suites
813-262-6511 800-821-0196

Location: On Beach; Naples: 3 miles
Airport: 10 miles
Near: Boutiques, Restaurants, Residential area, Marina
Walking Distance To: Beach, Gulf
Area Attractions: Old Naples Shopping Area

Price Range & Credit Cards: 1 Bedroom Suite $$, 2 Bedrooms $$$$, AmEx/MC/Visa/Other CC, Children Free, TAC 10%

Hotel Amenities: Valet Park, Free Parking, Grocery Service, Handicap (2)

Business Facilities: Conf. Rm. Cap. 80, Banquet Fac., Sec. Serv., Copier, Aud/Vis., Telex

Recreational Facilities: Pool, Fitn. Ctr., Fishing, Boating; Golf and Tennis nearby

Restaurant/Bar: Crystal Parrot, Mistrals, Piano bar

Room Amenities: Room Service, Free Paper, TV, Phone in Rm., Cable TV, Radio, Kitchen, Ind. Heat Ctl., Ind. AC Ctl.

The Edgewater is directly on the beach of the Gulf of Mexico and offers the discerning business traveler or vacationer a once-in-a-lifetime experience. Imagine yourself dining in the exquisite Crystal Parrot on the 6th floor overlooking the Gulf of Mexico and a spectacular Naples sunset. Make the most of many fun activities, unique shops and boutiques.

--- ORLANDO ---

Enclave Suites at Orlando
6165 Carrier Drive
Orlando, FL 32819

321 Suites
305-351-1155 800-457-0077

Location: Central; Downtown: 10 min.
Airport: 15 minutes
Near: International Cove
Walking Distance To: Shopping, Restaurants, Movies
Area Attractions: 10 min. to Disney/EPCOT, 5 min. to Convention Center

Price Range & Credit Cards: 2 Bedrooms $$$$, Junior $$$, AmEx/MC/Visa/Other CC, Children Free, TAC 15%

Hotel Amenities: Laundry, Gift Shop, TV Lounge, Handicap (2)

Business Facilities: Conf. Rm. Cap. 50-75, Banquet Fac., Copier, Aud/Vis., Telex, Comp. Hook-up

Recreational Facilities: Pool, Sauna, Whirlpool, Fitn. Ctr., Tennis, Fishing; Golf nearby.

Restaurant/Bar: Enclave Beach Cafe/Hammerhead Lounge, Entertainment

Comps: Hors d'oeuvres

Room Amenities: Free Paper, TV, Phones in Rm. (2), Cable TV, VCR, Radio, Full Kitchen, Ind. Heat Ctl., Ind. AC Ctl.

All suites have private balconies overlooking Sandy Lake. Maid service includes washing of dishes & utensils. Located in the heart of Central Florida, we are minutes from all area attractions, shopping, golf, and major business communities. Our indoor recreational facility includes an indoor pool, jacuzzi, sauna and executive workout room.

--- ORLANDO ---

Park Suite Hotel
8978 International Dr.
Orlando, FL 32819

245 Suites
407-352-1400 800-432-SARA

Location: Central; Downtown: 10 min.
Airport: 20 minutes
Near: Shops
Walking Distance To: Convention Center
Area Attractions: Epcot, Disney World, Sea World

Price Range & Credit Cards: 1 Bedroom Suite $$$, AmEx/MC/Visa/Other CC, Children Free, TAC 9%

Hotel Amenities: Laundry, Gift Shop, Service Desk, Handicap (6)

Business Facilities: Conf. Rm. Cap. 500, Banquet Fac., Copier, Telex, FAX

Recreational Facilities: Pool, Sauna, Whirlpool, Fitn. Ctr., Golf, Tennis nearby

Restaurant/Bar: Park Cafe (24 hrs), Plaza on the Green, Danielle's, Entertainment

Comps: Full Breakfast, Welcome Cocktail

Room Amenities: Room Service, TV, Phones in Rm. (2), Microwave, Cable TV, Wet Bar, Refrigerator, Ind. Heat Ctl., Ind. AC Ctl.

At Park Suite you'll be minutes from all the major attractions in Florida, while still being able to enjoy all the unique aspects of this Mediterranean style hotel. In the morning complimentary American breakfast awaits you. In the evening, you will enjoy award-winning cuisine at the Plaza on the Green.

Burnt Store Marina Resort, Punta Gorda, FL

─────────────── ORLANDO ───────────────

The Residence Inn by Marriott
7610 Canada Ave.
Orlando, FL 32819

176 Suites
305-345-0117 800-331-3131

Location: Central; Downtown: 10 min.
Airport: 20 minutes
Near: Sand Lake Rd., International Drive
Walking Distance To: Shops and Restaurants
Area Attractions: Sea World, Wet n'Wild, Disney World

Price Range & Credit Cards: 1 Bedroom Suite $$$, 2 Bedrooms $$$, Junior $$, AmEx/MC/Visa/Other CC, Children Free, TAC 10%

Hotel Amenities: Laundry, Parking, Handicap (2)

Business Facilities: Conf. Rm. Cap. 50, Telex

Recreational Facilities: 5 Whirlpools, Heated Pool

Comps: Continental Breakfast

Room Amenities: TV, Phone in Rm., Cable TV, Radio, Kitchen, Ind. Heat Ctl., Ind. AC Ctl.

The comfort, convenience, and location of the Residence Inn make this quaint English Tudor style hotel the perfect headquarters for an exciting family vacation. Taking care of business is easy with the 2 conference rooms. The contemporary home-like environment of each suite is relaxing at day's end. Discounted rates for extended stay.

-------------------------------- ORLANDO --------------------------------

Sonesta Village Hotel
10000 Turkey Lake Rd.
Orlando, FL 32819

370 Suites
305-352-8051 800-343-7170

Location: Resort; Orlando: 4 miles
Airport: 10 miles
Near: 97 Acres with lakes, Marketplace 2 miles
Walking Distance To: Lakeside
Area Attractions: Disney, EPCOT, Sea World

Price Range & Credit Cards: 1 Bedroom Suite $$$, 2 Bedrooms $$$$, AmEx/MC/ Visa/Other CC, Children Free, TAC 10%

Hotel Amenities: Laundry, Parking, TV Lounge, Pets Allowed

Business Facilities: Conf. Rm. Cap. 200, Banquet Fac., Mess. Ctr., Sec. Serv., Aud/Vis., Telex

Recreational Facilities: Pool, Sauna, Whirlpool, Fitn. Ctr., Tennis, Volleyball, Shuffleboard, Game Area; Jogging Trail

Restaurant/Bar: Greenhouse, Terrace Lounge, Entertainment

Room Amenities: TV, Phone in Rm., Cable TV, Kitchen, Ind. Heat Ctl., Ind. AC Ctl.

Located just 10 minutes from Disney World and EPCOT center and 5 minutes from Sea World, the informal Spanish tiled villas spread across 100 beautifully landscaped acres of the picturesque shore of Sand Lake. A cornucopia of recreational activities including tennis, shuffleboard, and jetskiing can be found at the hotel.

-------------------------------- PUNTA GORDA --------------------------------

Burnt Store Marina Resort
3150 Matecumbe Key Rd.
Punta Gorda, FL 33955

100 Suites
813-639-4151 800-237-4255

Location: Gulf of Mexico
Airport: RSW-Ft.Myers: 35 mi.
Near: Cape Coral, I-75
Walking Distance To: Golf, Tennis, Marina
Area Attractions: Barrier Islands

Price Range & Credit Cards: 1 Bedroom Suite $$$, 2 Bedrooms $$$$, AmEx/MC/ Visa/Other CC, Children Free, TAC 10%

Hotel Amenities: Laundry, Pets Allowed

Business Facilities: Conf. Rm. Cap. 250, Banquet Fac., Mess. Ctr., Copier, Aud/Vis.

Recreational Facilities: Pool, Bicycles, Tennis, Golf, Motorboats, Sailboats, Driving Range; Fishing excursions

Restaurant/Bar: Salty's Harborside Restaurant, Castaways Lounge

Room Amenities: TV, Phone in Rm., Cable TV, Radio, Kitchen, Ind. Heat Ctl., Ind. AC Ctl.

Located on the Gulf of Mexico, tucked inside Charlotte Harbor. Suite accommodations, 423-slip, full-service marina. Boating, deep sea fishing, sailing charters, bicycling, tennis, 27-hole golf course. Salty's Harborside Restaurant and Castaways Lounge. Conference center to accommodate groups up to 250. Easily accessible from I-75, exit 28.

——————————————— SANIBEL ISLAND ———————————————

Sundial Beach & Tennis Resort
1246 Middle Gulf Dr.
Sanibel Island, FL 33957

180 Suites
813-472-4151   800-237-4184

Location: Beachside; Downtown: 30 min.
Airport: Half hour
Near: Shelling Tours, Trolley Pickup for shopping
Walking Distance To: Gulf of Mexico
Area Attractions: Thomas Edison Winter
Estate, Wildlife Refuge

Price Range & Credit Cards: 1 Bedroom Suite $$$, 2 Bedrooms $$$$, AmEx/MC/ Visa/Other CC, Children Free, TAC 10%

Hotel Amenities: Laundry, Parking, TV Lounge, Handicap (all)

Business Facilities: Conf. Rm. Cap. 100, Banquet Fac., Mess. Ctr., Sec. Serv., Copier, Aud/Vis., Comp. Hook-up

Recreational Facilities: Pool, Golf, Sailboats, Game Area; Deep Sea Fishing

Restaurant/Bar: Morgan's, Entertainment

Comps: Hors d'oeuvres

Room Amenities: TV, Phone in Rm., Wet Bar, Kitchen, Ind. Heat Ctl., Ind. AC Ctl.

The exquisite accommodations and rare beauties that abound make Sundial a marvel. Many business services and a meeting facility with over 10,000 square feet. A host of different leisure activities and an excellent childcare program. Also enjoy fine steak and seafood while relishing the panoramic view of the Gulf.

——————————————— ST. PETERSBURG BEACH ———————————————

The Mariner Beach Club
4220 Gulf Blvd.
St. Petersburg Beach, FL 33706

30 Suites
813-367-3721

Location: Beachside; Downtown: 2 miles
Airport: 1 hour
Near: Restaurants
Walking Distance To: Shopping Center
Area Attractions: Beach, Tiki Gardens 5 miles

Price Range & Credit Cards: 1 Bedroom Suite $$, 2 Bedrooms $$$, AmEx/MC/ Visa/Other CC, Children Free, TAC 10%

Hotel Amenities: Laundry, Parking, Handicap (1)

Business Facilities: Mess. Ctr.

Recreational Facilities: Pool, Whirlpool, Tennis, Golf, Game Area

Room Amenities: TV, Phone in Rm., Cable TV, Radio, Kitchen, Ind. Heat Ctl., Ind. AC Ctl.

Overlooking the Gulf of Mexico stands the Mariner; with its four styles of luxury suites, roomy living and dining areas, spacious bedrooms and decorator extras like track lighting and ceiling fans. The kitchens come fully equipped with microwave ovens, refrigerators with ice-makers, dishwashers, ample glassware, cooking utensils, and dishes.

---------------------- ST. PETERSBURG BEACH ----------------------

TradeWinds St.Petersburg Beach   **Location:** Beachside; Downtown: 2 miles
5500 Gulf Blvd.   **Airport:** Tampa Int'l 35 min.
St. Petersburg Beach, FL 33706   **Near:** Navigable Waterways
                                                              Walking Distance To: Shops & Boutiques,
114 Suites   Beaches
813-367-6461 800-237-0707   **Area Attractions:** Waterways throughout
                                                              property, Deep Sea Fishing

Price Range & Credit Cards: 1 Bedroom Suite $$$, 2 Bedrooms $$$$+, AmEx/MC/
Visa/Other CC, Children Free, TAC 10%

Hotel Amenities: Laundry, Concierge, Parking, Car Hire, Children's games

Business Facilities: Conf. Rm. Cap. 750, Banquet Fac., Mess. Ctr., Sec. Serv., Copier,
Aud/Vis., Teleconf., Telex

Recreational Facilities: Sauna, Whirlpool, Fitn. Ctr., 4 Pools, Golf, Tennis, Fishing,
Gondolas, Windsurfing, Racquetball, Paddleboats

Restaurant/Bar: Flying Bridge floating restaurant, Sea Breeze Cafe, Entertainment

Room Amenities: Room Service, TV, Phones in Rm. (3), Cable TV, Radio, Kitchen, Ind.
Heat Ctl., Ind. AC Ctl.

*TradeWinds is a magnificent suite hotel with outstanding service and facilities; offering
every business service including 25 meeting rooms and a convention center seating 750;
abundant recreational activities on grounds or nearby; superb dining cuisine. Shopping
is footsteps away and daily activities are available for children.*

---------------------- TAMPA ----------------------

Embassy Suites Hotel   **Location:** Northeast; Downtown: 7 miles
11310 N. 30th. Street   **Airport:** 10 miles
Tampa, FL 33612   **Near:** Univ. of South Florida, Busch Gardens,
                                                              Museum of Science & Industry
129 Suites   **Walking Distance To:** University
813-971-7690 800-362-2779   **Area Attractions:** Florida State Fair

Price Range & Credit Cards: 1 Bedroom Suite $$, AmEx/MC/Visa/Other CC, Children Free, TAC 10%

Hotel Amenities: Laundry, TV Lounge, Handicap (3)

Business Facilities: Conf. Rm. Cap. 150, Copier, Aud/Vis.

Recreational Facilities: Pool, Whirlpool

Comps: Full Breakfast, Refreshments

Room Amenities: Free Paper, TV, Phones in Rm. (2), Cable TV, Radio, Wet Bar, Kitchen,
Ind. Heat Ctl., Ind. AC Ctl.

*In the mornings at Embassy you can open your door and see the charming courtyard
atrium filled with plants and waterfalls, then walk into the courtyard cafe for a complimentary breakfast! A favorite among corporate and visiting travelers Embassy is conveniently
located from the airport. While there, take advantage of Busch Gardens discount package.*

---------------------------- TAMPA ----------------------------

Embassy Suites Hotel
4400 W. Cypress Ave.
Tampa, FL 33607

260 Suites
813-873-8675 800-362-2779

Location: Airport; Downtown: 5 miles
Airport: 2 miles
Near: Westshore Business District, I-275, Tampa Stadium-2 miles
Area Attractions: Florida State Fair, Busch Gardens, Performing Arts Center

Price Range & Credit Cards: 1 Bedroom Suite $$$, AmEx/MC/Visa/Other CC, Children Free, TAC 10%

Hotel Amenities: Laundry, Gift Shop, Parking, Car Hire, TV Lounge, Handicap (7)

Business Facilities: Conf. Rm. Cap. 500, Banquet Fac., Copier, Aud/Vis., Teleconf., Telex, Comp. Hook-up

Recreational Facilities: Pool, Sauna, Whirlpool, Fitn. Ctr., Game Area; Golf and Tennis nearby

Restaurant/Bar: Swan Court, Zachary's, Entertainment

Comps: Full Breakfast, Refreshments, Airport Van Service

Room Amenities: Room Service, Free Paper, TV, Phones in Rm. (2), Cable TV, Radio, Wet Bar, Kitchen, Ind. Heat Ctl., Ind. AC Ctl.

Ideally located in the heart of Westshore business district, close to Busch Gardens, and less than 2 miles from Tampa International Airport, Embassy provides convenience and comfort in a relaxing ambiance. Socialize during the complimentary cocktail reception in the tropical rain forest styled atrium.

---------------------------- TAMPA ----------------------------

Guest Quarters Suite Hotel
555 N. Westshore Blvd.
Tampa, FL 33609

221 Suites
813-875-1555 800-424-2900

Location: Central; Downtown: 5 min.
Airport: 2 miles
Near: Westshore Business District, Gulf Beaches
Walking Distance To: Shops and Restaurants
Area Attractions: Busch Gardens

Price Range & Credit Cards: 1 Bedroom Suite $$$$, 2 Bedrooms $$$$, AmEx/MC/Visa/Other CC, TAC 10%

Hotel Amenities: Laundry, Library, Parking, Pets Allowed

Business Facilities: Conf. Rm. Cap. 200, Banquet Fac., Sec. Serv., Copier, Aud/Vis., FAX, Telex

Recreational Facilities: Pool, Sauna, Whirlpool, Fitn. Ctr.; Golf and Tennis nearby

Restaurant/Bar: The Terrace Cafe and Bar

Comps: Breakfast Buffet, Manager's Reception, Airport Limo

Room Amenities: Room Service, TV, Phones in Rm. (2), Cable TV, Radio, Wet Bar, Kitchen, Ind. Heat Ctl., Ind. AC Ctl.

We invite you to experience Guest treatment in the heart of Tampa's Westshore business district. Just minutes from downtown shopping or the Gulf beaches, this luxury high-rise with a tropical pool deck, offers spacious suites decorated in pastel and wicker. For added convenience have your grocery and sundry shopping done for you.

Sailport Resort, Tampa, FL

--- TAMPA ---

Pickett Suite Hotel
3050 N. Rocky Point Dr. W.
Tampa, FL 33607

203 Suites
813-888-8800 800-742-5388

Location: Bayside; Downtown: 15 min.
Airport: 3 minutes
Near: Westshore Business District, Major Shopping Areas
Walking Distance To: Rocky Point
Area Attractions: Clearwater Beaches, Tampa Bay Stadium

Price Range & Credit Cards: 1 Bedroom Suite $$, 2 Bedrooms $$$, AmEx/MC/ Visa/Other CC, Child Free, TAC 10%

Hotel Amenities: Laundry, Library, Parking, Handicap (12)

Business Facilities: Conf. Rm. Cap. 100, Banquet Fac., Copier, Aud/Vis., Teleconf., Comp. Hook-up

Recreational Facilities: Pool, Sauna, Whirlpool, Fitn. Ctr., Golf, Racquetball, Deep sea fishing, All water sports

Restaurant/Bar: Galerie

Comps: Breakfast

Room Amenities: Room Service, Free Paper, TV, Phone in Rm., Cable TV, Radio, Wet Bar, Ind. Heat Ctl., Ind. AC Ctl.

A remarkable number of guest services for the traveling business person or vacationer are awaiting you at Pickett. Just 3 minutes from the airport, the Westshore area, and downtown, the 203 suites all offer dining room views of Old Tampa Bay. Socializing is easy in; the contemporary marble floored lobby, the hotel library, or the health center.

———————————————— TAMPA ————————————————

Sailport Resort
2506 Rocky Point Dr.
Tampa, FL 33607

237 Suites
813-886-9599 800-255-9599

Location: Bayside; Downtown: 8 min.
Airport: 3 minutes
Near: Rocky Point Area, great shopping, restaurants
Area Attractions: Dali Museum, Olde Hyde Park Village

Price Range & Credit Cards: 1 Bedroom Suite $$, 2 Bedrooms $$$, AmEx/MC/Visa/Other CC, Children Free, TAC 10%

Hotel Amenities: Laundry, Parking, Car Hire, Handicap

Business Facilities: Conf. Rm. Cap. 60, Banquet Fac., Mess. Ctr., Copier, Aud/Vis.

Recreational Facilities: Pool, Tennis, Golf, Boating, Racquetball, Deep sea fishing

Comps: Continental Breakfast

Room Amenities: In-room movies, Free Paper, TV, Phone in Rm., Cable TV, Radio, Wet Bar, Kitchen, Ind. Heat Ctl., Ind. AC Ctl.

Directly on the Tampa coast, Sailport offers a picturesque view of the water from every suite. Many corporations are already taking advantage of the terrific value and convenient location—just 5 minutes from Westshore business district and even closer to the airport; 25 minutes to Busch Gardens, the Dali Museum; 10 minutes to Olde Hyde Park Village.

———————————————— TREASURE ISLAND ————————————————

Sea Castle All-Suite Hotel
10750 Gulf Boulevard
Treasure Island, FL 33706

42 Suites
813-367-2704

Location: Beachside; Downtown: 15 min.
Airport: 3 minutes
Near: St. Petersburg Beach, Shops
Walking Distance To: Beaches
Area Attractions: Epcot & Disney Tours available

Price Range & Credit Cards: 1 Bedroom Suite $$, AmEx/MC/Visa/Other CC, Children Free, TAC 10%

Hotel Amenities: Laundry, Car Hire, Handicap (2)

Business Facilities: Copier, Comp. Hook-up

Recreational Facilities: Pool, Tennis, Golf

Room Amenities: TV, Phone in Rm., Cable TV, VCR, Radio, Kitchen, Ind. Heat Ctl., Ind. AC Ctl.

The Sea Castle is an appropriate name of this hotel on the white friendly sands of the Gulf of Mexico. With tours leaving regularly for many of the famous Florida attractions, the pleasant white 3-story hotel makes the perfect springboard for a family vacation. You'll find a wide choice of restaurants nearby as well as shops and boutiques.

──────────── VERO BEACH ────────────

Vero Pickett Suite Resort
3500 Ocean Dr.
Vero Beach, FL 32963

55 Suites
305-231-5666 800-742-5388

Location: Beachside; Downtown: 10 min.
Airport: 45 minutes
Near: St. Petersburg Beaches, Business
Walking Distance To: Beaches, Shops
Area Attractions: 1.5 Hours to Cape Canaveral

Price Range & Credit Cards: 1 Bedroom Suite $$$$, 2 Bedrooms $$$$, AmEx/MC/ Visa/Other CC, Children Free, TAC 10%

Hotel Amenities: Laundry, Parking, Handicap (3)

Business Facilities: Conf. Rm. Cap. 50, Banquet Fac., Mess. Ctr., Sec. Serv., Copier, Aud/Vis.

Recreational Facilities: Pool, Whirlpool, Tennis, Golf

Comps: Full Breakfast

Room Amenities: Room Service, Free Paper, TV, Phone in Rm., Cable TV, Radio, Wet Bar, Kitchen, Ind. Heat Ctl., Ind. AC Ctl.

Directly on the lovely Florida coast rises the Pickett Resort. Its beautiful pool area with lush gardens is surrounded by the handsome Mediterranean style building complete with underground parking. Start the day with a complimentary breakfast buffet in the Lanai Room and end it in your elegantly furnished suite overlooking the ocean.

──────────── WEST PALM BEACH ────────────

Comfort Suites Airport Hotel
1808 S. Australian Ave.
West Palm Beach, FL 33409

174 Suites
407-689-6888 800-228-5050

Location: Airport; Downtown: 2 miles
Airport: 0.5 mile
Near: Worth Avenue Shopping, Palm Beach Kennel Club 3 miles
Area Attractions: Jai Alai, Beaches

Price Range & Credit Cards: 1 Bedroom Suite $$$$, Junior $$$, AmEx/MC/Visa/ Other CC, Children Free, TAC 10%

Hotel Amenities: Gift Shop, Pets Allowed, Handicap (4)

Business Facilities: Conf. Rm. Cap. 130, Banquet Fac., Mess. Ctr., Copier, Aud/Vis., Comp. Hook-up

Recreational Facilities: Pool, Sauna, Whirlpool, Fitn. Ctr.; Golf within 3 miles

Restaurant/Bar: Spangles Cafe 'n Deli/Spangles Lounge

Comps: Full Breakfast, Refreshments, Airport Van Service

Room Amenities: Room Service, Free Paper, TV, Phones in Rm. (2), Cable TV, VCR, Radio, Wet Bar, Ind. Heat Ctl., Ind. AC Ctl.

Comfort Suites Hotel features two types of guest rooms, Comfort and Quality suites. The larger Quality suites feature many amenities including 2 remote control cable TV's, two phones, stocked refrigerator, VCR, and stereo. The smaller Comfort suites also have the fully stocked refrigerator and remote control cable TV.

 Georgia

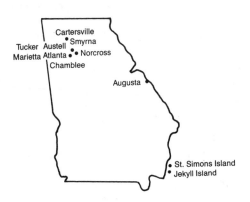

---------------------- ATLANTA ----------------------

Embassy Suites Hotel
2815 Akers Mill Rd.
Atlanta, GA 30339

261 Suites
404-984-9300 800-362-2779

Location: Northwest; Downtown: 12 min.
Airport: 23 miles
Near: Cumberland Mall, Chattahoochee Wild Life Park
Area Attractions: Six Flags, White Water Park

Price Range & Credit Cards: 1 Bedroom Suite $$$, 2 Bedrooms $$$, AmEx/MC/ Visa/Other CC, Children Free, TAC 10%

Hotel Amenities: Gift Shop, Parking, Car Hire, Pets Allowed, Handicap (8)

Business Facilities: Conf. Rm. Cap. 60, Banquet Fac., Mess. Ctr., Copier, Aud/Vis., Comp. Hook-up

Recreational Facilities: Pool, Sauna, Whirlpool, Golf, Game Area; Fitn. Center next door

Restaurant/Bar: Jaime's

Comps: Full Breakfast, Refreshments, Airport Limousine

Room Amenities: Room Service, Free Paper, TV, Phone in Rm., Cable TV, Radio, Wet Bar, Kitchen, Ind. Heat Ctl., Ind. AC Ctl.

The Embassy is an exceptional hotel because of their extensive business capacity; their complimentary limousine service to and from the airport; and their friendly staff. Located on the fashionable north side of Atlanta, the lobby area is a landscaped tropical atrium. The 261 suites include microwave ovens, wet bars, and refrigerator with ice makers.

---------------------- ATLANTA ----------------------

Embassy Suites Hotel
1030 Crown Pointe Pkwy.
Atlanta, GA 30338

241 Suites
404-394-5454 800-362-2779

Location: Northside; Downtown: 15 min.
Airport: 30 miles
Near: Dunwoody, Sandy Springs
Walking Distance To: Perimeter Mall
Area Attractions: Over 100 Specialty Shops

Price Range & Credit Cards: 1 Bedroom Suite $$$, AmEx/MC/Visa/Other CC, Children Free, TAC 10%

Hotel Amenities: Laundry, Parking, TV Lounge, Handicap (9)

Business Facilities: Conf. Rm. Cap. 100, Banquet Fac., Mess. Ctr., Copier, Aud/Vis., FAX

Recreational Facilities: Pool, Sauna, Whirlpool, Fitn. Ctr.; 19 Golf courses nearby

Restaurant/Bar: Alexander's Restaurant and Lounge

Comps: Full breakfast, Refreshments

Room Amenities: Room Service, Free Paper, TV, Phones in Rm. (2), Cable TV, Radio, Wet Bar, Kitchen, Ind. Heat Ctl., Ind. AC Ctl.

Embassy is proud of their award-winning hotel consisting of a 10-story structure around an atrium filled with tropical plants and a pool with a waterfall. The relaxed atmosphere continues into the suites decorated in muted mauves, blues, and greys. The furnishings are contemporary. Business or recreational facilities are plentiful. Tennis nearby.

---------------------- ATLANTA ----------------------

Executive Villas Hotel
5735 Roswell Rd. NE
Atlanta, GA 30342

131 Suites
404-252-2868 800-241-1013

Location: Northside; Downtown: 15 min.
Airport: Van Service
Near: Sandy Springs, Shopping malls
Walking Distance To: Dining
Area Attractions: Georgia World Congress Center

Price Range & Credit Cards: 1 Bedroom Suite $$, 2 Bedrooms $$$, AmEx/MC/Visa/Other CC, Children Free, TAC 10%

Hotel Amenities: Laundry, Library, Parking, Pets Allowed, Handicap (1)

Business Facilities: Conf. Rm. Cap. 45, Copier, Aud/Vis.

Recreational Facilities: Pool, Tennis, Game Area; Fitness Center

Comps: Airport Courtesy Van

Room Amenities: Free Paper, TV, Phone in Rm., Cable TV, Radio, Kitchen, Ind. Heat Ctl., Ind. AC Ctl.

With luxurious 1, 2, and 3 bedroom suites, Executive Villas is sure to satisfy your business and social needs. Centrally located in Sandy Springs, the gracious landscaping is composed of trees, azaleas, and constantly blooming plants. The inviting traditional lobby has hardwood floors & an oak front desk that welcomes each guest. Guest library.

——————————— ATLANTA ———————————

Guest Quarters Suite Hotel
111 Perimeter Center West
Atlanta, GA 30346

207 Suites
404-396-6800 800-424-2900

Location: Northside; Downtown: 20 min.
Airport: 4 miles
Near: Perimeter Shopping, Business District
Walking Distance To: Shopping Mall
Area Attractions: Stone Mountain Park, Six Flags

Price Range & Credit Cards: 1 Bedroom Suite $$$, 2 Bedrooms $$$$, AmEx/MC/ Visa/Other CC, TAC 10%

Hotel Amenities: Laundry, Library, Parking, Pets Allowed, Handicap (1)

Business Facilities: Conf. Rm. Cap. 80, Banquet Fac., Copier, Aud/Vis., FAX, Telex

Recreational Facilities: Pool, Sauna, Whirlpool, Fitn. Ctr., Golf; Tennis next to Hotel

Restaurant/Bar: Cafe One-Eleven

Comps: Breakfast Buffet, Manager's Reception

Room Amenities: Room Service, TV, Phone in Rm., Cable TV, Radio, Kitchen, Ind. Heat Ctl., Ind. AC Ctl.

Guest Quarters knows how important it is that hotel accommodations offer not only rest and comfort but flexibility for working and meeting as well. Well-located in the heart of the Perimeter Center (a business and shopping area), the suites will please you with live plants, handpainted graphics, and comfortable modern furnishings. Tennis and golf are nearby.

——————————— ATLANTA ———————————

The Granada All Suite Hotel
1302 West Peachtree Street
Atlanta, GA 30309

66 Suites
404-870-6700

Location: Midtown; Downtown: 2 min.
Airport: 15 minutes
Walking Distance To: High Museum & Woodruff Ct.
Area Attractions: Fox Theatre, Alliance Theatre, Restaurants

Price Range & Credit Cards: 1 Bedroom Suite $$$, 2 Bedrooms $$$$, Junior $$$, AmEx/MC/Visa/Other CC, Children Free, TAC 10%

Hotel Amenities: Laundry, Parking, TV Lounge, Pets Allowed, Handicap (6)

Business Facilities: Conf. Rm. Cap. 20, Banquet Fac., Sec. Serv., Copier, Aud/Vis., Telex, Comp. Hook-up

Recreational Facilities: Whirlpool, Fitn. Ctr.; Golf and Tennis nearby

Comps: Continental Breakfast, Refreshments, Hors d'oeuvres

Room Amenities: Free Paper, TV, Phones in Rm. (2), Cable TV, Radio, Wet Bar, Kitchen, Ind. Heat Ctl., Ind. AC Ctl.

The Granada Hotel, listed in the Prestigious Historic Register, combines the charm of old Spanish architecture with the convenience of a midtown Atlanta location. The 66 suites furnished in gracious 18th century style also provide kitchens and luxurious bath with whirlpool tub. The thoughtful attention of our well-trained staff is sure to please all.

──────────── ATLANTA ────────────

Marriott Suites Atlanta
6120 Peachtree-Dunwoody Road
Atlanta, GA 30328

224 Suites
404-668-0808 800-228-9290

Location: Northside; Downtown: 25 min.
Airport: 45 minutes
Near: Perimeter Shopping, Major Office Parks
Walking Distance To: Shopping Mall
Area Attractions: Civic Center, Stone Mountain, Six Flags Over Georgia Park

Price Range & Credit Cards: 1 Bedroom Suite $$$, AmEx/MC/Visa/Other CC, Children Free, TAC 10%

Hotel Amenities: Laundry, Parking, Pets Allowed, Handicap (10)

Business Facilities: Conf. Rm. Cap. 180, Mess. Ctr., Copier, Aud/Vis., FAX, Comp. Hook-up

Recreational Facilities: Pool, Sauna, Whirlpool, Health Club; Golf and Tennis nearby

Restaurant/Bar: Windows

Comps: Full Breakfast, Beverages & Snacks

Room Amenities: Room Service, Free Paper, TV, Phones in Rm. (2), Cable TV, Radio, Wet Bar, Refrigerator, Ind. Heat Ctl., Ind. AC Ctl.

Equipped with all the facilities and services business travelers need, Marriott Suites, with its inviting recreational facilities and elegant yet home-like suites, will also please vacationing families. The beautifully landscaped 4.5 acre site in suburban Atlanta is adjacent to Perimeter shopping and numerous business office parks.

──────────── ATLANTA ────────────

Mayfair Suites Hotel
7000 Roswell Road
Atlanta, GA 30328

244 Suites
404-394-6300 800-255-3019

Location: Northside; Downtown: 20 min.
Airport: 25 miles
Near: Perimeter Shopping, Night Life
Walking Distance To: Residential Areas
Area Attractions: Very Central Location

Price Range & Credit Cards: 1 Bedroom Suite $$$, 2 Bedrooms $$$$, AmEx/MC/Visa/Other CC, TAC 10%

Hotel Amenities: Laundry, Library, Pets Allowed, Handicap (2)

Business Facilities: Conf. Rm. Cap. 100, Banquet Fac., Mess. Ctr., Sec. Serv., Copier, Aud/Vis., Telex, FAX

Recreational Facilities: Pool, Fitn. Ctr., Tennis, Golf, Jogging, Volleyball, Health Center

Restaurant/Bar: Tyme Out Tavern

Comps: Continental Breakfast

Room Amenities: TV, Phone in Rm., Cable TV, Radio, Kitchen, Ind. Heat Ctl.

In the heart of Atlanta's bustling North side; great shopping, dining, and entertainment nearby. Close to many offices of Fortune 500 Corporations. The 14 acres of beautifully landscaped grounds resemble a neighborhood environment. Eleven conference rooms; ideal for regional meetings. Restaurant signing privileges. A full-service all-suite hotel.

—————————————— ATLANTA ——————————————

Pickett Suite Hotel
2999 Windy Hill Road
Atlanta, GA 30067

203 Suites
404-956-9999 800-742-5388

Location: Northwest; Downtown: 20 min.
Airport: 25 minutes
Near: Cumberland Area, Perimeter Center
Walking Distance To: Shops and Restaurants
Area Attractions: White Water, Six Flags

Price Range & Credit Cards: 1 Bedroom Suite $$$, AmEx/MC/Visa/Other CC, Children Free, TAC 10%

Hotel Amenities: Library, Parking, TV Lounge, Handicap (10)

Business Facilities: Conf. Rm. Cap. 100, Banquet Fac., Mess. Ctr., Sec. Serv., Copier, Aud/Vis., Teleconf., Telex, Comp. Hook-up, Bus. Ctr.

Recreational Facilities: Pool, Sauna, Whirlpool, Fitn. Ctr.; Health Club on property

Restaurant/Bar: Praline's

Comps: Full Breakfast

Room Amenities: Room Service, Free Paper, TV, Phones in Rm. (2), Cable TV, Radio, Wet Bar, refrigerator, Ind. Heat Ctl., Ind. AC Ctl.

Situated in the Northwest business area and close to fashionable shopping, The Pickett will help you rediscover the pleasure of traveling. The suites provide room to work efficiently and relax in comfort. If you're a business traveller, plan to spend some time in the library which is computer equipped and features the latest periodicals & reference books.

—————————————— ATLANTA ——————————————

Regency Suites Hotel
975 W. Peachtree St.
Atlanta, GA 30309

96 Suites
404-876-5003 800-642-3629

Location: Midtown;
Airport: 20 minutes
Near: MARTA Rapid Rail Station
Walking Distance To: Georgia Tech Campus
Area Attractions: Picturesque Midtown, Lenox
Square, Piedmont Park

Price Range & Credit Cards: All Suites $$$, AmEx/MC/Visa/Other CC, Children Free, TAC 10%

Hotel Amenities: Laundry, Library, Parking, Car Hire, TV Lounge, Handicap (4)

Business Facilities: Conf. Rm. Cap. 50, Banquet Fac., Mess. Ctr., Copier, Aud/Vis.

Recreational Facilities: Fitn. Ctr., Indoor Tennis; near Piedmont Park Jogging Trail

Comps: Continental Breakfast, Parking

Room Amenities: Free Paper, TV, Phone in Rm., Cable TV, VCR, Radio, Kitchen, Ind. Heat Ctl., Ind. AC Ctl.

Located in Atlanta's picturesque Midtown, Regency is at the hub of cultural and business activities of the city. An exercise room, a guest library, free home box office, a special electronic key and security system, and a jogging trail are all amenities to add to the ease and enjoyment of staying in Midtown. Convenient to 'Marta' (rapid transit).

──────────────── ATLANTA ────────────────

Terrace Garden Inn Suite Hotel
1500 Parkwood Circle
Atlanta, GA 30339

200 Suites
404-952-9595 800-338-7812

Location: Marrietta; Downtown: 12 mi.
Airport: 20 miles
Near: I-285 and 175, Cobb County, White Water Park
Area Attractions: Chattahochee River-Picnick areas, Cumberland Mall

Price Range & Credit Cards: 1 Bedroom Suite $$$, 2 Bedrooms $$$$, AmEx/MC/Visa/Other CC, TAC 10%

Hotel Amenities: Laundry, Library, Parking, Car Hire, TV Lounge, Pets Allowed

Business Facilities: Conf. Rm. Cap. 20-75, Banquet Fac., Mess. Ctr., Copier, Audio/Vis., Comp. Hook-up

Recreational Facilities: Pool, Whirlpool, Fitn. Ctr., Tennis, Fishing, Rafting, Jogging Trails, Game Area

Comps: Continental Breakfast, Refreshments, Fruit

Room Amenities: Room Service, TV, Phone in Rm., Cable TV, Radio, Kitchen, Ind. Heat Ctl., Ind. AC Ctl.

Terrace Garden Inn Suite Hotel is more than a hotel. Nestled in a Park-like setting, the hotel offers 200 spacious one and two bedroom suites, all with fully equiped kitchens; large living rooms and spacious bedrooms. Located in the Galleria area on Powers Ferry Road, and convenient to malls, movies and entertainment. Babysitting services available.

──────────────── ATLANTA/NORCROSS ────────────────

Amberley Suite Hotel
5885 Oakbrook Pkwy.
Atlanta/Norcross, GA 30093

170 Suites
404-263-0515 800-227-7229

Location: Northeast; Downtown: 20 min.
Airport: 25 miles
Near: County I-85
Walking Distance To: Shopping
Area Attractions: Stone Mountain, Lake Lanier

Price Range & Credit Cards: 1 Bedroom Suite $$, 2 Bedrooms $$$$, AmEx/MC/Visa/Other CC, Children Free, TAC 10%

Hotel Amenities: Laundry, Parking, TV Lounge, No-smoke suites, Handicap (8)

Business Facilities: Conf. Rm. Cap. 110, Banquet Fac., Mess. Ctr., Sec. Serv., Copier, Aud/Vis., Telex, FAX

Recreational Facilities: Pool, Sauna, Whirlpool, Exercise room, Game Area; 24 hour Fitness Center

Restaurant/Bar: Watson's Cafe/Deli

Comps: Hors d'oeuvres

Room Amenities: Refrigerator, Coffee maker, TV, Phones in Rm. (2), Cable TV, VCR, Radio, Wet Bar, Microwave, Ind. Heat Ctl., Ind. AC Ctl.

You will find Amberley ideal for a successful business meeting, family "getaway"'weekends, or relocating families. We offer special rates for weekends, and for stays of over 7 nights. Our suites feature Queen Anne furniture, microwave ovens, built-in coffee makers, and refrigerators. The Amberley, in prestigious Guinnett County, is ideally located.

Vero Pickett Suite Resort, Vero Beach, FL

— AUGUSTA —

Best Western Bradbury Suites
1062 Claussen Rd.
Augusta, GA 30907

116 Suites
404-733-4656 800-528-1234

Location: Suburbs; Downtown: 7 miles
Airport: 15 miles
Near: Residential Areas, Shops, Restaurants
Area Attractions: "The Masters"'-3 miles

Price Range & Credit Cards: 1 Bedroom Suite $$, 2 Bedrooms $$, AmEx/MC/Visa/ Other CC, Children Free, TAC 12%

Hotel Amenities: Pets Allowed, Handicap (6)

Business Facilities: Conf. Rm. Cap. 35, Copier, Aud/Vis.

Recreational Facilities: Pool, Whirlpool, Golf, Health Club

Comps: Continental Plus Breakfast, Refreshments, Hors d'oeuvres

Room Amenities: Free Paper, TV, Phone in Rm., Cable TV, Radio, Ind. Heat Ctl., Ind. AC Ctl.

A one-of-a-kind experience awaits you at Bradbury's. Choose from over 10 "Theme Suites" which are decorated in a particular style. Relax in the elegance of the Old South in the Gone With the Wind room, or have fun shooting pool in the Side Pocket Room. The friendly staff, business facilities, and cleanliness add to the real value of these suites.

--------------------------- TUCKER ---------------------------

Best Western Bradbury Suites
2060 Crescent Center Blvd.
Tucker, GA 30084

113 Suites
404-496-1070 800-528-1234

Location: Northlake; Downtown: 10 mi.
Airport: 20 miles
Near: Stone Mountain Park, Historical Sites, Downtown
Area Attractions: Beach, Hiking, Picnic, Golf, Shopping Malls, Atlanta Stadium

Price Range & Credit Cards: 1 Bedroom Suite $$, AmEx/MC/Visa/Other CC, Children Free, TAC 12%

Hotel Amenities: Laundry, Handicap (6)

Business Facilities: Conf. Rm. Cap. 140, Copier, Aud/Vis.

Recreational Facilities: Pool, Whirlpool, Fitn. Ctr., Golf, Hiking, Swimming; all sports nearby

Comps: Continental Plus Breakfast, Refreshments

Room Amenities: Room Service, Free Paper, TV, Phones in Rm. (2), Cable TV, Ind. Heat Ctl., Ind. AC Ctl.

In Atlanta's Northeast business district, The Bradbury offers a great value that includes amenities such as: complimentary buffet breakfast, evening cocktails (weekdays), indoor & outdoor whirlpools, exercise facility, and outdoor pool. Many suites offer a relaxing jacuzzi after a busy day. All suites feature a separate living and working area.

⚜ Hawaii

--------- HANALEI, KAUAI ---------

The Cliffs at Princeville
P. O. Box 1005
Hanalei, Kauai, HI 96714

202 Suites
808-826-6219 800-367-6046

Location: Shoreside; Downtown: 1 mile
Airport: 20 minutes
Near: Hanalei Mountains, Activity Center
Walking Distance To: Pacific Ocean
Area Attractions: 1 Mile to Shopping Center,
Princeville Championship Golf

Price Range & Credit Cards: 1 Bedroom Suite $$$$, 2 Bedrooms $$$$, AmEx/MC/
Visa/Other CC, TAC 10%

Hotel Amenities: Laundry, Parking, TV Lounge

Business Facilities: Mess. Ctr., Copier

Recreational Facilities: Pool, Sauna, Golf, Health Spa; 4 Tennis courts

Comps: Refreshments

Room Amenities: TV, Phone in Rm., Cable TV, Radio, Wet Bar, Kitchen

*Set between the majestic mountains and the Pacific, The Cliffs is perfect for the family vaca-
tion. Each tastefully appointed suite features a private lanai, wet bar and full kitchen. For
sports enthusiasts, a swimming pool and four tennis courts are available at the hotel.
Nearby, you'll find world-famous Princeville Championship Golf Course.*

―――――――――――――――― HONOLULU ――――――――――――――――

Colony Surf Hotel
2895 Kalakaua Ave.
Honolulu, HI 96815

50 Suites
808-923-5751 800-367-6046

Location: Resort; Downtown: nearby
Near: Diamond Head, Kapiolana Park
Walking Distance To: Waikiki
Area Attractions: Polynesian Cultural Center

Price Range & Credit Cards: 1 Bedroom Suite $$$$, 2 Bedrooms $$$$+, AmEx/MC/ Visa/Other CC, TAC 10%

Hotel Amenities: Laundry, Library, Parking, Handicap (50)

Business Facilities: Mess. Ctr., Sec. Serv., Copier, Telex

Recreational Facilities: Tennis, Golf; Water Sports in Waikiki

Restaurant/Bar: Michel's, Entertainment

Room Amenities: Room Service, Free Paper, TV, Phone in Rm., Radio, Kitchen

Situated on a magnificent beach, Colony Surf offers luxurious accommodations that provide the comfort and quiet you'll appreciate. For full enjoyment of the beautiful scenery, all suites have an entire wall of windows and breathtaking views of the Pacific, or Diamond Head and Kapiolani Park.

―――――――――――――――― HONOLULU ――――――――――――――――

Marine Surf Waikiki Hotel
364 Seaside Ave.
Honolulu, HI 96815

114 Suites
808-923-0277 800-367-5176

Location: Beachside; Downtown: Nearby
Airport: Half Hour
Near: Waikiki Beach, Shops, Restaurants
Walking Distance To: Waikiki Beach
Area Attractions: International Market Place

Price Range & Credit Cards: 1 Bedroom Suite $$$, Junior $, AmEx/MC/Visa/Other CC, Children Free, TAC 10%

Hotel Amenities: Laundry, Parking

Recreational Facilities: Pool, Tennis, Golf; All water sports

Restaurant/Bar: Matteo's

Room Amenities: TV, Kitchen, Ind. AC Ctl.

Offering "the best of Waikiki at your doorstep," Marine Surf is conveniently located within 2 blocks of Waikiki Beach and the International Market Place, and only half a mile from the Honolulu Zoo and Kapiolani Park. The beauty of Hawaii is brought indoors with the hotel's tropical decor accented with blue and gold color schemes.

---------------------- KAILUA-KONA ----------------------

Kanaloa at Kona
78-261 Manukai St.
Kailua-Kona, HI 96740

118 Suites
808-322-2272 800-367-6046

Location: Resort; Downtown: 5 miles
Airport: 15 miles
Near: Keauhou Bay, Golf, Fishing
Walking Distance To: Beach
Area Attractions: Beautiful Keauhou Bay

Price Range & Credit Cards: 1 Bedroom Suite $$$, 2 Bedrooms $$$$, AmEx/MC/Visa/Other CC, Children Free, TAC 10%

Hotel Amenities: Laundry, Parking, Handicap (2)

Business Facilities: Banquet Fac., Mess. Ctr., Copier

Recreational Facilities: Pool, Whirlpool, Tennis, Golf, Bowling, Game Area

Restaurant/Bar: The Terrace

Comps: Hors d'oeuvres

Room Amenities: TV, Phone in Rm., Cable TV, Wet Bar, Kitchen

An open and airy feeling is central to Kanaloa at Kona's decor, featuring open beam ceilings, with Koa wood accents, and plush furniture in every suite. A myriad of sports and recreational activities are available at the hotel and nearby. When hunger strikes, fire up the barbecue for some outdoor cooking, or relax at The Terrace.

---------------------- KAILUA-KONA ----------------------

Kona Bali Kai
76-6246 Alii Drive
Kailua-Kona, HI 96740

155 Suites
808-329-9381 800-367-6046

Location: Resort; Downtown: 20 min.
Airport: 20 minutes
Near: Kona Coast, Shops, Restaurants
Walking Distance To: Ocean
Area Attractions: Deep sea fishing, Mount Hualalai

Price Range & Credit Cards: 1 Bedroom Suite $$, 2 Bedrooms $$$$, Junior $$, AmEx/MC/Visa/Other CC, Children Free, TAC 10%

Business Facilities: Telex

Recreational Facilities: Pool, Sauna, Whirlpool, Tennis, Golf, Surfing, Snorkeling, Bowling

Room Amenities: TV, Phone in Rm., Kitchen

All accommodations face the blue Pacific, lushly landscaped gardens or Mt. Haulalai. Tradewinds during the day and cool mountain air at night create a very relaxing atmosphere. The weather in this famous Kona area of the Big Island is excellent year round. The hotel is designed for maximum comfort and located in the midst of an excellent fishing area.

────────────── KAPAA, KAUAI ──────────────

Lae Nani
410 Papaloa Rd.
Kapaa, Kauai, HI 96746

50 Suites
808-822-4938 800-367-6046

Location: Beachside; Downtown: 15 min.
Airport: 10 miles
Near: Wailua Area, Restaurants, Shops
Walking Distance To: Beach, Cinemas
Area Attractions: Fern Grotto, Waimea Canyon

Price Range & Credit Cards: 1 Bedroom Suite $$$$, 2 Bedrooms $$$$+, AmEx/MC/Visa/Other CC, Children Free, TAC 10%

Hotel Amenities: Laundry, Library, Parking, Car Hire

Business Facilities: Copier

Recreational Facilities: Pool, Tennis, Golf, Game Area

Comps: Refreshments

Room Amenities: TV, Phone in Rm., Cable TV, Radio, Kitchen

Every suite at the Lae Nani offers rich decor, distinctive furnishings, and complete kitchen facilities, not to mention a spectacular ocean view. On-site recreational facilities are at your disposal—including a large swimming pool and lighted tennis courts. Be sure to visit The Market Place next door, and enjoy evening entertainment with luau shows.

────────────── KAPAA, KAUAI ──────────────

Lanikai
390 Papaloa Rd.
Kapaa, Kauai, HI 96746

18 Suites
808-822-7457 800-367-6046

Location: Beachside; Downtown: 15 min.
Airport: 10 miles
Near: Wailua Area, The Market Place, Restaurants
Walking Distance To: Beaches
Area Attractions: Opaekaa Falls, Coconut Plantation

Price Range & Credit Cards: 2 Bedrooms $$$$, AmEx/MC/Visa/Other CC, Children Free, TAC 10%

Hotel Amenities: Laundry, Parking, Car Hire, Handicap

Recreational Facilities: Pool, Surfing, Snorkeling, Boogie board

Room Amenities: TV, Phone in Rm., Wet Bar, Kitchen

This location on Wailau Beach is one of Kauai's best for water sports-swimming, sunning, snorkeling, and more. The elegant Polynesian decor is carried throughout. The famous Opaekaa Falls is nearby as is the Coconut Plantation's famed Market Place. Even the drive from the airport is breathtaking.

―――――――――――――――― KAUAI ――――――――――――――――

Kiahuna Plantation Resort
RR 1 Box 73
Kauai, HI 96756

255 Suites
808-742-6411 800-367-7052

Location: Beachside; Downtown: 18 mi.
Airport: 21 miles
Near: Poipu Beach, Old Koloa Town
Walking Distance To: Plantation Gardens
Area Attractions: Waimea Canyon, Fern Grotto

Price Range & Credit Cards: 1 Bedroom Suite $$$, 2 Bedrooms $$$$, AmEx/MC/ Visa/Other CC, Children Free, TAC 10%

Hotel Amenities: Laundry, Parking

Business Facilities: Copier, Mess. Ctr.

Recreational Facilities: Pool, Fitn. Ctr., Golf; 10 Tennis courts, Beach

Restaurant/Bar: Plantation Gardens Restaurant

Room Amenities: TV, Phone in Rm., Cable TV, Radio, Kitchen

The charming touches of Koa wood, ceiling fans and wicker furniture welcome you to the lush tropical seclusion of Kiahuna Plantation. Be as playful or peaceful as you like. Take surfing and snorkeling lessons or just work on your tan poolside. Indulge yourself at the Plantation Gardens Restaurant, or create your favorite dishes in the privacy of your own suite.

―――――――――――――――― KIHEI, MAUI ――――――――――――――――

Kamaole Sands
2695 S. Kihei Rd.
Kihei, Maui, HI 96753

440 Suites
808-879-0666 800-367-6046

Location: Oceanside; Downtown: 5 min.
Airport: 15 miles
Near: Chain of beaches, Kapoli Springs
Walking Distance To: Excellent Restaurants
Area Attractions: Lava Flows, Beach, Burial Caves

Price Range & Credit Cards: 1 Bedroom Suite $$$, 2 Bedrooms $$$$, AmEx/MC/ Visa/Other CC, Children Free, TAC 10%

Hotel Amenities: Laundry, Parking, Car Hire

Business Facilities: Telex

Recreational Facilities: Pool, Whirlpool, Golf, Surfing, Snorkeling; Scuba diving

Restaurant/Bar: Sandpiper Grill

Room Amenities: TV, Phone in Rm., Kitchen

The Kamaole Sands is set in a 15-acre garden estate surrounded by lush gardens and fronted by white sand beach. Along this nine-mile chain of beaches is every sport Hawaii is known for-snorkeling, scuba diving, sailing and deep sea fishing to name a few. Suites are each individually done but all share an elegant Polynesian design.

—————————— LAHAINA, MAUI ——————————

Napili Shores Resort
5315 Honoapiilani Hwy.
Lahaina, Maui, HI 96761

106 Suites
808-669-8061　800-367-6046

Location: Rural Napili; Lahaina: 8 miles
Airport: 38 miles
Near: Serene Napili Bay, Kapalua
Walking Distance To: Beaches
Area Attractions: Shops & Restaurants

Price Range & Credit Cards: 1 Bedroom Suite $$$$, 2 Bedrooms $$$$, Junior $$$, AmEx/MC/Visa/Other CC, Children Free, TAC 10%

Hotel Amenities: Laundry, Parking

Recreational Facilities: Pool, Whirlpool, Tennis; Kapalua Golf course

Restaurant/Bar: Orient Express

Comps: Refreshments

Room Amenities: TV, Phone in Rm., Cable TV, Kitchen

Ceiling fans and the charm of wicker furniture in your suite contribute to the overall feeling of tropical serenity at the Napili Shores. Beautifully landscaped gardens provide the setting for a variety of outdoor activities. In the evening, treat yourself to a quiet dinner at the Orient Express or cook up your own feast at one of the barbecues.

Pickett Suite Hotel, Atlanta, GA

---------------- MAKENA, MAUI ----------------

Polo Beach Club
20 Makena Road
Makena, Maui, HI 96753

71 Suites
808-879-8847   800-367-6046

Location: Oceanside; Downtown: 6 miles
Airport: Half Hour
Near: Wailea District, Golf & Tennis
Walking Distance To: Beaches
Area Attractions: Golf courses, Famous "Fun
Spot"'

Price Range & Credit Cards: 1 Bedroom Suite $$$$, 2 Bedrooms $$$$+, AmEx/MC/
Visa/Other CC, Children Free, TAC 10%

Hotel Amenities: Laundry, Car Hire

Business Facilities: Telex

Recreational Facilities: Pool, Whirlpool; Tennis Club 2 miles

Room Amenities: TV, Phone in Rm., VCR, Radio, Kitchen

This is a very upscale hotel located in an enclave that affords special privacy. The crescent-shape white sand beach and sculptured gardens are home to many beautiful varieties of palm trees. Marble entranceways and Koa wood accents add to the posh ambiance. Secluded and private, but only 2 miles from Wailea, an internationally famous "fun spot".

---------------- MAUI ----------------

Hololani Condominium
4401 Honoapiilani Rd.
Maui, HI 96761

63 Suites
808-669-8021 800-367-5032

Location: Oceanside; Downtown: Nearby
Airport: 35 miles
Near: Kahana Area
Walking Distance To: 5 Restaurants, Beach
Area Attractions: Beautiful Sunsets, Enter-
tainment

Price Range & Credit Cards: 2 Bedrooms $$$, TAC 10%

Hotel Amenities: Laundry, Library, Parking

Business Facilities: Copier

Recreational Facilities: Pool, Tennis, Golf, Fishing, Snorkeling

Room Amenities: TV, Phone in Rm., Cable TV, Kitchen

This ocean-front property offers the rare combination of spacious apartment living in a superb location. Not only does Hololani's golden swimming beach stretch for a mile along the ocean, but every apartment has a Bali-Hai like view of Molokai Island across the Pailolo Channel, where several species of whales spend their winter.

─────────────── MAUNALOA, MOLOKAI ───────────────

Kaluakoi Hotel & Golf Course
P.O.Box 1977
Maunaloa, Molokai, HI 96770

288 Suites
800-552-2555 800-367-6046

Location: Resort
Airport: 20 minutes
Near: 13,000 Green Acres, Resort Area
Walking Distance To: Sea Shore
Area Attractions: Kepuhi Beach, Golf

Price Range & Credit Cards: 1 Bedroom Suite $$, 2 Bedrooms $$$$, AmEx/MC/ Visa/Other CC, Children Free, TAC 10%

Hotel Amenities: Laundry, Parking, Car Hire, Handicap (1)

Business Facilities: Conf. Rm. Cap. 300, Banquet Fac., Telex

Recreational Facilities: Pool, Whirlpool, Golf

Restaurant/Bar: Paniolo Broiler, Ohia Lodge, Entertainment

Room Amenities: TV, Phone in Rm., Cable TV, Radio

This is a "total living resort" that is all-encompassing with everything needed for a complete vacation. Romantic Polynesian decor, spectacular views of Kepuhi Beach from the casually elegent Ohia Lodge restaurant, combined with the friendly atmosphere Molokai is known for, make this the setting for a great vacation.

─────────────── MAUNALOA, MOLOKAI ───────────────

Ke Nani Kai Resort
P. O. Box 126 Kepuhi Road
Maunaloa, Molokai, HI 96770

60 Suites
808-552-2761 800-367-7040

Location: Resort; Downtown: 6 miles
Airport: 16 miles
Near: 15 Acre Garden
Walking Distance To: Horseback Riding
Area Attractions: Hawaii's Longest Waterfall

Price Range & Credit Cards: 1 Bedroom Suite $$, 2 Bedrooms $$$, AmEx/MC/Visa/ Other CC, Children Free, TAC 10%

Recreational Facilities: Pool, Whirlpool, Tennis, Golf, Fishing, Boating

Restaurant/Bar: Sheraton

Room Amenities: TV, Phone in Rm., Cable TV, Radio, Kitchen

All suites are spacious and richly furnished in tropical decor with fully equipped kitchens and large lanais offering magnificent views. Activities abound—a free-form swimming pool and tennis courts are surrounded by the Championship Kaluakoi Golf Course and Papohaku, Hawaii's largest white sand beach. World famous mule ride on Kalaupapa Trail.

⚜ Idaho

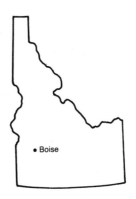

• Boise

BOISE

The Residence Inn by Marriott
1401 Lusk Street
Boise, ID 83706

104 Suites
208-344-1200   800-331-3131

Location: Southside; Downtown: 1 mi.
Airport: 3 miles
Near: Community District, 2 Restaurants
Walking Distance To: Boise State Univ.
Area Attractions: Zoo, Performing Arts, Museum

Price Range & Credit Cards: 1 Bedroom Suite $$, 2 Bedrooms $$, AmEx/MC/Visa/ Other CC, Children Free, TAC 10%

Hotel Amenities: Laundry, Library, Parking, TV Lounge, Pets Allowed, Handicap (2)

Business Facilities: Conf. Rm. Cap. 50, Mess. Ctr., Copier

Recreational Facilities: Pool, Whirlpool, Golf, Skiing, Game Area; Water sports

Comps: Continental Plus Breakfast

Room Amenities: Free Paper, TV, Phone in Rm., Cable TV, Radio, Kitchen, Ind. Heat Ctl., Ind. AC Ctl.

Walkways, lawns and beautiful landscaping give this hotel the feel of home. The Gatehouse, where complimentary buffet breakfast is served daily, features a fireplace and comfortable couches that add to the relaxing and unpretentious atmosphere you'll love. The same comfortable decor is carried through to your suite.

⚜ Illinois

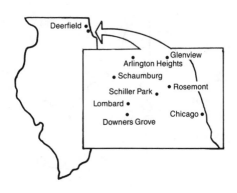

─────────────── ARLINGTON HEIGHTS ───────────────

Best Western Bradbury Suites   ***Location:*** Northeast
2111 So. Arlington Heights Rd.
Arlington Heights, IL 60005

114 Suites
800-528-1234

Price Range & Credit Cards: 1 Bedroom Suite $$, 2 Bedrooms $$, AmEx/MC/Visa/
Other CC, Children Free, TAC 12%

Hotel Amenities: Laundry, Parking, TV Lounge, Pets Allowed, Handicap (6)

Business Facilities: Conf. Rm. Cap. 35, Banquet Fac., Copier, Aud/Vis.

Recreational Facilities: Pool, Sauna, Whirlpool, Fitn. Ctr., Game Area

Comps: Breakfast, Refreshments, Hors d'oeuvres

Room Amenities: Free Paper, TV, Phone in Rm., Cable TV, Radio, Wet Bar, Kitchen, Ind.
Heat Ctl., Ind. AC Ctl.

*A great lodging value that includes a variety of amenities such as complimentary break-
fasts and evening cocktail parties daily. Each suite is furnished with a working desk and
refrigerator for your convenience. You can also book a little adventure by choosing one of
several theme rooms, decorated in "jungle," "harbor," or "mountain side" decor.*

──────────── CHICAGO ────────────

The Barclay Chicago Hotel
166 E. Superior St.
Chicago, IL 60611

120 Suites
312-787-6000 800-621-8004

Location: Central; Downtown: Nearby
Airport: 15 miles
Near: Neiman Marcus, Lake & Loop
Walking Distance To: Many Boutiques
Area Attractions: Magnificent Mile, Museum, Art

Price Range & Credit Cards: 1 Bedroom Suite $$$$, Junior $$$, AmEx/MC/Visa/ Other CC, Children Free, TAC 10%

Hotel Amenities: Laundry, Parking

Business Facilities: Conf. Rm. Cap. 50, Banquet Fac., Mess. Ctr., Sec. Serv., Copier, Aud/Vis., Telex, Comp. Hook-up

Recreational Facilities: Pool; Sports, see Concierge

Restaurant/Bar: The Barclay, Entertainment

Comps: Hors d'oeuvres

Room Amenities: Room Service, Free Paper, TV, Phone in Rm., Hair dryer, Radio, Wet Bar, Kitchen, Ind. Heat Ctl., Ind. AC Ctl.

Located in Chicago's Magnificent Mile, exclusive shops, fine restaurants, and the beautiful lakefront are only minutes from your door. An intimate lobby—decorated with rich woodwork and glittering brass—speaks for the elegance of the Barclay Chicago. Spacious suites provide deluxe accommodations, furnished with period furniture.

──────────── CHICAGO ────────────

The Lenox House
616 No. Rush St.
Chicago, IL 60611

330 Suites
312-337-1000 800-445-3669

Location: Goldcoast; Downtown: Nearby
Airport: 15 miles
Near: Pizzaria Due, Museum
Walking Distance To: Many Boutiques
Area Attractions: Magnificent Mile, Art

Price Range & Credit Cards: 1 Bedroom Suite $$$$, Junior $$$, AmEx/MC/Visa/ Other CC, Children Free, TAC 10%

Hotel Amenities: Laundry, Handicap (1)

Business Facilities: Conf. Rm. Cap. 30, Sec. Serv., Copier, Aud/Vis.

Recreational Facilities: All sports close by

Restaurant/Bar: Houstons/Lenox Coffee Shop

Room Amenities: Room Service, Free Paper, TV, Phone in Rm., Kitchen, Ind. Heat Ctl., Ind. AC Ctl.

When you arrive at The Lenox Hotel a uniformed doorman greets you, making you feel immediately welcome. All services and appointments are designed to assure your complete comfort, from the charming and distinctive lobby to warm and welcoming accommodations. To make business a pleasure, all suites provide well-lighted work areas.

─────────────── CHICAGO ───────────────

The Talbott Hotel
20 E. Delaware Place
Chicago, IL 60611

147 Suites
312-944-4970 800-621-8506

Location: Gold Coast; Downtown: 5 min.
Airport: 25 minutes
Near: Michigan Avenue, Oak Street
Area Attractions: Lake Michigan

Price Range & Credit Cards: 1 Bedroom Suite $$$$, 2 Bedrooms $$$$, Junior $$$$, AmEx/MC/Visa/Other CC, Children Free, TAC 10%

Hotel Amenities: Laundry, Barber Shop, Handicap (2)

Business Facilities: Conf. Rm. Cap. 70, Banquet Fac., Mess. Ctr., Sec. Serv., Copier, Aud/Vis., Telex, Comp. Hook-up

Recreational Facilities: Tennis, Golf, Outdoor Track; Health Club privileges

Restaurant/Bar: Talbott Bar

Comps: Toiletries, Coffee

Room Amenities: Free Paper, TV, Phones in Rm. (3), Radio, Wet Bar, Kitchen, Ind. AC Ctl.

Set in the prestigious Gold Coast, The Talbott offers traditional European service and ambiance in combination with modern amenities. Each suite includes separate sleeping and living rooms, honor bars, remote control TV's and 3 phones, with turn-down service nightly. Our personalized service and intimate lobby provide an elegant home while you travel.

─────────────── DEERFIELD ───────────────

Embassy Suites Hotel
1445 Lake Cook Road
Deerfield, IL 60015

237 Suites
312-945-4500 800-362-2779

Location: North Shore; Downtown: 30 mi.
Airport: 17 miles
Near: Northbrook Court-4 miles, Ravania-4 miles
Area Attractions: Great America-11 miles

Price Range & Credit Cards: 1 Bedroom Suite $$$$, 2 Bedrooms $$$$+, AmEx/MC/Visa/Other CC, Children Free, TAC 10%

Hotel Amenities: Laundry, Gift Shop, Car Hire, TV Lounge

Business Facilities: Conf. Rm. Cap. 15, Banquet Fac., Mess. Ctr., Copier, Aud/Vis., Telex, Comp. Hook-up

Recreational Facilities: Pool, Sauna, Whirlpool, Fitn. Ctr.

Restaurant/Bar: Tropical Cafe

Comps: Refreshments, Full Breakfast

Room Amenities: Room Service, Free Paper, TV, Phones in Rm. (2), Cable TV, Radio, Wet Bar, Microwave, Ind. Heat Ctl., Ind. AC Ctl.

Embassy Suites features luxurious living room, a spacious private bedroom, and a wet bar with refrigerator, microwave & coffeemaker. A great cooked-to-order breakfast is served in our lush tropical atrium, and 2-hour cocktail reception every evening. Extraordinary extras include meeting space, indoor pool, whirlpool, sauna, and free local limousine.

Regency Suites Hotel, Atlanta, GA

--------- DOWNERS GROVE ---------

Radisson Suite Hotel
2111 Butterfield Rd.
Downers Grove, IL 60515

256 Suites
312-971-2000

Location: Suburbs; Downtown: 20 mi.
Airport: O'Hare 14 miles
Near: West Side, Oakbrook Center Mall
Area Attractions: Morton Arboretum, York-town Mall, Finley Square Mall

Price Range & Credit Cards: 1 Bedroom Suite $$$, AmEx/MC/Visa/Other CC, Children Free, TAC 10%

Hotel Amenities: Laundry, Gift Shop, Parking, Handicap (8)

Business Facilities: Conf. Rm. Cap. 12, Banquet Fac., Copier

Recreational Facilities: Pool, Sauna, Whirlpool, Fitn. Ctr.; Golf Course nearby

Restaurant/Bar: Willy's, Entertainment

Comps: Breakfast, Refreshments, Hors d'oeuvres

Room Amenities: Room Service, Free Paper, TV, Phones in Rm. (2), Cable TV, Radio, Wet Bar, Kitchen, Ind. Heat Ctl., Ind. AC Ctl.

What sets The Radisson Suite Hotel apart from the rest is the luxurious all-suite concept, cook-to-order breakfast and cocktails in the evening, which are complimentary. The Radisson is located near the beautiful Morton Arboretum and the world famous Oakbrook Center Mall. There are four area golf courses as well as swimming facilities.

––––––––––––––––––––––––– LOMBARD –––––––––––––––––––––––––

The Residence Inn by Marriott   **Location:** W. Suburbs; Chicago: 20 miles
2001 S. Highland Ave.   **Airport:** O'Hare-18 miles
Lombard, IL 60148   **Near:** Greater Oak Brook Area
          Area Attractions: Oakbrook Mall-3 miles
144 Suites
312-629-7800 800-331-3131

Price Range & Credit Cards: 1 Bedroom Suite $$$, 2 Bedrooms $$$$, AmEx/MC/ Visa, Children Free, TAC 10%

Hotel Amenities: Laundry, TV Lounge, Pets Allowed, Handicap (2)

Business Facilities: Conf. Rm. Cap. 25, Mess. Ctr., Copier, Aud/Vis.

Recreational Facilities: Pool, Whirlpool, Tennis; Golf & Fitn.Ctr. nearby

Comps: Continental Plus Breakfast, Refreshments, Hors d'oeuvres

Room Amenities: Free Paper, TV, Phone in Room, Cable TV, Radio, Kitchen, Ind. Heat Ctl., Ind. AC Ctl.

Located just minutes from Oak Brook, The Residence Inn offers suites so inviting they're more home than hotel. Each suite has a fully equipped kitchen and separate livingroom area with wood-burning fireplace. The spaciousness of a one- or two-bedroom suite with all the amenities of home assures you a relaxing stay. Discounted rates for extended stays.

––––––––––––––––––––––––– ROSEMONT –––––––––––––––––––––––––

Embassy Suites Hotel   **Location:** Rosemont O'Hare
6501 No. Mannheim Rd.   **Airport:** 3 minutes
Rosemont, IL 60018   **Near:** Business Complex, O'Hare Expo Center
          Walking Distance To: Airport
300 Suites   **Area Attractions:** Rosemont Horizon Stadium
312-699-6300 800-362-2779

Price Range & Credit Cards: 1 Bedroom Suite $$$$, AmEx/MC/Visa, Children Free, TAC 10%

Hotel Amenities: Laundry, Parking, Car Hire, TV Lounge, Handicap (7)

Business Facilities: Conf. Rm. Cap. 400, Banquet Fac., Mess. Ctr., Sec. Serv., Copier, Aud/Vis., Teleconf., Comp. Hook-up

Recreational Facilities: Pool, Sauna, Whirlpool, Fitn. Ctr.; Golf nearby

Restaurant/Bar: Ellingtons, Whispers, Entertainment

Comps: Full Breakfast, Refreshments, Hors d'oeuvres

Room Amenities: Room Service, Free Paper, TV, Phones in Rm. (3), Cable TV, Radio, Wet Bar, Ind. Heat Ctl., Ind. AC Ctl.

Embassy Suites provides convenient and luxurious accommodations for business travelers. Situated in O'Hare International Center, with the airport just across the street, convention centers are only minutes away. After a busy day, return to the comfort of your private suite and enjoy the "extras" we offer, including a complimentary cocktail party.

─────────────── ROSEMONT ───────────────

Marriott Suites Chicago O'Hare
6155 North River Road
Rosemont, IL 60018

260 Suites
312-696-4400 800-228-9290

Location: Airport; Downtown: 20 min.
Airport: 5 minutes
Near: Rosemont's Horizon and Convention Center
Area Attractions: Brookfield Zoo, Fine Shopping at Oakbrook Center

Price Range & Credit Cards: 1 Bedroom Suite call for $, Junior call for $, AmEx/MC/Visa/Other CC, Children Free, TAC 10%

Hotel Amenities: Laundry, Parking, Gift Shop, Small Pets only, Handicap (10)

Business Facilities: Conf. Rm. Cap. 150, Mess. Ctr., Copier, Aud/Vis., FAX, Telex, Comp. Hook-up

Recreational Facilities: Pool, Sauna, Whirlpool, Fitn. Ctr.; Golf & Tennis nearby

Restaurant/Bar: Windows Restaurant/Windows Lounge

Comps: Full Breakfast, Beverages & Snacks, Toiletries

Room Amenities: Room Service, Free Paper, TV, Phones in Rm. (2), Cable TV, Radio, Wet Bar, Ind. Heat Ctl., Ind. AC Ctl.

Ideally located just minutes from Chicago's O'Hare International Airport, Marriott Suites is the perfect choice for the business traveler who requires extra space to work, entertain, or just relax. The luxury, comfort, and convenience of the elegant yet home-like suites, and the on-site business meeting facilities make it an exceptional value.

─────────────── SCHAUMBURG ───────────────

Embassy Suites Hotel
1939 No. Meacham Rd.
Schaumburg, IL 60173

209 Suites
312-397-1313 800-362-2779

Location: Northwest; Downtown: 30 mi.
Airport: O'Hare-12 miles
Near: Woodfield Shopping Mall 1 mile
Area Attractions: Poplar Creek Music Theatre, Arlington Park Race Track

Price Range & Credit Cards: 1 Bedroom Suite $$$$, AmEx/MC/Visa/Other CC, Children Free, TAC 10%

Hotel Amenities: Laundry, Parking, Car Hire, Handicap (7)

Business Facilities: Conf. Rm. Cap. 700, Banquet Fac., Copier, Aud/Vis., Teleconf., Comp. Hook-up, FAX

Recreational Facilities: Pool, Sauna, Whirlpool, Jogging path, Fitness Facility, Game Area; Golf and Tennis-2 miles

Restaurant/Bar: Willy's Restaurant and Lounge, Entertainment

Comps: Full Breakfast, Refreshments, Hors d'oeuvres, Limousine Service

Room Amenities: Room Service, Free Paper, TV, Phones in Rm. (2), Cable TV, Radio, Wet Bar, Kitchen, Ind. Heat Ctl., Ind. AC Ctl.

Stay in the lush garden atmosphere of a tropical paradise all year long at Embassy Suites, where every suite overlooks the open interior courtyard topped by a brilliant, sky-lighted ceiling. Within you'll find everything you need to conduct business, entertain or just relax. For your dining pleasure, Willy's Restaurant features a superb Sunday Brunch.

 **Indiana**

Fort Wayne •
• Remington

Carmel
⋮
Indianapolis

CARMEL

Pickett Suite Inn
11355 North Meridian Street
Carmel, IN 46032

138 Suites
317-844-7994 800-PICKETT

Location: Northside; Downtown: 20 min.
Airport: 30 minutes
Near: 5 min. to Keystone at the Crossing
Area Attractions: 15 min. to Indianapolis
Motor Speedway

Price Range & Credit Cards: 1 Bedroom Suite $$, AmEx/MC/Visa/Other CC, Children Free, TAC 10%

Hotel Amenities: Laundry, Parking, Car Hire, TV Lounge, Handicap (7)

Business Facilities: Conf. Rm. Cap. 75, Banquet Fac., Mess. Ctr., Sec. Serv., Copier, Aud/Vis., Teleconf., Comp. Hook-up

Recreational Facilities: Pool, Whirlpool, Fitn. Ctr., Tennis, Golf, Racquetball

Restaurant/Bar: Deli Cafe

Comps: Full Breakfast, Hors d'oeuvres

Room Amenities: Free Paper, TV, Phones in Rm. (2), Radio, Wet Bar, Ind. Heat Ctl., Ind. AC Ctl.

Our Inn reflects the perfect combination of convenient location, luxurious accommodations and personal service. Our courteous staff cater to our guests' every need. Guests enjoy a breakfast buffet, indoor/outdoor pool, health club, and more! All suites have a coffee/tea maker, complimentary juices, and 2 TV's. Pickett Suite Inn-your home away from home!

———————————————— FORT WAYNE ————————————————

The Residence Inn by Marriott
4919 Lima Rd.
Fort Wayne, IN 46808

80 Suites
219-484-4700 800-331-3131

Location: Northwest
Airport: Few miles
Near: Industrial Park, 3 miles to Shopping
Walking Distance To: Suburbs
Area Attractions: Glenbrook Square, Magna-
vox Tech Center

Price Range & Credit Cards: 1 Bedroom Suite $$, 2 Bedrooms $$, AmEx/MC/Visa/
Other CC, Children Free, TAC 10%

Hotel Amenities: Laundry, TV Lounge, Pets Allowed, Handicap (2)

Business Facilities: Conf. Rm. Cap. 40, Mess. Ctr., Copier, Comp. Hook-up

Recreational Facilities: Pool, Whirlpool, Fitn. Ctr., Sportcourt; Local health facilities

Comps: Continental Breakfast, Hors d'oeuvres

Room Amenities: Free Paper, TV, Phone in Rm., Cable TV, Radio, Kitchen, Ind. Heat
Ctl., Ind. AC Ctl.

*Residence Inn has just the type of "home-away-from-home" atmosphere travelers weary
of typical hotel rooms appreciate. Every suite is designed for comfort, quality and afford-
ability, with fully-equipped kitchens and comfortable living areas. For your recreation,
you'll find an outdoor heated pool and hot tub. Discounted rates for extended stay.*

———————————————— INDIANAPOLIS ————————————————

Embassy Suites Hotel
3912 W.Vincennes Road
Indianapolis, IN 46268

222 Suites
317-872-7700 800-362-2779

Location: Northside; Downtown: 15 mi.
Airport: 13 miles
Near: College Park, Fortune Park, Children's
Museum
Walking Distance To: Shops & Restaurants
Area Attractions: Indianapolis Motor Speed-
way, Raceway Park, Indianapolis Zoo

Price Range & Credit Cards: 1 Bedroom Suite $$$, AmEx/MC/Visa/Other CC, Chil-
dren Free, TAC 10%

Hotel Amenities: Parking, TV Lounge, Pets Allowed

Business Facilities: Conf. Rm. Cap. 200, Banquet Fac., Mess. Ctr., Sec. Serv., Copier,
Aud/Vis., Teleconf., Comp. Hook-up

Recreational Facilities: Pool, Sauna, Whirlpool, Golf; Racquet club 10 min.

Restaurant/Bar: Ellington's Restaurant/Whispers Lounge

Comps: Full Breakfast, Refreshments, Hors d'oeuvres

Room Amenities: Room Service, Free Paper, TV, Phones in Rm. (2), Cable TV, Radio,
Wet Bar, Kitchen, Ind. Heat Ctl., Ind. AC Ctl.

*Embassy Suites is conveniently located in Fortune Park Business Center, near many busi-
ness and shopping areas. An indoor atrium lobby with tropical plants and fountains wel-
comes you to suite living. You will be pleased with your accommodations, decorated in
a choice of 3 color schemes, and furnished with such amenities as a microwave and
refrigerator.*

─────────────── INDIANAPOLIS ───────────────

Embassy Suites Hotel
110 W. Washington St.
Indianapolis, IN 46204

360 Suites
317-635-1000 800-362-2779

Location: Central
Airport: 7 miles
Near: Monument Circle, Market Square
Walking Distance To: Fine Shopping
Area Attractions: Union Station, Hoosier Dome

Price Range & Credit Cards: 1 Bedroom Suite $$$, 2 Bedrooms $$$$+, AmEx/MC/ Visa/Other CC, Children Free, TAC 10%

Hotel Amenities: Laundry, Parking, TV Lounge, Handicap (6)

Business Facilities: Conf. Rm. Cap. 1500, Banquet Fac., Mess. Ctr., Sec. Serv., Copier, Aud/Vis., Teleconf., Comp. Hook-up, Bus. Ctr.

Recreational Facilities: Pool, Sauna, Whirlpool, Fitn. Ctr., Racquetball; Golf and Tennis nearby

Restaurant/Bar: Ellington's Restaurant, Entertainment

Comps: Full Breakfast, Refreshments, Hors d'oeuvres, Limo Service

Room Amenities: Room Service, TV, Phones in Rm. (2), Cable TV, Radio, Wet Bar, Kitchen, Ind. Heat Ctl., Ind. AC Ctl.

The hotel is decorated throughout in a modified Art Deco design. Enter the lobby and find rich mahogany and marble accented by an Indiana Limestone fountain with a beautiful cascading plant tier. Treat yourself to lunch or dinner at Embassy's own Ellington's Restaurant, where soft pastels, create an intimate and warm dining atmosphere.

─────────────── INDIANAPOLIS ───────────────

Radisson Suite/Plaza Hotel
8787 Keystone Crossing
Indianapolis, IN 46240

160 Suites
317-846-2700 800-333-3333

Location: Office Park; Downtown: 20 min.
Airport: 25 minutes
Walking Distance To: Shopping and Entertainment
Area Attractions: Hoosier Dome

Price Range & Credit Cards: 1 Bedroom Suite $$$, Junior $$$, AmEx/MC/Visa/ Other CC, Children Free, TAC 10%

Hotel Amenities: Laundry, Gift shop, Parking, Car Hire, Pets Allowed, Handicap (20)

Business Facilities: Conf. Rm. Cap. 200, Banquet Fac., Copier, Aud/Vis., Teleconf., Telex, Comp. Hook-up

Recreational Facilities: Pool, Sauna, Whirlpool, Tennis, Racquet Club, Game Area; Golf nearby

Restaurant/Bar: Keystone Cafe, Waterson's, Whirligigs, Entertainment

Comps: Full breakfast, Refreshments, Hors d'oeuvres

Room Amenities: Room Service, Free Paper, TV, Phones in Rm. (2), Cable TV, VCR, Radio, Wet Bar, Ind. Heat Ctl., Ind. AC Ctl.

The Suite side of the Radisson Plaza Hotel complex features 157 suites with many bilevel and boardroom suites. Conveniently located in an exclusive shopping and entertainment complex, it is convenient for both business and vacation travellers.

INDIANAPOLIS

Riverpointe Suites Hotel
1150 N. White River Pkwy. West
Indianapolis, IN 46222

139 Suites
317-638-9866   800-777-8483

Location: Westedge; Downtown: 5 min.
Airport: 15 minutes
Near: White River, Convention Center, Hoosier Dome
Walking Distance To: IUPUI Facility
Area Attractions: Indianapolis Sports Center, Indianapolis Zoo

Price Range & Credit Cards: 1 Bedroom Suite $$, 2 Bedrooms $$, AmEx/MC/Visa/Other CC, Children Free, TAC 10%

Hotel Amenities: Laundry, Parking, Food Store, Shuttle Serv, Pets Allowed, Handicap (139)

Business Facilities: Conf. Rm. Cap. 200, Banquet Fac., Mess. Ctr., Sec. Serv., Copier, Teleconf.

Recreational Facilities: Pool, Sauna, Whirlpool, Fitn. Ctr., Tennis, Golf, Volleyball, Basketball, Jogging Track; Eagle Creek Park

Restaurant/Bar: The Westbank

Room Amenities: TV, Phone in Rm., Cable TV, Radio, Kitchen, Ind. Heat Ctl., Ind. AC Ctl.

Whether you're travelling alone, with family, or in a group, Riverpointe's friendly staff makes you feel right at home. You'll enjoy the relaxing atmosphere of its 8-acre grounds, complete with tennis, basketball and volleyball courts, a seasonal pool, a half mile jogging track and several picnic areas. All just minutes from many downtown attractions!

 **Kansas**

---------- LENEXA ----------

Guesthouse Apartment Hotel
9775 Lenexa Drive
Lenexa, KS 66215

39 Suites
913-541-4000

Location: Johnson Cty; Downtown: 30 min.
Near: 5 minutes away from all amenities needed
for long term stay

Price Range & Credit Cards: 1 Bedroom Suite $, 2 Bedrooms $, AmEx/MC/Visa/
Other CC, Children Free, TAC 10%

Hotel Amenities: Laundry, Pets Deposit, Handicap (3)

Business Facilities: Conf. Rm. Cap. 10, Mess. Ctr., Copier, Comp. Hook-up

Recreational Facilities: ; Free Health Club nearby

Room Amenities: TV, Phones in Rm. (2), Cable TV, Radio, Kitchen, Ind. Heat Ctl., Ind.
AC Ctl.

*Conveniently located in the Lenexa/Overland Park corridor of the Kansas City metro area,
the Guesthouse offers all the comforts of home at a budget price. New in 1988, all suites
are decorator furnished and feature completely equipped kitchens with microwave.
Whether staying for a day, week, or more, you'll agree that now there is "Someplace Like
Home."*

——————————— OVERLAND PARK ———————————

Embassy Suites Hotel
10601 Metcalf Rd. I-435
Overland Park, KS 66212

199 Suites
913-649-7060 800-362-2779

Location: I-435; Downtown: 25 min.
Airport: 45 minutes
Near: Shopping Mall-1 mile, Corporate Woods, Sports Complex-17 miles
Area Attractions: County Club Plaza-12 miles, Worlds of Fun-25 miles

Price Range & Credit Cards: 1 Bedroom Suite $$$, 2 Bedrooms $$$$+, Junior $$$, AmEx/MC/Visa/Other CC, Children Free, TAC 10%

Hotel Amenities: Gift Shop, TV Lounge, Small Pets only, Handicap (3)

Business Facilities: Conf. Rm. Cap. 30, Banquet Fac., Copier, Aud/Vis.

Recreational Facilities: Pool, Sauna, Whirlpool, Game Area; Tennis and Golf nearby

Restaurant/Bar: Embassy Court Restaurant and Bar

Comps: Full Breakfast, Refreshments

Room Amenities: Room Service, Free Paper, TV, Phones in Rm. (2), Cable TV, Radio, Wet Bar, Ind. Heat Ctl., Ind. AC Ctl.

A beautiful open atrium with the ambiance of plants enhanced with brass and glass provides an attractive focus for the 199 suites. The suites include livingroom with dining table and chairs with the option of a sofa sleeper, kitchen facilities, bedroom, and bath. A complimentary breakfast and manager's reception each evening are served in the atrium.

——————————— WICHITA ———————————

Inn @ Tallgrass Club
2400 Tallgrass
Wichita, KS 67226

40 Suites
316-684-4110 316-684-2222

Location: Northwest; Downtown: 30 min.
Airport: 10 minutes
Near: Country Club, Restaurants
Walking Distance To: Shopping Center

Price Range & Credit Cards: 1 Bedroom Suite $$$, 2 Bedrooms $$$, Junior $$, AmEx/MC/Visa, Children Free, TAC 10%

Hotel Amenities: Laundry, TV Lounge

Business Facilities: Conf. Rm. Cap. 65, Banquet Fac., Mess. Ctr., Copier, Aud/Vis., Telex

Recreational Facilities: Pool, Whirlpool, Fitn. Ctr., Tennis, Golf

Restaurant/Bar: Tallgrass

Comps: Continental Breakfast

Room Amenities: Free Paper, TV, Phone in Rm., Cable TV, Radio, Kitchen, Ind. Heat Ctl., Ind. AC Ctl.

Listen to the quiet at The Inn at Tallgrass Club, where you'll find comfort and convenience in a relaxed country club setting. All services and facilities are attuned to your needs—from meeting rooms to a myriad of sports facilities. Professional staff will provide the personal service that will guarantee a pleasant and comfortable stay.

Hana Maui, Maui, HI

WICHITA

The Talavera Hotel
658 West Dale
Wichita, KS 67209

50 Suites
316-945-2600

Location: Westside; Downtown: 10 min.
Airport: 5 minutes
Near: Town West Mall
Walking Distance To: Shopping Center

Price Range & Credit Cards: 1 Bedroom Suite $$, AmEx/MC/Visa/Other CC, Children Free

Hotel Amenities: Parking, Car Hire, Pets Allowed, Handicap (2)

Business Facilities: Conf. Rm. Cap. 40, Banquet Fac., Mess. Ctr., Copier, Aud/Vis.

Recreational Facilities: Pool, Sauna, Whirlpool, Tennis, Golf, Bowling, Racquetball, Jogging

Restaurant/Bar: The Cafe, Entertainment

Comps: Full Breakfast, Hors d'oeuvres

Room Amenities: Room Service, Free Paper, TV, Phone in Rm., Cable TV, Wet Bar, Ind. Heat Ctl., Ind. AC Ctl.

An indoor courtyard accented with an atrium secluded by tropical plants surrounds The Cafe's Restaurant and Club, where you can enjoy fine dining or your favorite cocktail while listening to the music of a classical guitarist. Each suite provides a bedroom, living room, and work/dining area. Use the space to handle business matters or entertain.

 Kentucky

Louisville
Lexington

LEXINGTON

The Residence Inn by Marriott
1080 Newtown Pike
Lexington, KY 40511

80 Suites
606-252-7500   800-331-3131

Location: Northside; Downtown: 2 miles
Airport: 3 miles
Near: Farm Areas, Industrial Area
Walking Distance To: Countryside
Area Attractions: New Circle Road

Price Range & Credit Cards: 1 Bedroom Suite $$$, 2 Bedrooms $$$, AmEx/MC/Visa/ Other CC, Children Free, TAC 10%

Hotel Amenities: Laundry, Parking, Car Hire, TV Lounge, Pets Allowed, Handicap (2)

Business Facilities: Conf. Rm. Cap. 25, Mess. Ctr., Copier, Aud/Vis., Comp. Hook-up

Recreational Facilities: Pool, Whirlpool, Fitn. Ctr., Golf, Riding, Ky. Horse Park, Keeneland Track, Game Area; all sports nearby

Comps: Continental Breakfast, Refreshments, Hors d'oeuvres

Room Amenities: Free Paper, TV, Phone in Rm., Cable TV, Radio, Kitchen, Ind. Heat Ctl., Ind. AC Ctl.

Curbside parking, private entrances, a fully-equipped kitchen, and a fireplace or patio are among the amenities you'll appreciate at The Residence Inn. Enjoy complimentary breakfast served daily at the Gatehouse, and a weekly complimentary cocktail party. Take advantage of a variety of recreational facilities. Rates discounted for extended stay.

──────────────── LOUISVILLE ────────────────

The Galt House Hotel East
141 North 4th Street
Louisville, KY 40202

600 Suites
502-589-3300

Location: Riverfront; Downtown
Airport: Standiford-6 miles
Near: Financial area
Walking Distance To: Galleria Mall
Area Attractions: Center for Arts, Museum of History & Science, Churchill Downs

Price Range & Credit Cards: 1 Bedroom Suite $$, 2 Bedrooms $$$$+, AmEx/MC/Visa/Other CC, Children Free

Hotel Amenities: Gift Shop, Parking, Barber Shop, Beauty Parlor, Handicap (52)

Business Facilities: Conf. Rm. Cap. 5000, Banquet Fac., Mess. Ctr., Copier, Aud/Vis.

Recreational Facilities: Pool, TV Lounge; Horseracing, baseball

Restaurant/Bar: Flagship/Fountain Room/Lobby Bar/D'Marie Lounge, Entertainment

Comps: Hors d'oeuvres

Room Amenities: Room Service, TV, Phones in Rm. (2), Cable TV, Radio, Wet Bar, Refrigerator, Ind. Heat Ctl., Ind. AC Ctl.

The Galt House Hotel East is the handsome all-suite tower of this famous riverfront hotel, first opened in the early 1800's. Your suite provides the comforts of a livingroom, separate bedroom, many closets, wet bar and refrigerator. Then enjoy fine cuisine or stroll in the beautifully landscaped park overlooking the Ohio River.

Louisiana

BATON ROUGE

Embassy Suites Hotel
4914 Constitution Ave.
Baton Rouge, LA 70808

224 Suites
504-924-6566 800-362-2779

Location: Downtown: 8 miles
Airport: 12 miles
Near: Corporate Square Mall, Heart of City
Area Attractions: Mississippi River Steamboats, Louisiana State Univ.

Price Range & Credit Cards: 1 Bedroom Suite $$$, AmEx/MC/Visa/Other CC, Children Free, TAC 9%

Hotel Amenities: Laundry, Parking, TV Lounge, Handicap (14)

Business Facilities: Conf. Rm. Cap. 450, Banquet Fac., Mess. Ctr., Sec. Serv., Copier, Aud/Vis., Bus. Ctr.

Recreational Facilities: Pool, Sauna, Whirlpool, Tennis, Golf, Racquetball

Restaurant/Bar: Branberry's/Brandies, Entertainment

Comps: Breakfast, Refreshments, Airport Transport

Room Amenities: Room Service, Free Paper, TV, Phone in Rm., Cable TV, Radio, Wet Bar, Kitchen, Ind. Heat Ctl., Ind. AC Ctl.

Embassy caters to all your needs—including complimentary full breakfast in the landscaped atrium courtyard and complete business facilities that make business a pleasure. Enjoy exceptional continental cuisine at Branberry's, then retire to the quiet of your own luxurious suite, decorated in custom-crafted mahogany.

───────────────── KENNER ─────────────────

Garden Vue Square
2438 Veterans Blvd.
Kenner, LA 70062

78 Suites
504-469-2800 800-824-0800

Location: Xerox Ct.; Downtown: 12 mi.
Airport: 2 miles
Near: Interstate-10, Largest Mall in Area
Walking Distance To: Rivertown
Area Attractions: Jefferson Downs' Race Track

Price Range & Credit Cards: 1 Bedroom Suite $$, Junior $$, AmEx/MC/Visa/Other CC, Children Free, TAC 10%

Hotel Amenities: Laundry, Parking, Car Hire, TV Lounge, Handicap (3)

Business Facilities: Copier

Recreational Facilities: Pool, Sauna, Whirlpool, Fitn. Ctr., Golf, Fishing, Boating; Lake: 2 miles

Restaurant/Bar: Cabana Cafe/Garden Vue Lounge

Room Amenities: Room Service, TV, Phones in Rm. (2), Cable TV, Wet Bar, Kitchen, Ind. Heat Ctl., Ind. AC Ctl.

You're only minutes away from Rivertown, Esplanade, and Jefferson Downs' Race Track when you stay at Garden Vue Square. A full compliment of superb facilities plus the spaciousness and convenience of a condominium await you here. Set in a tropical garden courtyard you'll have access to a variety of on-site recreational facilities.

───────────────── NEW ORLEANS ─────────────────

Hotel De La Monnaie
405 Esplanade Ave.
New Orleans, LA 70116

48 Suites
504-942-3700 800-445-3204

Location: French Qtr.; Royal St.: 3 blks
Airport: One Hour
Near: Mississippi River, Bourbon Street
Walking Distance To: Old New Orleans
Area Attractions: SuperDome, Museum, Arts, Music, River Tours

Price Range & Credit Cards: 1 Bedroom Suite $$$$, 2 Bedrooms $$$$, AmEx/MC/ Visa/Other CC, Children Free, TAC 15%

Hotel Amenities: Laundry, Library, Parking, Car Hire

Business Facilities: Conf. Rm. Cap. 200, Mess. Ctr., Sec. Serv., Copier, Aud/Vis.

Recreational Facilities: Pool, Sauna, Whirlpool, Fitn. Ctr., Tennis, Stables, Game Area; Health Spa nearby

Comps: Continental Breakfast, Refreshments

Room Amenities: Free Paper, TV, Phone in Rm., Cable TV, Radio, Wet Bar, Kitchen, Ind. Heat Ctl., Ind. AC Ctl.

French and English antiques, oriental carpets, chandeliers, and imported objets d'art in the lobby of this hotel introduce you to the ambiance of a private continental club, devoted to the ultimate in elegance and service. You can expect the same standards of excellence in each exquisite suite.

─────────────── NEW ORLEANS ───────────────

Radisson Suite Hotel
315 Julia St.
New Orleans, LA 70130

227 Suites
504-525-1993 800-333-3333

Location: Central; Downtown: 5 min.
Airport: 15 miles
Near: Convention Center, Waterfront
Walking Distance To: Historic Areas
Area Attractions: Children's Museum, Riverwalk

Price Range & Credit Cards: 1 Bedroom Suite $$$$, 2 Bedrooms $$$$+, AmEx/MC/Visa/Other CC, Children Free, TAC 10%

Hotel Amenities: Laundry, Parking, Concierge, Pets Allowed, Handicap (12)

Business Facilities: Conf. Rm. Cap. 200, Banquet Fac., Mess. Ctr., Copier, Aud/Vis., Teleconf., Comp. Hook-up

Recreational Facilities: Pool, Whirlpool; Golf and Tennis nearby

Restaurant/Bar: Sugar House, Entertainment

Comps: Full American Buffet Breakfast, Cocktail Reception

Room Amenities: Room Service, Free Paper, TV, Phone in Rm., Cable TV, Radio, Wet Bar, Ind. Heat Ctl., Ind. AC Ctl.

Step inside the Radisson Suite Hotel to discover a new world of luxury, comfort and convenience. You'll enjoy a spacious, elegantly decorated suite with Country French furnishings and the convenience of a built-in wet bar. Here the emphasis is on catering to each individual's requests, so just relax and enjoy every moment of your stay.

─────────────── SHREVEPORT ───────────────

Chateau Suite Hotel
201 Lake St.
Shreveport, LA 71161

49 Suites
318-222-7620 800-845-9334

Location: Central; Donwtown
Near: Business District, Entertainment
Walking Distance To: Red River
Area Attractions: Shopping, Business, Nightlife

Price Range & Credit Cards: 1 Bedroom Suite $$, 2 Bedrooms $$$$, AmEx/MC/Visa/Other CC, Children Free, TAC 10%

Hotel Amenities: Parking

Business Facilities: Conf. Rm. Cap. 200, Banquet Fac., Sec. Serv., Copier, Aud/Vis.

Recreational Facilities: Pool, Hot Tubs; Jogging trails

Restaurant/Bar: Normandy Room

Comps: Full Breakfast, Refreshments, Courtesy Van

Room Amenities: Free Paper, TV, Phones in Rm. (2), Cable TV, Radio, Kitchen, Ind. Heat Ctl., Ind. AC Ctl.

The convenient Chateau Suite Hotel puts you at only walking distance from the business district and a variety of entertainment spots. Business facilities that accommodate from 21 to 200 are available so you'll be able to conduct business right in the hotel. After hours of meetings, enjoy a leisurely meal in the Normandy Room or simply relax in a hot tub.

 Maryland

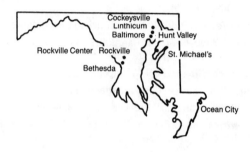

BALTIMORE

The Tremont Hotel
8 East Pleasant St.
Baltimore, MD 21202

62 Suites
301-576-1200 800-638-6266

Location: Central; Downtown
Airport: 25 minutes
Near: Business and Financial Districts
Walking Distance To: Downtown
Area Attractions: Baltimore's Inner Harbor

Price Range & Credit Cards: 1 Bedroom Suite $$$, Junior $$$, AmEx/MC/Visa/Other CC, Children Free, TAC 10%

Hotel Amenities: Laundry, Parking, Handicap (1)

Business Facilities: Conf. Rm. Cap. 120, Banquet Fac., Mess. Ctr., Sec. Serv., Copier, Aud/Vis., Teleconf., Comp. Hook-up

Recreational Facilities: ; Athletic Club passes

Restaurant/Bar: 8 East Restaurant/Celebrities Lounge

Comps: Continental Breakfast

Room Amenities: Room Service, Free Paper, TV, Phone in Rm., Radio, Mini Bar, Full Kitchen, Ind. Heat Ctl., Ind. AC Ctl.

You'll appreciate the service and intimate atmosphere at the Tremont. Each richly decorated suite provides a luxurious setting for business or pleasure. The staff and personal service make each visit special. The Tremont's central city location puts you only a few blocks from Baltimore's best business addresses, and attractions at Inner Harbor.

—————————————— BETHESDA ——————————————

Guest Quarters Suite Hotel
7335 Wisconsin Ave.
Bethesda, MD 20814

187 Suites
301-961-6400 800-424-2900

Location: Central; D.C.: 6 miles
Near: Business and Financial Districts
Walking Distance To: Business Area
Area Attractions: Metro Red Line to Historic D.C.

Price Range & Credit Cards: 1 Bedroom Suite $$$$, 2 Bedrooms $$$$, AmEx/MC/ Visa/Other CC, Children Free, TAC 10%

Hotel Amenities: Laundry, Library, Parking, Car Hire, Pets Allowed

Business Facilities: Conf. Rm. Cap. 200, Banquet Fac., Mess. Ctr., Sec. Serv., Copier, Aud/Vis., Teleconf., Telex, FAX

Recreational Facilities: Pool, Sauna, Fitn. Ctr., Tennis, Golf, Racquetball, Running track

Restaurant/Bar: Yorkshire Grill and Bar

Comps: Breakfast Buffet, Manager's Reception

Room Amenities: Room Service, TV, Phone in Rm., VCR, Radio, Wet Bar, Kitchen, Ind. Heat Ctl., Ind. AC Ctl.

A variety of recreational facilities await you when you stay at Guest Quarters. After a day of activity, enjoy the privacy of your comfortable suite, and the special advantages of having a complete kitchen and groceries delivered to your door. Other Guest Quarters in the DC area are in Alexandria, VA., and on Pennsylvania and New Hampshire Avenues.

—————————————— COCKEYSVILLE ——————————————

The Residence Inn by Marriott
10710 Beaver Dam Rd.
Cockeysville, MD 21030

96 Suites
301-584-7370 800-331-3131

Location: Hunt Valley; Downtown: 18 mi.
Airport: 35 miles
Near: I-83 and Shawan Road, Hunt Valley Mall
Area Attractions: Maryland State Fairgrounds, Timonium Race Track, Aquarium

Price Range & Credit Cards: 1 Bedroom Suite $$$, 2 Bedrooms $$$$, AmEx/MC/ Visa/Other CC, Children Free, TAC 10%

Hotel Amenities: Laundry, Library, Parking, TV Lounge, Pets Allowed, Handicap (4)

Business Facilities: Conf. Rm. Cap. 50, Mess. Ctr., Sec. Serv., Copier

Recreational Facilities: Pool, Whirlpool, Sport Court, Basketball, Volleyball, Badminton, Barbeque Area

Comps: Continental Plus Breakfast, Refreshments, Hors d'oeuvres

Room Amenities: Room Service, Free Paper, TV, Phones in Rm. (2), Cable TV, Radio, Kitchen, Ind. Heat Ctl., Ind. AC Ctl.

The Residence Inn is ideal for business or pleasure with beautifully decorated 1-bedroom studio and 2-bedroom penthouse suites, all with full kitchens, most with fireplaces. Area attractions include 800-acre Oregan Ridge Park, historic Hampton Mansion, Boordy Vineyards and Hunt Valley Mall shopping. Rates are discounted for extended stays.

———————————— HUNT VALLEY ————————————

Embassy Suites Hotel
213 International Circle
Hunt Valley, MD 21030

223 Suites
301-584-1400 800-362-2779

Location: Suburban; Downtown: 18 mi.
Airport: 30 miles
Near: Hunt Valley, Entertainment
Walking Distance To: Hunt Valley Mall
Area Attractions: Oregon Ridge Dinner Theater

Price Range & Credit Cards: 1 Bedroom Suite $$$, AmEx/MC/Visa, Children Free, TAC 10%

Hotel Amenities: Parking, TV Lounge, Handicap (22)

Business Facilities: Conf. Rm. Cap. 10, Banquet Fac., Copier, Aud/Vis., Teleconf., FAX, Comp. Hook-up

Recreational Facilities: Pool, Sauna, Whirlpool, Fitn. Ctr., Game Area; Golf & Tennis nearby

Restaurant/Bar: Ellington's, Entertainment

Comps: Full Breakfast, Refreshments, Hors d'oeuvres

Room Amenities: Room Service, Free Paper, TV, Phones in Rm. (2), Cable TV, Radio, Wet Bar, Kitchen, Ind. Heat Ctl., Ind. AC Ctl.

An atrium filled with beautiful foliage and waterfall, with walkways throughout the courtyard is the centerpiece of this hotel. Modern Art Deco decor combined with spacious suites provides a sophisticated atmosphere for conducting business, while a variety of sport and recreational facilities allow you to relax and enjoy your stay.

———————————— LINTHICUM ————————————

Guest Quarters Suite Hotel
1300 Concourse Dr.
Linthicum, MD 21090

251 Suites
301-850-0747 800-424-2900

Location: Gateway; Downtown: 8 miles
Airport: adjacent
Near: Baltimore's Inner Harbor-8 miles, Pimlico Race Track-10 miles
Area Attractions: Washington D.C.-30 mi., John Hopkins Univ., Naval Academy

Price Range & Credit Cards: 2 Bedrooms $$$$, AmEx/MC/Visa/Other CC, Children Free, TAC 10%

Hotel Amenities: Laundry, Gift Shop, Parking, Handicap (11)

Business Facilities: Conf. Rm. Cap. 160, Banquet Fac., Sec. Serv.

Recreational Facilities: Pool, Sauna, Whirlpool, Game Area

Restaurant/Bar: Atrium Cafe/Atrium Lounge, Piano Entertainment

Comps: Full Breakfast, Drinks & Snacks, Airport Van

Room Amenities: TV, Phones in Rm. (2), Cable TV, Radio, Wet Bar, Kitchen, Ind. Heat Ctl., Ind. AC Ctl.

Only 1.5 miles from BWI, Guest Quarters is in the heart of the exciting Baltimore/Washington corridor. Executive meeting suites, banquet halls and meeting rooms both small and large accommodate the business traveller in the most convenient location. Any meeting or conference can be expertly arranged by the helpful staff, assuring a successful meeting.

─────────────── ROCKVILLE ───────────────

Woodfin Suites Hotel
1380 Piccard Dr.
Rockville, MD 20850

203 Suites
301-590-9880 800-237-8811

Location: Rockville; D.C.: 16 miles
Airport: National-21 miles
Near: Suburban Business Center
Walking Distance To: Central Business Area
Area Attractions: Metro-1 mile

Price Range & Credit Cards: 1 Bedroom Suite $$$, 2 Bedrooms &$$$, AmEx/MC/ Visa/Other CC, Children Free, TAC 10%

Hotel Amenities: Laundry, Gift Shop, Parking, Pets/Fee, Handicap (9)

Business Facilities: Conf. Rm. Cap. 150, Banquet Fac., Mess. Ctr., Sec. Serv., Copier, Comp. Hook-up, Bus. Ctr.

Recreational Facilities: Pool, Whirlpool; Fitness Center, golf nearby

Restaurant/Bar: Normandie Cafe and Bar, Player Grand Piano

Comps: Full Breakfast, Refreshments, Hors d'oeuvres

Room Amenities: Free Paper, TV, Phones in Rm. (3), VCR, Radio, Kitchen, Ind. Heat Ctl., Ind. AC Ctl.

Conveniently located in Rockville's business center, Woodfin Suites offers a new standard for the discriminating traveller. Spacious, beautiful suites with full kitchens, dining areas, large desks and every amenity of home provide a relaxing environment for business or family travel. Full business center available. Our staff will assist with any request.

The Barclay Chicago Hotel, Chicago, IL

⚜ Massachusetts

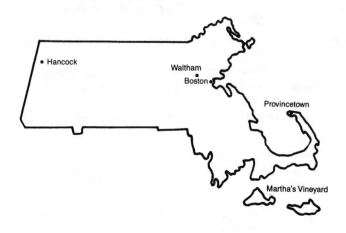

--- BOSTON ---

Guest Quarters Suite Hotel
400 Soldiers Field Rd.
Boston, MA 02134

310 Suites
617-783-0090

Location: Central; Downtown: 3 miles
Airport: 4 miles
Near: Charles River, Theatre District
Area Attractions: Harvard Business School, Harvard Square

Price Range & Credit Cards: 1 Bedroom Suite $$$$, AmEx/MC/Visa/Other CC, Children Free, TAC 10%

Hotel Amenities: Laundry, Parking, TV Lounge, Handicap (15)

Business Facilities: Conf. Rm. Cap. 175, Banquet Fac., Sec. Serv., Copier, Aud/Vis., Teleconf., Comp. Hook-up

Recreational Facilities: Pool, Sauna, Whirlpool, Jogging track

Restaurant/Bar: Scullers Grill & Lounge, Entertainment

Comps: Full Breakfast

Room Amenities: Room Service, TV, Phone in Rm., Cable TV, Radio, Wet Bar, Ind. Heat Ctl., Ind. AC Ctl.

Whether you're here for a weekend escape, a business convention, or touring local colleges and universities, Guest Quarters provides perfect accommodations. Ideally located on the Boston/Cambridge line, you'll be minutes away from cherished landmarks and walking distance from Harvard Business School, Boston University and MIT.

---------------------------- HANCOCK ----------------------------

The Country Inn Jiminy Peak   ***Location:*** Resort; Pittsfield:12 mi.
Carey Rd.   ***Airport:*** 12 miles
Hancock, MA 01237   ***Near:*** Mountain & Valley, Rural Resort
                                     Walking Distance To: Lift system
105 Suites   ***Area Attractions:*** Skiing, Theatre Festival
413-738-5500 413-445-5500

Price Range & Credit Cards: 1 Bedroom Suite $$, AmEx/MC/Visa, Children Free,
TAC 10%

Hotel Amenities: Laundry, Parking, TV Lounge, Pets Allowed, Handicap (10)

Business Facilities: Conf. Rm. Cap. 400, Banquet Fac., Mess. Ctr., Aud/Vis.

Recreational Facilities: Pool, Sauna, Whirlpool, Fitn. Ctr., Golf, Skiing, Ice skating,
Game Area; Cross country skiing

Restaurant/Bar: Drummonds, Entertainment

Room Amenities: TV, Phone in Rm., Cable TV, Radio, Kitchen, Ind. Heat Ctl., Ind.
AC Ctl.

*Come to the Country Inn for a mix of modern amenities and old New England charm. At
the foot of Jiminy Peak, where ski programs abound, you'll also find swimming, tennis,
boating, fishing, bicycling, hiking, golf. Relax before the massive stone fireplace in the
lobby, set out for music at Tanglewood, or dance concerts at Jacob's Pillow.*

---------------------------- WALTHAM ----------------------------

Guest Quarters Suite Hotel   ***Location:*** Route 128; Downtown: 10 mi.
550 Winter Street   ***Airport:*** 13 miles
Waltham, MA 02154   ***Near:*** High Tech Corridor, easy access by free-
                                     way to Boston, north & south shore
275 Suites
617-890-6767 800-424-2900

Price Range & Credit Cards: AmEx/MC/Visa/Other CC, Children Free, TAC 10%

Hotel Amenities: Laundry, Gift Shop, Parking, Car Hire, Handicap (14)

Business Facilities: Conf. Rm. Cap. 180, Banquet Fac., Mess. Ctr., Sec. Serv., Copier,
Aud/Vis., Comp. Hook-up

Recreational Facilities: Pool, Sauna, Whirlpool, Fitn. Ctr.

Restaurant/Bar: Piano Entertainment

Comps: Full Breakfast, Hors d'oeuvres

Room Amenities: Room Service, TV, Phones in Rm. (3), Cable TV, Radio, Wet Bar, Ind.
Heat Ctl., Ind. AC Ctl.

*In the heart of Boston's suburban high-technology corridor, Guest Quarters offers business
travellers every amenity, plus their unmatched standard of service and guest treatment.
Rich woods, fine tapestries and lush greenery contribute to the elegance of this hotel's decor.*

☙ Michigan

Grand Rapids •
Lansing •
East Lansing
Ann Arbor
Troy
Southfield
Madison Heights
Farmington Hills

ANN ARBOR

The Residence Inn by Marriott
800 Victors Way
Ann Arbor, MI 48104

72 Suites
313-996-5666 800-331-3131

Location: Southside; Downtown: 7 miles
Airport: 25 miles
Near: Business/Residential Areas, Farmers Market
Walking Distance To: Mall, Movies
Area Attractions: Central Campus, Fall Art Festival

Price Range & Credit Cards: 1 Bedroom Suite $$$, 2 Bedrooms $$$, AmEx/MC/Visa/Other CC, Children Free, TAC 10%

Hotel Amenities: Laundry, Library, Parking, Car Hire, TV Lounge, Pets Allowed, Handicap (3)

Business Facilities: Conf. Rm. Cap. 30, Mess. Ctr., Copier, Aud/Vis.

Recreational Facilities: Pool, Whirlpool, Game Area; Golf Courses 15 min.

Comps: Continental Breakfast, Airport Van

Room Amenities: Free Paper, TV, Phone in Rm., Cable TV, Radio, Kitchen, Ind. Heat Ctl., Ind. AC Ctl.

The spacious, homey suites at the Inn are a great place to stretch out and relax, each with its full kitchen and cosy fireplace. Extra touches are free transportation to and from Detroit Metropolitan Airport and throughout the city of Ann Arbor, complimentary continental breakfast, laundry facilities and sport court. Discounted rates for extended stays.

-------------------- EAST LANSING --------------------

The Residence Inn by Marriott
1600 E. Grand River
East Lansing, MI 48823

60 Suites
517-332-7711   800-331-3131

Location: Eastside; Downtown: 6 miles
Airport: 8 miles
Near: Red Cedar River, Meridian Mall
Walking Distance To: Michigan State Univ.
Area Attractions: Science Museum, Wharton Center, State Capitol

Price Range & Credit Cards: 1 Bedroom Suite $$, 2 Bedrooms $$$, AmEx/MC/Visa/Other CC, Children Free, TAC 10%

Hotel Amenities: Laundry, Parking, TV Lounge, Pets Allowed, Handicap (3)

Business Facilities: Mess. Ctr., Copier

Recreational Facilities: Pool, Whirlpool, Tennis, Golf, Skiing, Racquetball, Ice skating, Game Area

Comps: Continental Breakfast, Valet Service, Grocery Service

Room Amenities: Free Paper, TV, Phone in Rm., Cable TV, Radio, Kitchen, Ind. Heat Ctl., Ind. AC Ctl.

One block from Michigan State University, the Inn is on the banks of the Red Cedar River. You'll stay in lovely, contemporary suites, with fireplace and fully equipped kitchen. Enjoy freshly popped corn by the Hearthroom's cozy fire and complimentary continental breakfast daily. Try the Inn's many sports facilities. Rates discounted for extended stay.

-------------------- SOUTHFIELD --------------------

Embassy Suites Hotel
28100 Franklin Road
Southfield, MI 48034

240 Suites
313-350-2000   800-362-2779

Location: Southfield; Downtown: 20 min.
Airport: 30 minutes
Near: Greenfield Village and Henry Ford Museum-20 minutes
Area Attractions: Detroit Grand Prix (June)

Price Range & Credit Cards: 1 Bedroom Suite $$$$, AmEx/MC/Visa/Other CC, Children Free, TAC 10%

Hotel Amenities: Laundry, Gift Shop, Parking, TV Lounge, Handicap (8)

Business Facilities: Conf. Rm. Cap. 200, Banquet Fac., Copier, Aud/Vis., Telex

Recreational Facilities: Pool, Sauna, Whirlpool, Fitn. Ctr., Skiing-45 min.; Golf nearby

Restaurant/Bar: Wellington's/La Salles, Entertainment

Comps: Full Breakfast, Refreshments

Room Amenities: Room Service, Free Paper, TV, Phones in Rm. (2), Cable TV, Radio, Wet Bar, Microwave, Ind. Heat Ctl., Ind. AC Ctl.

Enjoy the Suite Life at the Embassy Suites Hotel. Our 2- room luxurious suites overlook the tropical atrium and include a wet bar, refrigerator, 2 TV's, and 3 phones. The Suite Life also includes an indoor pool, jacuzzi, sauna, and exercise equipment. Complimentary, full, cooked-to-order breakfast is served mornings and evening complimentary cocktails.

―――――――――――― SOUTHFIELD ――――――――――――

The Residence Inn by Marriott
26700 Central Park Blvd.
Southfield, MI 48076

144 Suites
313-352-8900 800-331-3131

Location: Southfield; Downtown: 15 mi.
Airport: 20 miles
Near: US-10 and I-696, Business, Entertainment, Shopping and Restaurants

Price Range & Credit Cards: 1 Bedroom Suite $$, 2 Bedrooms $$$, AmEx/MC/Visa/Other CC, Children Free, TAC 10%

Hotel Amenities: Laundry, Library, Parking, TV Lounge, Small pets/fee, Handicap (6)

Business Facilities: Conf. Rm. Cap. 30, Banquet Fac., Mess. Ctr., Copier, Aud/Vis.

Recreational Facilities: Pool, Whirlpool, Tennis, Game Area; Golf & Fitn. Ctr. near

Comps: Continental Plus Breakfast, Refreshments, Dinner on Thursday

Room Amenities: Free Paper, TV, Phones in Rm. (2), Cable TV, Radio, Kitchen, Ind. Heat Ctl., Ind. AC Ctl.

At the Residence Inn, you will experience the warm, comfortable feeling of home. All suites include comfortable living areas with wood-burning fireplaces and fully-equipped kitchens. We offer complimentary, a continental buffet breakfast, weekly social hour, grocery shopping, daily newspaper, and satellite television. Extended stay rate discount.

―――――――――――― TROY ――――――――――――

Guest Quarters Suite Hotel
850 Tower Dr.
Troy, MI 48098

251 Suites
313-879-7500 800-424-2900

Location: Northfield; Downtown: 15 mi.
Airport: 30 miles
Near: Business District, exclusive shops, Greenfield Village, Somerset Mall
Walking Distance To: Business Area
Area Attractions: Silverdome, Henry Ford Museum, Walsh College

Price Range & Credit Cards: 1 Bedroom Suite $$$$, AmEx/MC/Visa/Other CC, Children Free, TAC 10%

Hotel Amenities: Laundry, Gift Shop, Parking, Car Hire, Handicap (11)

Business Facilities: Conf. Rm. Cap. 190, Banquet Fac., Mess. Ctr., Sec. Serv., Copier, Aud/Vis., FAX, Comp. Hook-up

Recreational Facilities: Pool, Sauna, Whirlpool, Fitn. Ctr., Game Area; Golf and Tennis nearby

Restaurant/Bar: Atrium Cafe/Atrium Lounge, Piano Entertainment

Comps: Full Breakfast, Refreshments, Hors d'oeuvres

Room Amenities: Room Service, TV, Phones in Rm. (2), Cable TV, Radio, Wet Bar, Ind. Heat Ctl., Ind. AC Ctl.

Combining the recreational facilities of a vacation retreat with the comforts and amenities of a business hotel, Guest Quarters-Troy is perfect for work and play. Nearby, the Pontiac Silverdome, Cultural Center and superb retail shops provide ample diversion. A highly acclaimed restaurant and handsome suites are among this hotel's outstanding features.

⚜ Minnesota

BLOOMINGTON

Embassy Suites Hotel
2800 W. 80th St.
Bloomington, MN 55431

219 Suites
612-884-4811 800-362-2779

Location: Suburbs; Downtown: 20 min.
Airport: 8 miles
Near: Many fine shops, Major Highway
Walking Distance To: Fine Restaurants
Area Attractions: Amusement Park, Metro-dome Race Track

Price Range & Credit Cards: 1 Bedroom Suite $$$, AmEx/MC/Visa/Other CC, Children Free, TAC 10%

Hotel Amenities: Laundry, Parking, Car Hire, Pets Allowed, Handicap (4)

Business Facilities: Conf. Rm. Cap. 12, Banquet Fac., Copier, Aud/Vis., FAX, Notary Public

Recreational Facilities: Pool, Sauna, Whirlpool, Skiing, Jogging trail; Golf nearby

Restaurant/Bar: Woolley's, Entertainment

Comps: Full Breakfast, Refreshments

Room Amenities: Room Service, Free Paper, TV, Phones in Rm. (2), Cable TV, Radio, Wet Bar, Kitchen, Ind. Heat Ctl., Ind. AC Ctl.

Step out on your patio to enjoy a panoramic view of the city. Visit the Embassy Suites' central garden atrium with its Spanish murals, tiles and fountains and sip a complimentary cocktail with friends. Canterbury Downs Race Track and Valley Fair Amusement Park are just a short drive, Chanhassen and Guthrie theatres even closer. Golf and skiing nearby.

The Residence Inn by Marriott, Omaha, NE

--- BLOOMINGTON ---

Embassy Suites Hotel
7901 34th Ave. So.
Bloomington, MN 55425

311 Suites
612-854-1000 800-362-2779

Location: Airport; Downtown: 12 mi.
Airport: 2 miles
Near: Bloomington, Met Sport Center
Area Attractions: Valley Fair Amusement Park, Canterbury Downs Race Track

Price Range & Credit Cards: 1 Bedroom Suite $$$, AmEx/MC/Visa/Other CC, Children Free, TAC 10%

Hotel Amenities: Laundry, Parking, Car Hire, TV Lounge, Pets Allowed, Handicap (18)

Business Facilities: Conf. Rm. Cap. 200, Banquet Fac., Mess. Ctr., Copier, Aud/Vis., FAX, Comp. Hook-up

Recreational Facilities: Pool, Sauna, Whirlpool, Golf, Skiing; Health Club nearby

Restaurant/Bar: Woolley's Too, Entertainment

Comps: Full Breakfast, Refreshments

Room Amenities: Room Service, Free Paper, TV, Phone in Rm., Cable TV, Radio, Wet Bar, Kitchen

Art Deco mode is highlighted in the contemporary design of the airport Embassy Suites. 3,000 plants and trees harmonize with shades of mauve, lavender and teal in the atrium courtyard. A stream meanders through, fed by spectacular waterfalls. Your complimentary breakfast will be cooked to order, & the manager invites you to a cocktail party each evening.

———————————————————— EDEN PRAIRE ————————————————————

The Residence Inn by Marriott
7780 Flying Cloud Dr.
Eden Praire, MN 55344

128 Suites
612-829-0033 800-331-3131

Location: Southwest; Downtown: 20 min.
Airport: 10 minutes
Near: Shopping Mall, Dinner Theatre, Health Clubs
Walking Distance To: Suburban Area
Area Attractions: Canterbury Downs Race Track, Renaissance Festival

Price Range & Credit Cards: 1 Bedroom Suite $$, 2 Bedrooms $$$, AmEx/MC/Visa/Other CC, Children Free, TAC 10%

Hotel Amenities: Laundry, Library, TV Lounge, Pets Allowed

Business Facilities: Conf. Rm. Cap. 15, Mess. Ctr., Sec. Serv., Copier, Aud/Vis.

Recreational Facilities: Pool, Whirlpool, Volleyball, Sportcourt, Paddle Tennis

Comps: Continental Breakfast, Wednesday Dinner

Room Amenities: Free Paper, TV, Phone in Rm., HBO, Radio, Kitchen, Ind. Heat Ctl., Ind. AC Ctl.

The Residence Inn staff wants to reduce the stress of long-term travel by providing a "home" at the price of a hotel room. They will do your shopping for you, direct you to the Sport Court, and invite you to the Gatehouse Gathering Wednesday nights for complimentary food and beverages. Just check in and relax. Discounted rates for extended stays.

———————————————————— MINNEAPOLIS ————————————————————

Best Western Bradbury Suites
7770 Johnson Ave.
Minneapolis, MN 55435

126 Suites
612-893-9999 800-528-1234

Location: Suburbs; Downtown: 20 min
Airport: 7 miles
Near: Business district, Health Clubs
Walking Distance To: Business, Restaurants
Area Attractions: Met Center, Zoo, Canterbury Downs Racetrack, Valley Fair

Price Range & Credit Cards: 1 Bedroom Suite $$, AmEx/MC/Visa/Other CC, Children Free, TAC 12%

Hotel Amenities: Laundry, Parking, Handicap (6)

Business Facilities: Conf. Rm. Cap. 20 to 35, Copier, Aud/Vis.

Recreational Facilities: Whirlpool; Fitness Center Complex

Comps: Breakfast Buffet

Room Amenities: Room Service, Free Paper, TV, Phones in Rm. (2), Cable TV, Radio, Ind. Heat Ctl., Ind. AC Ctl.

The staff at Bradbury Suites is eager to serve you with hospitality and quality. The morning newspaper is complimentary and you can enjoy a complimentary breakfast in the lobby/cafe area. The nearby Fitness Center Complex is available for your use. The airport business district, and shopping centers are easily accessible.

—————————————— MINNEAPOLIS ——————————————

Embassy Suites Hotel
425 So. 7th St.
Minneapolis, MN 55415

219 Suites
612-333-3111 800-362-2779

Location: Central; Downtown
Airport: 12 miles
Near: Centre Village, Metrodome
Walking Distance To: Business, Dining
Area Attractions: Orchestra Hall, Theatre, Shops

Price Range & Credit Cards: 1 Bedroom Suite $$$, 2 Bedrooms $$$, AmEx/MC/ Visa/Other CC, Children Free, TAC 10%

Hotel Amenities: Laundry, Parking, Pets Allowed, Handicap (10)

Business Facilities: Conf. Rm. Cap. 60, Banquet Fac., Mess. Ctr., Copier, Aud/Vis., Teleconf., Comp. Hook-up

Recreational Facilities: Pool, Sauna, Whirlpool; Golf-3 miles; Skiing: 40 minutes

Restaurant/Bar: Ellington's

Comps: Full Breakfast, Refreshments, Hors d'oeuvres

Room Amenities: Room Service, Free Paper, TV, Phone in Rm., Radio, Wet Bar, Kitchen

Families are as welcome at the Embassy Suites as the business person, with no charge for children under 12 and cribs available for infants. Ski facilities are just a 40-minute drive away, and you can walk to the Hubert Humphrey Metrodome. You'll admire the Art Deco pinks, mauves and blacks at Ellington's Restaurant, as well as excellent food.

—————————————— MINNEAPOLIS ——————————————

Hotel Luxeford Suites
1101 La Salle
Minneapolis, MN 55403

230 Suites
612-332-6800 800-662-3232

Location: Central; Downtown
Airport: 15 minutes
Near: Orchestra Hall, Nicollet Mall
Walking Distance To: Fine Shops
Area Attractions: Orchestra Hall

Price Range & Credit Cards: 1 Bedroom Suite $$, AmEx/MC/Visa/Other CC, Children Free, TAC 10%

Hotel Amenities: Laundry, Library, Parking, TV Lounge, Handicap (11)

Business Facilities: Conf. Rm. Cap. 25, Banquet Fac., Mess. Ctr., Sec. Serv., Copier, Aud/Vis.

Recreational Facilities: Sauna, Whirlpool, Fitn. Ctr.

Restaurant/Bar: Cafe Luxeford

Comps: Continental Breakfast, Downtown Shuttle

Room Amenities: Room Service, Free Paper, TV, Phone in Rm., Radio, Wet Bar, Kitchen, Ind. Heat Ctl., Ind. AC Ctl.

Spend your honeymoon at the Hotel Luxeford and enjoy complimentary champagne and fresh flowers. Orange juice and morning newspaper delivered to your suite. Exquisite complimentary breakfast in the comfortable clubroom goes beyond Continental. In the evening, enjoy a concert at the Orchestra Hall only a block away.

─────────────────── ST. PAUL ───────────────────

Embassy Suites Hotel
175 E. 10th St.
St. Paul, MN 55101

210 Suites
612-224-5400 800-362-2779

Location: Central; Downtown
Airport: 15 minutes
Near: Downtown Business, State Capitol
Walking Distance To: Omni Theatre
Area Attractions: St. Paul Cathedral, Museum,
Shops

Price Range & Credit Cards: 1 Bedroom Suite $$$, AmEx/MC/Visa/Other CC, Children Free, TAC 10%

Hotel Amenities: Laundry, Parking, Car Hire, Pets Allowed, Handicap (7)

Business Facilities: Conf. Rm. Cap. 200, Banquet Fac., Copier, Aud/Vis., Teleconf., Telex, Comp. Hook-up

Recreational Facilities: Pool, Sauna, Whirlpool, Steam Room, Game Room; Jogging & Golf nearby

Restaurant/Bar: Woolleys, Entertainment

Comps: Full Breakfast, Refreshments, Airport Transit

Room Amenities: Room Service, Free Paper, TV, Phone in Rm., Cable TV, Radio, Kitchen, Ind. Heat Ctl., Ind. AC Ctl.

In view of the State Capitol, the Embassy Suites of St.Paul offers many extras. Enjoy your complimentary, cooked-to-order breakfast, beverages in the evening, & free airport transportation. All 8 floors overlook the atrium with its waterfall, 10,000 plants, and live ducks! Evenings, enjoy your favorite dance music in Woolley's Lounge.

─────────────────── ST. PAUL ───────────────────

The Residence Inn by Marriott
3040 Eagandale Place
St. Paul, MN 55121

120 Suites
612-688-0363 800-331-3131

Location: Eagan; Downtown: 10 mi.
Airport: 4 miles NW
Near: Burnsville Shopping Mall, Met Center, Valley Fair Amusement Park
Area Attractions: Minnesota Zoo, Canterbury Downs, Buck Hill Ski Area

Price Range & Credit Cards: 1 Bedroom Suite $$, 2 Bedrooms $$$, AmEx/MC/Visa/Other CC, Children Free, TAC 10%

Hotel Amenities: Laundry, Library, Parking, TV Lounge, Pets Allowed, Handicap (5)

Business Facilities: Conf. Rm. Cap. 50, Banquet Fac., Mess. Ctr., Sec. Serv., Copier, Aud/Vis., Telex, Comp. Hook-up, Bus. Ctr.

Recreational Facilities: Pool, Whirlpool, Fitn. Ctr., Jogging, Sportcourt, Game Area; Golf & Riding nearby

Comps: Continental+ breakfast, Refreshments, Hors d'oeuvres (Tues & Thurs.)

Room Amenities: Room Service, Free Paper, TV, Phones in Rm. (2), Cable TV, VCR, Radio, Wet Bar, Kitchen, Ind. Heat Ctl., Ind. AC Ctl.

The Residence Inn by Marriott will invite you to return often with its thoughtful staff offering home-like service. Enjoy daily complimentary breakfast, meet new friends at Tuesday and Thursday evening hospitality hour while relaxing by the fireplace. The Hotel is located in a quiet suburban neighborhood. Rates discounted for extended stay.

⚜ Mississippi

Jackson

JACKSON

The Diplomat
500 Northpointe Parkway
Jackson, MS 39211

20 Suites
601-956-9411

Location: Northeast; Downtown: 15 min.
Airport: 12 miles
Near: Shopping Malls & Office Complex
Walking Distance To: Business Areas
Area Attractions: Reservoir, Entertainment, Shops

Price Range & Credit Cards: 1 Bedroom Suite $, 2 Bedrooms $, MC/Visa

Hotel Amenities: Laundry, TV Lounge

Business Facilities: Conf. Rm. Cap. 60

Recreational Facilities: Pool, Whirlpool, Fitn. Ctr., Golf, Skiing, Fishing, Nature trails nearby, Game Area

Room Amenities: TV, Phone in Rm., Cable TV, Wet Bar, Kitchen, Ind. Heat Ctl., Ind. AC Ctl.

The Diplomat is noted for its classic conservative ambiance and lovely interiors (9 foot ceilings with crown mouldings). This is an adult apartment community with only 20 suites for rent, set amidst formal gardens. Suite guests enjoy the courtyard pool area and the clubhouse which can also be reserved for parties or meetings.

---------------------------------- JACKSON ----------------------------------

The Residence Inn by Marriott
881 East River Place
Jackson, MS 39202

96 Suites
601-355-3599 800-331-3131

Location: Central; Downtown: 1 mi.
Airport: 12 miles
Near: Shops, Restaurants, Davis Planetarium
Walking Distance To: Downtown
Area Attractions: MS Trade Mart, Coliseum, Museums

Price Range & Credit Cards: 1 Bedroom Suite $$, 2 Bedrooms $$$, AmEx/MC/ Visa/Other CC, Children Free, TAC 10%

Hotel Amenities: Laundry, Library, TV Lounge, Pets Allowed, Handicap (2)

Business Facilities: Conf. Rm. Cap. 35, Mess. Ctr., Sec. Serv., Copier, Aud/Vis.

Recreational Facilities: Pool, Sauna, Whirlpool, Fitn. Ctr., Golf, Jogging trails, Game Area; Full service YMCA

Comps: Continental Breakfast, Refreshments, Hors d'oeuvres

Room Amenities: Free Paper, TV, Phone in Rm., Cable TV, VCR, Radio, Wet Bar, Kitchen, Ind. Heat Ctl., Ind. AC Ctl.

When you step inside your suite you'll appreciate the fireplace, kitchen, and lovely teal and mauve decor—so home-like. You're minutes from the Davis Planetarium and the Jackson Zoological Park. Residence Inn's Gatehouse offers a place to congregate and relax, and there's even a 24-hour delicatessen. Rates discounted for extended stays.

⚜ Missouri

─────────────── CHESTERFIELD ───────────────

The Residence Inn by Marriott
15431 Conway Rd.
Chesterfield, MO 63017

104 Suites
314-537-1444 800-331-3131

Location: Suburban; Downtown: 15 min.
Airport: 9 miles
Near: Wooded area, Arena: 16 miles
Walking Distance To: Residential Areas
Area Attractions: Busch Stadium, St.Louis Arch

Price Range & Credit Cards: 1 Bedroom Suite $$, 2 Bedrooms $$$, AmEx/MC/ Visa/Other CC, Children Free, TAC 10%

Hotel Amenities: Laundry, TV Lounge, Handicap (2)

Business Facilities: Conf. Rm. Cap. 25, Copier, Teleconf.

Recreational Facilities: Pool, Whirlpool, Fitn. Ctr., Game Area; Health Club privileges

Comps: Continental Breakfast, Refreshments, Hors d'oeuvres

Room Amenities: Free Paper, TV, Phone in Rm., Cable TV, Radio, Wet Bar, Kitchen, Ind. Heat Ctl., Ind. AC Ctl.

The Residence Inn Chesterfield is located in a beautifully wooded, quiet residential neighborhood. Travel just twenty minutes to see the famous St. Louis Arch and Busch Wildlife Center, while Babler State Park and a fabulous shopping mall are even closer. You will appreciate the special attentiveness of the staff. Discounted rates for extended stays.

──────────── KANSAS CITY ────────────

Embassy Suites Hotel
I-29 at Tiffany Springs Prkwy
Kansas City, MO 64190

Location: Airport; Downtown: 25 min.
Airport: 4 minutes
Area Attractions: 10 minutes to Worlds of Fun

237 Suites

Price Range & Credit Cards: 1 Bedroom Suite $$$, AmEx/MC/Visa/Other CC, Children Free, TAC 10%

Hotel Amenities: Laundry, Gift Shop, Parking, Car Hire, TV Lounge, Barber Shop, Handicap (5)

Business Facilities: Conf. Rm. Cap. 500, Banquet Fac., Copier, Aud/Vis., Teleconf., Telex, Comp. Hook-up, Bus. Ctr.

Recreational Facilities: Pool, Sauna, Whirlpool, Fitn. Ctr., Game Area

Restaurant/Bar: Park Place/Fountain Court, Entertainment

Comps: Full Breakfast, Refreshments, Hors d'oeuvres

Room Amenities: Room Service, Free Paper, TV, Phones in Rm. (2), Cable TV, VCR, Radio, Wet Bar, Kitchen, Ind. Heat Ctl., Ind. AC Ctl.

A full service atrium hotel with a luxuriously appointed interior, Embassy Suites Hotel features oversized two-room suites, exquisitely decorated. Indoor pool and complete health club facilites available. Be sure to enjoy complimentary breakfast, complimentary cocktails each evening, or the American style restaurant and high energy dance club.

──────────── KANSAS CITY ────────────

The Residence Inn by Marriott
2975 Main Street
Kansas City, MO 64108

96 Suites
816-561-3000 800-331-3131

Location: Union Hill; Downtown: 1.5 mi.
Airport: 20 miles
Near: Crown Center
Walking Distance To: Shops, Restaurants, Theatres
Area Attractions: Country Club Plaza 2 miles, Westport 1 mi.

Price Range & Credit Cards: 1 Bedroom Suite $$$, 2 Bedrooms $$$$, AmEx/MC/Visa/Other CC, Children Free, TAC 10%

Hotel Amenities: Laundry, Library, Parking, Gift Shop, TV Lounge, Pets Fee, Handicap (2)

Business Facilities: Conf. Rm. Cap. 35, Mess. Ctr., Copier, Aud/Vis.

Recreational Facilities: Pool, Whirlpool, Fitn. Ctr., Tennis, Outdoor Skating; all sports nearby

Comps: Continental Plus Breakfast, Refreshments, Hors d'oeuvres

Room Amenities: Free Paper, TV, Phone in Rm., Cable TV, VCR, Radio, Kitchen, Ind. Heat Ctl., Ind. AC Ctl.

The Residence Inn by Marriott/Union Hill is well-located to visit the shops, restaurants and theatres in Crown Center, or to explore Country Club Plaza. The hotel features Victorian design and decor in attractive shades of blue, spruce and rose. Discounted rates for extended stays.

─────────────────── ST. LOUIS ───────────────────

Embassy Suites Hotel
901 No. 1st St.
St. Louis, MO 63102

298 Suites
314-241-4200 800-922-2120

Location: Riverside; Downtown
Airport: 15 minutes
Near: Laclede's Landing, Convention Center
Walking Distance To: Riverfront, Convention Center
Area Attractions: Gateway Arch, Laclede's Landing

Price Range & Credit Cards: 1 Bedroom Suite $$$, AmEx/MC/Visa/Other CC, Children Free, TAC 10%

Hotel Amenities: Parking, Pets Allowed, Handicap (4)

Business Facilities: Conf. Rm. Cap. 6, Banquet Fac., Copier, Aud/Vis., Teleconf., Comp. Hook-up

Recreational Facilities: Pool, Sauna, Whirlpool, Fitn. Ctr., Golf, Game Area; Forest Park course

Restaurant/Bar: Joe B's, The Landings Lounge

Comps: Cook to order breakfast, Refreshments

Room Amenities: Room Service, Free Paper, TV, Phones in Rm. (2), Cable TV, Radio, Wet Bar, Ind. Heat Ctl., Ind. AC Ctl.

A perfect location in the heart of downtown St. Louis and so many special extras make Embassy Suites a wonderful place to stay. Complimentary breakfast and cocktails in the garden atrium, dancing in the lounge, and the opportunity for a good workout or a relaxing swim at the health club all contribute to your stay.

─────────────────── ST. LOUIS ───────────────────

Guesthouse Apartment Hotel
810 Dunn Road
St. Louis, MO 63042

40 Suites
314-895-1835

Location: I-270; Downtown: 30 min.
Airport: 10 minutes
Area Attractions: Within 5 minutes of all amenities

Price Range & Credit Cards: 1 Bedroom Suite $, 2 Bedrooms $, AmEx/MC/Visa/Other CC, Children Free, TAC 10%

Hotel Amenities: Laundry, Parking, Pets Deposit, Handicap (3)

Business Facilities: Conf. Rm. Cap. 10, Mess. Ctr., Copier, Comp. Hook-up

Recreational Facilities: ; Health Club privileges

Room Amenities: TV, Phones in Rm. (2), Cable TV, Radio, Kitchen, Ind. Heat Ctl., Ind. AC Ctl.

Conveniently located adjacent to West County corridor of the St. Louis metro area, the Guesthouse offers all the comforts of home at a budget price. New in 1988, all suites are decorator furnished and feature completely equipped kitchens with microwave. Whether staying for a day, week, or more, you'll agree that now there is "Someplace Like Home."

Geneva On The Lake, Geneva, NY

———————————— ST. LOUIS ————————————

The Residence Inn by Marriott
1881 Craigshire Rd.
St. Louis, MO 63146

128 Suites
314-469-0060   800-331-3131

Location: Suburbs; Downtown: 10 min.
Airport: 10 minutes
Near: Business, Shops
Walking Distance To: Westport Plaza
Area Attractions: The Westport Playhouse,
Funny Bone Comedy Club

Price Range & Credit Cards: 1 Bedroom Suite $$, 2 Bedrooms $$$, AmEx/MC/
Visa/Other CC, Children Free, TAC 10%

Hotel Amenities: Laundry, TV Lounge, Handicap (2)

Business Facilities: Conf. Rm. Cap. 20, Mess. Ctr., Copier, Aud/Vis.

Recreational Facilities: Pool, Whirlpool, Game Area; Health Club privileges

Comps: Continental Breakfast, Cocktails & Snacks, Airport Van

Room Amenities: Free Paper, TV, Phone in Rm., Cable TV, Radio, Kitchen, Ind. Heat
Ctl., Ind. AC Ctl.

*You'll feel right at home during your travels when you stay at the Residence Inn—But the
extras!—free grocery shopping by the courteous staff; complimentary breakfast and cocktail hour; and a cozy fireplace and kitchen in your suite. Enjoy the entertainment at the
Plaza nearby, or see comedy, a play, or a movie! Rates discounted for extended stays.*

———————————————— ST. LOUIS ————————————————

The Residence Inn by Marriott
1100 McMorrow
St. Louis, MO 63117

128 Suites
314-862-1900 800-331-3131

Location: Suburban; Downtown: 10 mi.
Airport: 9 miles
Near: Clayton, Business, Shops, Restaurants, Theatre
Walking Distance To: Galleria
Area Attractions: Forest Park, St. Louis Zoo, Muny Opera

Price Range & Credit Cards: 1 Bedroom Suite $$, 2 Bedrooms $$$, AmEx/MC/Visa/Other CC, Children Free, TAC 10%

Hotel Amenities: Laundry, Handicap (2)

Business Facilities: Conf. Rm. Cap. 15, Mess. Ctr., Copier, Aud/Vis., Teleconf.

Recreational Facilities: Pool, Sauna, Whirlpool, Sportscourt, Tennis, Volleyball, Basketball, Barbeque Area

Comps: Continental Breakfast, Beverages & Snacks, Airport Shuttle

Room Amenities: Free Paper, TV, Phones in Rm. (2), Fireplaces, Radio, Cable TV, Kitchen, Ind. Heat Ctl., Ind. AC Ctl.

Imagine a hotel environment with beautiful landscaping, garden and penthouse suites, and refreshing recreational activities. All these things make the Residence Inn very special. Complimentary breakfast and social hour are enjoyed amid pleasant surroundings. Transportation daily to airport and other nearby locations. Discounted rates for extended stays

 Nebraska

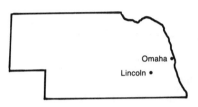

---------- OMAHA ----------

Embassy Suites Hotel
7270 Cedar St.
Omaha, NE 68124

190 Suites
402-397-5141 800-362-2779

Location: Central Omaha
Near: Ak-Sar-Ben Racetrack
Walking Distance To: 3 Restaurants
Area Attractions: Crossroads Shopping Center

Price Range & Credit Cards: 1 Bedroom Suite $$, AmEx/MC/Visa/Other CC, Children Free, TAC 10%

Hotel Amenities: Laundry, Handicap (1)

Business Facilities: Conf. Rm. Cap. 150, Banquet Fac., Copier, Aud/Vis., FAX, Comp. Hook-up

Recreational Facilities: Pool, Sauna, Whirlpool, Tennis, Golf, Game Area; Track nearby

Restaurant/Bar: New York Style Deli

Comps: Full Breakfast, Refreshments, Airport Shuttle

Room Amenities: Free Paper, TV, Phone in Rm., Cable TV, VCR, Radio, Wet Bar, Kitchen, Ind. Heat Ctl., Ind. AC Ctl.

Whether you're in Omaha for business or vacation, you'll find that Embassy Suites has everything you need. The spacious two-room suites, complimentary breakast, and 2-hr cocktails are all included in one affordable price. The lovely ambiance will please you too; glass elevators rise through the garden atrium, and suites are tastefully decorated.

---------------------------- OMAHA ----------------------------

The Residence Inn by Marriott
6990 Dodge St.
Omaha, NE 68132

80 Suites
402-553-8898 800-331-3131

Location: Suburban; Downtown: 5 miles
Airport: 10 miles
Near: 72nd. & Dodge St., Westroads Mall
Walking Distance To: Suburbs
Area Attractions: Westroads Shopping Center

Price Range & Credit Cards: 1 Bedroom Suite $$, 2 Bedrooms $$$, AmEx/MC/ Visa/Other CC, Children Free, TAC 10%

Hotel Amenities: Laundry, Library, Parking, TV Lounge, Pets Allowed, Handicap (1)

Business Facilities: Conf. Rm. Cap. 20, Mess. Ctr., Sec. Serv., Copier, Aud/Vis., Teleconf., Comp. Hook-up

Recreational Facilities: Pool, Whirlpool, Fitn. Ctr., Sportcourt, Game Area

Comps: Continental Plus Breakfast, Hors d'oeuvres

Room Amenities: Free Paper, TV, Phone in Rm., Cable TV, Radio, Kitchen, Ind. Heat Ctl., Ind. AC Ctl.

At the Residence Inn you can have guests share your suite at no extra charge. All suites have private entrances and parking at the door. The quiet atmosphere of the suburban setting, close to shopping, restaurants and entertainment, make the Inn perfect for business and leisure travel. Rates are discounted for extended stays.

---------------------------- OMAHA ----------------------------

The Residence Inn by Marriott
11025 "M" St.
Omaha, NE 68137

86 Suites
402-331-0101 800-331-3131

Location: Southwest; Downtown: 10 mi.
Airport: 10 miles
Near: Just off I-80 & 680 Interchange, Westroads Mall, AT & T Omaha Works
Walking Distance To: Restaurants, Shops
Area Attractions: Zoo, Dog Tracks, Boys Town, AK-SAR-BEN

Price Range & Credit Cards: 1 Bedroom Suite $$, 2 Bedrooms $$, AmEx/MC/Visa/ Other CC, Children Free, TAC 10%

Hotel Amenities: Laundry, Library, Parking, TV Lounge, Pets Allowed, Handicap (1)

Business Facilities: Mess. Ctr., Sec. Serv., Copier, Aud/Vis., Teleconf., Comp. Hook-up

Recreational Facilities: Pool, Whirlpool, Fitn. Ctr., Sportcourt, Game Area

Comps: Continental Plus Breakfast, Hors d'oeuvres

Room Amenities: Free Paper, TV, Phone in Rm., Cable TV, Radio, Kitchen, Ind. Heat Ctl., Ind. AC Ctl.

At the Residence Inn you can bring guests along to share your suite at no extra charge. After conferences in the extensive business facilities, you and your guests can take a walk around the courtyard to enjoy the flowers, play a game of racquetball nearby, or relax in front of the fireplace in the Gatehouse. Rates are discounted for extended stays.

 Nevada

Stateline

Las Vegas

LAS VEGAS

Alexis Park Resort Hotel
375 E. Harmon Ave.
Las Vegas, NV 89109

500 Suites
702-796-3300 800-223-0888

Location: Resort; Downtown: 1 mile
Airport: 2 minutes
Near: Golf Course, Shops, Bally's
Walking Distance To: Casinos, Dining, Entertainment
Area Attractions: The Las Vegas "Strip"'

Price Range & Credit Cards: 1 Bedroom Suite $$$, 2 Bedrooms $$$$+, AmEx/MC/ Visa/Other CC, Children Free

Hotel Amenities: Laundry, Parking, Car Hire, Handicap (20)

Business Facilities: Conf. Rm. Cap. 1000, Banquet Fac., Mess. Ctr., Copier, Aud/Vis., Teleconf., Telex

Recreational Facilities: Sauna, Whirlpool, Fitn. Ctr., Tennis, Weight room, 3 pools; 9 hole putting green

Restaurant/Bar: Pegasus Room, Cafinao Garden, Pisces Lounge, Entertainment

Comps: Limousine to: Airport/The Strip

Room Amenities: Room Service, TV, Phone in Rm., Cable TV, Wet Bar

500 luxurious suites surrounded by lush gardens, streams and waterfalls; 3 pools with heated spas, tennis courts, health club, putting green; 17,000 sq. feet of divisible meeting and convention space, and suites perfect for smaller gatherings. Complimentary limousine to and from airport and to Las Vegas Strip. Pegasus Room awarded Mobile 4 Star award!

──────────── LAS VEGAS ────────────

Best Western Mardi Gras Inn
3500 Paradise Rd.
Las Vegas, NV 89109

315 Suites
702-731-2020 800-634-6501

Location: Central; Downtown: 3 miles
Airport: 2 miles
Near: Las Vegas Strip Area, Shopping, Restaurants
Walking Distance To: "The Strip"', Convention Center
Area Attractions: Resort, Entertainment, Sports, Casinos

Price Range & Credit Cards: 1 Bedroom Suite $$, AmEx/MC/Visa/Other CC, Children Free, TAC 15%

Hotel Amenities: Laundry, Gift Shop, Parking, Car Hire, TV Lounge, Valet, Beauty Shop

Business Facilities: Conf. Rm. Cap. 200, Banquet Fac., Copier, Aud/Vis., Telex

Recreational Facilities: Pool, Spa, Tennis, Golf, Skiing, Mini-Casino, Video Games; Fishing nearby

Restaurant/Bar: Mardi Gras Restaurant and Lounge

Comps: Hors d'oeuvres-Happy Hour, Airport Shuttle

Room Amenities: Eurobath, TV, Phone in Rm., Cable TV, HBO, Radio, Wet Bar, Refrigerator, Ind. Heat Ctl., Ind. AC Ctl.

This hotel features Best Western's mini-suite concept. Each 415 square feet suite has a queen-sized bed, separate living room with queen hide-a-bed, wet bar/refrigerator. Resort atmosphere together with mini casino and its close proximity to shopping, sports, gambling, and entertainment makes this hotel a real guest-pleaser!

──────────── LAS VEGAS ────────────

Sheffield Inn
3970 Paradise Rd.
Las Vegas, NV 89109

171 Suites
702-796-9000 800-632-4040

Location: Central; Downtown: 3 mi.
Airport: 2 miles
Near: Las Vegas Strip Area, Shopping, Restaurants
Walking Distance To: "The Strip"
Area Attractions: Resort, Entertainment, Sports

Price Range & Credit Cards: 1 Bedroom Suite $$$, 2 Bedrooms $$$$, Junior $$, AmEx/MC/Visa/Other CC, Children Free, TAC 15%

Hotel Amenities: Laundry, Parking, Handicap (6)

Business Facilities: Conf. Rm. Cap. 200, Banquet Fac., Copier, Aud/Vis.

Recreational Facilities: Pool, Whirlpool, Tennis, Golf

Comps: Continental Breakfast, Refreshments

Room Amenities: TV, Phone in Rm., Cable TV, Radio, Wet Bar, Kitchen, Ind. Heat Ctl., Ind. AC Ctl.

At the Sheffield Inn you're just one mile from the "Strip" and three minutes from the L. V. Convention Center. Your suite will have a calming effect with its soft pinks and greens, light oak woods and your own private Jacuzzi. You can enjoy the pleasures of a heated pool or sauna, and golf and tennis are a few steps away.

⚜ New Hampshire

Waterville Valley

Merrimack ·

———————————— MERRIMACK ————————————

The Residence Inn by Marriott
246 Daniel Webster Highway
Merrimack, NH 03054

96 Suites
603-424-8100 800-331-3131

Location: Nashua: 4 miles
Airport: Manchester 15 min.
Area Attractions: Anheuser Busch Brewery, Pheasant Lane Mall, Ski Area

Price Range & Credit Cards: 1 Bedroom Suite $$, 2 Bedrooms $$$, AmEx/MC/ Visa/Other CC, Children Free, TAC 10%

Hotel Amenities: Laundry, Library, Parking, Car Hire, TV Lounge, Pets Allowed, Handicap (2)

Business Facilities: Conf. Rm. Cap. (2) 40 each, Banquet Fac., Mess. Ctr., Sec. Serv., Copier, Aud/Vis., Bus. Ctr.

Recreational Facilities: Pool, Whirlpool, Volleyball, Basketball, Game Area; Fitn.Center privileges

Comps: Lite meal, Tues. and Thur., Refreshments, Cont. Plus Breakfast

Room Amenities: Free Paper, TV, Phone in Rm., Cable TV, VCR, Radio, Wet Bar, Kitchen, Ind. Heat Ctl., Ind. AC Ctl.

The Residence Inn by Marriott, an all-suite hotel with homelike buildings, private entrances, trees and landscaped walkways, is located off Route 3 between Manchester and Nashua. Travellers enjoy complimentary breakfast buffet, grocery shopping service, fully equipped kitchens, separate living areas. Rates discounted for extended stays.

✿ New Jersey

Morris Plains
Secaucus • Parsippany
Piscataway •
Somerset • •
• Tinton Falls
Mt. Laurel
Pennsauken
Brigantine Beach
Somers Point • • Atlantic City

ATLANTIC CITY

The Admirals Quarters
655 Absecon Blvd.
Atlantic City, NJ 08401

70 Suites
609-344-2201 800-833-3242

Location: Central; Downtown: 10 min.
Airport: 15 minutes
Near: Marina Area, Casinos, Shops
Walking Distance To: Beaches
Area Attractions: Convention Center, Harrahs,
   Historic Smithville-15 miles

Price Range & Credit Cards: 1 Bedroom Suite $$$, 2 Bedrooms $$$$, Junior $$,
   AmEx/MC/Visa/Other CC, Children Free, TAC 10%

Hotel Amenities: Laundry, Parking, Pets Allowed

Business Facilities: Conf. Rm. Cap. 40, Mess. Ctr., Sec. Serv., Copier, Aud/Vis., Telex

Recreational Facilities: Pool, Golf, Beaches; Health Clubs

Comps: Continental Breakfast

Room Amenities: Free Paper, TV, Phone in Rm., Kitchen, Ind. Heat Ctl., Ind. AC Ctl.

The Admirals Quarters is located on the quiet and relaxed side of the island, but you can jump on the Atlantic City jitney and be at the casinos in minutes. Complimentary breakfast is served in the Captain's Galley and the newspaper is delivered to your suite each morning. The decor is high-tech and the service is warm and friendly.

──────────────── ATLANTIC CITY ────────────────

The Enclave Suite Resort
3851 Boardwalk Ave.
Atlantic City, NJ 08401

232 Suites
609-347-0400 800-362-5283

Location: Southside; Downtown
Near: Boardwalk, Ocean, Convention Center
Walking Distance To: Shopping Center
Area Attractions: Beaches, Casinos, Entertainment

Price Range & Credit Cards: 1 Bedroom Suite $$$$, 2 Bedrooms $$$$+, Junior $$$$, AmEx/MC/Visa/Other CC, Children Free, TAC 10%

Hotel Amenities: Laundry, Parking, TV Lounge

Business Facilities: Conf. Rm. Cap. 250, Banquet Fac., Mess. Ctr., Copier, Aud/Vis., Comp. Hook-up

Recreational Facilities: Pool, Sauna, Whirlpool, Fitn. Ctr.

Restaurant/Bar: Cafe Orleans

Room Amenities: TV, Phone in Rm., Cable TV, Radio, Kitchen, Ind. Heat Ctl., Ind. AC Ctl.

What could be more exciting than being right on the Boardwalk, near casinos, shopping, the convention center and—the beach! The decor is contemporary and luxurious; amenities and conveniences abound. Personal computer terminals are available and each suite offers a whirlpool, stereo/television, even a washer and dryer!

──────────────── PARSIPPANY ────────────────

Embassy Suites Hotel
909 Parsippany Road
Parsippany, NJ 07054

274 Suites
800-362-2779

Location: I-80 & I-287; Downtown: 1 mile
Airport: Newark-25 miles
Near: All North Morris County business locations
Area Attractions: Washington's Headquarters & Jockey Hollow-both 5 miles away

Price Range & Credit Cards: 1 Bedroom Suite $$$, AmEx/MC/Visa/Other CC, Children Free, TAC 10%

Hotel Amenities: Laundry, Gift Shop, TV Lounge, Handicap (6)

Business Facilities: Conf. Rm. Cap. 150, Banquet Fac., Copier, Aud/Vis., Telex

Recreational Facilities: Pool, Sauna, Whirlpool, Fitn. Ctr.; Pocono Mtns. Skiing near

Restaurant/Bar: Vivande Restaurant and Bar

Comps: Full Breakfast, Refreshments, Popcorn

Room Amenities: Room Service, TV, Phones in Rm. (2), Cable TV, Radio, Wet Bar, Kitchen, Ind. Heat Ctl., Ind. AC Ctl.

The Embassy is adjacent to a lake in suburban area with easy access to Interstate & convenient to Manhattan. We offer 274 one-bedroom suites and conference facilities for up to 150. Complimentary breakfast & evening cocktails are served daily in the landscaped atrium. Recreation facilities include indoor heated pool, whirlpool, sauna and exercise room.

—————————— PISCATAWAY ——————————

Embassy Suites Hotel
121 Centennial Ave.
Piscataway, NJ 08854

225 Suites
201-980-0500 800-362-2779

Location: Corp. Park; New Brunswick:6mi
Airport: Newark-25 miles
Near: Centennial Corporate Park, Rutgers-2 mi.
Area Attractions: Flemington Outlet Shopping-25 mi., New Jersey Beaches-45 mi.

Price Range & Credit Cards: 1 Bedroom Suite $$$$, AmEx/MC/Visa/Other CC, Children Free, TAC 10%

Hotel Amenities: Laundry, Gift Shop, Parking, Handicap (10)

Business Facilities: Conf. Rm. Cap. 12, Banquet Fac., Copier, Aud/Vis.

Recreational Facilities: Pool, Sauna, Whirlpool

Restaurant/Bar: Ellington's Food & Fun/Ellington's Piano Lounge, Quiet Piano Music

Comps: Full Breakfast, Refreshments, Popcorn

Room Amenities: Room Service, Free Paper, TV, Phones in Rm. (2), Microwave, Cable TV, Wet Bar, Refrigerator, Ind. Heat Ctl., Ind. AC Ctl.

All suites offer a living room with wet bar, microwave oven, refrigerator, full-size sofa bed, dining/conference table, sitting area, spacious bathroom, private bedroom, two telephones, and two televisions. Complimentary full cooked-to-order breakfast and two-hour cocktail party are offered daily in the attractively landscaped and lush atrium.

Eastgate Tower Hotel, New York, NY

──────────── SECAUCUS ────────────

Embassy Suites Hotel
455 Plaza Dr.
Secaucus, NJ 07094

261 Suites
201-864-7300 800-362-2779

Location: Central; N.Y.C.: 5 miles
Airport: 12 miles
Near: 30 Mall Shops, Movie Theatres
Walking Distance To: Shops, Restaurants
Area Attractions: Discount Outlet Shopping
Center

Price Range & Credit Cards: 1 Bedroom Suite $$$$, 2 Bedrooms $$$$+, Junior $$$,
AmEx/MC/Visa/Other CC, Children Free, TAC 10%

Hotel Amenities: Laundry, Parking, Car Hire, TV Lounge, Handicap (16)

Business Facilities: Conf. Rm. Cap. 100, Banquet Fac., Mess. Ctr., Copier, Aud/Vis.,
Teleconf.

Recreational Facilities: Pool, Sauna, Whirlpool, Game Area; Meadowland Racetrack

Restaurant/Bar: Caffe Sport, Entertainment

Comps: Full Breakfast, Refreshments, Airport Shuttle

Room Amenities: Room Service, Free Paper, TV, Phone in Rm., Cable TV, Radio, Wet
Bar, Kitchen, Ind. Heat Ctl., Ind. AC Ctl.

*When you stay at the Embassy Suites Hotel you're just 5 miles from midtown Manhattan
or the Javits Convention Center. Choose from four nearby airports. The Meadowlands
Racetrack and the Giants Stadium are a mere two miles away. Spacious suites and com-
plimentary, cooked-to-order breakfasts are among the amenities which make Embassy
a special hotel.*

──────────── SOMERSET ────────────

Madison Suites Hotel
25 Cedar Grove Lane
Somerset, NJ 08873

86 Suites
201-563-1000

Location: Hiway I-287; N. Brunswick:2 mi
Airport: Newark: 40 minutes
Near: Flemington Outlet Center-15 miles,
Bridgewater Commons-4 miles
Area Attractions: Rutgers Univ.-1.5 miles,
Meadowlands Arena-25 miles

Price Range & Credit Cards: 1 Bedroom Suite $$$, 2 Bedrooms $$$$, Junior $$,
AmEx/MC/Visa/Other CC, Children Free, TAC 10%

Hotel Amenities: Laundry, Handicap (2)

Business Facilities: Conf. Rm. Cap. 2-60, Banquet Fac., Mess. Ctr., Copier, Aud/Vis.,
Comp. Hook-up

Recreational Facilities: Pool, Sauna, Whirlpool, Fitn. Ctr., Tennis; all sports nearby

Restaurant/Bar: Madison Corte

Comps: Full or Cont. Plus Breakfasts, Refreshments, Hors d'oeuvres

Room Amenities: Room Service, Free Paper, TV, Phones in Rm. (2), Cable TV, VCR,
Radio, Wet Bar, Kitchen, Ind. Heat Ctl., Ind. AC Ctl.

*A natural combination of sophistication and easy convenience. Beautifully detailed, quietly
continental. Designed to care for the discerning traveler. The Deluxe Duplex Suites offer
a new perspective to room design. Accented with cantilevered bedrooms and skylights,
kitchenettes, and wet bars. Located in the heart of Central New Jersey corp. centers.*

---------------------------- TINTON FALLS ----------------------------

The Residence Inn by Marriott *Location:* Shore area; Eatontown: 2 mi.
90 Park Rd. *Airport:* La Guardia 55 mi., Newark 40 mi.
Tinton Falls, NJ 07724 *Near:* Exit 105 Garden State Parkway
  Area Attractions: Beach, Garden State Arts
96 Suites Center, Monmouth Park Race Track
201-389-8100 800-331-3131

Price Range & Credit Cards: 1 Bedroom Suite $$$, 2 Bedrooms $$$, AmEx/MC/
Visa/Other CC, Children Free, TAC 10%

Hotel Amenities: Laundry, Library, Parking, TV Lounge, Pets Allowed, Handicap (2)

Business Facilities: Conf. Rm. Cap. 40, Banquet Fac., Mess. Ctr., Copier, Aud/Vis.,
Comp. Hook-up, Bus. Ctr.

Recreational Facilities: Pool, Whirlpool, Sports Court, Game Area; Fitness Center
nearby

Comps: Continental Plus breakfast, Refreshments

Room Amenities: Room Service, Free Paper, TV, Phones in Rm. (2), Cable TV, VCR,
Radio, Wet Bar, Kitchen, Ind. Heat Ctl., Ind. AC Ctl.

*The hotel is conveniently located off exit 105 of the Garden State Parkway. With fully
equipped kitchens, living rooms—most with fireplaces—our suites are more home than
hotel. We offer complimentary continental breakfast, morning newspaper, and grocery
shopping service. Enjoy our outdoor pool and jacuzzi. Rates discounted for extended stay.*

New Mexico

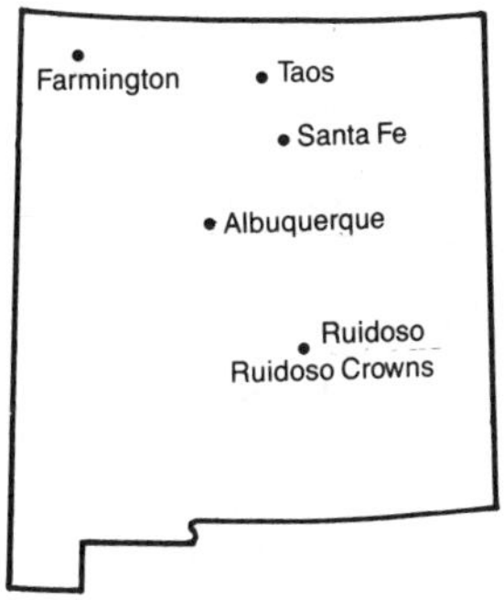

Farmington
Taos
Santa Fe
Albuquerque
Ruidoso
Ruidoso Crowns

ALBUQUERQUE

Amberley Suites Hotel
7620 Pan American Frwy. NE
Albuquerque, NM 87109

170 Suites
505-823-1300 800-227-7229

Location: Northeast
Near: Northeast Heights, Sandia Mountain
Walking Distance To: International Balloon Center
Area Attractions: Sandia Peak Tram & Ski Area

Price Range & Credit Cards: 1 Bedroom Suite $$, 2 Bedrooms $$$$, Junior $$, AmEx/MC/Visa/Other CC, Children Free, TAC 10%

Hotel Amenities: Laundry, Parking, TV Lounge, Pets Allowed, Handicap (2)

Business Facilities: Conf. Rm. Cap. 100, Banquet Fac., Mess. Ctr., Sec. Serv., Copier, Aud/Vis., Teleconf., Comp. Hook-up

Recreational Facilities: Pool, Sauna, Whirlpool, Fitn. Ctr., Tennis, Golf, Skiing, Hiking; Mountain climbing

Restaurant/Bar: Watson's Cafe

Comps: Hors d'oeuvres

Room Amenities: TV, Phone in Rm., Cable TV, Radio, Kitchen, Ind. Heat Ctl., Ind. AC Ctl.

Your suite at the Amberley is just 15 minutes from Sandia Peak where you can board the longest tram in North America. Enjoy the view of the mountain from your window or float serenely above the area in a balloon! Go for a hike, play a game of tennis or golf. Then relax in the lovely southwestern atmosphere of the Fireplace Lounge.

——————————————— ALBUQUERQUE ———————————————

Best Western Barcelona Court
900 Louisiana Ave. NE
Albuquerque, NM 87110

164 Suites
505-255-5556 800-222-1122

Location: Uptown
Airport: 6 miles
Near: New Mexico Fairgrounds, Skiing
Walking Distance To: Shopping
Area Attractions: Sandia Mountains

Price Range & Credit Cards: 1 Bedroom Suite $$, AmEx/MC/Visa/Other CC, Children Free, TAC 10%

Hotel Amenities: Parking, Handicap 2

Business Facilities: Conf. Rm. Cap. 150, Copier

Recreational Facilities: Pool, Sauna, Whirlpool, Tennis, Golf, Skiing

Comps: Full Breakfast, Refreshments, Popcorn

Room Amenities: Room Service, TV, Phone in Rm., Radio, Wet Bar, Ind. Heat Ctl., Ind. AC Ctl.

At the Barcelona Court each suite opens onto a garden gallery and, if you choose Plaza Rosa, yours will be decorated in a soft warm rose. Or you may choose from Plaza Verde, Blanca or Azul. The Fountain Court where you'll relax has a spectacular staircase flanked by two glass elevators. Plaza Blanca suites have a view of the lovely Sandia Mountains.

New York

BINGHAMTON

The Residence Inn by Marriott
4610 Vestal Parkway East
Binghamton, NY 13903

72 Suites
607-770-8500 800-331-3131

Location: Central; Downtown: 2 miles
Airport: 10 miles
Walking Distance To: State Univ. of New York
Area Attractions: Corning Glass Works, Greek Peak Ski Resort, Roberson Center

Price Range & Credit Cards: 1 Bedroom Suite $$$, 2 Bedrooms $$$, AmEx/MC/Visa/Other CC, Children Free, TAC 10%

Hotel Amenities: Laundry, Parking, Car Hire, TV Lounge, Pets Allowed, Handicap (4)

Business Facilities: Conf. Rm. Cap. 20, Catering, Mess. Ctr., Sec. Serv., Copier, Aud/Vis., Comp. Hook-up

Recreational Facilities: Pool, Whirlpool, Racquetball, Sportcourt, Skiing nearby, Fitn/Ctr. access, Game Area; Tennis, Golf privileges

Restaurant/Bar: Restaurant of the Week Club, Summer Barbeques

Comps: Continental Plus Breakfast, Hospitality Hour, Hors d'oeuvres

Room Amenities: Room Service, Free Paper, TV, Phone in Rm., Cable TV, VCR, Radio, Kitchen, Ind. Heat Ctl., Ind. AC Ctl.

At the Residence Inn you have the comforts of home. It features one bedroom and penthouse suites with fully equipped kitchen, living area with fireplace, generous closets. Complimentary amenities include European breakfast, hospitality hour, transportation and grocery shopping. All suites have private entrances. Rates discounted for extended stay.

––––––––––––––––––––– FISHKILL –––––––––––––––––––––

The Residence Inn by Marriott
Rt. 9 Interstate 84
Fishkill, NY 12524

104 Suites
914-896-5210 800-331-3131

Location: Wilderness; Downtown: 10 mi.
Airport: 20 minutes
Near: Suburban District, IBM 10 miles
Walking Distance To: Fine Restaurants
Area Attractions: U.S.Military Academy,
Wineries

Price Range & Credit Cards: 1 Bedroom Suite $$$, 2 Bedrooms $$$$, AmEx/MC/Visa/Other CC, Children Free, TAC 10%

Hotel Amenities: Laundry, TV Lounge, Handicap (5)

Business Facilities: Conf. Rm. Cap. 30, Mess. Ctr., Sec. Serv., Copier, Aud/Vis.

Recreational Facilities: Pool, Whirlpool, Fitn. Ctr., Bowling, Game Area; Golf and Skiing nearby

Comps: Continental Breakfast, Refreshments, Hors d'oeuvres

Room Amenities: Free Paper, TV, Phones in Rm. (2), Cable TV, VCR, Radio, Kitchen, Ind. Heat Ctl., Ind. AC Ctl.

The special attention at the Residence Inn will make you want to go back again and again—the staff is interested in making you feel at home. You'll find yourself centrally located for skiing, wine-tasting, dining in fine restaurants or vising Manhattan for all the exciting things one can do in the Big Apple. Discounted rates for extended stays.

––––––––––––––––––––– GENEVA –––––––––––––––––––––

Geneva on the Lake
1001 Lochland Rd. Rt. 14S
Geneva, NY 14456

29 Suites
315-789-7190 800-225-5536

Location: Resort; Downtown: 0.5 mi.
Airport: 10 miles
Near: Lake, Wineries, Corning Glass
Walking Distance To: Historic Area
Area Attractions: Rose Hill Mansion, Museum

Price Range & Credit Cards: 1 Bedroom Suite $$$$, 2 Bedrooms $$$$, Junior $$$, AmEx/MC/Visa, Children Free, TAC 10%

Hotel Amenities: Laundry, Library, Handicap (1)

Business Facilities: Conf. Rm. Cap. 35, Banquet Fac., Mess. Ctr., Sec. Serv., Copier, Aud/Vis.

Recreational Facilities: Pool, Game Area; Bristol Mt. Ski Center 29 mi.

Restaurant/Bar: Villa Lancellotti, Entertainment

Comps: Full Breakfast, Refreshments, Hors d'oeuvres

Room Amenities: Room Service, Free Paper, TV, Phone in Rm., Cable TV, Radio, Kitchen, Ind. Heat Ctl., Ind. AC Ctl.

When you first enter your suite at the Geneva you'll be greeted with a complimentary bottle of wine, fresh fruit and flowers! The New York Times will be delivered with your continental breakfast. You may choose from sailing, windsurfing, water skiing, canoeing, fishing and three kinds of lawn games, in this elegant Italian Renaissance Villa.

Shelburne Murray Hill, New York, NY

NEW YORK

Beekman Tower
3 Mitchell Place
New York, NY 10017

160 Suites
212-355-7300 800-637-8483

Location: Eastside; Downtown: 20 min.
Airport: 30 minutes
Near: Midtown, East River, Restaurants, Shopping
Walking Distance To: 42nd Street
Area Attractions: United Nations Plaza, Shops

Price Range & Credit Cards: 1 Bedroom Suite $$$$, 2 Bedrooms $$$$+, AmEx/MC/ Visa/Other CC, Children Free, TAC 10%

Hotel Amenities: Laundry, Car Hire

Business Facilities: Banquet Fac., Mess. Ctr., Copier, Telex

Restaurant/Bar: Mondial, Coq d'Or, Top of the Tower, Entertainment

Comps: Hors d'oeuvres

Room Amenities: Room Service, TV, Phone in Rm., Radio, Kitchen

Gracious service is the byword at Beekman Tower. This Art Deco masterpiece of marble floors, brass chandeliers and Persian rugs is home to world dignitaries. Walk to United Nations Plaza or to elegant shops, theatres and restaurants. Return to the Top of the Tower for cocktails and breathtaking views of the city. Many extras offered for business guests.

──────────────── NEW YORK ────────────────

Dumont Plaza Hotel
150 E. 34th St.
New York, NY 10016

251 Suites
212-481-7600 800-637-8483

Location: Eastside; Downtown: 15 min.
Airport: 30 minutes
Near: Empire State Building, Shopping, Convention Center
Walking Distance To: Fine Shops, Offices
Area Attractions: Heart of Midtown Manhattan

Price Range & Credit Cards: 1 Bedroom Suite $$$$, 2 Bedrooms $$$$+, Junior $$$$, AmEx/MC/Visa/Other CC, Children Free, TAC 10%

Hotel Amenities: Laundry, Car Hire

Business Facilities: Conf. Rm. Cap. 75, Mess. Ctr., Sec. Serv., Copier, Aud/Vis., Telex, Comp. Hook-up, Bus. Ctr.

Recreational Facilities: Sauna, Fitn. Ctr., Racquetball; Local Club facilities

Room Amenities: Free Paper, TV, Phone in Rm., Cable TV, Radio, Kitchen, Ind. Heat Ctl., Ind. AC Ctl.

The beautifully appointed suites and high level of personalized guest service, as well as spectacular views of the East River and Chrysler Building, combine to make your stay at the Dumont Plaza Hotel unforgettable. Relax after a busy New York day in beautiful, spacious living and working areas, or use the complete in-hotel exercise equipment.

──────────────── NEW YORK ────────────────

Eastgate Tower Hotel
222 E. 39th St.
New York, NY 10016

192 Suites
212-687-8000 800-637-8483

Location: Eastside; Downtown: 15 min.
Airport: 30 minutes
Near: Midtown, Empire State Building
Walking Distance To: East River, 42nd Street
Area Attractions: Mid-Manhattan Location

Price Range & Credit Cards: 1 Bedroom Suite $$$$, 2 Bedrooms $$$$+, Junior $$$$, AmEx/MC/Visa/Other CC, Children Free, TAC 10%

Hotel Amenities: Laundry, Garage, Car Hire

Business Facilities: Mess. Ctr., Copier, Telex

Recreational Facilities: Racquetball Club nearby

Restaurant/Bar: Marmalade Park

Room Amenities: Room Service, TV, Phone in Rm., Cable TV, Radio, Kitchen, Ind. Heat Ctl., Ind. AC Ctl.

You'll be greeted by elegance in the Eastgate's lobby, where intimate furniture groupings, amid gold leaf, marble and warm woods offer privacy and comfort. From your beautiful suite with its fully appointed kitchen and luxurious bath, you'll have a special view of the East River. Eastgate staff's first priority is warm and gracious personal service.

―――――――――――― NEW YORK ――――――――――――

Lyden Gardens Hotel
215 E. 64th St.
New York, NY 10021

133 Suites
212-355-1230 800-637-8483

Location: Upper East Side; Downtown: 30 min.
Airport: 30 minutes
Near: Residential Area, Galleries
Walking Distance To: Eastside Shops
Area Attractions: Theatre District, Fine Foods

Price Range & Credit Cards: 1 Bedroom Suite $$$$, 2 Bedrooms $$$$+, Junior $$$$, AmEx/MC/Visa/Other CC, Children Free, TAC 10%

Hotel Amenities: Laundry, Car Hire

Business Facilities: Mess. Ctr., Copier, Telex

Room Amenities: TV, Phone in Rm., Cable TV, Radio, Kitchen, Ind. Heat Ctl., Ind. AC Ctl.

The exterior is that of a stately townhouse, and sophistication is evident in the stunning lobby where chrome, glass, leather and marble accent the silver and black interior. The suites are classic with traditional elegance. Guests at Lyden Gardens feel truly at home. Personal attention from the staff is the key, right down to the smallest detail.

―――――――――――― NEW YORK ――――――――――――

Lyden House
320 E. 53rd St.
New York, NY 10022

81 Suites
212-888-6070 800-637-8483

Location: Midtown; Downtown: 20 min.
Airport: 30 minutes
Near: Celebrated Shops, Midtown
Walking Distance To: Central Park
Area Attractions: Bloomingdales, Galleries, Theatres

Price Range & Credit Cards: 1 Bedroom Suite $$$$, Junior $$$$, AmEx/MC/Visa/Other CC, Children Free, TAC 10%

Hotel Amenities: Laundry, Car Hire

Business Facilities: Mess. Ctr., Copier, Telex

Room Amenities: TV, Phone in Rm., Radio, Kitchen, Ind. Heat Ctl., Ind. AC Ctl.

A special tranquility is found in the charming, tree-lined neighborhood of Lyden House, where you're within walking distance of famous shops and restaurants. Amenities abound in each suite, with fully appointed kitchen and luxury bath. Comfort and understated elegance are all around you, including the highest standards of service.

---------------------------- NEW YORK ----------------------------

Plaza Fifty
155 E. 50th St.
New York, NY 10022

206 Suites
212-751-5710 800-637-8483

Location: Midtown; Downtown: 20 min.
Airport: 30 minutes
Near: Excellent Restaurants, Heart of The City, Fifth Avenue
Walking Distance To: Central Park
Area Attractions: Finest Stores, Museums, Theatres

Price Range & Credit Cards: 1 Bedroom Suite $$$$, 2 Bedrooms $$$$+, Junior $$$$, AmEx/MC/Visa/Other CC, Children Free, TAC 10%

Hotel Amenities: Laundry, Parking, Car Hire

Business Facilities: Mess. Ctr., Sec. Serv., Copier, Aud/Vis., Telex

Room Amenities: TV, Phone in Rm., Cable TV, Radio, Kitchen, Ind. Heat Ctl., Ind. AC Ctl.

In the most exciting part of the city, the Plaza Fifty's excellent service and sleek environment make it a special place to stay. The spacious suites with their lacquer furniture, writing desks, fully appointed kitchens and direct dial phones will charm you into believing you're really in a chic home. The staff is always eager to help you.

---------------------------- NEW YORK ----------------------------

Shelburne Murray Hill
303 Lexington Ave.
New York, NY 10016

251 Suites
212-689-5200 800-637-8483

Location: Midtown; Downtown: 15 min.
Airport: 30 minutes
Near: Murray Hill Section, Midtown
Walking Distance To: Empire State, Chrysler Bldg.
Area Attractions: Grand Central Station, Macy's Department Store

Price Range & Credit Cards: 1 Bedroom Suite $$$$, 2 Bedrooms $$$$+, Junior $$$$, AmEx/MC/Visa/Other CC, Children Free, TAC 10%

Hotel Amenities: Laundry, Parking, Car Hire

Business Facilities: Mess. Ctr., Copier, Aud/Vis., Telex

Restaurant/Bar: Billy Budd

Room Amenities: Room Service, TV, Phone in Rm., Kitchen, Ind. Heat Ctl., Ind. AC Ctl.

Set in the center of historic Murray Hill, the Shelburne is a charming hotel where the accent is on individual attention to each guest. The spacious elegance of beautifully furnished suites with all the amenities of home will make your stay relaxing and luxurious. Lovely classic wood furniture and tasteful upholstery add a touch of grace to your suite.

---------------------- NEW YORK ----------------------

Southgate Tower Hotel
371 7th Ave.
New York, NY 10001

525 Suites
212-563-1800 800-637-8483

Location: Midtown; Downtown: 15 min.
Airport: 45 minutes
Near: Penn Station, Convention Center
Walking Distance To: Business Areas
Area Attractions: Madison Square Garden, Theatres, Shopping

Price Range & Credit Cards: 1 Bedroom Suite $$$$, Junior $$$$, AmEx/MC/Visa/ Other CC, Children Free, TAC 10%

Hotel Amenities: Laundry, Concierge, Parking, Car Hire

Business Facilities: Conf. Rm. Cap. 300, Mess. Ctr., Sec. Serv., Copier, Aud/Vis., Telex

Restaurant/Bar: Penn Garden

Room Amenities: Room Service, TV, Phone in Rm., Radio, Kitchen, Ind. Heat Ctl., Ind. AC Ctl.

Crystal chandeliers, marble floors, and two lovely fountains are the elegant setting of the lobby in Southgate Tower. Throughout your stay you'll notice the extra-special service the staff is always ready to give. Ask them to arrange dinner or theatre, limousines and airline tickets. There's even a fitness center and a driving range for your enjoyment.

---------------------- NEW YORK ----------------------

Surrey Hotel
20 E. 76th St.
New York, NY 10021

115 Suites
212-288-3700 800-637-8483

Location: Upper East Side; Downtown: 30 min.
Airport: 30 minutes
Near: Art Galleries, Museums, Gourmet Dining
Walking Distance To: Central Park
Area Attractions: Madison Avenue Boutiques, Art

Price Range & Credit Cards: 1 Bedroom Suite $$$$+, 2 Bedrooms $$$$+, Junior $$$$, AmEx/MC/Visa/Other CC, Children Free, TAC 10%

Hotel Amenities: Laundry, Valet, Car Hire

Business Facilities: Conf. Rm. Cap. 75, Banquet Fac., Mess. Ctr., Copier, Aud/Vis., Telex

Restaurant/Bar: Les Pleiades

Room Amenities: Room Service, TV, Phone in Rm., Cable TV, Radio, Kitchen, Ind. AC Ctl.

The charm and grace of the lobby and suites of the Surrey make every visit a unique pleasure. You'll love the moulded ceilings, beveled mirrors and antique accents; they'll make you feel like a guest in a beautiful and gracious home. Each suite has so many extras— an executive-sized mahogany desk, a completely appointed kitchen, a luxury bath and more.

WILLIAMSVILLE

The Residence Inn by Marriott
100 Maple Rd.
Williamsville, NY 14221

112 Suites
716-632-6622 800-331-3131

Location: Suburban; Downtown: 15 min.
Airport: 9 miles
Near: All Major Shopping, Dining
Walking Distance To: Suburbs, University, Shopping
Area Attractions: Quiet Neighborhood Area

Price Range & Credit Cards: 1 Bedroom Suite $$, 2 Bedrooms $$$, AmEx/MC/ Visa/Other CC, Children Free, TAC 13%

Hotel Amenities: Laundry, Parking, Car Hire, TV Lounge, Pets Allowed, Handicap (6)

Business Facilities: Conf. Rm. Cap. 20, Mess. Ctr., Sec. Serv., Copier, Aud/Vis., FAX, Comp. Hook-up

Recreational Facilities: Pool, Whirlpool, Fitn. Ctr.; Skiing-20 mi., Game Area

Restaurant/Bar: Charlie Bubbles

Comps: Continental Breakfast, Cocktails & Snacks, Airport Shuttle

Room Amenities: Free Paper, TV, Comp. Local Calls, Cable TV, Radio, Kitchen, Ind. Heat Ctl., Ind. AC Ctl.

Whether you travel for business or pleasure, you will be relaxed and comfortable at The Residence Inn by Marriott, which offers one and two bedroom fully-equipped suites. Travellers are minutes from recreational activities such as golf, skiing, boating, a fitness center; theatres, shopping, and fine dining. Rates discounted for extended stays.

⚜ North Carolina

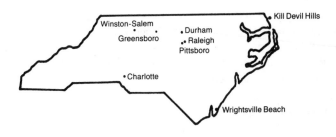

Winston-Salem
•
Greensboro
• Durham
.• Raleigh
Pittsboro
• Kill Devil Hills

• Charlotte

Wrightsville Beach

─────────────────── CHARLOTTE ───────────────────

Guest Quarters Suite Hotel
6300 Morrison Blvd.
Charlotte, NC 28211

208 Suites
704-364-2400 800-424-2900

Location: Southside; Downtown: 10 min.
Airport: 13 miles
Near: Southpark Mall, Specialty Shops
Walking Distance To: Southpark Mall
Area Attractions: Prestigious Business District

Price Range & Credit Cards: 1 Bedroom Suite $$$, 2 Bedrooms $$$$, AmEx/MC/ Visa/Other CC, TAC 10%

Hotel Amenities: Laundry, Library, Parking, Pets Allowed, Handicap (7)

Business Facilities: Conf. Rm. Cap. 200, Banquet Fac., Mess. Ctr., Copier, Aud/Vis., FAX

Recreational Facilities: Pool, Sauna, Whirlpool, Fitn. Ctr.; Racquetball, Golf and Tennis nearby

Restaurant/Bar: Arbour Cafe and Bar

Room Amenities: Room Service, Free Paper, TV, Phone in Rm., Cable TV, Radio, Kitchen, Ind. Heat Ctl., Ind. AC Ctl.

At Guest Quarters-Charlotte you will discover the real meaning of Southern Hospitality! Here is the perfect spot for business entertaining, with everything you need for your meeting, and fine banquet facilities for after-hours gatherings. A luxury hotel with full service.

─────────────────── DURHAM ───────────────────

Meredith Guest House
300 Meredith Drive
Durham, NC 27713

100 Suites
919-361-4663

Location: Central; Raleigh: 20 min.
Airport: 10 minutes
Near: Research Triangle Park, Minutes to Shop
Walking Distance To: Triangle Park
Area Attractions: Univ. of North Carolina,
Duke Univ.

Price Range & Credit Cards: 1 Bedroom Suite $$$, 2 Bedrooms $$$, AmEx/MC/ Visa/Other CC, TAC 10%

Hotel Amenities: Laundry, Parking

Business Facilities: Conf. Rm. Cap. 120, Banquet Fac., Mess. Ctr., Sec. Serv., Copier, Aud/Vis.

Recreational Facilities: Pool, Basketball, Football-3 Univ.; Golf

Restaurant/Bar: Garden Terrace, After The Hunt, Entertainment

Comps: Full Breakfast, Airport Van, Hors d'oeuvres

Room Amenities: Room Service, Free Paper, TV, Phone in Rm., Movies, Radio, Wet Bar, Kitchen, Ind. Heat Ctl., Ind. AC Ctl.

The Garden Terrace Restaurant at Meredith Guest House offers fine dining; choose from the international menu, enjoy the Queen Anne decor in mauve and rose and the Impressionist paintings on the walls. Or dine outside on the canopied terrace. Just 20 minutes from Durham and Raleigh, this area is noted for year-round golf courses nearby.

─────────────────── GREENSBORO ───────────────────

Embassy Suites Hotel
I-40 and Highway 68
Greensboro, NC 27410

214 Suites

Location: Airport
Airport: 3 miles

Price Range & Credit Cards: 1 Bedroom Suite $$$, AmEx/MC/Visa/Other CC, Children Free, TAC 10%

Hotel Amenities: Laundry, Gift Shop, Parking, Car Hire, TV Lounge, Barber Shop, Handicap (5)

Business Facilities: Conf. Rm. Cap. 500, Banquet Fac., Copier, Aud/Vis., Teleconf., Telex, Comp. Hook-up, Bus. Ctr.

Recreational Facilities: Pool, Sauna, Whirlpool, Fitn. Ctr., Game Area

Restaurant/Bar: Park Place/Fountain Court, Dance Club

Comps: Full Breakfast, Refreshments, Hors d'oeuvres

Room Amenities: Room Service, Free Paper, TV, Phones in Rm. (2), Cable TV, VCR, Radio, Wet Bar, Kitchen, Ind. Heat Ctl., Ind. AC Ctl.

This full service hotel has luxuriously appointed interior, oversized 2-room suites, exquisitely decorated. Indoor pool and complete health club; full meeting and conference facilities; an American style restaurant; and high energy dance club are just some of the features. Complimentary breakfast and manager's reception with free cocktails every evening.

Guest Quarters Suite Hotel, Charlotte, NC

---------------------------------- GREENSBORO ----------------------------------

Mayfair Suites Hotel
5929 W. Friendly Ave.
Greensboro, NC 27410

132 Suites
919-292-9821 800-637-4009

Location: Northwest; Downtown: 10 min.
Airport: 10 minutes
Near: Guilford College, Minutes To Shop, Restaurants
Area Attractions: Winston/Salem, Coliseum, Music

Price Range & Credit Cards: 1 Bedroom Suite $$$, 2 Bedrooms $$$, AmEx/MC/Visa/Other CC, Children Free, TAC 10%

Hotel Amenities: Laundry, Library, Parking, Car Hire, Pets Allowed

Business Facilities: Conf. Rm. Cap. 100, Banquet Fac., Sec. Serv., Copier, Aud/Vis., FAX

Recreational Facilities: Pool, Tennis, Golf; Health Club privileges

Comps: Continental Breakfast, Airport Shuttle, Restaurant Signing Privileges

Room Amenities: Coffee Maker, TV, Phone in Rm., Cable TV, Radio, Kitchen, Ind. Heat Ctl., Ind. AC Ctl.

Whether you travel to Greensboro for business or pleasure, you can suite yourself at Mayfair. Accompanied by friendly personal service, our attractively decorated suites offer fully-equipped kitchens, pleasant dining area, large walk-in closets and satellite TV with 24-hr movie channel. Begin each morning with a complimentary continental breakfast.

RALEIGH

Embassy Suites Hotel
4700 Creedmoor Road
Raleigh, NC 27612

225 Suites
919-881-0000 800-362-2779

Location: Crabtree Vly; Downtown: 5 miles
Airport: 12 miles
Near: N.C. Museum of Art-3 miles
Walking Distance To: Crabtree Valley Mall
Area Attractions: State Capital, Museums

Price Range & Credit Cards: 1 Bedroom Suite $$$, AmEx/MC/Visa/Other CC, Children Free, TAC 10%

Hotel Amenities: Gift Shop, Parking, Handicap (12)

Business Facilities: Conf. Rm. Cap. 200, Banquet Fac., Copier, Aud/Vis., Teleconf., Telex, Comp. Hook-up

Recreational Facilities: Pool, Sauna, Whirlpool, Fitn. Ctr., Sundeck; State Park-5 miles

Restaurant/Bar: Ferguson's

Comps: Full Breakfast, Airport Shuttle, Refreshments

Room Amenities: Room Service, Free Paper, TV, Phones in Rm. (2), Cable TV, Radio, Wet Bar, Microwave, Refrigerator, Ind. Heat Ctl., Ind. AC Ctl.

This all-suite hotel has 9 floors and 225 suites, two of which are Presidential Suites. Embassy provides both non-smoking and handicapped suites; meeting facilities for 200 people, & 2 boardrooms. Complimentary breakfast and evening beverages are served in the atrium. Located in Crabtree Valley, minutes away from Universities, shopping, and downtown.

WINSTON-SALEM

The Residence Inn by Marriott
7835 No. Point Rd.
Winston-Salem, NC 27106

88 Suites
919-727-1777 800-331-3131

Location: Northwest; Downtown: 4 miles
Airport: 20 minutes
Near: Suburban District, Reynolds Garden
Walking Distance To: Restaurants, Shops
Area Attractions: R.J. Reynolds Headquarters

Price Range & Credit Cards: 1 Bedroom Suite $$$, 2 Bedrooms $$$, AmEx/MC/Visa/Other CC, Children Free, TAC 10%

Hotel Amenities: Laundry, Library, Parking, Handicap (4)

Business Facilities: Conf. Rm. Cap. 20, Mess. Ctr., Copier

Recreational Facilities: Pool, Whirlpool, Fitn. Ctr., Sportcourt

Room Amenities: Free Paper, TV, Phone in Rm., Cable TV, Radio, Kitchen, Ind. Heat Ctl., Ind. AC Ctl.

You are sure to appreciate the homey comforts at this Residence Inn by Marriott. Recreational facilities are extensive-swimming pool, whirlpool, sportcourt and fitness center. Among the many nearby attractions are: R. J. Reynolds, Old Salem and Reynolds Gardens. Rates are discounted for extended stay.

⚜ Ohio

Toledo
Middleburg Heights
Westlake
• Akron

• Columbus

• Dayton
• Miamisburg

• Cincinnati
Blue Ash

AKRON

The Residence Inn by Marriott
120 Montrose West Ave.
Akron, OH 44321

88 Suites
216-666-4811 800-331-3131

Location: Copley; Downtown: 9 miles
Airport: Akron Canton-18 mi.
Near: Fine Shopping & Restaurants-15 min.,
Cleveland Hopkins Airport-28 miles
Area Attractions: Sea World & Geauga Lake-
20 miles, Richfield Coliseum-9 miles

Price Range & Credit Cards: 1 Bedroom Suite $$, 2 Bedrooms $$$, AmEx/MC/
Visa/Other CC, Children Free, TAC 10%

Hotel Amenities: Laundry, TV Lounge, Pets Allowed, Handicap (4)

Business Facilities: Conf. Rm. Cap. 25, Banquet Fac., Mess. Ctr., Copier

Recreational Facilities: Pool, Whirlpool; Skiing-30 min.; 12 Golf Courses-30 min.

Comps: Continental Plus Breakfast, Refreshments, Hors d'oeuvres

Room Amenities: Free Paper, TV, Phone in Rm., Cable TV, Radio, Kitchen, Ind. Heat
Ctl., Ind. AC Ctl.

*When you stay in a tastefully decorated one- or two-bedroom suite at The Residence Inn,
there is no charge for an extra guest. Each suite has a woodburning fireplace, livingroom
area, full kitchen, & barbecue area available. For relaxation, enjoy the outdoor pool, hot
tub, & sportcourt, or visit nearby shopping area. Discounted rates for extended stays.*

———————————— BLUE ASH ————————————

Embassy Suites Hotel-Blue Ash
4554 Lake Forest Drive
Blue Ash, OH 45202

240 Suites
800-362-2779

Location: Bus. Park; Cincinnati: 12 mi.
Airport: 28 miles
Near: Prudential Business Park
Area Attractions: Kings Island-14 miles

Price Range & Credit Cards: 1 Bedroom Suite $$$, Junior $$$, AmEx/MC/Visa/ Other CC, Children Free, TAC 15%

Hotel Amenities: Gift Shop, Parking, Car Hire, TV Lounge, Handicap (3)

Business Facilities: Conf. Rm. Cap. 300, Banquet Fac., Mess. Ctr., Sec. Serv., Copier, Aud/Vis., Telex, Comp. Hook-up, Bus. Ctr.

Recreational Facilities: Pool, Sauna, Whirlpool, Fitn. Ctr.; Golf; Jogging Trails nearby

Restaurant/Bar: Terraces/Encounters, Music & Dancing

Comps: Full Breakfast, Refreshments, Hors d'oeuvres

Room Amenities: Room Service, Free Paper, TV, Phones in Rm. (2), Cable TV, Wet Bar, Microwave, Refrigerator, Ind. Heat Ctl., Ind. AC Ctl.

The Embassy is located in Blue Ash, close to Kings Island; 240 suites surrounding a tropical atrium, featuring cascading waterfalls, streams and wandering paths. Terraces Restaurant serves unique Ohio cuisine. Encounter Bar features dancing nightly. The swimming pool, whirlpool, and exercise room are available 24 hours. Conference facilities available.

———————————— CINCINNATI ————————————

The Residence Inn by Marriott
11689 Chester Rd.
Cincinnati, OH 45246

144 Suites
513-771-2525 800-331-3131

Location: Northside; Downtown: 12 mi.
Airport: 28 miles
Near: Hub of Entertainment, Floating Restaurant
Walking Distance To: Suburbs, Restaurants
Area Attractions: Amusement Park, Kings Island

Price Range & Credit Cards: 1 Bedroom Suite $$, 2 Bedrooms $$$, AmEx/MC/ Visa/Other CC, Children Free, TAC 10%

Hotel Amenities: Laundry, Parking, TV Lounge, Pets Allowed, Handicap (5)

Business Facilities: Conf. Rm. Cap. 35, Banquet Fac., Mess. Ctr., Copier

Recreational Facilities: Pool, Whirlpool, Game Area; Racquet Club access

Comps: Continental Breakfast, Refreshments, Hors d'oeuvres

Room Amenities: Room Service, Free Paper, TV, Phone in Rm., Cable TV, Radio, Kitchen, Ind. Heat Ctl., Ind. AC Ctl.

Residence Inn offers comfortable, home-like accommodations for a single traveler or a whole family. Each suite is fully equipped with all the amenities of home; most suites even include a woodburning fireplace. Join other guests at the hotel pool and sportcourt, or enjoy direct access to nearby golf and Racquet Club. Rates discounted for extended stays.

—————————————— COLUMBUS ——————————————

Embassy Suites Hotel
2700 Corporate Exchange Drive
Columbus, OH 43229

217 Suites
614-890-8600   800-362-2779

Location: Northeast; Downtown: 15 min.
Airport: 20 minutes
Near: Linclay Corporate Park
Walking Distance To: Running Path

Price Range & Credit Cards: 1 Bedroom Suite $$$, AmEx/MC/Visa/Other CC, Children Free, TAC 10%

Hotel Amenities: Laundry, Parking

Business Facilities: Conf. Rm. Cap. 375, Banquet Fac., Copier, Aud/Vis.

Recreational Facilities: Pool, Sauna, Whirlpool, Fitn. Ctr.; Athletic Club

Restaurant/Bar: Delphines, Exchange Pub, Entertainment

Comps: Full Breakfast, Refreshments

Room Amenities: Room Service, Free Paper, TV, Phones in Rm. (2), Cable TV, Radio, Wet Bar, Kitchen, Ind. Heat Ctl., Ind. AC Ctl.

Upon arrival, you will be greeted with the elegance of waterways and bridges, live plants, and glass top tables done in a mauve and rose color scheme. For the athlete, the hotel provides an indoor/outdoor heated pool, outdoor jogging track, and nearby golf. In the evening, enjoy award-winning dining in Delphines Restaurant.

—————————————— COLUMBUS ——————————————

Pickett Suite Hotel
50 So. Front St.
Columbus, OH 43215

194 Suites
614-228-4600   800-742-5388

Location: Central; Downtown
Airport: 25 minutes
Near: Scioto River, Theatres, Restaurants, Ohio Statehouse
Walking Distance To: C.O.S.I.
Area Attractions: Entertainment, Museum, Ohio State Univ.

Price Range & Credit Cards: 1 Bedroom Suite $$$$, AmEx/MC/Visa/Other CC, Children Free, TAC 10%

Hotel Amenities: Laundry, Library, Parking, TV Lounge, Handicap (9)

Business Facilities: Conf. Rm. Cap. 125, Banquet Fac., Mess. Ctr., Sec. Serv., Copier, Aud/Vis., Comp. Hook-up

Recreational Facilities: Sauna, Whirlpool, Fitn. Ctr.; Health Club nearby

Restaurant/Bar: Caucus Room

Comps: Full Breakfast, Juices, Coffee/Tea, Hors d'oeuvres

Room Amenities: Room Service, Free Paper, TV, Phones in Rm. (2), Cable TV, Radio, Kitchen, Wet Bar, Hairdryer, Ind. Heat Ctl., Ind. AC Ctl.

Linked to the Ohio Statehouse and other downtown state offices by a network of underground walkways, Pickett conveniently accommodates the business traveler, with a variety of meeting rooms, well-stocked library, and an IBM PC. Start your day with complimentary breakfast, and unwind at day's end in the Caucus Room with complimentary hors d'oeuvres.

─────────────── COLUMBUS ───────────────

The Residence Inn by Marriott
6191 West Zumstein Drive.
Columbus, OH 43229

96 Suites
614-431-1819 800-331-3131

Location: Downtown: 20 min.
Airport: Port Columbus; 20 min.
Near: French Market, The Continent
Walking Distance To: Theaters, Restaurants
Area Attractions: Fairgrounds, Specialty Shops. O.S.U.

Price Range & Credit Cards: 1 Bedroom Suite $$, 2 Bedrooms $$$, AmEx / MC / Visa / Other CC, TAC 10 %

Hotel Amenities: Laundry, TV Lounge, Pets Allowed, Handicap (2)

Business Facilities: Mess. Ctr., Copier

Recreational Facilities: Pool, Whirlpool, Fitn. Ctr.; Athletic Club access

Comps: Continental Breakfast, Refreshments, Hors d'oeuvres

Room Amenities: Free Paper, TV, Phone in Rm., Cable TV, Radio, Kitchen, Fireplaces, Ind. Heat Ctl., Ind. AC Ctl.

Located next door to the famous French Market, the Residence Inn's lobby continues the theme with French decor. The comfortable Hearthroom lobby provides the perfect gathering place after spending the day exploring the 19th Century European village. Our expert staff ensure a pleasant stay in this homelike atmosphere. Rates discounted for extended stays.

─────────────── COLUMBUS ───────────────

The Residence Inn by Marriott
2084 S. Hamilton Rd.
Columbus, OH 43232

80 Suites
614-864-8844 800-331-3131

Location: Port Columbus; Downtown: 10 min.
Airport: 15 minutes
Near: Eastland Shopping Mall, Central Business
Walking Distance To: Theaters, Restaurants
Area Attractions: Fairgrounds, Specialty Shops

Price Range & Credit Cards: 1 Bedroom Suite $$$, 2 Bedrooms $$$, AmEx / MC / Visa / Other CC, Children Free, TAC 10 %

Hotel Amenities: Laundry, Library, TV Lounge, Pets Allowed, Handicap (1)

Business Facilities: Conf. Rm. Cap. 15, Mess. Ctr., Copier

Recreational Facilities: Pool, Whirlpool, Health Club, Miniature Golf; all sports nearby

Comps: Continental Breakfast, Refreshments, Hors d'oeuvres

Room Amenities: Free Paper, TV, Phone in Rm., Cable TV, Radio, Kitchen, Ind. Heat Ctl., Ind. AC Ctl.

The "home-away-from-home" environment of this hotel and the amenities provided in each suite makes it especially well-suited to the extended-stay traveler. The lobby, decorated in contemporary decor, has a fireplace and television for your enjoyment, or relax in the hotel's swimming pool and whirlpool. Rates discounted for extended stays.

---------------------- MIDDLEBURG HEIGHTS ----------------------

The Residence Inn by Marriott
17525 Rosbough Dr.
Middleburg Heights, OH 44130

104 Suites
216-234-6688 800-331-3131

Location: Airport/I-71; Downtown: 20 min.
Airport: 4 miles
Near: 3 Miles to Metropolitan Parks
Area Attractions: Great Northern Mall-10 miles

Price Range & Credit Cards: 1 Bedroom Suite $$, 2 Bedrooms $$$, AmEx/MC/ Visa/Other CC, Children Free, TAC 10%

Hotel Amenities: Laundry, Library, Car Hire, TV Lounge, Pets Allowed

Business Facilities: Conf. Rm. Cap. 15-20, Banquet Fac., Mess. Ctr., Copier

Recreational Facilities: Pool, Whirlpool, Sport Court, Tennis, Golf nearby

Comps: Continental Plus Breakfast, Refreshments, Hors d'oeuvres

Room Amenities: Free Paper, TV, Phone in Rm., Cable TV, Radio, Kitchen, Ind. Heat Ctl., Ind. AC Ctl.

The Residence Inn offers business and vacation travellers the comfortable feeling of home. The living room, separate bedroom and fully-equipped kitchen provide attractively decorated accommodations to conduct business or welcome friends. Outdoor exercise is available in pool or on the sports court. Discounted rates are offered for extended stays.

---------------------- WESTLAKE ----------------------

The Residence Inn by Marriott
30100 Clemans Road
Westlake, OH 44145

104 Suites
216-892-2254 800-331-3131

Location: I-90; Downtown: 20 min.
Airport: 10 miles
Walking Distance To: Running Track
Area Attractions: Great Northern Mall-8 miles, Lake Erie Beaches-5 miles

Price Range & Credit Cards: 1 Bedroom Suite $$, 2 Bedrooms $$$, AmEx/MC/ Visa/Other CC, Children Free, TAC 10%

Hotel Amenities: Laundry, Library, TV Lounge, Pets Allowed

Business Facilities: Conf. Rm. Cap. 15-20, Banquet Fac., Mess. Ctr., Copier, Telex

Recreational Facilities: Pool, Whirlpool, Sport Court, Tennis, Volleyball, Basketball; Many Local Golf Courses

Comps: Continental Plus Breakfast, Refreshments, Hors d'oeuvres

Room Amenities: Free Paper, TV, Phone in Rm., Cable TV, Kitchen, Ind. Heat Ctl., Ind. AC Ctl.

The Residence Inn/Cleveland West has the look and feel of home with its comfortably furnished living room with fireplace and well-equipped kitchen and bath. Right outside you can relax in the pool and heated spa. Daily complimentary breakfast and hospitality hour (Mon.-Thur.) are offered in the gatehouse. Discounted rates for extended stays.

⚜ Oklahoma

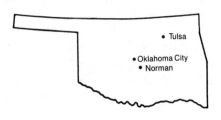

--------------------- OKLAHOMA CITY ---------------------

Governors Inn of Oklahoma City
2308 S. Meridian
Oklahoma City, OK 73108

50 Suites
405-682-5299 800-443-9350

Location: Downtown: 7 min.
Airport: 5 minutes
Near: Reno-Meridian Area, Hotels, Restaurants
Area Attractions: Cowboy Hall of Fame, Museums

Price Range & Credit Cards: 1 Bedroom Suite $$, 2 Bedrooms $$, AmEx/MC/Visa/ Other CC, Children Free, TAC 10%

Hotel Amenities: Handicap (2)

Business Facilities: Conf. Rm. Cap. 42, Banquet Fac.

Recreational Facilities: Pool, Sauna, Whirlpool

Restaurant/Bar: Silvers, Entertainment

Comps: Full Breakfast, Hors d'oeuvres

Room Amenities: Room Service, Free Paper, TV, Phone in Rm., Cable TV, Ind. Heat Ctl., Ind. AC Ctl.

Governors Inn provides a pleasing combination of the personal attention found in small hotels and the larger hotel's VIP services. This suite hotel is decorated throughout in elegant English decor—from the central Atrium filled with plants and iron patio furniture, to comfortable stuffed couches, a marble-topped wet bar, and country style bed.

OKLAHOMA CITY

Park Suite Hotel
1815 S. Meridian
Oklahoma City, OK 73108

236 Suites
405-682-6000 800-654-7000

Location: Southwest; Downtown: 1 mi.
Airport: 2 miles
Near: Will Rogers Airport, Airport Prop.
Area Attractions: Myriad Gardens, White Water

Price Range & Credit Cards: 1 Bedroom Suite $$$, 2 Bedrooms $$$$, AmEx/MC/Visa/Other CC, Children Free, TAC 10%

Hotel Amenities: Laundry, Parking, Car Hire, TV Lounge, Pets Allowed, Handicap (8)

Business Facilities: Conf. Rm. Cap. 700, Banquet Fac., Copier, Teleconf., Comp. Hook-up

Recreational Facilities: Pool, Sauna, Whirlpool, Fitn. Ctr.

Restaurant/Bar: The Atrium, Burgandy's, The Looking Glass Club

Comps: Full Breakfast, Hors d'oeuvres

Room Amenities: Room Service, Free Paper, TV, Phones in Rm. (2), Cable TV, Radio, Wet Bar, Ind. Heat Ctl., Ind. AC Ctl.

The Park Suite offers many of the amenities of a world class hotel—including full-concierge service—at affordable rates. Suites are decorated in either French Provincial or Honey-Oak wood decor to suit your mood. Also, enjoy casual dining in the lovely Atrium Courtyard filled with exotic plants and trees and after hours entertainment.

Embassy Suites Hotel, Raleigh, NC

---------------------------- TULSA ----------------------------

Embassy Suites Hotel
3332 S. 79th East Ave.
Tulsa, OK 74145

248 Suites
918-622-4000 800-362-2779

Location: Airport; Downtown: 10 min.
Airport: 10 minutes
Near: Big Splash Water Park/Expo Square, Philbrook Art Museum, Tulsa Garden Ctr.
Area Attractions: Gilcrease Museum-10 miles, Mayfest & October Fest-10 miles

Price Range & Credit Cards: 1 Bedroom Suite $$, 2 Bedrooms $$$, AmEx/MC/Visa/Other CC, Children Free, TAC 10%

Hotel Amenities: Laundry, Gift Shop, Parking, Car Hire, Pets Allowed, Handicap (4)

Business Facilities: Conf. Rm. Cap. 300, Banquet Fac., Mess. Ctr., Sec. Serv., Copier, Aud/Vis., Comp. Hook-up

Recreational Facilities: Pool, Sauna, Whirlpool, Fitn. Ctr., Steamroom, Jogging; Tennis & Golf nearby

Restaurant/Bar: Cattleman's Steakhouse & Chocolate Factory/Harveys, Entertainment

Comps: Full Breakfast, Airport Limousine, Refreshments

Room Amenities: Room Service, Free Paper, TV, Phones in Rm. (2), Cable TV, Radio, Wet Bar, Ind. Heat Ctl., Ind. AC Ctl.

Embassy Suites Hotel is centrally located in Tulsa, convenient to Tulsa International airport, downtown, and all suburban business districts. Tulsa's newest and only full-service suite hotel is situated near all major expressways and within 3 miles of 4 shopping malls. Embassy's restaurant, Cattleman's, was named "Best Steakhouse in Tulsa."

---------------------------- TULSA ----------------------------

Lexington Hotel Suites
8525 East 41st St.
Tulsa, OK 74145

162 Suites
918-627-0030 800-527-1877

Location: Central; Downtown: 9 miles
Airport: 10 miles
Near: Suburbs, Raceway, Malls
Walking Distance To: University
Area Attractions: Fairgrounds

Price Range & Credit Cards: 1 Bedroom Suite $, 2 Bedrooms $$, Junior $, AmEx/MC/Visa/Other CC, Children Free, TAC 15%

Hotel Amenities: Laundry, Pets Allowed, Handicap (4)

Business Facilities: Conf. Rm. Cap. 80, Aud/Vis.

Recreational Facilities: Pool, Tennis, Golf 5 mi.; Water Skiing 30 miles

Comps: Continental Breakfast

Room Amenities: TV, Phone in Rm., Radio, Kitchen, Ind. Heat Ctl., Ind. AC Ctl.

Centrally located, and accessible to major expressways, restaurants, clubs, tourist attractions, and less than ten minutes from downtown Tulsa, Lexington is the perfect choice for business, leisure, or relocation. Decorated in traditional decor, the variety of suite sizes and meeting facilities is tailored to your needs.

 # Oregon

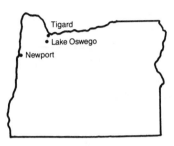

LAKE OSWEGO

The Residence Inn by Marriott
15200 S.W. Bangy Rd.
Lake Oswego, OR 97035

112 Suites
503-684-2603 800-331-3131

Location: Southwest; Downtown: 8 miles
Airport: 20 miles
Near: Suburbs, Wineries 5 miles
Area Attractions: Washington Square Shopping Center

Price Range & Credit Cards: 1 Bedroom Suite $$, 2 Bedrooms $$$, AmEx/MC/ Visa/Other CC, Children Free, TAC 10%

Hotel Amenities: Laundry, Library, Parking, Car Hire, TV Lounge, Pets Allowed, Handicap (5)

Business Facilities: Conf. Rm. Cap. 30, Copier

Recreational Facilities: Pool, Whirlpool, Golf 4 mi., Game Area; year-round Skiing: 1 hr

Comps: Continental Breakfast, Refreshments, Hors d'oeuvres

Room Amenities: Free Paper, TV, Phone in Rm., Cable TV, Radio, Kitchen, Ind. Heat Ctl., Ind. AC Ctl.

The Tudor-style exteriors of the buildings and nicely landscaped grounds create a townhouse feeling. The lobby has contemporary country decor accented by a vaulted ceiling, cathedral windows, and a double-sided fireplace. Or, enjoy popcorn provided in your "first nighter kit" before a fire in your suite. Rates discounted for extended stay.

—————————————— TIGARD ——————————————

Embassy Suites Hotel
9000 S.W. Washington Square
Tigard, OR 97223

253 Suites
503-644-4000 800-362-2779

Location: Westside; Downtown: 8 miles
Airport: 20 miles
Near: Regional Shopping Center, Wine Country
Walking Distance To: Shopping Mall
Area Attractions: Sunset Corridor (Electronics)

Price Range & Credit Cards: 1 Bedroom Suite $$, AmEx/MC/Visa/Other CC, Children Free, TAC 10%

Hotel Amenities: Handicap (13)

Business Facilities: Conf. Rm. Cap. 300, Banquet Fac., Copier, Aud/Vis., FAX

Recreational Facilities: Pool, Sauna, Whirlpool, Fitn. Ctr., Tennis, Golf, Racquetball

Restaurant/Bar: Crossroads, Entertainment

Comps: Full Breakfast, Refreshments, Hors d'oeuvres

Room Amenities: Room Service, TV, Phones in Rm. (2), Cable TV, Radio, Wet Bar, Ind. Heat Ctl., Ind. AC Ctl.

Located in Portland's Westside, Embassy Suites is adjacent to Washington Square Shopping Center, only 5 miles from Oregon wineries. Elegant teal and mauve color schemes and mahogony woods with brass accents are carried throughout the hotel. Join other guests in the Atrium for complimentary breakfast and the evening cocktail party.

⚜ Pennsylvania

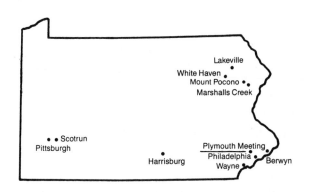

─────────────────── HARRISBURG ───────────────────

The Residence Inn by Marriott
4480 Lewis Road
Harrisburg, PA 17111

80 Suites
717-561-1900 800-331-3131

Location: I-83; Downtown: 8 miles
Airport: Harrisburg 8 miles
Near: Penn National Race Track 15 miles, Mall
& Theatres 2 miles
Area Attractions: Hershey Park, State Capitol,
City Island Park

Price Range & Credit Cards: 1 Bedroom Suite $$, 2 Bedrooms $$$, AmEx/MC/
Visa/Other CC, Children Free, TAC 10%

Hotel Amenities: Laundry, Library, TV Lounge, Pets Allowed, Handicap (2)

Business Facilities: Conf. Rm. Cap. 24, Sec. Serv., Copier, FAX, Comp. Hook-up

Recreational Facilities: Pool, Whirlpool, Badminton, Volleyball, Basketball; Golf and
Tennis nearby

Restaurant/Bar: Barbeque area

Comps: Continental Plus Breakfast, Refreshments, Hors d'oeuvres

Room Amenities: Free Paper, TV, Phone in Rm., Cable TV, VCR, Radio, Kitchen, Ind.
Heat Ctl., Ind. AC Ctl.

*The Inn provides one-and-two bedroom suites, tastefully furnished with everything needed
for business, entertainment and relaxation, including fully equipped kitchen and often a
fireplace. Within a short drive are the State Capitol, Penn Museum, Hershey Park, Zoo,
Amish Country, Gettysburg, and Reading's outlet shopping. Rate discount for extended
stay.*

──────────────── PHILADELPHIA ────────────────

Guest Quarters Suites Hotel
1 Gateway Center
Philadelphia, PA 19153

250 Suites
215-365-6600 800-424-2900

Location: Downtown: 8 miles
Airport: 2 miles
Near: Airport Area, Sports Complex
Walking Distance To: Scott Paper Center
Area Attractions: Historic Center City, Veterans Stadium

Price Range & Credit Cards: 1 Bedroom Suite $$$$, 2 Bedrooms $$$$+, AmEx/MC/Visa/Other CC, Children Free, TAC 10%

Hotel Amenities: Laundry, Parking, Handicap (7)

Business Facilities: Conf. Rm. Cap. 200, Banquet Fac., Copier, Aud/Vis., Comp. Hookup, Bus. Ctr.

Recreational Facilities: Pool, Sauna, Whirlpool

Restaurant/Bar: Cafe, Lounge, Entertainment

Comps: Full Breakfast, Refreshments

Room Amenities: Free Paper, TV, Phones in Rm. (3), Cable TV, Radio, Wet Bar, Ind. Heat Ctl., Ind. AC Ctl.

Guest Quarters is conveniently located minutes from the airport, the Philadelphia Sports Complexes, and the excitement of Center City. In your suite, you'll find all the amenities of home, with the privileges to the hotel's swimming pool.

──────────────── PITTSBURGH ────────────────

The Bigelow
1 Bigelow Square
Pittsburgh, PA 15219

450 Suites
412-281-5800 800-225-5858

Location: Central; Downtown
Airport: 40 minutes
Near: Golden Triangle, Heart of Town
Walking Distance To: Convention Center
Area Attractions: Art Festival, Regatta, Stadium

Price Range & Credit Cards: 1 Bedroom Suite $$$, 2 Bedrooms $$$$, Junior $$, AmEx/MC/Visa/Other CC, Children Free, TAC 10%

Hotel Amenities: Laundry, Parking

Business Facilities: Conf. Rm. Cap. 100, Banquet Fac., Copier, Aud/Vis.

Recreational Facilities: Pool, Sauna, Whirlpool, Fitn. Ctr., Golf, Skiing, Football, Baseball

Restaurant/Bar: The Ruddy Duck

Comps: Full Breakfast, Hors d'oeuvres

Room Amenities: Room Service, TV, Phone in Rm., Cable TV, Radio, Kitchen

Only three blocks from most of Pittsburgh's major businesses and easily accessible to downtown locations via the Pittsburgh Subway system just across the street, the Bigelow is very convenient. During your stay, be certain to visit the hotel's own famed Ruddy Duck restaurant and lounge. The ambiance is that of a private club.

———————————— WAYNE ————————————

Guest Quarters Suite Hotel
888 Chesterbrook Blvd.
Wayne, PA 19087

230 Suites
215-647-6700 800-424-2900

Location: Chesterbrook; Philadephia: 12mi
Airport: 20 miles
Near: Valley Forge National Park-3 miles
Area Attractions: Veterans Stadium/Spectrum-12 miles

Price Range & Credit Cards: 1 Bedroom Suite $$$$, AmEx/MC/Visa/Other CC, Children Free, TAC 10%

Hotel Amenities: Laundry, Gift Shop, Car Hire, Handicap (4)

Business Facilities: Conf. Rm. Cap. 125, Banquet Fac., Mess. Ctr., Sec. Serv., Copier, Aud/Vis., Comp. Hook-up

Recreational Facilities: Pool, Sauna, Whirlpool, Fitn. Ctr., Game Area; Jogging Trail nearby

Restaurant/Bar: The Grille At Chesterbrook/Atrium & Terrace Lounge, Piano Entertainment

Comps: Full Breakfast, Hors d'oervres

Room Amenities: Room Service, TV, Phones in Rm. (3), Cable TV, Radio, Wet Bar, Ind. Heat Ctl., Ind. AC Ctl.

The Guest Quarters-Valley Forge is set amid the natural wooded landscapes of the Chesterbrook Corp. Center. Lush greenery abounds in the atriums. Enjoy the award-winning cuisine at the Grille At Chesterbrook. Guest Quarters invites you to come and experience unparalleled Guest treatment. There are Guest Hotels at Philadelphia Airport & Plymouth Meeting.

❧ Rhode Island

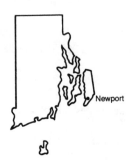

Newport

NEWPORT

Inn on Long Wharf
142 Long Wharf
Newport, RI 02840

40 Suites
401-847-7800 800-343-3413

Location: Wharfside; Downtown
Airport: 40 minutes
Near: Newport Harbor, Shops, Beaches
Walking Distance To: Quaint Shops
Area Attractions: Mansion Tours, Boating

Price Range & Credit Cards: 1 Bedroom Suite $$$, AmEx/MC/Visa/Other CC, Children Free, TAC 10%

Hotel Amenities: Laundry, Parking, TV Lounge, Handicap (3)

Business Facilities: Conf. Rm. Cap. 35, Mess. Ctr., Sec. Serv., Copier, Aud/Vis.

Recreational Facilities: Whirlpool, Fitn. Ctr., Tennis, Golf, Boating, Sailing; YMCA Services nearby

Restaurant/Bar: Spinnakers

Room Amenities: Free Paper, TV, Phone in Rm., Radio, Wet Bar, Kitchenette, Ind. Heat Ctl., Ind. AC Ctl.

Situated on Newport Harbor, this all-suite hotel offers a private enclave surrounded by intimate shops. Make this your home while you take advantage of all the nearby recreational facilities, including golf, tennis, sailing. Enjoy cocktails in Spinnakers while watching the sunset over Narragansett Bay.

———————————————— NEWPORT ————————————————

Mill Street Inn
75 Mill Street
Newport, RI 02840

23 Suites
401-849-9500

Location: Central; Downtown
Airport: 40 minutes
Near: Newport Harbor, Historic Hill Buildings
Walking Distance To: Antiques, Shops
Area Attractions: International Tennis Hall
of Fame

Price Range & Credit Cards: 1 Bedroom Suite $$$$, AmEx/MC/Visa/Other CC, Children Free, TAC 10%

Hotel Amenities: Laundry, Parking, Handicap (1)

Business Facilities: Conf. Rm. Cap. 50, Copier, Aud/Vis.

Recreational Facilities: Tennis, Golf, Fishing, Sailing; Surfing

Comps: Continental Plus Breakfast

Room Amenities: Free Paper, TV, Phone in Rm., Radio, Wet Bar, Ind. Heat Ctl.

The Inn has an excellent in-town location, one and a half blocks from harbor shops, restaurants and points of interest. An AIA design award winner for 1987, the hotel is an innovative synthesis of old and new. Dramatic contemporary interiors blend with original brick and beams. Townhouse suites offer a spectacular view of the bay from private decks.

⚜ South Carolina

CHARLESTON

Ansonborough Inn
21 Hasell St.
Charleston, SC 29401

38 Suites
803-723-1655 800-522-2073

Location: Ansonborough; Historic District
Airport: 25 minutes
Walking Distance To: Best Shopping and Restaurants
Area Attractions: Two blocks from famous market area

Price Range & Credit Cards: 1 Bedroom Suite $$$, AmEx/MC/Visa, Children Free, TAC 10%

Hotel Amenities: Pets Allowed

Business Facilities: Mess. Ctr.

Recreational Facilities: Historic tours; Golf and Tennis nearby

Comps: Continental Breakfast, Refreshments, Hors d'oeuvres

Room Amenities: Room Service, Free Paper, TV, Phone in Rm., Cable TV, VCR, Radio, Kitchen, Ind. Heat Ctl., Ind. AC Ctl.

Located conveniently in Charleston's renowned Historic District, our inn is a converted 1900 warehouse featuring massive exposed beams and original brickwork throughout. Classic pine reproductions, colorful chintz fabrics and local art complete the interior decor. Afternoon wine and free film library complement your visit. Walk to many attractions.

──────────────────── COLUMBIA ────────────────────

Best Western Bradbury Suites   ***Near:*** Interstate
7525 Two Notch Road
Columbia, SC 29223

116 Suites
803-736-6666 800-528-1234

Price Range & Credit Cards: 1 Bedroom Suite $$, AmEx/MC/Visa/Other CC, Children Free, TAC 12%

Hotel Amenities: Handicap (6)

Business Facilities: Conf. Rm. Cap. 35, Copier, Aud/Vis.

Recreational Facilities: Pool, Whirlpool

Comps: Continental Breakfast, Refreshments

Room Amenities: Free Paper, TV, Phone in Rm., Radio, Ind. Heat Ctl., Ind. AC Ctl.

Reserve one of the exciting theme suites when you stay at Bradbury Suites. In the morning, join other guests in the lobby and cafe area for breakfast, compliments of the hotel, and in the evening, return here for the nightly cocktail party. Be sure to take advantage of the hotel's own outdoor pool and whirlpool during your stay.

──────────────────── COLUMBIA ────────────────────

Embassy Suites Hotel   ***Location:*** St. Andrews; Downtown: 8 miles
200 Stoneridge Drive   ***Airport:*** 10 minutes
Columbia, SC 29210   ***Near:*** Shopping Mall-3 miles
                               Walking Distance To: Zoo
214 Suites   ***Area Attractions:*** Lake Murray-10 miles
803-252-8700 800-362-2779

Price Range & Credit Cards: 1 Bedroom Suite $$, AmEx/MC/Visa/Other CC, Children Free, TAC 10%

Hotel Amenities: Laundry, Gift Shop, Parking, Handicap (12)

Business Facilities: Conf. Rm. Cap. 1095, Banquet Fac., Mess. Ctr., Copier, Aud/Vis., Telex, Comp. Hook-up

Recreational Facilities: Pool, Sauna, Whirlpool, Fitn. Ctr., Billards Room, Game Area

Restaurant/Bar: Park Place/Fountain Court-Nite Lites

Comps: Full Breakfast, Refreshments, Hors d'oeuvres

Room Amenities: Room Service, Free Paper, TV, Cable TV, Radio, Wet Bar, Kitchen, Ind. Heat Ctl., Ind. AC Ctl.

The Embassy Suites Hotel has two-room suites competitively priced and includes full breakfast and hosted Manager's reception. The Hotel has an interior atrium with live plants, beautiful fountains; 13,000 sq. ft. of meeting space; restaurant, piano lounge, dance club; indoor pool, whirlpool, sauna, & sun decks. Group rates and weekend package rates.

Pickett Suite Hotel, Columbus, OH

HILTON HEAD ISLAND

Hilton Head Island Resort
40 Folly Field Rd.
Hilton Head Island, SC 29928

300 Suites
803-842-4402 800-845-9508

Location: Northend; Savannah: 40 mi.
Airport: 40 miles
Near: 42 Acre Complex, Resort Area
Walking Distance To: Shops, Restaurants
Area Attractions: Major Tennis Tournaments, Historic Plantations

Price Range & Credit Cards: 1 Bedroom Suite $$, 2 Bedrooms $$$$, AmEx/MC/Visa, Children Free, TAC 15%

Hotel Amenities: Laundry, Parking, TV Lounge

Business Facilities: Conf. Rm. Cap. 950, Banquet Fac., Sec. Serv., Copier, Aud/Vis.

Recreational Facilities: Pool, Tennis; 13 Golf Courses nearby

Restaurant/Bar: Napa Valley Cafe & Bar, Entertainment

Comps: Hors d'oeuvres

Room Amenities: TV, Phone in Rm., Wet Bar, Kitchen, Ind. Heat Ctl., Ind. AC Ctl.

Located on legendary Hilton Head Island, this resort offers affordable quality accommodations directly on the ocean. Business becomes pleasure in this ideal setting, a Convention Center only a walk from your villa. In between and after meetings, relax on white sand beaches, and hone your athletic skills on championship tennis courts and golf courses.

─────────── MYRTLE BEACH ───────────

Sands Beach Club
1000 Shore Dr.
Myrtle Beach, SC 29577

225 Suites
803-449-1531 800-845-6999

Location: Arcadian Shores
Airport: 40 minutes
Near: Directly on Ocean, Resort Beach, Downtown-20 minutes
Walking Distance To: Beachside
Area Attractions: Beaches, Local Art, Dunes

Price Range & Credit Cards: 1 Bedroom Suite $$$, 2 Bedrooms $$$$, AmEx/MC/Visa/Other CC, Children Free, TAC 10%

Hotel Amenities: Laundry, Parking, TV Lounge

Business Facilities: Conf. Rm. Cap. 50, Banquet Fac., Mess. Ctr., Sec. Serv., Copier, Aud/Vis., Comp. Hook-up

Recreational Facilities: Pool, Whirlpool, Fitn. Ctr., Golf, Fishing; Dinner Cruise

Restaurant/Bar: Toppers, Entertainment

Comps: Airport Limousine, Hors d'oeuvres

Room Amenities: TV, Phone in Rm., Cable TV, Wet Bar, Kitchen, Ind. Heat Ctl., Ind. AC Ctl.

All suites, individually decorated by their owners, combine tasteful contemporary decor with all the conveniences necessary for your comfort. Enjoy a variety of on-site recreational facilities and try your hand at deep sea fishing. Then lift your spirits and feed your appetite at Topper's Lounge & Restaurant with a panoramic view of the ocean and beach.

─────────── MYRTLE BEACH ───────────

The Palace Suite Resort
1605 South Ocean Blvd.
Myrtle Beach, SC 29577

298 Suites
803-448-4300 800-334-1397

Location: Central; Downtown: 5 min.
Airport: 2 miles
Near: Carolina Opera, Located directly on the Ocean
Walking Distance To: Beachside
Area Attractions: Brookgreen Gardens, Plantation Tours, Golf

Price Range & Credit Cards: 1 Bedroom Suite $, 2 Bedrooms $$$, AmEx/MC/Visa/Other CC, Children Free, TAC 10%

Hotel Amenities: Laundry, Parking

Business Facilities: Conf. Rm. Cap. 180, Banquet Fac., Mess. Ctr., Copier, Aud/Vis., FAX

Recreational Facilities: Pool, Sauna, Whirlpool, Fitn. Ctr., Tennis, Golf, Fishing, Game Area

Restaurant/Bar: Ocean front Palace Cafe Restaurant and Lounge, Entertainment

Comps: Refreshments, Hors d'oeuvres

Room Amenities: Room Service, Free Paper, TV, Phone in Rm., Cable TV, Radio, Kitchen, Ind. Heat Ctl., Ind. AC Ctl.

A classic suite resort, The Palace features a beautiful 3-story lobby waterfall and spacious suites, with contemporary decor and private oceanfront balconies. A wide variety of area attractions are available for the entire family. Complete meeting facilities will please business travelers. The Palace Restaurant provides fine dining with ocean view.

--------------------- NORTH CHARLESTON ---------------------

The Residence Inn by Marriott **Location:** Airport; Downtown: 12 mi.
7645 Northwoods Blvd.   **Airport:** 8 miles
North Charleston, SC 29418   **Near:** 12 miles to Historic Downtown district
                                    Area Attractions: 17 miles to Beaches
96 Suites
803-572-5757 800-331-3131

Price Range & Credit Cards: 1 Bedroom Suite $$, 2 Bedrooms $$$, AmEx/MC/
Visa/Other CC, Children Free

Hotel Amenities: Laundry, TV Lounge, Pets Allowed, Handicap (3)

Business Facilities: Conf. Rm. Cap. 15, Copier, Aud/Vis.

Recreational Facilities: Pool, Whirlpool, Sports court

Comps: Continental Plus Breakfast, Refreshments, Hors d'oeuvres

Room Amenities: Free Paper, TV, Phone in Rm., Cable TV, Radio, Kitchen, Ind. Heat
Ctl., Ind. AC Ctl.

*The Residence Inn offers the comfort of Studio and Penthouse Suites. Relax in a spacious
living room featuring a cosy woodburning fireplace, with a fully-equipped kitchen. Complimentary continental breakfast and evening Get-together are offered at the Gatehouse.
For outside pleasure we suggest the pool or heated spa. Rates discounted for extended stay.*

--------------------- NORTH MYRTLE BEACH ---------------------

Clarion Beach Cove Resort   **Location:** Resort; Downtown: 5 min.
4800 So. Ocean Blvd.   **Airport:** 15 miles
North Myrtle Beach, SC 29582   **Near:** Windy Hill Section, Restaurant Row
                                Walking Distance To: Oceanside
260 Suites   **Area Attractions:** Amusement Park, Shop-
803-272-4044 800-331-6533   ping Area

Price Range & Credit Cards: 1 Bedroom Suite $$, AmEx/MC/Visa/Other CC, Chil-
dren Free, TAC 20%

Hotel Amenities: Laundry, Parking, TV Lounge, Handicap (10)

Business Facilities: Conf. Rm. Cap. 50, Banquet Fac., Mess. Ctr., Sec. Serv., Copier,
Aud/Vis., Teleconf., Telex, Comp. Hook-up, Bus. Ctr.

Recreational Facilities: Pool, Sauna, Whirlpool, 30 Tennis Courts, Game Area; 40 Golf
Courses

Restaurant/Bar: Tradewinds Cafe, Coral Room, Chasers, Entertainment

Comps: Hors d'oeuvres

Room Amenities: Room Service, TV, Phone in Rm., Cable TV, Radio, Wet Bar, Kitchen,
Ind. Heat Ctl., Ind. AC Ctl.

*Suites are elegantly decorated in French Country decor with beautiful stained glass panels
at each entry and spacious private patios which overlook the ocean and poolscape below.
Offering a complete business service center as well as the ultimate in outdoor and indoor
recreation, the Beach Cove easily accommodates both business and pleasure travelers.*

NORTH MYRTLE BEACH

Ocean Creek Resort & Conf. Ct.
10700 King Hiway
North Myrtle Beach, SC 29598

335 Suites
803-272-7724 800-845-0353

Location: Windy Hill; Downtown: 15 min.
Airport: 10 minutes
Near: Minutes From Area Shopping Malls
Area Attractions: Brookgreen Gardens (largest sculpture garden in world)

Price Range & Credit Cards: 1 Bedroom Suite $$$, 2 Bedrooms $$$$, Junior $$$, AmEx/MC/Visa/Other CC, Children Free, TAC 10%

Hotel Amenities: Laundry, Library, Parking, Gift Shop, TV Lounge

Business Facilities: Conf. Rm. Cap. 250, Banquet Fac., Copier, Aud/Vis., Telex

Recreational Facilities: Pool, Whirlpool, Tennis, Sailing, Horseback Riding, Game Area; Golf & Fishing nearby

Restaurant/Bar: Four Seasons

Room Amenities: TV, Phones in Rm. (2), Cable TV, Wet Bar, Kitchen, Ind. Heat Ctl., Ind. AC Ctl.

In 7 acres of protected space. Enjoy 8 indoor/outdoor/oceanfront swimming pools, the elevated oceanfront pool bar; 7 tennis courts with on-site tennis pro at the Tennis Center; 45 golf courses and a putting green; gourmet restaurant & lounge. Many boutiques, malls, & outlets are nearby. Choose either an oceanfront tower or a Villa in a woodsy setting.

PAWLEY'S ISLAND

Waccamaw House Resort
Highway 17 South
Pawley's Island, SC 29585

96 Suites
803-237-8402 800-845-1897

Location: Resort; Downtown: 22 mi.
Airport: 20 miles
Near: Litchfield Beach, Quaint Shops
Walking Distance To: Shopping Center
Area Attractions: Brookgreen Gardens, Ocean

Price Range & Credit Cards: 1 Bedroom Suite $$$, /MC/Visa, Children Free, TAC 10%

Hotel Amenities: Laundry, Parking, Handicap (2)

Business Facilities: Conf. Rm. Cap. 250, Banquet Fac., Sec. Serv., Copier, Aud/Vis., Comp. Hook-up

Recreational Facilities: Pool, Sauna, Whirlpool, Fitn. Ctr., Tennis, Golf, Fishing, Surfing, Sailing

Restaurant/Bar: J.R.Webster's, Entertainment

Comps: Hors d'oeuvres

Room Amenities: Room Service, TV, Phone in Rm., Cable TV, Radio, Wet Bar, Ind. Heat Ctl., Ind. AC Ctl.

The Waccamaw House enjoys close proximity to quaint shops in several shopping areas and Brookgreen Gardens, a sculpture and floral garden. There are on-site theaters, fitness center, and racquetball courts. Enjoy a leisurely lunch at J.R. Webster's Restaurant, decorated to create a garden effect-part of this hotel's Low Country charm.

 Tennessee

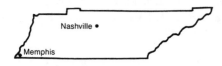

Nashville •

Memphis

MEMPHIS

Governors Inn of Memphis
2305 Airport Interchange
Memphis, TN 38116

50 Suites
901-396-4321 800-443-9350

Location: Airport; Downtown: 20 min.
Airport: 5 minutes
Near: Whitehaven, Suburbs
Area Attractions: Graceland, Memphis Festival

Price Range & Credit Cards: 1 Bedroom Suite $$, 2 Bedrooms $$, AmEx/MC/Visa/ Other CC, Children Free, TAC 10%

Hotel Amenities: Laundry, TV Lounge, Handicap (2)

Business Facilities: Conf. Rm. Cap. 20, Banquet Fac., Mess. Ctr., Sec. Serv., Copier, Aud/Vis.

Recreational Facilities: Pool, Sauna, Whirlpool, Golf

Comps: Full Breakfast, Hors d'oeuvres

Room Amenities: Room Service, Free Paper, TV, Phone in Rm., Cable TV, Wet Bar

Each suite, decorated with wrought iron and wood accents, gives you ample space for working, relaxing, or entertaining. Start your day in the Atrium with your complimentary newspaper and a breakfast buffet to suit all tastes. And, after a busy day, relax completely in the hotel's whirlpool or steamroom, or enjoy a refreshing swim in the outdoor pool.

──────────────── MEMPHIS ────────────────

Lexington Hotel Suites
4300 American Way
Memphis, TN 38118

121 Suites
901-366-9333 800-537-8483

Location: SE I-240; Downtown: 9 miles
Airport: 4 miles
Near: Largest Mall in Memphis
Area Attractions: Graceland

Price Range & Credit Cards: 1 Bedroom Suite $$, 2 Bedrooms $$$, Junior $$, AmEx/ MC/Visa/Other CC, Children Free

Hotel Amenities: Laundry, Handicap (7)

Business Facilities: Conf. Rm. Cap. 100, Banquet Fac., Mess. Ctr., Copier, Aud/Vis.

Recreational Facilities: Pool, Whirlpool; Riviera Spa nearby

Comps: Continental Plus Breakfast, Check-in Soft Drinks

Room Amenities: TV, Phone in Room, Cable TV, Radio, Kitchen, Ind. Heat Ctl., Ind. AC Ctl.

"A Suite for the Price of a Room"—and each suite includes a living room, one or two bedrooms, kitchen and bath. This fine accommodation is within walking distance to the largest mall in Memphis and is minutes from downtown, airport and Graceland. Enjoy complimentary breakfast in the atrium overlooking a heated pool and whirlpool. Meeting rooms available.

──────────────── NASHVILLE ────────────────

Elm Hill Inn
2615 Elm Hill Pike
Nashville, TN 37214

50 Suites
615-883-0114

Location: Airport; Downtown: 2 mi.
Airport: One mile
Near: Opryland-Donelson, Two Large Malls
Walking Distance To: Suburbs
Area Attractions: Grand Ole Opry, Riverboats

Price Range & Credit Cards: 1 Bedroom Suite $$$, Junior $$, AmEx/MC/Visa/Other CC, Children Free, TAC 10%

Hotel Amenities: Laundry, TV Lounge, Pets Allowed, Handicap (2)

Business Facilities: Conf. Rm. Cap. 40, Banquet Fac., Mess. Ctr., Copier

Recreational Facilities: Pool, Sauna, Whirlpool, Wave Pool; Old Hickory Golf Course

Restaurant/Bar: Elm Hill

Comps: Full Breakfast, Hors d'oeuvres

Room Amenities: Room Service, Free Paper, TV, Phone in Rm., Cable TV, Radio, Wet Bar, Ind. Heat Ctl., Ind. AC Ctl.

A highly trained, professional staff set the tone of this quaint, elegant hotel. In your suite, everything from coffee maker to bath robes makes you feel right at home. The Atrium is a favorite gathering place, with its lighted dome sky light and globed lanterns, all amidst beautiful plants.

---------------- NASHVILLE ----------------

Lexington Hotel Suites
2425 Atrium Way
Nashville, TN 37210

120 Suites
615-883-5201 800-537-8483

Location: Central; Downtown:.5 miles
Airport: 2 miles
Near: Shops, Restaurants
Area Attractions: Country Music Hall, Twitty City, Opryland

Price Range & Credit Cards: 1 Bedroom Suite $$, 2 Bedrooms $$$, Junior $$, AmEx/ MC/Visa/Other CC, Children Free, TAC 15%

Hotel Amenities: Laundry, Handicap (2)

Business Facilities: Conf. Rm. Cap. 50

Recreational Facilities: Pool, Whirlpool, Tennis, Golf, Skiing, Boating; Health Club nearby

Comps: Continental breakfast

Room Amenities: TV, Phone in Rm., Cable TV, Radio, Kitchen, Ind. Heat Ctl., Ind. AC Ctl.

Lexington Hotel Suites has attractive American decor with paintings and plenty of beautiful green plants in the lobby. Start your day by joining other guests in the Atrium for a complimentary breakfast. And take advantage of the recreational facilities—relax in the whirlpool, or enjoy an invigorating swim.

---------------- NASHVILLE ----------------

Park Suite Hotel
10 Century Blvd.
Nashville, TN 37214

294 Suites
615-871-0033 800-432-7272

Location: Airport; Downtown: 7 miles
Airport: 2 miles
Near: Opryland Amusement Park, Music Row, Downtown Business District
Area Attractions: The Hermitage, Home of President Andrew Jackson

Price Range & Credit Cards: 1 Bedroom Suite $$$, 2 Bedrooms $$$$+, AmEx/MC/ Visa/Other CC, Children Free, TAC 10%

Hotel Amenities: Laundry, Gift Shop, Parking, Car Hire, Handicap (16)

Business Facilities: Conf. Rm. Cap. 16, Banquet Fac., Mess. Ctr., Copier, Aud/Vis., Comp. Hook-up

Recreational Facilities: Pool, Sauna, Whirlpool, Fitn. Ctr., Tennis, Golf; Waterpark nearby

Restaurant/Bar: Plaza On The Green/Aviators, D.J. & Live Acts

Comps: Refreshments, Hors d'oeuvres, Airport Shuttle, Full Breakfast

Room Amenities: Room Service, Free Paper, TV, Phones in Rm. (2), Cable TV, Radio, Wet Bar, Ind. Heat Ctl., Ind. AC Ctl.

Located 2 miles from Nashville Airport, in the Century City Complex, Park Suite's exceptional value provides the comfort and luxury of a suite at the price of a room. A complimentary full buffet breakfast is served each morning in our lavish 9-story atrium restaurant. When you stay at the Park Suite, you'll experience a new standard of hotel excellence.

─────────────────── NASHVILLE ───────────────────

The Hermitage Hotel
231 6th Ave. No.
Nashville, TN 37219

112 Suites
615-244-3121 800-251-1908

Location: Heart of Downtown
Airport: 5 minutes
Near: Historic District, Capitol Plaza
Walking Distance To: Business Area
Area Attractions: State Capitol, Convention Center

Price Range & Credit Cards: 1 Bedroom Suite $$$, 2 Bedrooms $$$$, AmEx/MC/Visa/Other CC, Children Free, TAC 15%

Hotel Amenities: Laundry, Parking, Car Hire, TV Lounge, Pets Allowed, Handicap (9)

Business Facilities: Conf. Rm. Cap. 250, Banquet Fac., Mess. Ctr., Sec. Serv., Copier, Aud/Vis.

Recreational Facilities: Pool, Sauna, Whirlpool, Running track; Free access to YMCA

Restaurant/Bar: The Hermitage, Veranda Bar, Entertainment

Comps: Full Breakfast, Hors d'oeuvres

Room Amenities: Room Service, TV, Phones in Rm. (3), Radio, Wet Bar, Ind. Heat Ctl., Ind. AC Ctl.

Experience the elegance of another era in this historic hotel, built in 1910 in the ornate style of Beaux Arts Classicism. From the lobby's richly marbled floors to luxuriously decorated suites every effort is made to ensure a pleasant stay. Find excellent gourmet dining in the Hermitage Dining Room, surrounded by rich paneling and handcrafted ceiling.

─────────────────── NASHVILLE ───────────────────

The Residence Inn by Marriott
2300 Elm Hill Pike
Nashville, TN 37210

168 Suites
615-889-8600 800-331-3131

Location: Northeast; Downtown: 10 min.
Airport: 2 minutes
Near: Opryland Corridor, Music City
Area Attractions: Museums, Country Hall of Fame

Price Range & Credit Cards: 1 Bedroom Suite $$, 2 Bedrooms $$, AmEx/MC/Visa/Other CC, Children Free, TAC 10%

Hotel Amenities: Laundry, Library, Parking, TV Lounge, Pets Allowed, Handicap (16)

Business Facilities: Conf. Rm. Cap. 70, Mess. Ctr., Sec. Serv., Copier, Aud/Vis., Telex, Comp. Hook-up

Recreational Facilities: Pool, Whirlpool, Tennis, Golf, Skiing, Fishing, Game Area; Health Spa access

Comps: Continental Breakfast, Refreshments, Hors d'oeuvres

Room Amenities: Room Service, Free Paper, TV, Phone in Rm., Cable TV, VCR, Radio, Wet Bar, Kitchen, Ind. Heat Ctl., Ind. AC Ctl.

One of twelve 4-Diamond rated hotels in Tennessee, this hotel offers country-style ambiance with professional service. Your suite has all the comforts of home—from a full kitchen to a fireplace and VCR. For your enjoyment, there is a swimming pool, whirlpool, multiple-use sportcourt, picnic and barbeque areas. Rates discounted for extended stays.

❖ Texas

ABILENE

Embassy Suites Hotel
4250 Ridgemont Dr.
Abilene, TX 79606

176 Suites
915-698-1234 800-362-2779

Location: Southwest; Downtown: 5 miles
Airport: 9 miles
Near: Mall of Abilene, Western Village
Walking Distance To: Shopping
Area Attractions: Zoo, Dyess A.F.B., SW Golf Classic

Price Range & Credit Cards: 1 Bedroom Suite $$, AmEx/MC/Visa/Other CC, Children Free, TAC 10%

Hotel Amenities: Laundry, Parking, TV Lounge, Small Pets only, Handicap (2)

Business Facilities: Conf. Rm. Cap. 60, Banquet Fac., Sec. Serv., Copier, Aud/Vis., Comp. Hook-up

Recreational Facilities: Pool, Sauna, Whirlpool, Game Area; Tennis and Golf nearby

Restaurant/Bar: Remington's, Entertainment

Comps: Full Breakfast, Refreshments, Hors d'oeuvres

Room Amenities: Room Service, Free Paper, TV, Phones in Rm. (2), Cable TV, Radio, Wet Bar, Kitchen, Ind. Heat Ctl., Ind. AC Ctl.

Spanish style architecture and plenty of lush plants and trees throughout this hotel provide a beautiful and airy atmosphere. Each suite comes complete with all the amenities of home and a parlor that's perfect for entertaining or work. Full complimentary breakfast is served in the Atrium, and after a busy day, enjoy a leisurely dinner at Remington's.

―――――――――――――――――――――― ARLINGTON ――――――――――――――――――――――

Lexington Hotel Suites
1075 E. Waldrop Dr.
Arlington, TX 76011

132 Suites
817-261-8900 800-527-1877

Location: Central; Ft.Worth: 11 mi.
Airport: 6 miles
Near: Wet-N-Wild Park, City Center
Walking Distance To: Ranger Stadium
Area Attractions: Wax Museum, Six Flags, International Wildlife Park

Price Range & Credit Cards: 1 Bedroom Suite $$, 2 Bedrooms $$, Junior $, AmEx/ MC/Visa/Other CC, Children Free, TAC 15%

Hotel Amenities: Laundry, Airport Shuttle, Handicap (2)

Business Facilities: Conf. Rm. Cap. 50, Aud/Vis., FAX

Recreational Facilities: Pool, Whirlpool

Comps: Continental Breakfast

Room Amenities: TV, Phone in Rm., Radio, Kitchen, Ind. Heat Ctl., Ind. AC Ctl.

Within a mile of Six Flags Over Texas and Wet-N-Wild Park, Lexington is perfectly located for vacationers. Each room has a complete kitchen with all the appliances you'll need. Complimentary continental breakfast is served daily in the Solarium overlooking a two-tiered heated swimming pool with jacuzzi. There is also a playground for children.

―――――――――――――――――――――― ARLINGTON ――――――――――――――――――――――

Radisson Suite Hotel
700 Ave. H. East
Arlington, TX 76011

203 Suites
817-640-0440 800-228-9822

Location: Northside; Dallas: 15 min.
Airport: 15 minutes
Near: I-30 & Hiway 360, Six Flags Over Texas Amusement Park
Walking Distance To: North Arlington
Area Attractions: Ranger Stadium, Wet N'Wild Park

Price Range & Credit Cards: 1 Bedroom Suite $$, 2 Bedrooms $$$$, AmEx/MC/ Visa/Other CC, Children Free, TAC 10%

Hotel Amenities: Laundry, Handicap (3)

Business Facilities: Conf. Rm. Cap. 250, Banquet Fac., Aud/Vis.

Recreational Facilities: Pool, Sauna, Whirlpool, Steamroom, Game Area; Indoor sunning area

Restaurant/Bar: Mandolins, Entertainment

Comps: Full Breakfast, Refreshments

Room Amenities: Room Service, TV, Phones in Rm. (2), Cable TV, Radio, Wet Bar

The simple white exterior of the Radisson contrasts excitingly with the seven-story atrium featuring a glass pyramid ceiling and forty-foot brass cage lobby bar amidst water and greenery. Enjoy fine dining in the romantic atmosphere of Mandolins, surrounded by marble, etched mirrored glass, touches of brass, and soft-toned live entertainment.

──────────── AUSTIN ────────────

Embassy Suites Hotel
300 So. Congress Ave.
Austin, TX 78704

261 Suites
512-469-9000 800-362-2779

Location: Downtown; Townlake
Airport: 7 miles
Near: Recreational Area, Sixth Street Shops
Walking Distance To: Business Areas
Area Attractions: State Capitol, LBJ Library

Price Range & Credit Cards: 1 Bedroom Suite $$$, 2 Bedrooms $$$$, AmEx/MC/ Visa/Other CC, Children Free, TAC 10%

Hotel Amenities: Parking, Pets Allowed, Handicap (10)

Business Facilities: Conf. Rm. Cap. 100, Banquet Fac., Copier, Aud/Vis., Comp. Hook-up

Recreational Facilities: Pool, Sauna, Whirlpool, Game Area; Golf 5 miles

Restaurant/Bar: Embassy Suites Restaurant and Lounge, Entertainment

Comps: Full Breakfast, Refreshments, Hors d'oeuvres

Room Amenities: Room Service, Free Paper, TV, Phone in Rm., Cable TV, Radio, Wet Bar, Kitchen, Ind. Heat Ctl., Ind. AC Ctl.

The comforts of a fully-equipped suite for the price of most hotel "singles" is only one benefit of staying here. You'll find meeting facilities just as accommodating, with a variety of room sizes to suit your needs. Enjoy fine cuisine—featuring continental dishes—in an atmosphere of casual elegance at the Embassy Suites restaurant off the atrium.

──────────── AUSTIN ────────────

Embassy Suites Hotel
5901 No. I.H. 35
Austin, TX 78723

261 Suites
512-454-8004 800-362-2779

Location: IH-35 Access; Downtown: 5 miles
Airport: 4 miles
Near: Capitol Plaza
Walking Distance To: Highland Mall
Area Attractions: Sixth Street Entertainment, Zilker Park, Univ. of Texas

Price Range & Credit Cards: 1 Bedroom Suite $$$, AmEx/MC/Visa/Other CC, Children Free, TAC 10%

Hotel Amenities: Laundry, Gift Shop, Parking, Valet, Pets Fee, Handicap (10)

Business Facilities: Conf. Rm. Cap. 15, Banquet Fac., Copier, Aud/Vis.

Recreational Facilities: Pool, Sauna, Whirlpool, Steamroom; Fitness Center nearby

Restaurant/Bar: Steak & Ale's Plaza Grill, Lynx Lounge

Comps: Full Breakfast, Refreshments, Airport Limousine

Room Amenities: Room Service, USA Today, TV, Phones in Rm. (2), Cable TV, Clock, Radio, Wet Bar, Microwave

You will receive a warm welcome with the comfortable appeal of the lobby, decorated in a Spanish motif enhanced by warm earth tones. The same attention to comfort is carried through to your suite, where you'll find all the amenities of home. Enjoy your breakfast amidst the lush tropical surroundings of the atrium, which features a beautiful waterfall.

Palace Hotel, Philadelphia, PA

—————————————————— AUSTIN ——————————————————

Guest Quarters Suite Hotel
303 West 15th St.
Austin, TX 78701

191 Suites
512-478-7000 800-424-2900

Location: Downtown
Airport: 15 minutes
Near: City Hall
Walking Distance To: State Capitol, Univ. of Texas
Area Attractions: Stadium 1 mile; Convention Ctr. 2 mi.

Price Range & Credit Cards: 1 Bedroom Suite $$$, 2 Bedrooms $$$$, AmEx/MC/ Visa/Other CC, Children Free, TAC 10%

Hotel Amenities: Laundry, Library, Gift Shop, Car Hire, Pets Allowed, Handicap (2)

Business Facilities: Conf. Rm. Cap. 180, Banquet Fac., Mess. Ctr., Sec. Serv., Copier, Aud/Vis., Comp. Hook-up

Recreational Facilities: Pool, Sauna, Whirlpool, Fitn. Ctr.; Golf and Tennis nearby

Restaurant/Bar: 15th Street Cafe/15th Street Lounge

Comps: Full Breakfast, Refreshments, Hors d'oeuvres

Room Amenities: TV, Phones in Rm. (2), Cable TV, Radio, Kitchen, Ind. Heat Ctl., Ind. AC Ctl.

Right in the center of downtown Austin, Guest Quarters offers Guest treatment to business travellers and tourists. Pleasant conference facilities, a landscaped recreational area and exceptional dining round out the amenities of this fine hotel. Spacious one- and two-bedroom suites, complete with full kitchens, are sure to make your stay a relaxing one.

———————————————————— AUSTIN ————————————————————

Habitat Hotel
500 Highland Mall Blvd.
Austin, TX 78750

96 Suites
512-467-6000 800-553-4663

Location: Northeast; Downtown: 5 min.
Airport: 3 miles
Near: Lincoln Village, Highland Mall
Walking Distance To: Dining, Shops
Area Attractions: Over 150 Fine Shops, Theatres

Price Range & Credit Cards: 1 Bedroom Suite $, 2 Bedrooms $$, AmEx/MC/Visa/ Other CC, Children Free, TAC 10%

Hotel Amenities: Laundry, Car Hire, Pets Allowed, Handicap (1)

Business Facilities: Conf. Rm. Cap. 45, Banquet Fac., Mess. Ctr., Copier, Aud/Vis.

Recreational Facilities: Pool, Whirlpool, Fitn. Ctr., Tennis, Golf, Soccer, Game Area; Bike & Hike Trails

Comps: Full Breakfast, Refreshments

Room Amenities: Free Paper, TV, Phones in Rm. (2), Cable TV, Radio, Wet Bar, Kitchen, Ind. Heat Ctl., Ind. AC Ctl.

These home-like complexes have beautiful brick and wood exteriors and the Guest House, the center of all activity, features vaulted ceilings, wall-size window, and an inviting over-sized fireplace. The open and airy feeling of your suite provides a perfect place to spend some private time. If you prefer, fire up the barbecue and cook up your own feast.

———————————————————— AUSTIN ————————————————————

Hawthorn Suites Austin Central
935 La Posada Drive
Austin, TX 78752

70 Suites
512-459-3335 800-527-1133

Location: I-35/Airport; Downtown: nearby
Airport: Robert Mueller-4 min
Near: Univ. of Texas-5 minutes
Area Attractions: State Capitol

Price Range & Credit Cards: 1 Bedroom Suite $$, 2 Bedrooms $$$

Hotel Amenities: Pets Allowed

Business Facilities: Conf. Rm. Cap. 45

Recreational Facilities: Pool; Outdoor Sports Center

Restaurant/Bar: Hawthorn Room/Hawthorn Bar

Comps: Full Breakfast, Refreshments, Hors d'oeuvres

Room Amenities: Free Paper, TV, Phone in Rm., Cable TV, VCR, Radio, Wet Bar, Kitchen, Ind. Heat Ctl., Ind. AC Ctl.

Hawthorn Suites offers detailed attention to executive meetings or training sessions with 12-45 attendance. Comfortable suites with restful decor provide privacy and relaxation. Complimentary full breakfast buffet and evening hospitality hour with drinks and hors d'oeuvres complete your business or pleasure stay.

──────────────────── AUSTIN ────────────────────

Hawthorn Suites Austin N.W.
8888 Tallwood Dr.
Austin, TX 78759

105 Suites
512-343-0008   800-527-2360

Location: Northwest; Downtown: 7 miles
Airport: 5 miles
Near: High-tech area, Arboretum Plaza
Area Attractions: Northcross Mall, I.B.M., T.I.

Price Range & Credit Cards: 1 Bedroom Suite $$, 2 Bedrooms $$$, AmEx/MC/Visa/Other CC, Children Free, TAC 13%

Hotel Amenities: Laundry, VCR Rental, Parking, Grocery Serv, Pets Allowed, Handicap (1)

Business Facilities: Conf. Rm. Cap. 50, Banquet Fac., Copier, Aud/Vis., Teleconf., FAX, Comp. Hook-up

Recreational Facilities: Pool, Whirlpool, Fitn. Ctr.; Golf 4 miles

Comps: Full Breakfast, Refreshments, Hors d'oeuvres

Room Amenities: Conv. snacks, Free Paper, TV, Phones in Rm. (2), Cable TV, Radio, Wet Bar, Kitchen, Ind. Heat Ctl., Ind. AC Ctl.

You'll find comfortable accommodations in this beautiful garden suite hotel. Breakfast daily, and evening cocktail parties are all compliments of the hotel. The Activity Room's decor is particularly attractive with all rattan and glass furniture, a stained glass window on one wall and another window looking out onto the patio deck and the pool.

──────────────────── AUSTIN ────────────────────

Highland Village Hotel
803 Tirado
Austin, TX 78752

49 Suites
512-459-3333

Location: Northwest; Downtown: 7 miles
Airport: 5 miles
Near: Highland Mall, Shops, Restaurants
Walking Distance To: Hilton Inn
Area Attractions: Zilker Gardens, Clubs, Sixth Street Shops

Price Range & Credit Cards: 1 Bedroom Suite $, 2 Bedrooms $, Junior $, AmEx/MC/Visa/Other CC, Children Free, TAC 10%

Hotel Amenities: Laundry, Parking, Pets Allowed, Handicap (1)

Business Facilities: Conf. Rm. Cap. 35, Mess. Ctr., Copier

Recreational Facilities: Pool, Whirlpool

Comps: A Bottle of Wine

Room Amenities: TV, Phones in Rm. (2), Cable TV, Kitchen, Ind. Heat Ctl., Ind. AC Ctl.

The Highland Village offers well-appointed, spacious suites complete with fully-equipped kitchens, that make it the perfect option for relocating families or hotel weary businessmen. Unwind with a complimentary bottle of wine, stretch your muscles with an invigorating swim in the beautifully landscaped pool, or simply relax in the hot tub.

──────── AUSTIN ────────

Lexington Hotel Suites
8300 IH 35 North
Austin, TX 78753

217 Suites
512-835-5050 800-527-1877

Location: Northside; Downtown: 4 miles
Airport: 6 miles
Near: City Center, Highland Mall
Walking Distance To: Suburbs
Area Attractions: Capitol, Univ. of Texas

Price Range & Credit Cards: 1 Bedroom Suite $, 2 Bedrooms $$, Junior $, AmEx/ MC/Visa/Other CC, Children Free, TAC 15%

Hotel Amenities: Laundry, Pets Allowed, Handicap (3)

Business Facilities: Conf. Rm. Cap. 75, Copier, Aud/Vis.

Recreational Facilities: Pool, Tennis, Golf; Health Club privileges

Comps: Continental Breakfast, Airport shuttle

Room Amenities: TV, Phone in Rm., Radio, Kitchen, Ind. Heat Ctl., Ind. AC Ctl.

Conveniently located near I-35, Lexington offers the affordable alternative to single room lodging. Spacious suites feature complete kitchen and dining areas, giving you the freedom to have meal, snack, and beverages whenever you choose. The back lobby is a comfortable conversation area for gatherings.

──────── AUSTIN ────────

Woodfin Suites Hotel & Bus.Ctr
7685 Northcross Drive
Austin, TX 78757

180 Suites
512-452-9391

Location: Northside; Downtown: 12 min.
Airport: 15 minutes
Near: Movie Theatre, Restaurants
Walking Distance To: Northcross Mall, Shopping
Area Attractions: Austin's only Ice Skating Rink

Price Range & Credit Cards: 1 Bedroom Suite $$$, 2 Bedrooms $$$, AmEx/MC/ Visa/Other CC, Children Free, TAC 10%

Hotel Amenities: Laundry, Library, Pets Allowed, Handicap (2)

Business Facilities: Conf. Rm. Cap. 80, Banquet Fac., Mess. Ctr., Sec. Serv., Copier, Aud/Vis., Comp. Hook-up, Bus. Ctr.

Recreational Facilities: Pool, Whirlpool, Tennis, Golf, Jogging, Bowling; all sports 10 min.

Restaurant/Bar: Solarium

Comps: Airport Shuttle (Reservation), Full Breakfast, Snacks, Refreshments

Room Amenities: Free Paper, TV, Phones in Rm. (2), VCR, Radio, Kitchen, Ind. Heat Ctl., Ind. AC Ctl.

Woodfin Suites Hotel is a luxury condominium-style hotel featuring one & two bedroom suites. Suites have woodburning fireplaces, full kitchens, two TV's with complimentary VCR and movie rental at the clubhouse. Also enjoy a full, hot breakfast daily and complimentary social hour M-T, 5-7pm. Guest business center with IBM Wheelwriter 5 available.

──────────── CORPUS CHRISTI ────────────

Embassy Suites Hotel
4337 S. Padre Island Drive
Corpus Christi, TX 78411

154 Suites
512-853-7899 800-362-2779

Location: Downtown: 11 mi.
Airport: 9 miles
Near: Marina-11 miles
Walking Distance To: Entertainment and Restaurants
Area Attractions: Padre Island National Seashore, Convention Center, Shopping

Price Range & Credit Cards: 1 Bedroom Suite $$, AmEx/MC/Visa/Other CC, Children Free, TAC 10%

Hotel Amenities: Laundry, Parking, No-smoke suites, Handicap (2)

Business Facilities: Conf. Rm. Cap. 100, Banquet Fac., Mess. Ctr., Sec. Serv., Copier, Aud/Vis.

Recreational Facilities: Pool, Sauna, Whirlpool, Game Area; Kings Crossing Country Club & YMCA

Restaurant/Bar: Atrium Deli/Bar

Comps: Full Breakfast, Shoeshine, Refreshments, Airport Shuttle

Room Amenities: TV, Phones in Rm. (2), Cable TV, Radio, Wet Bar, Kitchen

Lush tropical greenery and a large atrium combined with Spanish decor provides a pleasing mix of luxury and comfort. Each suite has galley kitchen and wet bar, perfect for private meals or a quiet nightcap. Join other guest for a delicious cooked-to-order breakfast and unwind at the Manager's complimentary cocktail party in the atrium.

──────────── CORPUS CHRISTI ────────────

Villa Del Sol
3938 Surfside Blvd.
Corpus Christi, TX 78402

411 Suites
512-883-9748 800-242-3291

Location: Beachside; Downtown: 11 mi.
Airport: 9 miles
Near: Resort setting, Galleries, Shopping, Restaurants
Walking Distance To: Beaches
Area Attractions: The Artist Colony, Wild Life

Price Range & Credit Cards: 1 Bedroom Suite $$, AmEx/MC/Visa/Other CC, Children Free, TAC 10%

Hotel Amenities: Laundry, Parking

Business Facilities: Conf. Rm. Cap. 35, Mess. Ctr., Aud/Vis.

Recreational Facilities: Pool, Whirlpool; Boat rentals available

Room Amenities: TV, Phone in Rm., Cable TV, Radio, Kitchen, Ind. Heat Ctl., Ind. AC Ctl.

Much of Villa del Sol's appeal is the diversity of its guests—from long-term guests to weekend business travelers. The comforts of suites and the warm climate make this a favorite place for winter get-aways. The beach is just a few steps away.

---------------------------- DALLAS ----------------------------

Bristol Suites Hotel
7800 Alpha Road
Dallas, TX 75240

295 Suites
214-233-7600 800-922-9222

Location: Park Central; Downtown: 20 min.
Airport: 20 minutes
Near: 500 Stores in 4 Shopping Malls-10 min.,
Cotton Bowl, West End Historic Dist.
Area Attractions: Southfork Ranch-12 miles,
J.F.Kennedy Memorial-14 miles

Price Range & Credit Cards: 1 Bedroom Suite $$$$, 2 Bedrooms $$$$+, AmEx/
MC/Visa/Other CC, Children Free, TAC 10%

Hotel Amenities: Laundry, Parking, Gift Shop, Pets Allowed, Handicap (8)

Business Facilities: Conf. Rm. Cap. 400, Banquet Fac., Mess. Ctr., Copier, Aud/Vis.,
Teleconf.

Recreational Facilities: Pool, Whirlpool, Fitn. Ctr.; Jogging nearby; Golf & Tennis

Restaurant/Bar: Cafe Biarritz/Atrium Bar, Piano

Comps: Full Breakast, Refreshments, Hors d'oeuvres

Room Amenities: Microwave, Free Paper, TV, Phones in Rm. (2), Cable TV, Radio, Wet
Bar, Coffee Maker, Ind. Heat Ctl., Ind. AC Ctl.

*Bristol Suites combines the comfort of a fine home with the services of a luxury hotel.
Located at the crossroads of the North Dallas business and residential areas, Bristol Suites
is convenient to a vast array of the finest shopping, dining, and entertainment in the Southwest. Cafe Biarritz, featuring country French cuisine, is a Dallas favorite.*

---------------------------- DALLAS ----------------------------

Embassy Suites Hotel
2727 Stemmons Freeway
Dallas, TX 75207

248 Suites
214-630-5332 800-362-2779

Location: Central; Downtown: 5 miles
Airport: Love Field-6 miles
Near: Market Center, World Trade Center
Walking Distance To: Restaurants
Area Attractions: Apparel Mart, Westend Mar-
ketplace

Price Range & Credit Cards: 1 Bedroom Suite $$$, 2 Bedrooms $$$$, AmEx/MC/
Visa/Other CC, Children Free, TAC 10%

Hotel Amenities: Laundry, Parking, Car Hire, TV Lounge, Pets Allowed, Handicap (4)

Business Facilities: Conf. Rm. Cap. 30, Banquet Fac., Conf.Suites, Copier, Aud/Vis.,
FAX

Recreational Facilities: Pool, Sauna, Whirlpool, Steamroom, Game Area

Restaurant/Bar: Embassy Ristorante, piano lounge, Entertainment

Comps: Full Breakfast, Refreshments

Room Amenities: Room Service, TV, Phones in Rm. (2), Cable TV, Radio, Wet Bar,
Kitchen, Ind. Heat Ctl., Ind. AC Ctl.

*A lush tropical atrium lobby with a spectacular Old World fountain will greet you upon
arrival at Embassy. Enjoy a cooked-to-order breakfast in the calm surroundings of the
atrium. In the evening, join other guests at the Manager's Complimentary Cocktail Party.
Enjoy dinner in the Southwestern atmosphere of Embassy Ristorante.*

─────────────── DALLAS ───────────────

Embassy Suites Hotel
3880 W. Northwest Highway
Dallas, TX 75220

248 Suites
214-357-4500 800-362-2779

Location: Airport; Downtown: 8 miles
Airport: Love Field-1 mile
Near: Bachman Lake, World Trade Center
Area Attractions: Texas Stadium, Convention Center

Price Range & Credit Cards: 1 Bedroom Suite $$$, 2 Bedrooms $$$$+, AmEx/MC/ Visa/Other CC, Children Free, TAC 11%

Hotel Amenities: Laundry, Concierge, Parking, Gift Shop, Handicap (8)

Business Facilities: Conf. Rm. Cap. 200, Banquet Fac., Mess. Ctr., Sec. Serv., Copier, Aud/Vis., Teleconf., Comp. Hook-up, Bus. Ctr.

Recreational Facilities: Pool, Sauna, Whirlpool, Fitn. Ctr., Jogging Trails; Golf, Paddle boats near

Restaurant/Bar: Cafe on Bachman Creek, Belmont's Bar, Entertainment

Comps: Breakfast, Refreshments, Airport Transport

Room Amenities: Room Service, Free Paper, TV, Phones in Rm. (2), Cable TV, Radio, Wet Bar, Kitchen, Ind. Heat Ctl., Ind. AC Ctl.

Embassy provides ideal accommodations for both pleasure and business travelers. Exercise enthusiasts will appreciate the hotel's two lap pools, a weight room, and a paved jogging path encircling Bachman Lake. All business needs are met here, with a convenient business center and professional staff who will help with arrangements.

─────────────── DALLAS ───────────────

Lexington Hotel Suites
4150 Independence Dr.
Dallas, TX 75237

108 Suites
214-298-7014 800-537-8483

Location: Southwest; Downtown: 14 mi.
Airport: 15 miles
Near: Suburban Area, Red Bird Mall
Walking Distance To: Shops
Area Attractions: Wax Museum, Six Flags, Stadium

Price Range & Credit Cards: 1 Bedroom Suite $, 2 Bedrooms $$, Junior $, AmEx/ MC/Visa/Other CC, Children Free, TAC 15%

Hotel Amenities: Laundry

Business Facilities: Conf. Rm. Cap. 80, Aud/Vis.

Recreational Facilities: Pool, Whirlpool, Boating; Skiing 20 miles

Comps: Continental breakfast

Room Amenities: TV, Phone in Rm., Radio, Kitchen, Ind. Heat Ctl., Ind. AC Ctl.

Suites at this hotel feature a complete living room and kitchen/dining area that make you feel right at home while you attend to business. Equipped with meeting facilities to suit almost any need, Lexington specializes in catering to corporations. When the work is done, stretch those muscles with a few laps in the pool or relax in the whirlpool.

──────────── DALLAS ────────────

Park Suite Hotel
13131 N. Central Expressway
Dallas, TX 75243

280 Suites
214-234-3300 800-432-7272

Location: Northside; Downtown: 8 miles
Airport: 35 miles
Near: Business District, North Dallas
Walking Distance To: Shops & Restaurants
Area Attractions: Greenville Avenue nightlife

Price Range & Credit Cards: 1 Bedroom Suite $$, AmEx/MC/Visa/Other CC, Children Free, TAC 10%

Hotel Amenities: Laundry, Parking, Car Hire, TV Lounge, Pets Allowed, Handicap (6)

Business Facilities: Conf. Rm. Cap. 600, Banquet Fac., Mess. Ctr., Sec. Serv., Copier, Aud/Vis., Telex, Comp. Hook-up

Recreational Facilities: Pool, Sauna, Whirlpool, Fitn. Ctr., Racquetball; Running track

Restaurant/Bar: Plaza On The Green, Entertainment

Comps: Full Breakfast

Room Amenities: Room Service, Free Paper, TV, Phone in Rm., Cable TV, Radio, Wet Bar, Kitchen, Ind. Heat Ctl., Ind. AC Ctl.

Step through mahogany doors with etched glass into the elegant atmosphere of yesteryear. The hotel has Mediterranean decor throughout, with unique antique furnishings in the lobby. You'll find your suite just as elegant, with light oak furnishings and a pale rose marble vanity. Dine in the relaxing atmosphere of the award-winning Plaza On The Green.

Lexington Hotel Suites, Memphis, TN

─────────────────── DALLAS ───────────────────

Preston House Hotel
6104 LBJ Freeway
Dallas, TX 75240

95 Suites
214-458-2626 800-524-7038

Location: Northside; Downtown: 10 mi.
Airport: 9 miles
Near: North Dallas, One Block to Galleria
Walking Distance To: Shops & Restaurants
Area Attractions: Night Spots, Shopping Malls

Price Range & Credit Cards: 1 Bedroom Suite $$, 2 Bedrooms $$$, Junior $$, AmEx/ MC/Visa/Other CC, Children Free, TAC 10%

Hotel Amenities: Laundry, Parking, TV Lounge, Pets Allowed

Business Facilities: Conf. Rm. Cap. 60, Copier, Aud/Vis.

Recreational Facilities: Pool, Whirlpool; Golf 8 miles

Comps: Continental Plus Breakfast, Refreshments, Hors d'oeuvres

Room Amenities: TV, Phone in Rm., Cable TV, Radio, Wet Bar, Kitchen, Ind. Heat Ctl., Ind. AC Ctl.

Conveniently situated in the heart of the busiest area of North Dallas (perfect for business travelers), Preston is also near the Galleria and other prestigious shopping and dining places. All suites have private entrances and offer home-like features, equipped kitchen, separate dining area, a garden-style patio.

─────────────────── DALLAS ───────────────────

The Residence Inn by Marriott
13636 Goldmark Drive
Dallas, TX 75240

70 Suites
214-669-0478 800-331-3131

Location: North Dallas; Downtown: 12 mi.
Airport: 20 miles
Near: High Tech Area
Area Attractions: Galleria Shopping Mall

Price Range & Credit Cards: 1 Bedroom Suite $$, 2 Bedrooms $$$, AmEx/MC/ Visa/Other CC, Children Free, TAC 10%

Hotel Amenities: Pets Allowed, Handicap (1)

Business Facilities: Conf. Rm. Cap. 10, Copier

Recreational Facilities: Pool, Sauna; Access to Health Club

Comps: Breakfast, Refreshments, Hors d'oeuvres

Room Amenities: Free Paper, TV, Phones in Rm. (2), Cable TV, Radio, Kitchen, Ind. Heat Ctl., Ind. AC Ctl.

The Residence Inn by Marriott is well-located in North Dallas for travelers with business in nearby high tech area or vacationers who will enjoy the Galleria Shopping Mall. Suites are tastefully appointed in a modern mauve and blue decor. Daily breakfast and evening refreshments (Mon.-Thur.) are complimentary. Rates discounted for extended stay.

─────────────── EL PASO ───────────────

Embassy Suites Hotel
6100 Gateway East
El Paso, TX 79905

185 Suites
915-779-6222 800-362-2779

Location: Central; Downtown: 7 miles
Airport: 2 miles
Near: Rio Grande, Shopping Center
Walking Distance To: Bassett Mall
Area Attractions: Juarez, Coliseum, Zoo, Stadium

Price Range & Credit Cards: 1 Bedroom Suite $$$, AmEx/MC/Visa/Other CC, Children Free, TAC 15%

Hotel Amenities: Laundry, Pets Allowed

Business Facilities: Conf. Rm. Cap. 275, Banquet Fac., Mess. Ctr., Sec. Serv., Copier, Aud/Vis.

Recreational Facilities: Pool, Sauna, Whirlpool, Sun Deck, Tennis, Golf; Health Spas

Restaurant/Bar: Isabella's, Entertainment

Comps: Full Breakfast, Refreshments, Airport Transport

Room Amenities: Room Service, Free Paper, TV, Phones in Rm. (2), Cable TV, Radio, Wet Bar, Kitchen

Centrally located directly off Interstate 10 at Geronimo, Embassy is conveniently situated and close to many fascinating attractions. The handsome Spanish-style hotel offers complimentary limo service to and from the airport. Four flexible conference rooms make social or business meetings easy. In the mornings enjoy a full breakfast in the atrium.

─────────────── EL PASO ───────────────

The Residence Inn by Marriott
6791 Montana
El Paso, TX 79925

200 Suites
915-772-8000 800-331-3131

Location: Airport; Downtown: 7 miles
Airport: 5 minutes
Near: Raytheon Headquarter, Shopping Center
Walking Distance To: Business
Area Attractions: Race Track, Juarez-Mexico, Tigua Indian Reservation

Price Range & Credit Cards: 1 Bedroom Suite $$$, 2 Bedrooms $$$, AmEx/MC/Visa/Other CC, Children Free, TAC 10%

Hotel Amenities: Laundry, Library, Parking

Business Facilities: Conf. Rm. Cap. 120, Copier, Aud/Vis., FAX

Recreational Facilities: Pool, Whirlpool, Tennis, Golf, Game Area; Country Club

Comps: Continental Breakfast, Refreshments

Room Amenities: Room Service, Free Paper, TV, Phone in Rm., Cable TV, Radio, Kitchen, Ind. Heat Ctl., Ind. AC Ctl.

Adjacent to the airport and providing shuttle service to Cielo Vista Shopping Mall, and Bassett Shopping Center, The Residence Inn caters to travelers making extended stays for business, relocation, or leisure. The spacious and peaceful suites have modern kitchens, a color T.V., and well-placed telephone jacks. Discounted rates for extended stays.

FORT WORTH

The Residence Inn by Marriott
1701 S. University
Fort Worth, TX 76107

120 Suites
817-870-1011   800-331-3131

Location: Westside; Downtown: 5 min.
Airport: 5 minutes
Near: Log Cabin Village, Will Rogers Equestrian Center
Walking Distance To: Zoo, Park
Area Attractions: Botanical Gardens, Omni Theatre, Texas Christian Univ.

Price Range & Credit Cards: 1 Bedroom Suite $$, 2 Bedrooms $$$, AmEx/MC/ Visa/Other CC, Children Free, TAC 10%

Hotel Amenities: Laundry, Library, Parking, TV Lounge, Handicap (2)

Business Facilities: Conf. Rm. Cap. 30, Mess. Ctr., Copier, Aud/Vis., Teleconf., FAX, Comp. Hook-up

Recreational Facilities: Pool, Whirlpool, Fitn. Ctr., Golf, Ice Skating, Paddle Boats, Game Area, Bikes nearby

Comps: Continental Plus Breakfast, Refreshments, Hors d'oeuvres

Room Amenities: Free Paper, TV, Phone in Rm., Cable TV, Radio, Full Kitchen, Ind. Heat Ctl., Ind. AC Ctl.

Close to the Will Rogers Equestrian Center and Texas Christian U., Residence Inn by Marriott is the best choice whether you are on business or vacation. Your suite is fully equipped with a kitchen, living and bedroom areas, as well as a wood-burning fireplace. For recreation, enjoy the pool, spas, sportcourt or the scenic Trinity River jogging path.

GALVESTON

The Victorian Condotel
6300 Seawall Blvd.
Galveston, TX 77551

216 Suites
409-740-3555   800-231-6363

Location: Seawall; Downtown: 5 min.
Airport: 30 minutes
Near: Beach Area, Restaurants
Walking Distance To: Shopping Mall
Area Attractions: Sea-Arama, Railroad Museum

Price Range & Credit Cards: 1 Bedroom Suite $$, 2 Bedrooms $$, AmEx/MC/Visa/ Other CC, Children Free, TAC 15%

Hotel Amenities: Laundry, Parking

Business Facilities: Conf. Rm. Cap. 80

Recreational Facilities: Pool, Whirlpool, Game Area; Fishing Pier

Comps: Continental Breakfast

Room Amenities: Room Service, TV, Phone in Rm., Cable TV, Radio, Kitchen, Ind. Heat Ctl., Ind. AC Ctl.

Each cozy suite at The Victorian Condotel features a T.V., stereo, microwave oven and a private patio overlooking the breathtaking Mexican Gulf. If you don't feel like strolling the beautiful beach, visit the historic Strand, turn of the century homes, museums, and attractions galore.

——————————————————— HOUSTON ———————————————————

Embassy Suites Hotel
9090 Southwest Freeway
Houston, TX 77074

248 Suites
713-995-0123   800-362-2779

Location: Southwest; Downtown: 15 mi.
Airport: 30 miles
Near: Sharpstown Complex, Restaurants
Walking Distance To: Shopping Mall
Area Attractions: Astroworld/Waterworld

Price Range & Credit Cards: 1 Bedroom Suite $$$, 2 Bedrooms $$$, AmEx/MC/
Visa/Other CC, Children Free, TAC 15%

Hotel Amenities: Laundry, Parking, TV Lounge, Handicap (8)

Business Facilities: Conf. Rm. Cap. 200, Banquet Fac., Mess. Ctr., Sec. Serv., Copier,
Aud/Vis., Comp. Hook-up

Recreational Facilities: Pool, Sauna, Whirlpool, Fitn. Ctr., Tennis, Golf, Racquetball;
Jogging Track

Comps: Full Breakfast, Refreshments

Room Amenities: Free Paper, TV, Phones in Rm. (2), Cable TV, Radio, Wet Bar, Kitchen,
Ind. Heat Ctl., Ind. AC Ctl.

Conveniently located ten minutes from the Galleria, Embassy Suites puts you within easy driving distance to all the city has to offer. Treat yourself to your favorite drink at the Manager's complimentary cocktail party held nightly in the beautiful all weather atrium courtyard rich with tropical plants. Golf, tennis and racquetball are all nearby.

——————————————————— HOUSTON ———————————————————

Galleria Executive Inn
4723 W. Alabama
Houston, TX 77027

52 Suites
713-621-2797

Location: Galleria; Downtown: 15 min.
Airport: 30 minutes
Near: Shopping Mecca, Restaurants
Area Attractions: Heart of very modern mall

Price Range & Credit Cards: 1 Bedroom Suite $, 2 Bedrooms $$, Junior $, AmEx/
MC/Visa/Other CC, Children Free, TAC 10%

Hotel Amenities: Laundry, Parking, Car Hire, Pets Allowed, Handicap (26)

Business Facilities: Mess. Ctr., Sec. Serv., Copier

Recreational Facilities: Pool; Athletic Club nearby

Comps: Coffee Service

Room Amenities: TV, Phone in Rm., Cable TV, Kitchen, Ind. Heat Ctl., Ind. AC Ctl.

This intimate 52 unit all-suite hotel is located in the heart of the Galleria area on a quiet oak-shaded street. Suites feature Williamsburg bedroom furniture with a plum color scheme, traditional livingroom with oriental screens, and a contemporary kitchen and dining area. Close to the educational and medical areas.

—————————————— HOUSTON ——————————————

Galleria Oaks Corporate Inn
5151 Richmond Ave.
Houston, TX 77056

70 Suites
713-629-7120

Location: Galleria; Downtown: 10 min.
Airport: 30 minutes
Near: Windsor Plaza, Restaurants, Shops
Walking Distance To: Theatres
Area Attractions: Night Life, Astrodome

Price Range & Credit Cards: 1 Bedroom Suite $, 2 Bedrooms $$, AmEx/MC/Visa/ Other CC, Children Free, TAC 10%

Hotel Amenities: Laundry, Parking, Car Hire, TV Lounge, Pets Allowed

Business Facilities: Conf. Rm. Cap. 75, Mess. Ctr., Sec. Serv., Copier, Telex

Recreational Facilities: Pool, Sauna, Whirlpool, Fitn. Ctr., Golf, Game Area

Comps: Continental Breakfast, Refreshments, Hors d'oeuvres

Room Amenities: TV, Phone in Rm., Cable TV, Radio, Kitchen, Ind. Heat Ctl., Ind. AC Ctl.

Amidst high-rise buildings and fast-paced life, tranquility is offered at Galleria Oaks. Suites feature large walk-in closets, and fully-equipped kitchens. Hotel amenities include 24-hour security, covered complimentary parking, and daily maid service. Excellent business and recreational facilities make this 2-story garden style hotel a great value.

—————————————— Houston ——————————————

Guest Quarters Suite Hotel
5353 Westheimer Rd.
Houston, TX 77056

335 Suites
713-961-9000 800-424-2900

Location: Uptown; Downtown: 15 min.
Airport: 30 minutes
Near: The prestigious Galleria, Uptown Houston
Walking Distance To: Everything
Area Attractions: Heart of Houston's finest shopping center

Price Range & Credit Cards: 1 Bedroom Suite $$$, 2 Bedrooms $$$$, AmEx/MC/ Visa/Other CC, TAC 10%

Hotel Amenities: Laundry, Library, Parking, Car Hire, Pets Allowed

Business Facilities: Banquet Fac., Mess. Ctr., Sec. Serv., Copier, Aud/Vis., FAX, Telex

Recreational Facilities: Pool, Fitn. Ctr., Tennis 5 min.; Golf 5 min.

Restaurant/Bar: McKinley's

Comps: Breakfast Buffet, Managers Reception

Room Amenities: Room Service, TV, Phones in Rm. (2), Cable TV, Radio, Kitchen, Ind. Heat Ctl., Ind. AC Ctl.

This 26-story towering high-rise secluded from the street by a courtyard satisfies every guest's needs. Relax in the casual restaurant adorned with hanging plants and cacti. Business is easy with the many services and facilities available. One block to the famous Galleria Mall containing Macy's, Neiman Marcus, Lord and Taylor, and more.

───────────────── HOUSTON ─────────────────

Hotel Luxeford Suites
1400 Old Spanish Trail
Houston, TX 77054

191 Suites
713-796-1000 800-662-3232

Location: Southmain; Downtown: 5 mi.
Airport: 15 minutes
Near: Astrodome, Medical Center, Convention Center, Business District
Area Attractions: Herman Park, Galleria, Astroworld

Price Range & Credit Cards: 1 Bedroom Suite $$, AmEx/MC/Visa/Other CC, Children Free, TAC 10%

Hotel Amenities: Laundry, Parking, TV Lounge, Handicap (11)

Business Facilities: Conf. Rm. Cap. 185, Banquet Fac., Mess. Ctr., Sec. Serv., Copier, Telex, Bus. Ctr.

Recreational Facilities: Pool, Sauna, Whirlpool, Fitn. Ctr., Tennis, Golf, Scuba, Game Area; Deep Sea Fishing

Restaurant/Bar: Cafe Luxeford

Comps: Continental Breakfast, Shoeshine

Room Amenities: Free Paper, TV, Phones in Rm. (2), VCR, Radio, Wet Bar, Ind. Heat Ctl., Ind. AC Ctl.

Tucked between the Medical Center and the Astrodome, the Luxeford is close to major freeways which lead to the airport, Galleria, and downtown. Many business and recreational facilities are available at this handsome brick hotel. By focusing attention on the suites and amenities the Luxeford has increased individual comfort at an affordable price.

───────────────── HOUSTON ─────────────────

Lexington Hotel Suites
16410 N. Freeway 45
Houston, TX 77090

250 Suites
713-821-1000 800-537-8483

Location: Northside; Downtown: 15 mi.
Airport: 8 miles
Near: Greenspoint Mall 4 miles, Golf course, Old Town Spring
Walking Distance To: Suburbs, Restaurants
Area Attractions: Woodlands, Goodyear Blimp Base

Price Range & Credit Cards: 1 Bedroom Suite $, 2 Bedrooms $$, Junior $, AmEx/MC/Visa/Other CC, Children Free, TAC 15%

Hotel Amenities: On-site laundry, Handicap (4)

Business Facilities: Conf. Rm. Cap. 10, Banquet Fac., Mtg. cap. 50, Aud/Vis.

Recreational Facilities: Pool, Boating/Skiing 20 mi.; Golf 15 mi.

Comps: Continental Breakfast, Airport shuttle

Room Amenities: TV, Phone in Rm., Radio, Kitchen, Ind. Heat Ctl., Ind. AC Ctl.

Lexington Hotel Suites can easily accommodate the business traveler or vacationer with 3 sizes of suites available. Located only 8 miles from the airport, the 250 suites are traditionally furnished and have full kitckens. Complimentary continental breakfast is served 6:00am-8:30am in the spacious Hospitality Room. Play golf at the Woodlands' TPC.

The Hermitage, Nashville, TN

HOUSTON

The Residence Inn by Marriott
7710 S. Main
Houston, TX 77030

290 Suites
713-660-7993 800-331-3131

Location: Downtown: 2 miles
Airport: Houston: 45 minutes
Near: Jogging Trail, Texas Medical Center, Hobby
Airport-25 min., Shopping Malls
Walking Distance To: Suburbs, Restaurants
Area Attractions: Astroworld, Waterworld, Zoo

Price Range & Credit Cards: 1 Bedroom Suite $, 2 Bedrooms $$, AmEx/MC/Visa/
Other CC, Children Free, TAC 14%

Hotel Amenities: Laundry, Parking, TV Lounge, Pets Allowed, Handicap (14)

Business Facilities: Conf. Rm. Cap. 60, Mess. Ctr., Copier

Recreational Facilities: Pool, Whirlpool, Sportcourt; Jogging trail nearby

Comps: Continental Breakfast, Cocktails & Snacks, Local Phone Calls

Room Amenities: Free Paper, TV, Phone in Rm., Cable TV, Radio, Kitchen, Ind. Heat
Ctl., Ind. AC Ctl.

*Close to Rice University, Downtown, Texas Medical Center and Astrodome, the Residence
is ideal for a relocating family or an extended business stay. All suites have fully-equipped
kitchens and separate livingroom. Enjoy a year-round heated pool. Complimentary breakfast, snacks & cocktails served daily except Sunday. Rates discounted for extended stays.*

─────────────── HOUSTON ───────────────

The Residence Inn by Marriott
6910 So. West Freeway
Houston, TX 77074

151 Suites
713-785-3415 800-331-3131

Location: Southwest; Downtown: 12 mi.
Airport: 45 minutes
Near: Sharpstown Mall, Regency Park
Area Attractions: Astrodome, Museums, Galleria

Price Range & Credit Cards: 1 Bedroom Suite $$$, 2 Bedrooms $$$, AmEx/MC/Visa/Other CC, Children Free, TAC 10%

Hotel Amenities: Laundry, Library, Parking, Car Hire, TV Lounge, Pets Allowed, Handicap (4)

Business Facilities: Conf. Rm. Cap. 50, Mess. Ctr., Sec. Serv., Copier, Aud/Vis.

Recreational Facilities: Pool, Whirlpool, Game Area; Health Club privileges

Comps: Continental Breakfast, Refreshments, Hors d'oeuvres

Room Amenities: Free Paper, TV, Phone in Rm., Cable TV, VCR, Radio, Wet Bar, Kitchen, Ind. Heat Ctl., Ind. AC Ctl.

The Residence Inn Southeast is beautifully landscaped with a grass picnic area. The inner courtyard includes a pool and deck adjacent to the sportscourt for basketball, paddletennis, and volleyball. Business needs are well-served with three conference rooms, a message center, audio-visual capabilities, and a copier. Discounted rates for extended stays.

─────────────── HOUSTON ───────────────

Wyndham Hotel Travis Center
6633 Travis St.
Houston, TX 77030

145 Suites
713-524-6633 800-822-4200

Location: West Univ.; Downtown: 10 min.
Airport: 45 minutes
Near: Rice Univ., Village Shops
Walking Distance To: Rice Stadium
Area Attractions: Texas Medical Center, Museums

Price Range & Credit Cards: 1 Bedroom Suite $$$, 2 Bedrooms $$$$+, Junior $$$, AmEx/MC/Visa/Other CC, Children Free, TAC 14%

Hotel Amenities: Laundry, Parking, Pets Allowed, Handicap (27)

Business Facilities: Conf. Rm. Cap. 200, Banquet Fac., Mess. Ctr., Sec. Serv., Copier, Aud/Vis., Telex

Recreational Facilities: Pool, Sauna, Whirlpool, Fitn. Ctr., Aerobics; Jogging Paths

Restaurant/Bar: Garden Court, Lobby Lounge, Entertainment

Room Amenities: Room Service, TV, Phones in Rm. (2), Cable TV, Radio, Wet Bar, Coffee Makers, Ind. Heat Ctl., Ind. AC Ctl.

Next door to the Texas Medical Center, the Wyndham's distinctive 18-story structure is an elegant hotel for business executives or the perfect retreat for visiting travelers. Work out in the fitness center, then relax while floating in the rooftop pool. The many opportunities for leisure activity are only surpassed by the myriad of business facilities.

─────────────────── IRVING ───────────────────

Embassy Suites Hotel
4650 W. Airport Freeway
Irving, TX 75062

308 Suites
214-790-0093 800-362-2779

Location: DFW Airport; Downtown: 20 mi.
Airport: 5 minutes
Near: Shopping Malls
Area Attractions: Texas Stadium, Wet N'Wild Park, Ranger Stadium, Six Flags

Price Range & Credit Cards: 1 Bedroom Suite $$$, AmEx/MC/Visa/Other CC, Children Free, TAC 10%

Hotel Amenities: Valet Laundry, Handicap Rooms

Business Facilities: Conf. Rm. Cap. 450, Banquet Fac., Aud/Vis., Conf.Suites

Recreational Facilities: Pool, Sauna, Whirlpool, Steamroom, Golf, Racquetball; Tennis 5 min. away

Restaurant/Bar: Restaurant, Lounge, Entertainment

Comps: Full Breakfast, Refreshments, Airport Transport

Room Amenities: TV, Phones in Rm. (2), Cable TV, Radio, Wet Bar, Kitchen, Ind. Heat Ctl., Ind. AC Ctl.

With free 24-hour airport transportation, a good location and many business services, Embassy makes a great place for taking care of business. The 10-story atrium with a large cascading waterfall and tropical plants creates a relaxed atmosphere that any vacationer can appreciate after a busy day at the many nearby attractions.

─────────────────── IRVING ───────────────────

Lexington Hotel Suites
4100 W. John Carpenter Freeway
Irving, TX 75063

90 Suites
214-929-4008 800-527-1877

Location: Westside; Downtown: 15 mi.
Airport: 5 minutes
Near: Airport DFW, Las Colinas
Walking Distance To: Suburbs
Area Attractions: World Trade Center, Stockyards, Dallas West End Market Place

Price Range & Credit Cards: 1 Bedroom Suite $$, 2 Bedrooms $$$, Junior $$, AmEx/MC/Visa/Other CC, Children Free, TAC 15%

Hotel Amenities: Laundry, Handicap (1)

Business Facilities: Conf. Rm. Cap. 65, Banquet Fac., Mess. Ctr., Sec. Serv., Copier, Aud/Vis., FAX

Recreational Facilities: Pool, Whirlpool; Las Colinas Country Club

Comps: Continental Breakfast, Airport Shuttle

Room Amenities: Free Paper, TV, Phone in Rm., Cable TV, Radio, Kitchen, Ind. Heat Ctl., Ind. AC Ctl.

The Lexington features a beautiful atrium overlooking a lighted pool & jacuzzi courtyard. Close to downtown Dallas, downtown Fort Worth, and The World Trade Center, this hotel has 2 conference rooms & several business services including secretarial and FAX. Whether you are staying for business or leisure the staff is eager to extend "Texas Hospitality."

──────────── MCALLEN ────────────

Embassy Suites Hotel
1800 S. Second St.
McAllen, TX 78503

168 Suites
512-686-3000 800-362-2779

Location: Central; Downtown: 1 mile
Airport: ½ mile
Near: Expressway 83, La Plaza Mall
Walking Distance To: Medical Center
Area Attractions: Convention Center, South
Padre Island, Reynosa Mexico

Price Range & Credit Cards: 1 Bedroom Suite $$, 2 Bedrooms $$$$, AmEx/MC/
Visa/Other CC, Children Free, TAC 10%

Hotel Amenities: Laundry, Parking, TV Lounge, Handicap (10)

Business Facilities: Conf. Rm. Cap. 500, Banquet Fac., Mess. Ctr., Sec. Serv., Copier,
Aud/Vis., Telex, FAX

Recreational Facilities: Pool, Sauna, Whirlpool, Fitn. Ctr., Racquetball, Game Area;
Golf and Tennis nearby

Restaurant/Bar: Remington's, Entertainment

Comps: Full Breakfast, Refreshments, Hors d'oeuvres

Room Amenities: Room Service, Free Paper, TV, Phones in Rm. (2), Cable TV, Radio,
Wet Bar, Kitchen, Ind. Heat Ctl., Ind. AC Ctl.

*Embassy Suites McAllen is the only all-suite, full service, luxury hotel in the Rio Grande
Valley. The hotel is convenient to McAllen Medical Center and Mexico. The nine story trop-
ical atrium is the perfect place to congregate for a complimentary full breakfast and cock-
tails. Remington's Restaurant in the hotel features mesquite broiled specialties.*

──────────── MIDLAND ────────────

Lexington Hotel Suites
1003 S. Midkiff
Midland, TX 79701

305 Suites
915-697-3155 800-442-7682

Location: Central; Downtown: 3 miles
Airport: 5 miles
Near: Suburbs, Midland Mall
Walking Distance To: Shops, Restaurants
Area Attractions: Petroleum Museum, Theatre

Price Range & Credit Cards: 1 Bedroom Suite $, 2 Bedrooms $$, Junior $, AmEx/
MC/Visa/Other CC, Children Free, TAC 15%

Hotel Amenities: Laundry, Pets Allowed, Handicap (4)

Business Facilities: Conf. Rm. Cap. 175, Aud/Vis.

Recreational Facilities: Pool, Whirlpool; Golf & Bowling 2 miles

Comps: Continental Breakfast

Room Amenities: TV, Phone in Rm., Radio, Kitchen, Ind. Heat Ctl., Ind. AC Ctl.

*Well located in Midland, the Lexington Hotel Suites can easily accommodate the business
traveler or vacationer with three sizes of suites available to meet almost any need. The
decor is bright and cheerful and the atrium and beautiful lobby seating area provide places
to congregate. The pool area is surrounded by attractive gardens.*

—————————————— MONTGOMERY ——————————————

Walden on Lake Conroe
14001 Walden Rd.
Montgomery, TX 77356

220 Suites
713-353-9737   409-582-6441

Location: Country; Downtown: 20 mi.
Airport: 15 miles
Near: Resort Area, Marina, Two Restaurants
Walking Distance To: Lakeside
Area Attractions: Tranquil Setting, Wooded Area

Price Range & Credit Cards: 1 Bedroom Suite $$, 2 Bedrooms $$$, AmEx/MC/Visa/Other CC, Children Free, TAC 10%

Hotel Amenities: Laundry, Library, Parking, Car Hire, TV Lounge

Business Facilities: Conf. Rm. Cap. 350, Banquet Fac., Mess. Ctr., Sec. Serv., Copier, Aud/Vis., Teleconf., Comp. Hook-up

Recreational Facilities: Pool, Fitn. Ctr., Golf, 16 Tennis Courts, Game Area; Marina

Restaurant/Bar: Commodore, Retreat, 19th Hole, Entertainment

Room Amenities: TV, Phone in Rm., Cable TV, Radio, Wet Bar, Kitchen, Ind. Heat Ctl., Ind. AC Ctl.

If you are looking for a tranquil setting for serious relaxation or productive business at an affordable price, Walden is for you. Compete on the Von Hagge-Devlin par 72 golf course, or on one of the 16 Laykold tennis courts, or enjoy the many opportunities a sparkling lake provides. Many "500" companies do business here. Excellent facilities

—————————————— ODESSA ——————————————

Lexington Hotel Suites
3031 E. Highway 80
Odessa, TX 79761

144 Suites
915-333-9678   800-527-1877

Location: Central; Downtown: 3 miles
Airport: 6 miles
Near: Restaurants, Shops, Permian Basin
Walking Distance To: Univ. of Texas
Area Attractions: Permian Basin Mall, Art Institute

Price Range & Credit Cards: 1 Bedroom Suite $, 2 Bedrooms $, AmEx/MC/Visa/Other CC, Children Free, TAC 15%

Hotel Amenities: Laundry, Pets Allowed, Handicap (2)

Recreational Facilities: Pool

Comps: Continental Breakfast, Refreshments, Courtesy Airport Car

Room Amenities: TV, Phone in Rm., Radio, Kitchen, Ind. Heat Ctl., Ind. AC Ctl.

This traditional 144-suite hotel offers 2 types of suites and is situated close to Petroleum Museum and Art Institute. A continental breakfast is served daily from 6:30-8:30 in the Hospitality Room. Relax by the swimming pool and tan in the big Texas sun. Be sure to ask about the special rates for extended stays.

─────────── PORT ARANSAS ───────────

Port Royal "By the Sea"
P. O. Box 336
Port Aransas, TX 78373

210 Suites
512-749-5011 800-847-5659

Location: Beachside; Downtown: 7 miles
Airport: 7 miles
Near: All water facilities, Mustang Island
Walking Distance To: Gulf of Mexico
Area Attractions: Marine Science Institute,
Wildlife Refuge

Price Range & Credit Cards: 1 Bedroom Suite $$$$, 2 Bedrooms $$$$, AmEx/MC/
Visa/Other CC, Children Free, TAC 10%

Hotel Amenities: Laundry, Parking, TV Lounge, Handicap (1)

Business Facilities: Conf. Rm. Cap. 700, Banquet Fac., Copier, Aud/Vis.

Recreational Facilities: Pool, Whirlpool, Fitn. Ctr., Golf, Boating, Pier Fishing, Horses

Restaurant/Bar: Royale Beachcomber, Entertainment

Room Amenities: TV, Phone in Rm., Radio, Wet Bar, Kitchen, Ind. Heat Ctl., Ind. AC Ctl.

Imagine a water wonderland on the Gulf shore where you can swim, walk the beach, wind surf or sail. Closer to your own ocean-view suite at Port Royal by the Sea are waterfalls, grottoes, whirlpools and a water slide, even swim-up cabana bars! Within easy reach by car are such pleasures as national beaches, a fishing village, and Corpus Christi.

─────────── SAN ANTONIO ───────────

Embassy Suites Hotel
7750 Briaridge St.
San Antonio, TX 78230

217 Suites
512-340-5421 800-362-2779

Location: Northwest; Downtown: 15 min.
Airport: 5 minutes
Near: North Star Mall
Area Attractions: Seaworld, The Alamo, River-
Walk

Price Range & Credit Cards: 1 Bedroom Suite $$$, AmEx/MC/Visa/Other CC, Chil-
dren Free, TAC 10%

Hotel Amenities: Laundry, Parking, Car Hire, Pets Allowed

Business Facilities: Conf. Rm. Cap. 48, Banquet Fac., Copier, Aud/Vis., Telex, Comp.
Hook-up

Recreational Facilities: Pool, Sauna, Whirlpool, Fitn. Ctr.; President's Health Club

Restaurant/Bar: Deli/Restaurant and Lounge

Comps: Full Breakfast, Refreshments, Hors d'oeuvres

Room Amenities: Room Service, Free Paper, TV, Phones in Rm. (2), Cable TV, Radio,
Wet Bar, Kitchen

Embassy Suites features tastefully furnished, homelike accommodations with mauve and dusty rose decor, and kitchens with stove and oven. Complimentary breakfast is served in the plant-filled atrium, an attractive place to socialize at any time. Guest privileges at the Health Club provide additional relaxation.

———————————————— SAN ANTONIO ————————————————

Embassy Suites Hotel
10110 U.S. Hiway 281 North
San Antonio, TX 78216

261 Suites
512-525-9999 800-362-2779

Location: Northside; Downtown: 9 miles
Airport: 2 minutes
Near: Airport, North Star Mall
Walking Distance To: Airport Shops
Area Attractions: Seaworld, The Alamo, River-Walk

Price Range & Credit Cards: 1 Bedroom Suite $$$, 2 Bedrooms $$$$, AmEx/MC/Visa/Other CC, Children Free, TAC 10%

Hotel Amenities: Parking, Pets Allowed, Handicap (4)

Business Facilities: Conf. Rm. Cap. 100, Banquet Fac., Sec. Serv., Copier, FAX, Telex

Recreational Facilities: Pool, Sauna, Whirlpool, Game Area

Restaurant/Bar: Ellington's, Entertainment

Comps: Full Breakfast, Refreshments

Room Amenities: Room Service, TV, Phone in Rm., Cable TV, Radio, Wet Bar, Kitchen, Ind. Heat Ctl., Ind. AC Ctl.

The staff at Embassy goes out of its way to make your stay memorably pleasant. And you'll appreciate the complimentary full breakfast, cooked to order, and the two-hour Manager's reception each evening. If you want to shop, you have free transportation to and from San Antonio's finest specialty malls, North Star and Central Park.

———————————————— SAN ANTONIO ————————————————

Lexington Hotel Suites
4934 N.W. Loop 410
San Antonio, TX 78229

212 Suites
512-680-3351 800-527-1877

Location: Central; Downtown: 7 miles
Airport: 8 miles
Near: City Center, Military Bases
Walking Distance To: Suburb Shops
Area Attractions: Hemisphere Plaza, Medical Center, Zoo, Sea World

Price Range & Credit Cards: 1 Bedroom Suite $, 2 Bedrooms $$, Junior $, AmEx/MC/Visa/Other CC, Children Free, TAC 15%

Hotel Amenities: Laundry, Pets Allowed, Handicap (3)

Business Facilities: Conf. Rm. Cap. 50, Board Room, Aud/Vis.

Recreational Facilities: Pool, Athletic Fac, Tennis 3 miles, Skiing 10 miles, Golf 4 miles

Comps: Continental Breakfast, Airport Shuttle

Room Amenities: TV, Phone in Rm., Radio, Kitchen, Ind. Heat Ctl., Ind. AC Ctl.

Conveniently located just 15 minutes from the airport, the Lexington is also close enough for you to explore the beauty and history of downtown San Antonio. Enjoy your complimentary continental breakfast in the lovely Atrium or beside the heated pool. Golf, tennis and horseback riding are easily accesible from the hotel.

---------------------------------- SAN ANTONIO ----------------------------------

Texas Guestel
13101 E. Loop 1604 N.
San Antonio, TX 78233

103 Suites
512-655-9491

Location: Northwest; Downtown: 7 miles
Airport: 7 miles
Near: Live Oak District
Walking Distance To: Randolph A.F.B.
Area Attractions: Breckenridge Park Zoo, Alamo, Seaworld of Texas

Price Range & Credit Cards: 1 Bedroom Suite $, 2 Bedrooms $, AmEx/MC/Visa/ Other CC

Hotel Amenities: Laundry, Parking, Pets Allowed

Business Facilities: Conf. Rm. Cap. 100, Mess. Ctr., Copier

Recreational Facilities: Pool, Fitn. Ctr.

Comps: Continental Breakfast, Airport Transport

Room Amenities: TV, Phone in Rm., Cable TV, Radio, Kitchen, Ind. Heat Ctl., Ind. AC Ctl.

The staff at Guestel is always ready to serve you with a smile. And you'll love your home-like suite which has a fully-equipped kitchen—there's even a dishwasher, and a well-lit desk, bar and game table. There's a complimentary continental breakfast and transportation to and from the airport.

---------------------------------- SAN ANTONIO ----------------------------------

The Residence Inn by Marriott
4041 Bluemel Rd.
San Antonio, TX 78240

128 Suites
512-692-9600 800-331-3131

Location: Northwest; Downtown: 20 min.
Airport: 20 minutes
Near: U.S.Auto Association, Medical Center
Walking Distance To: Restaurants
Area Attractions: The Alamo, Seaworld of Texas

Price Range & Credit Cards: 1 Bedroom Suite $$, 2 Bedrooms $$$, AmEx/MC/ Visa/Other CC, Children Free, TAC 10%

Hotel Amenities: Laundry, Parking, TV Lounge, Pets Allowed, Handicap (1)

Business Facilities: Conf. Rm. Cap. 15

Recreational Facilities: Pool, Whirlpool, Sport Court, Golf; Water Skiing nearby

Comps: Continental Breakfast, Airport Shuttle, Cocktails & Snacks

Room Amenities: Free Paper, TV, Phone in Rm., Cable TV, Radio, Kitchen, Ind. Heat Ctl., Ind. AC Ctl.

Everything about the Residence Inn will make you feel at home, from the tastefully furnished and spacious suites, each with a kitchen and fireplace, to the central fireplace and cozy meeting area of the Gatehouse. Visit the lakes for water skiing, see the beautiful Texas hill country, and don't forget Seaworld! Rates discounted for extended stays!

 **Utah**

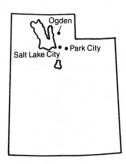

--- OGDEN ---

Radisson Suite Hotel Ogden
2510 Washington Blvd.
Ogden, UT 84401

104 Suites
801-627-1900 800-228-9822

Location: Central; Downtown
Airport: 40 miles
Near: Ogden City Park
Walking Distance To: Shops
Area Attractions: City Mall, Art Center, Library

Price Range & Credit Cards: 1 Bedroom Suite $$, AmEx/MC/Visa/Other CC, Children Free, TAC 10%

Hotel Amenities: Laundry, Parking, Car Hire, TV Lounge, Handicap (2)

Business Facilities: Conf. Rm. Cap. 350, Banquet Fac., Mess. Ctr., Sec. Serv., Copier, Aud/Vis.

Recreational Facilities: Whirlpool, Golf, Water Skiing, Game Area; 3 Ski resorts 20 miles

Restaurant/Bar: The Radisson, P.J. Kilpatricks, Entertainment

Room Amenities: Room Service, Free Paper, TV, Phones in Rm. (2), Cable TV, Radio, Wet Bar, Ind. Heat Ctl., Ind. AC Ctl.

One of the tallest and most majestic buildings in Ogden, the Radisson offers spectacular vistas in all directions. Built in 1927 and completely restored to its original beauty, it boasts marble floors, mirrors and chandeliers. Each suite is different, but all offer two telephones, two TV's, a wet bar and refrigerator. Full gym facilities-one block.

The Residence Inn by Marriott, Nashville, TN

PARK CITY

Prospector Square Hotel
2200 Sidewinder Drive
Park City, UT 84060

180 Suites
801-649-7100   800-453-3812

Location: Resort; Downtown: 6 miles
Airport: 45 minutes
Near: Wasatch Mountains, Resort Area, Prospector Square
Walking Distance To: Ski Trails
Area Attractions: Arts Festival, Balloon Festival

Price Range & Credit Cards: 1 Bedroom Suite $$$$, 2 Bedrooms $$$$, Junior $$, AmEx/MC/Visa/Other CC, Children Free, TAC 10%

Hotel Amenities: Handicap (30)

Business Facilities: Conf. Rm. Cap. 330, Banquet Fac., Mess. Ctr., Sec. Serv., Copier, Aud/Vis., Telex

Recreational Facilities: Pool, Sauna, Whirlpool, Fitn. Ctr., Golf, Skiing; Hot Air Balloon

Restaurant/Bar: Grub Steak, Entertainment

Room Amenities: TV, Phone in Rm., Cable TV, Kitchen, Ind. Heat Ctl., Ind. AC Ctl.

Park City's resort within a resort with all the luxuries of a world class hotel. The home of the ever popular Grub Steak Restaurant, a full service athletic club, and Park City's largest conference center-whether for business or pleasure your stay is certain to be a memorable one.

———————————————— SALT LAKE CITY ————————————————

Embassy Suites Hotel
W. Temple St. 6th.South St.
Salt Lake City, UT 84101

241 Suites
801-359-7800 800-325-7643

Location: Central; Downtown
Airport: 10 minutes
Near: Salt Palace Center, Major Shopping
Walking Distance To: Convention Center
Area Attractions: L.D.S. Mormon Temple

Price Range & Credit Cards: 1 Bedroom Suite $$$, 2 Bedrooms $$$$+, AmEx/MC/ Visa/Other CC, Children Free, TAC 10%

Hotel Amenities: Laundry, Parking, TV Lounge, Handicap (5)

Business Facilities: Conf. Rm. Cap. 100, Banquet Fac., Mess. Ctr., Copier, Aud/Vis., FAX, Comp. Hook-up

Recreational Facilities: Pool, Sauna, Whirlpool, Fitn. Ctr.; Skiing 30-45 minutes

Restaurant/Bar: The Plum, Clouseau's, Entertainment

Comps: Full breakfast, Refreshments, Hors d'oeuvres

Room Amenities: Room Service, Free Paper, TV, Phone in Rm., Cable TV, Radio, Wet Bar, Kitchen, Ind. Heat Ctl., Ind. AC Ctl.

Special extras will make your stay at Embassy Suites memorable: a complimentary cooked-to-order breakfast, a two-hour social with cocktails and hors d'ouuvres in the evening, airport limousine service and a well-equipped exercise room, including a sauna and hydrotherapy pool.You may relax in the skylighted, plant filled atrium.

———————————————— SALT LAKE CITY ————————————————

The Residence Inn by Marriott
765 E. 400 So.
Salt Lake City, UT 84102

128 Suites
801-532-5511 800-331-3131

Location: Central; Downtown: 7 blks.
Airport: 8 miles
Near: Major Highways, Business District
Walking Distance To: Trolley Square
Area Attractions: Univ. of Utah, Ski Resorts, Temple Square

Price Range & Credit Cards: 1 Bedroom Suite $$, 2 Bedrooms $$$, AmEx/MC/ Visa/Other CC, Children Free, TAC 10%

Hotel Amenities: Laundry, Parking, TV Lounge, Grocery Shopping

Business Facilities: Conf. Rm. Cap. 30, Copier, FAX

Recreational Facilities: Pool, Whirlpools, Movie Rentals; Sportcourt & Equipment

Comps: Continental Plus Breakfast, Evening Specials

Room Amenities: Free Paper, TV, Phone in Rm., Cable TV, Kitchen, Ind. Heat Ctl., Ind. AC Ctl.

The Residence Inn is conveniently located between downtown Salt Lake City and University of Utah, walking distance to shops, restaurants and theatres. Easy access to major highways lets you reach 7 ski areas in under 45 min . . . The spacious accommodations with full kitchens are ideal for business or vacation travellers. Rates discounted for extended stays.

 # Vermont

• Williston

WILLISTON

The Residence Inn by Marriott
1 Hurricane Lane
Williston, VT 05495

96 Suites
802-878-2001 800-331-3131

Location: Taft's Cors.; Burlington: 7 mi.
Airport: Burlington: 4 miles
Near: Shelburne Museum-4 miles, Lake Champlain-7 miles
Area Attractions: Skiing-1 hour

Price Range & Credit Cards: 1 Bedroom Suite $$, 2 Bedrooms $$$, AmEx/MC/Visa/Other CC, Children Free, TAC 10%

Hotel Amenities: Laundry, Library, Parking, TV Lounge, Handicap (5)

Business Facilities: Conf. Rm. Cap. 40, Mess. Ctr., Copier, Aud/Vis., FAX, Comp. Hook-up

Recreational Facilities: Pool, Whirlpool, Basketball, Paddle Tennis, Volleyball, Game Area; Health Club nearby

Comps: Continental Plus Breakast, Refreshments, Hors d'oeuvres

Room Amenities: Free Paper, TV, Phones in Rm. (2), Cable TV, Radio, Kitchen, Ind. Heat Ctl., Ind. AC Ctl.

The Residence Inn by Marriott is a special new hotel. Suites with full kitchens and living areas along with a warm and friendly staff, will make your stay comfortably homelike. Our hotel is located minutes from downtown Burlington, Burlington International Airport, Lake Champlain, and an hour from the best skiing. Rates discounted for extended stay.

❦ Virginia

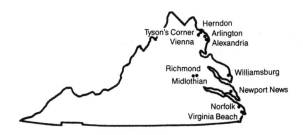

ARLINGTON

Embassy Suites Hotel
1300 Jefferson Davis Hiway
Arlington, VA 22202

267 Suites
703-979-9799 800-362-2779

Location: Central; Downtown: 5 miles
Airport: 1 mile
Walking Distance To: Metro, Shops
Area Attractions: Kennedy Center, Alexandria

Price Range & Credit Cards: 1 Bedroom Suite $$$$, 2 Bedrooms $$$$+, AmEx/ MC/Visa/Other CC, Children Free, TAC 10%

Hotel Amenities: Parking, Handicap (23)

Business Facilities: Conf. Rm. Cap. 80, Banquet Fac., Copier, Aud/Vis., Teleconf.

Recreational Facilities: Pool, Sauna, Whirlpool, Game Area; Outdoor Sun Deck

Restaurant/Bar: The Capitol Grille

Comps: Full Breakfast, Manager's Reception

Room Amenities: Room Service, Free Paper, TV, Phones in Rm. (2), Cable TV, Radio, Wet Bar, Ind. Heat Ctl., Ind. AC Ctl.

At the Embassy Suites Hotel you'll start the day with a complimentary breakfast cooked to your special order. Then set out for the nation's capital where you can visit the Smithsonian Institute, the Jefferson Memorial and the White House. Return to the Embassy in time for the manager's reception in the atrium at 5:30 and then dine at th Capitol Grille.

MIDLOTHIAN

Brandermill Inn & Conf. Ctr.
13550 Harbour Pointe Parkway
Midlothian, VA 23113

60 Suites
804-739-2777 800-441-3334

Location: Suburbs; Downtown: 8 miles
Airport: 15 minutes
Near: Brandermill, Three Restaurants, Planetarium
Walking Distance To: Market Square
Area Attractions: Cloverleaf Mall, Jazz Festival, Christopher Newport Festival

Price Range & Credit Cards: 1 Bedroom Suite $$, AmEx/MC/Visa/Other CC, Children Free, TAC 10%

Hotel Amenities: Parking, TV Lounge, Pets Allowed, Handicap (1)

Business Facilities: Conf. Rm. Cap. 150, Banquet Fac., Mess. Ctr., Sec. Serv., Copier, Aud/Vis.

Recreational Facilities: Pool, Sauna, Whirlpool, Fitn. Ctr., Tennis, Golf, Racquetball, Game Area; Boat Rentals

Restaurant/Bar: Nesting Place, Lobby Lounge, Entertainment

Comps: Hors d'oeuvres

Room Amenities: Room Service, TV, Phones in Rm. (2), Cable TV, Radio, Kitchen, Ind. Heat Ctl., Ind. AC Ctl.

You'll really enjoy the country charm at the Brandermill Inn! Tile floors, French Blue decor, carved figurines, Oriental rugs, wicker and natural wood add up to a comfortable and intimate environment, overlooking a 1700 acre lake.

NEWPORT NEWS

Governors Inn of Newport News
741 Thimble Shoals Blvd.
Newport News, VA 23606

50 Suites
804-873-1701 800-443-9350

Location: Suburbs; Downtown: 15 min.
Airport: 5 miles
Near: Industrial Park, Busch Gardens
Walking Distance To: Business Area
Area Attractions: Mariner's Museum, Jamestown

Price Range & Credit Cards: 1 Bedroom Suite $$, 2 Bedrooms $$, Junior $$, AmEx/MC/Visa/Other CC, Children Free, TAC 10%

Hotel Amenities: TV Lounge, Handicap (2)

Business Facilities: Conf. Rm. Cap. 50, Banquet Fac., Mess. Ctr., Sec. Serv., Copier, Aud/Vis.

Recreational Facilities: Pool, Sauna, Whirlpool, Tennis, Golf, Racquetball, Bowling

Restaurant/Bar: Governor's Inn

Comps: Full Breakfast, Hors d'oeuvres

Room Amenities: Room Service, Free Paper, TV, Phone in Rm., Cable TV, Radio, Wet Bar, Ind. Heat Ctl., Ind. AC Ctl.

Deep in the heart of an area of great historical significance, the Governors Inn will be your headquarters for wonderful sightseeing tours. Contrast the modern technology of NASA with a stroll through Colonial Williamsburg and the spectacular Busch Gardens; then take advantage of what the Atlantic shore offers, all within a radius of 25 miles.

──────── NORFOLK ────────

Lagniappe Inn Hotel
890 Poplar Hall Dr.
Norfolk, VA 23502

50 Suites
804-461-5956

Location: Central; Downtown: 1 mile
Airport: 5 miles
Near: 110 Store Mall, 14 Theatres
Walking Distance To: Restaurants, Shops
Area Attractions: Virginia Beach, Waterside

Price Range & Credit Cards: 1 Bedroom Suite $$$, Junior $$, AmEx/MC/Visa/Other CC, Children Free, TAC 10%

Hotel Amenities: Laundry, Parking, TV Lounge, Pets Allowed, Handicap (2)

Business Facilities: Conf. Rm. Cap. 30, Banquet Fac., Mess. Ctr., Sec. Serv., Copier, Aud/Vis., Comp. Hook-up

Recreational Facilities: Pool, Tennis, Golf; Fitness Center-3 miles

Restaurant/Bar: Lagniappe Cafe, Entertainment

Comps: Full Breakfast, Hors d'oeuvres

Room Amenities: Room Service, Free Paper, TV, Phone in Rm., Cable TV, Radio, Wet Bar, Ind. Heat Ctl., Ind. AC Ctl.

You'll find the New Orleans-style tropical atrium just the right place to relax. Or you can walk to a 110-store mall, or take in a play and stroll home to the Lagniappe Cafe for a nightcap.

Embassy Suites Hotel, Austin, TX

―――――――――――――――― RICHMOND ――――――――――――――――

Commonwealth Park Hotel
9th & Bank St.
Richmond, VA 23219

59 Suites
804-343-7300 800-343-7302

Location: Central; Downtown: 4 miles
Airport: 15 miles
Near: Financial District, Government Area
Walking Distance To: Downtown Shops
Area Attractions: Capitol Square, Historic Area

Price Range & Credit Cards: 1 Bedroom Suite $$$$, 2 Bedrooms $$$$+, AmEx/MC/ Visa/Other CC, Children Free, TAC 10%

Hotel Amenities: Laundry, Parking, Handicap (2)

Business Facilities: Conf. Rm. Cap. 75, Banquet Fac., Sec. Serv., Copier, Aud/Vis., Telex

Recreational Facilities: Sauna, Whirlpool, Fitn. Ctr., Tennis, Golf

Restaurant/Bar: Maxine's, The Assembly, Memories, Entertainment

Room Amenities: Room Service, Free Paper, TV, Phones in Rm. (3), Radio, Wet Bar, Ind. Heat Ctl., Ind. AC Ctl.

The Commonwealth is situated directly across from the state capitol in the heart of the financial, legal, governmental and historic districts of Richmond. This is truly a luxurious place to conduct your business, surrounded by 18th century atmosphere. All the charm and grace of the old South become real at this hotel.

―――――――――――――――― RICHMOND ――――――――――――――――

Embassy Suites Hotel
2925 Emerywood Parkway
Richmond, VA 23229

225 Suites
804-282-8585 800-362-2779

Location: Central; Downtown: 4 miles
Airport: 15 miles
Near: Brookfield Office Park, Commerce Center
Area Attractions: Coliseum, Shockoe Bottom Slip, Kings Dominion

Price Range & Credit Cards: 1 Bedroom Suite $$$, 2 Bedrooms $$$, AmEx/MC/ Visa/Other CC, Children Free, TAC 10%

Hotel Amenities: Laundry, Gift Shop, Parking, Car Hire, Handicap (8)

Business Facilities: Conf. Rm. Cap. 400, Banquet Fac., Mess. Ctr., Sec. Serv., Copier, Aud/Vis., Teleconf., Comp. Hook-up

Recreational Facilities: Pool, Sauna, Whirlpool, Fitn. Ctr.; Golf and Tennis nearby

Restaurant/Bar: Ellington's

Comps: Full Breakfast, Refreshments, Airport Transport

Room Amenities: Room Service, Free Paper, TV, Phones in Rm. (2), Cable TV, Radio, Wet Bar, Kitchen, Ind. Heat Ctl., Ind. AC Ctl.

Embassy Suites Hotel's 225 two-room suites overlook an 8-story garden atrium with fountains and walkways, located in the heart of Richmond. Enjoy a complimentary cooked-to-order breakfast, and in the evening, complimentary cocktails at the Manager's reception. Washington or Virginia Beach are within a one and a half hour drive.

TYSONS CORNER

The Residence Inn by Marriott
8616 Westwood Center Dr.
Tysons Corner, VA 22180

96 Suites
703-893-0120 800-331-3131

Location: Westside; Downtown: 5 miles
Airport: 15 minutes
Near: Major Corporate Headquarters, Washington D.C.
Walking Distance To: Many Shops
Area Attractions: Restaurants & Entertainment

Price Range & Credit Cards: 1 Bedroom Suite $$$, 2 Bedrooms $$$$, AmEx/MC/Visa/Other CC, Children Free, TAC 10%

Hotel Amenities: Laundry, Library, Parking, TV Lounge, Pets Allowed, Handicap (2)

Business Facilities: Conf. Rm. Cap. 30, Mess. Ctr., Sec. Serv., Copier

Recreational Facilities: Pool, Whirlpool; Golf Courses-10 mi.

Comps: Continental Plus Breakfast

Room Amenities: Free Paper, TV, Phone in Rm., Cable TV, VCR, Radio, Kitchen, Ind. Heat Ctl., Ind. AC Ctl.

13 garden-style buildings in a beautifully landscaped courtyard cluster around the pool, the gazebo, a sport court and a jogging trail here at the Residence Inn. The personal attention and friendliness of the staff give you a sense of being at home, but with all the fascination of the nation's capital nearby. Rates discounted for extended stays.

VIENNA

Embassy Suites Hotel
8517 Leesburg Pike
Vienna, VA 22180

232 Suites
703-883-0707 800-362-2779

Location: Central; D.C.: 15 miles
Airport: 12 miles
Near: Shopping Mall, Metro Station
Walking Distance To: Restaurants
Area Attractions: Wolf Trap Farm Park

Price Range & Credit Cards: 1 Bedroom Suite $$$$, 2 Bedrooms $$$$+, AmEx/MC/Visa/Other CC, Children Free, TAC 10%

Hotel Amenities: Gift Shop, Parking, Car Hire, TV Lounge, Handicap (2)

Business Facilities: Conf. Rm. Cap. 15, Copier, Aud/Vis., Teleconf., FAX

Recreational Facilities: Pool, Sauna, Whirlpool, Fitn. Ctr., Game Area; Health Club-full serv.

Restaurant/Bar: New York Carnegie Deli

Comps: Full Breakfast, Refreshments

Room Amenities: Room Service, Free Paper, TV, Phones in Rm. (2), Cable TV, Radio, Wet Bar, Refrigerator, Ind. Heat Ctl., Ind. AC Ctl.

The Embassy Suites Hotel at Tysons Corner is perfectly located for a variety of vacation activities. Comfortable suites and a lovely open atrium offer a great place to relax or meet associates. Travel five miles to Wolftrap Center for the Performing Arts and ten miles to the center of Washington, D.C., a sightseer's paradise.

—————————— VIRGINIA BEACH ——————————

Station One Hotel
2321 Atlantic Ave.
Virginia Beach, VA 23451

104 Suites
804-491-2400 800-435-2424

Location: Oceanside
Airport: Norfolk
Near: Resort Area
Walking Distance To: Public Beach
Area Attractions: Maritime Museum, Williamsburg

Price Range & Credit Cards: 1 Bedroom Suite $$$, AmEx/MC/Visa/Other CC, Children Free, TAC 10%

Hotel Amenities: Laundry, Parking, Handicap (10)

Business Facilities: Conf. Rm. Cap. 150, Banquet Fac., Copier, Aud/Vis.

Recreational Facilities: Pool, Sauna, Whirlpool, Tennis, Golf; Water Skiing

Restaurant/Bar: Unicorn by the Sea, Entertainment

Room Amenities: Room Service, Free Paper, TV, Phone in Rm., Cable TV, Radio, Wet Bar, Kitchen, Ind. Heat Ctl., Ind. AC Ctl.

Station One helps you make the most of Virginia Beach! The lobby overlooks the Maritime Museum, the hotel is located right on the ocean and in the immediate area are charter boats, a fishing pier, parasailing, lifeguarded beaches and the lovely Seashore State Park. Colonial Williamsburg and Busch Gardens are just an hour's drive away.

⚜ Washington

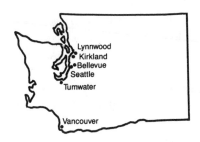

─────────────── BELLEVUE ───────────────

Holiday Court Hotel
10 100th Ave. NE
Bellevue, WA 98004

40 Suites
206-454-7018

Location: Central; Seattle: 10 min.
Airport: 20 minutes
Near: Lake Washington, Movie Theatres
Walking Distance To: Boutiques, Restaurants
Area Attractions: Near largest mall in the area

Price Range & Credit Cards: 1 Bedroom Suite $, 2 Bedrooms $$, AmEx/MC/Visa, Children Free, TAC 10%

Hotel Amenities: Laundry, Parking, Pets Allowed

Business Facilities: Mess. Ctr.

Recreational Facilities: Pool

Room Amenities: Free Paper, TV, Phone in Rm., Kitchen, Ind. Heat Ctl.

The Holiday Court Hotel loves children and your children will love it here. Each suite faces the garden and pool area and after their swim the kids can walk to the library, the movies, the bowling alley or the waterfront park. Take them to see the Space Needle in Seattle across Lake Washington and then shopping in the sumptuous Bellevue Square mall.

─── BELLEVUE ───

The Residence Inn by Marriott
14455 NE 29th. Place
Bellevue, WA 98007

120 Suites
206-882-1222　800-331-3131

Location: Suburban; Downtown: 10 min.
Airport: 17 miles
Near: High Tech Industries, Many Shops
Walking Distance To: Suburbs
Area Attractions: Bellevue Square, Puget Sound

Price Range & Credit Cards: 1 Bedroom Suite $$, 2 Bedrooms $$$, Junior $$, AmEx/MC/Visa/Other CC, Children Free, TAC 10%

Hotel Amenities: Laundry, Library, Parking, TV Lounge, Pets Allowed, Handicap (6)

Business Facilities: Conf. Rm. Cap. 25, Copier, Aud/Vis.

Recreational Facilities: Pool, Whirlpool, Golf, Game Area; Boating & Skiing nearby

Restaurant/Bar: Houlihan's

Comps: Continental Breakfast

Room Amenities: Free Paper, TV, Phone in Rm., Cable TV, Radio, Kitchen, Ind. Heat Ctl., Ind. AC Ctl.

Your First Nighter Kit at the Inn includes free popcorn, coffee and a log for your fireplace. There's endless shopping just three miles away at famed Bellevue Square and nearby wineries produce world-class wines. Visit the Space Needle, ride a ferry on Puget Sound, or just relax in the comfortable Gatehouse. Rates are discounted for extended stay.

─── KIRKLAND ───

The Club on Yarrow Bay
4311 Lake Washington Blvd.N.E.
Kirkland, WA 98033

35 Suites
206-827-4605

Location: Waterside; Downtown: 20 min.
Airport: 20 minutes
Near: Lakefront Location, Urban Resort
Walking Distance To: Fine Restaurants
Area Attractions: Lake side parks, Shops, Sports

Price Range & Credit Cards: 1 Bedroom Suite $$, 2 Bedrooms $$, AmEx/MC/Visa, Children Free

Hotel Amenities: Laundry, Parking, Pets Allowed, Handicap (20)

Business Facilities: Conf. Rm. Cap. 50, Mess. Ctr., Sec. Serv., Copier, Teleconf.

Recreational Facilities: Pool, Sauna, Whirlpool, Fitn. Ctr., Fishing, Boating, Sailing, Game Area; Skiing 45 min.

Room Amenities: TV, Phone in Rm., Cable TV, Radio, Wet Bar, Kitchen, Ind. Heat Ctl., Ind. AC Ctl.

Nestled among the trees on the shore of Lake Washington, The Club on Yarrow Bay is a boater's paradise. A thirty slip marina is a few steps from your door and power-yacht or sailboat cruises are available by day or week-end. Cross the Evergreen Pt. Bridge and you're in Seattle, a sightseer's dream.An ideal place for your conference.

---------------------------------- SEATTLE ----------------------------------

Doubletree Plaza
16500 Southcenter Parkway
Seattle, WA 98188

221 Suites
206-575-8220 800-528-0444

Location: Southside; Downtown: 20 min.
Airport: 5 minutes
Near: Southcenter Mall, Horse Racing, Major Shops
Walking Distance To: Shopping Mall
Area Attractions: Pike Street Market, Space Needle

Price Range & Credit Cards: 1 Bedroom Suite $$$, AmEx/MC/Visa/Other CC, Children Free, TAC 10%

Hotel Amenities: Laundry, Car Hire, Pets Allowed

Business Facilities: Conf. Rm. Cap. 610, Banquet Fac., Mess. Ctr., Sec. Serv., Copier, Aud/Vis., Telex

Recreational Facilities: Pool, Sauna, Whirlpool, Fitn. Ctr., Golf, Skiing; Horse Race Track

Restaurant/Bar: Peter B's, Infinity Lounge, Entertainment

Comps: Full Breakfast

Room Amenities: Room Service, TV, Phone in Rm., Cable TV, Radio, Wet Bar, Ind. Heat Ctl., Ind. AC Ctl.

Peter B's Restaurant, featuring fresh seafood, is located in the dramatic atrium area of the Doubletree Plaza. A plush seating area nearby is a great place to meet friends—the peaceful atmosphere enhanced by soft lights and sweet music. Relaxing beside the pool you'll have a spectacular view of snow-capped Mount Rainier.

---------------------------------- TUMWATER ----------------------------------

Shalimar Suites
5895 Capitol Blvd.
Tumwater, WA 98501

18 Suites
206-943-8391

Location: Southside; Downtown: 15 min.
Airport: 2 miles
Near: Exit 102, Highway 5, Residential Area
Walking Distance To: Barnes Lake
Area Attractions: State Capitol Campus, Malls

Price Range & Credit Cards: 1 Bedroom Suite $, 2 Bedrooms $, Junior $, MC/Visa, Children Free

Hotel Amenities: Laundry, Pets Allowed, Handicap (8)

Recreational Facilities: ; Golf Course one mile

Room Amenities: T.V., Cable TV, Kitchen, Ind. Heat Ctl

Shalimar Suites offers the comforts of home at a very moderate price. Among the features are twice-weekly maid service, a fully equipped kitchen (restaurants are nearby, too), and real closets. Close by the State Capitol Campus with its lovely grounds and fountains, Percival Park at the Puget Sound waterfront and 2 big regional shopping malls.

⚜ Washington D.C.

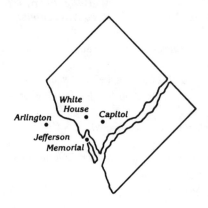

--- WASHINGTON ---

Embassy Suites Hotel
1250 22nd. Street NW
Washington, DC 20037

318 Suites
202-857-3388 800-362-2779

Location: West End; Downtown
Airport: 6 miles
Near: Blue-Red Metro Lines, Georgetown
Walking Distance To: Monuments, White House
Area Attractions: Galleries, Smithsonian, Zoo

Price Range & Credit Cards: 1 Bedroom Suite $$$$, Junior $$$$, AmEx/MC/Visa/Other CC, Children Free, TAC 10%

Hotel Amenities: Laundry, Gift Shop, Parking, No-smoke suites, Handicap (2)

Business Facilities: Conf. Rm. Cap. 20-400, Aud/Vis.

Recreational Facilities: Pool, Sauna, Whirlpool, Billards Room, Game Area; exercise facilities

Restaurant/Bar: Vivande Ristorante and Lounge

Comps: Full Cooked-to-order breakfast, Hospitality Hour

Room Amenities: Room Service, TV, Phones in Rm.(2), Radio, Wet Bar, Microwave, Ind. Heat Ctl., Ind. AC Ctl.

Recently opened in October, 1987, Embassy Suites welcomes guests to the comforts of the Suite Life and the conveniences of a downtown location. Full, cooked-to-order breakfast and evening Manager's Reception included in all rates! All suites offer a balcony view of our tropical atrium filled with greenery and waterfalls. Don't miss Vivande for dinner.

---------------------- WASHINGTON ----------------------

Georgetown Marbury Hotel
3000 "M" Street, N.W.
Washington, DC 20007

164 Suites
202-726-5000 800-368-5922

Location: Northwest; Downtown
Airport: 6 miles
Near: Historic Georgetown, Dining
Walking Distance To: Entertainment
Area Attractions: John F. Kennedy Center for Arts

Price Range & Credit Cards: 1 Bedroom Suite $$$, 2 Bedrooms $$$$, AmEx/MC/Visa/Other CC, Children Free, TAC 10%

Hotel Amenities: Laundry, Parking

Business Facilities: Conf. Rm. Cap. 300, Banquet Fac., Mess. Ctr., Sec. Serv., Copier, Aud/Vis., Telex

Recreational Facilities: Pool; Health Facilities near

Restaurant/Bar: Marbury, Lion's Gate, Entertainment

Comps: Refreshments

Room Amenities: Room Service, Free Paper, TV, Phone in Rm., Cable TV, Radio, Wet Bar, Ind. Heat Ctl., Ind. AC Ctl.

In the hub of Washington D.C. rises the contemporary Georgetown Marbury Hotel. Designed to accommodate any business need this prestigious hotel has the added attraction of being only footsteps away from some of the Capital's premiere dining, shopping, and entertainment. Later you can stop by the hotel restaurant, Marbury.

---------------------- WASHINGTON ----------------------

Hampshire Hotel
1310 New Hampshire Ave., N.W.
Washington, DC 20036

82 Suites
202-296-7600 800-368-5691

Location: Downtown
Airport: 6 miles
Near: Georgetown, Performing Arts
Walking Distance To: Theatres, Restaurants
Area Attractions: Embassy Row, Museums, Capitol

Price Range & Credit Cards: 1 Bedroom Suite $$$, 2 Bedrooms $$$$, AmEx/MC/Visa/Other CC, Children Free, TAC 10%

Hotel Amenities: Laundry, Parking

Business Facilities: Conf. Rm. Cap. 35, Banquet Fac., Mess. Ctr., Sec. Serv., Copier, Aud/Vis., Telex

Recreational Facilities: Health Facilities near

Restaurant/Bar: Lafitte

Comps: Refreshments

Room Amenities: Room Service, Free Paper, TV, Phone in Rm., Cable TV, Radio, Wet Bar, Kitchen, Ind. Heat Ctl., Ind. AC Ctl.

The Hampshire Hotel can easily accommodate any business need and still maintain a comfortable home-like environment. A myriad of interesting places to visit are minutes away from the lobby door including, The White House, the Capitol, Embassy Row, and major theatres and museums. The fine restaurant, Lafitte, provides an elegant ambiance.

Bristol Suites Hotel, Dallas, TX

WASHINGTON

Hotel Lombardy
2019 "I" St., N.W.
Washington, DC 20006

126 Suites
202-828-2600 800-424-5486

Location: Downtown
Airport: Dulles: 60 min.
Near: Kennedy Center, Museums, Monuments,
National Airport: 10 min.
Walking Distance To: White House,
Georgetown

Price Range & Credit Cards: 1 Bedroom Suite $$$, Junior $$$, AmEx/MC/Visa/
Other CC, Children Free, TAC 10%

Hotel Amenities: Laundry, Pets Allowed

Business Facilities: Conf. Rm. Cap. 45, Banquet Fac., Copier, Aud/Vis., FAX

Restaurant/Bar: Cafe Lombardy

Room Amenities: Free Paper, TV, Phone in Rm., Cable TV, VCR, Radio, Wet Bar, Kitchen, Ind. Heat Ctl., Ind. AC Ctl.

*A European style hotel located halfway between the White House and Georgetown. The
Lombardy offers spacious and well-equipped accommodations. Most have fully equipped
kitchens. All feature mini bars, large closets, and tastefully appointed decor. Complimentary newspapers and overnight shoeshine are also offered. The Cafe Lombardy is a local
favorite.*

—————————————— WASHINGTON ——————————————

One Washington Circle Hotel
1 Washington Circle, N.W.
Washington, DC 20037

151 Suites
202-872-1680 800-424-9671

Location: Foggy Bottom; Downtown
Airport: 6 miles
Near: Exclusive West End, Metro Station
Walking Distance To: White House
Area Attractions: Lincoln & Vietnam
Memorials

Price Range & Credit Cards: 1 Bedroom Suite $$$$, 2 Bedrooms $$$$+, Junior $$$$, AmEx/MC/Visa/Other CC, Children Free, TAC 10%

Hotel Amenities: Laundry, Parking, TV Lounge, Pets Allowed

Business Facilities: Conf. Rm. Cap. 100, Banquet Fac., Mess. Ctr., Sec. Serv., Copier, Aud/Vis., Telex, Comp. Hook-up

Recreational Facilities: Pool; Jogging Paths

Restaurant/Bar: West End Cafe, Entertainment

Comps: Continental Breakfast, Refreshments

Room Amenities: Room Service, Free Paper, TV, Phone in Rm., Kitchen, Ind. Heat Ctl., Ind. AC Ctl.

Overlooking a park, One Washington Circle is within easy walking distance of Georgetown, Metro, and downtown. Everything you want to do in Washington is right outside your door. The comfortable home-like atmosphere with oriental touches is perfect for meetings or carefree living. Visit the restaurant, West End Cafe, and relax in its airy surroundings.

—————————————— WASHINGTON ——————————————

The Canterbury Hotel
1733 "N" St., N.W.
Washington, DC 20036

99 Suites
202-393-3000 800-424-2950

Location: Central; Downtown
Airport: 6 miles
Near: Embassy Row, Major Theatres
Walking Distance To: Business
Area Attractions: Capitol, White House

Price Range & Credit Cards: 1 Bedroom Suite $$$$, 2 Bedrooms $$$$, AmEx/MC/Visa/Other CC, Children Free, TAC 10%

Hotel Amenities: Laundry, Parking

Business Facilities: Conf. Rm. Cap. 80, Banquet Fac., Mess. Ctr., Sec. Serv., Copier, Aud/Vis., Telex

Recreational Facilities: Health Facilities near

Restaurant/Bar: Chaucer's

Comps: Continental Breakfast, Refreshments, Hors d'oeuvres

Room Amenities: Room Service, Free Paper, TV, Phone in Rm., Cable TV, Radio, Wet Bar, Kitchen, Ind. Heat Ctl., Ind. AC Ctl.

The Canterbury offers a gracious and elegant ambiance; spacious and comfortable accommodations; personalized service; and a fine gourmet restaurant. Minutes from many points of interest, the hotel's furnishings and color scheme are 18th Century English. Consider dining at Chaucer's, an intimate grill restaurant with an understated decor.

─────────── WASHINGTON ───────────

The Carlyle Suites Hotel
1731 New Hampshire Ave., N.W.
Washington, DC 20009

170 Suites
202-234-3200

Location: Northwest; Downtown
Airport: 6 miles
Near: All Points of Interest, Smithsonian
Walking Distance To: Restaurants
Area Attractions: Shops and Boutiques

Price Range & Credit Cards: 1 Bedroom Suite $$$$, Junior $$, AmEx/MC/Visa/ Other CC, Children Free, TAC 10%

Hotel Amenities: Laundry, Parking, Pets Allowed

Business Facilities: Conf. Rm. Cap. 100, Banquet Fac., Mess. Ctr., Sec. Serv., Copier, Aud/Vis., Telex

Recreational Facilities: Game Area; Health Facilities near

Restaurant/Bar: Jimmy K's

Room Amenities: TV, Phone in Rm., VCR, Radio, Wet Bar, Kitchen, Ind. Heat Ctl., Ind. AC Ctl.

Located in one of Washington D.C.'s vintage neighborhoods, the Carlyle has combined the style of the past with modern renovation and convenience to create a great value. The impressive art deco motif is accented with grey, lavender, silver, white, and black. Beautiful art deco moldings and period furniture adorn the hotel.

─────────── WASHINGTON ───────────

The Ramada Inn Central
1430 Rhode Island Ave., N.W.
Washington, DC 20005

186 Suites
202-462-7777 800-368-5690

Location: Central; Downtown
Airport: 6 miles
Near: Scott Circle, Massachusetts Avenue
Walking Distance To: Theatres, Restaurants
Area Attractions: Minutes from White House

Price Range & Credit Cards: 1 Bedroom Suite $$, 2 Bedrooms $$, AmEx/MC/Visa/ Other CC, Children Free, TAC 10%

Hotel Amenities: Laundry, Parking

Business Facilities: Conf. Rm. Cap. 75, Banquet Fac., Mess. Ctr., Sec. Serv., Copier, Aud/Vis., Telex

Recreational Facilities: Pool; Jogging Paths

Restaurant/Bar: Kitchen Cabinet

Comps: Refreshments

Room Amenities: Room Service, TV, Phone in Rm., Cable TV, Radio, Wet Bar, Kitchen, Ind. Heat Ctl., Ind. AC Ctl.

The Ramada Inn Central's name is appropriate. Its central location is close to everything you would want to experience in Washington. After a long day of business or sightseeing, the rooftop pool offers a refreshing temptation. At dusk, treat yourself to the fine American fare you'll find at the Kitchen Cabinet, the hotel restaurant.

--------------------------------- WASHINGTON ---------------------------------

The St. James
950 24th. Street, N.W.
Washington, DC 20037

197 Suites
202-457-0500 800-852-8512

Location: Downtown
Airport: Dulles 30 min.
Near: National airport-20 minutes
Walking Distance To: Georgetown
Area Attractions: Kennedy Center, The
White House, Lincoln Memorial

Price Range & Credit Cards: 1 Bedroom Suite $$$$, 2 Bedrooms $$$$, Junior $$$, AmEx/MC/Visa/Other CC, Children Free, TAC 10%

Hotel Amenities: Laundry, Parking, Handicap (10)

Business Facilities: Conf. Rm. Cap. 90, Banquet Fac., Mess. Ctr., Copier, Aud/Vis., Telex

Recreational Facilities: Pool, Fitn. Ctr.

Comps: Continental breakfast

Room Amenities: TV, Phones in Rm. (2), Radio, Full kitchens, Ind. Heat Ctl., Ind. AC Ctl.

With everything the St. James provides it may come as a surprise that it's also one of the city's best values. Quietly situated in the heart of Foggy Bottom, accommodations are offered for about half what Washington's finest hotels charge. Minimun stay, 2 nights. An elegant alternative to commercial hotel accommodations.

--------------------------------- WASHINGTON ---------------------------------

Wyndham Bristol Hotel
2430 Pennsylvania Ave., N.W.
Washington, DC 20037

240 Suites
202-955-6400 800-822-4200

Location: West End
Airport: 7 miles
Near: Residential area, Kennedy Center
Walking Distance To: Metro-8 blocks
Area Attractions: Smithsonian, Georgetown

Price Range & Credit Cards: 1 Bedroom Suite $$$$, 2 Bedrooms $$$$+, Junior $$$$, AmEx/MC/Visa/Other CC, Children Free, TAC 10%

Hotel Amenities: Laundry, Parking, Car Hire

Business Facilities: Conf. Rm. Cap. 120, Banquet Fac., Mess. Ctr., Sec. Serv., Copier, Aud/Vis., Telex

Recreational Facilities: Health Facilities near

Restaurant/Bar: Bristol Grill

Room Amenities: Room Service, Free Paper, TV, Phone in Rm., Cable TV, Radio, Wet Bar, Kitchen, Ind. Heat Ctl., Ind. AC Ctl.

Appointed with elegant European and American art, textiles and furnishings, the Wyndham Bristol Hotel combines exquisite taste with the quality of service demanded by discerning travelers. Placed near the airport and close to all points of interest, the hotel provides ample facilities and services for business.

 **Wisconsin**

Egg Harbor

Green Bay

Brookfield
Glendale

Madison

──────────────── BROOKFIELD ────────────────

Embassy Suites Hotel
1200 So. Moorland Rd.
Brookfield, WI 53005

203 Suites
414-782-2900 800-362-2779

Location: Milwaukee-15 min.
Airport: 15 miles
Near: Suburban Area, State Fair Grounds, Milwaukee County Stadium
Walking Distance To: Fine Shops, Brookfield Mall
Area Attractions: Miller Brewery, Sports Complex, Milwaukee County Zoo

Price Range & Credit Cards: 1 Bedroom Suite $$$, AmEx/MC/Visa/Other CC, Children Free, TAC 11%

Hotel Amenities: Laundry, Car Hire, Handicap (20)

Business Facilities: Conf. Rm. Cap. 400, Banquet Fac., Sec. Serv., Copier, Aud/Vis., Teleconf., FAX, Comp. Hook-up

Recreational Facilities: Pool, Sauna, Whirlpool, Fitn. Ctr., Steamroom, X-Country Skiing; Golf and Tennis nearby

Restaurant/Bar: Tivoli's Restaurant and Lounge, Entertainment

Comps: Full Breakfast, Refreshments

Room Amenities: Room Service, TV, Phones in Rm. (2), Cable TV, Radio, Wet Bar, Kitchen, Ind. Heat Ctl., Ind. AC Ctl.

Whether golf, tennis or cross country skiing is your favorite sport, you'll find them near the Embassy in Brookfield. For conviviality afterward you'll enjoy complimentary beverages in the enchanting 5-story atrium and skywalk among lovely trees and fountains. In the morning, your complimentary breakfast will be cooked to order.

———————————— EGG HARBOR ————————————

Landmark Resort
7643 Hillside Rd.
Egg Harbor, WI 54209

292 Suites
414-868-3205

Location: Resort; Downtown: 30 min.
Airport: 20 miles
Near: Charming Waterfront, Resort District
Walking Distance To: Deep Woods
Area Attractions: Door Peninsula, Music, Wineries

Price Range & Credit Cards: 1 Bedroom Suite $$, 2 Bedrooms $$, AmEx/MC/Visa, Children Free, TAC 10%

Hotel Amenities: Laundry, Handicap (12)

Business Facilities: Conf. Rm. Cap. 500, Banquet Fac., Mess. Ctr., Sec. Serv., Copier, Aud/Vis.

Recreational Facilities: Pool, Whirlpool, Fitn. Ctr., Golf, Sailboat, Beaches, Game Area, Snowmobile

Restaurant/Bar: Landmark Club, Entertainment

Comps: Hors d'oeuvres

Room Amenities: Room Service, TV, Phone in Rm., VCR, Kitchen, Ind. Heat Ctl., Ind. AC Ctl.

The Landmark offers a complete year round family vacation and conference resort in a spectacular natural setting on the Door County peninsula with the quiet of the deep woods and breathtaking views of Egg Harbor. Every winter snow and summer water sport is here for you to explore. Come for the week-end and enjoy wine and cheese tasting Sat. night.

———————————— GREEN BAY ————————————

Embassy Suites Hotel
333 Main St.
Green Bay, WI 54301

223 Suites
414-432-4555 800-362-2779

Location: Central; Downtown
Airport: 7 miles
Near: Fox River, Regency Conference Center, Port Plaza Mall
Walking Distance To: Many Shops
Area Attractions: Museum, Packer Hall of Fame

Price Range & Credit Cards: 1 Bedroom Suite $$, 2 Bedrooms $$$$, Junior $$, AmEx/MC/Visa/Other CC, Children Free, TAC 10%

Hotel Amenities: Laundry, Parking, Pets Allowed, Handicap (6)

Business Facilities: Conf. Rm. Cap. 1600, Banquet Fac., Copier, Aud/Vis., Comp. Hook-up

Recreational Facilities: Pool, Sauna, Whirlpool, Fitn. Ctr.; Y.M.C.A.-2 blocks

Restaurant/Bar: Pepik's, Entertainment

Comps: Full Breakfast, Refreshments, Hors d'oeuvres

Room Amenities: Room Service, TV, Phones in Rm. (2), Cable TV, Radio, Wet Bar, Kitchen, Ind. Heat Ctl., Ind. AC Ctl.

Embassy Suites provides the "Old World" atmosphere of brick, tile and hand-carved wood. Complimentary cooked-to-order breakfast and two hours of complimentary beverages/cocktails are served each day. Free airport limousine service, skywalk connection to 118-store Port Plaza Mall, and 19 smaller conference rooms, all are advantages to travellers.

Wyoming

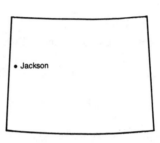

JACKSON

Spring Creek Ranch
P.O. Box 3154
Jackson, WY 83001

53 Suites
307-733-8833 800-443-6139

Location: Resort; Downtown: 3 miles
Airport: 12 miles
Near: East Gros Ventre Butte, Mountain Resorts
Walking Distance To: Ski Area
Area Attractions: Yellowstone, Grand Teton

Price Range & Credit Cards: 1 Bedroom Suite $$$$, 2 Bedrooms $$$$+, Junior $$$, AmEx/MC/Visa, Children Free, TAC 10%

Hotel Amenities: Handicap (1), Gift Shop

Business Facilities: Conf. Rm. Cap. 150, Banquet Fac., Copier, Aud/Vis.

Recreational Facilities: Pool, Whirlpool, Golf, River Rafting; Helicopter Skiing

Restaurant/Bar: Granary

Room Amenities: Room Service, TV, Phone in Rm., Cable TV, Radio, Wet Bar, Kitchen, Ind. Heat Ctl., Ind. AC Ctl.

Summer or winter you'll find plenty to do at Spring Creek Ranch. High atop the East Gros Ventre Butte, with breathtaking views in every direction, you'll relax in the rustic elegance. Close at hand are skiing, golfing, snowmobiling, river rafting and the South Grand Teton National Park. Snake River float trips.

JACKSON

The Wort Hotel
50 North Glenwood
Jackson, WY 83001

42 Suites
307-733-2190 800-322-2727

Location: Central; Downtown
Airport: 9 miles
Near: Town Square, Galleries, Shops
Walking Distance To: Center of town
Area Attractions: Grand Teton Music Festival

Price Range & Credit Cards: 1 Bedroom Suite $$$, Junior $$, AmEx/MC/Visa/
Other CC, TAC 10%

Hotel Amenities: Parking, Car Hire, Handicap (1)

Business Facilities: Conf. Rm. Cap. 400

Recreational Facilities: Sport facilities-2 mi.

Restaurant/Bar: Gold Piece Room, Silver Dollar, Entertainment

Room Amenities: TV, Phone in Rm., Ind. Heat Ctl., Ind. AC Ctl.

This Four Diamond award-winning hotel and convention center features all-out Old West ambiance in a cosmopolitan resort. The location at the gateway to the Grand Tetons and Yellowstone National Parks in the heart of the valley surrounded by majestic mountains is stunning! Floating the Snake River is a sports dream.

 **Canada**

CALGARY

International Hotel of Calgary
220-4th Avenue, SW
Calgary, T2P 0H5, Alta.

250 Suites
403-265-9600 800-223-0888

Location: Downtown
Airport: 20 minutes
Near: Business and Financial District
Walking Distance To: Shopping Malls, Dining
Area Attractions: Calgary Stampede, Canada Olympic Park

Price Range & Credit Cards: 1 Bedroom Suite $$$, 2 Bedrooms $$$, AmEx/MC/ Visa/Other CC, Children Free, TAC 10%

Hotel Amenities: Gift Shop, Parking, Barber Shop, Beauty Parlor

Recreational Facilities: Pool, Sauna, Whirlpool, Sport Deck; Ski & Ice Skate nearby

Restaurant/Bar: The 4th Avenue Cafe and Bar

Room Amenities: TV, Phone in Rm., Cable TV, Wet Bar, Ind. Heat Ctl.

The International Hotel of Calgary features 250 one- and two-bedroom suites, with separate living room, bar and bedroom areas. Within easy walking distance of business, shopping and cultural centers, Calgary offers access to excellent winter sports. Summer is highlighted by the famous Calgary Stampede. Enjoy Calgary in a comfortable International Suite.

EDMONTON

Edmonton House
10205-100 Avenue
Edmonton, T5J 4B5, Alta.

283 Suites
403-424-5555 800-661-6562

Location: Central
Walking Distance To: Business and Shopping
Area Attractions: Shuttle to West Edmonton

Price Range & Credit Cards: 1 Bedroom Suite $$, AmEx/MC/Visa/Other CC

Hotel Amenities: Gift Shop, Parking, Barber Shop, Beauty Parlor

Business Facilities: Conf. Rm. Cap. 50, Banquet Fac., Aud/Vis., Teleconf.

Recreational Facilities: Pool, Sauna, Billiards, Ping Pong, Shuffleboard, Fitn. Ctr.

Room Amenities: TV, Phone in Rm., Kitchen, Ind. Heat Ctl.

At Edmonton House your suite is designed for rest and relaxation or a place to invite clients and guests with pride. It features a tastefully furnished living room with private balcony to view the river valley or Edmonton's skyline; a fully equipped kitchen, and separate bedroom. Every amenity is offered for business meetings or after hours recreation.

--- MISSISSAUGA ---

Dodge Suites Hotel
2515 Eglinton Ave. East
Mississauga, ONT

187 Suites
416-238-9600

Location: Downtown: 30 min.
Airport: 5 minutes
Near: Industrial Park
Walking Distance To: Golf Course
Area Attractions: Wonderland Amusement
Center-2 miles, Zoo-5 miles

Price Range & Credit Cards: 1 Bedroom Suite $$, AmEx/Visa, TAC x%

Hotel Amenities: Laundry, Gift Shop, Handicap (2)

Business Facilities: Conf. Rm. Cap. 100, Banquet Fac., Mess. Ctr., Copier, FAX, Comp. Hook-up

Recreational Facilities: Golf Course nearby

Comps: Continental Plus Breakfast

Room Amenities: TV, Phone in Rm., Radio, Kitchen, Ind. Heat Ctl., Ind. AC Ctl.

"First True All Suite Hotel in Ontario." Adjacent to the hotel strip, Dodge Suites is a luxury, yet budget, all suite hotel where you can live in a suite for the price of a room; a hotel where people really count. At Dodge Suites, you are not properly dressed without a smile. Quality, service, cleanliness, and value is what the hotel stands for.

--- OTTAWA ---

Gallery Court
35 Murray Street
Ottawa, ONT

10 Suites
613-563-0002

Location: Downtown
Airport: 35-40 minutes
Near: Market Area, Business District
Walking Distance To: Parliament Buildings
Area Attractions: Parliament Buildings,
Shopping

Price Range & Credit Cards: 1 Bedroom Suite $$, 2 Bedrooms $$$, AmEx/MC/Visa/Other CC, Children Free, TAC 10%

Hotel Amenities: Laundry, Parking, Pets Allowed

Room Amenities: TV, Phones in Rm. (2), Cable TV, Radio, Kitchen, Ind. Heat Ctl., Ind. AC Ctl.

A new private apartment suite located on Murray Street in Ottawa's trendy market area (off Sussex Drive), Gallery Court is just one minute's walk from the Parliament Buildings, Ottawa's business district and convenient shopping and major attractions. This beautifully designed stone and glass building features luxurious one and two bedroom suites.

Hotel Luxeford Suites, Houston, TX

--- OTTAWA ---

The Portals
292 Laurier Avenue, East
Ottawa, ONT

10 Suites
613-563-0002

Location: Sandy Hill; Downtown: 10 min.
Airport: 35 minutes
Near: Residential Area
Walking Distance To: Parliament Buildings
Area Attractions: Parliament Buildings

Price Range & Credit Cards: 1 Bedroom Suite $$$, 2 Bedrooms $$$, Junior $$, AmEx/MC/Visa/Other CC, Children Free, TAC 10%

Hotel Amenities: Laundry, Parking, Pets Allowed

Room Amenities: TV, Phones in Rm. (2), Cable TV, Radio, Kitchen, Ind. Heat Ctl., Ind. AC Ctl.

A superb property situated on Laurier Avenue, The Portals is ideal for corporate and diplomatic travellers. Each uniquely designed suite is elegantly decorated and contains a full kitchen with dishwasher, microwave, and large living and dining areas ideal for entertaining or business meetings. All suites have fireplaces and some even have skylights.

————————————— TORONTO —————————————

Clarendon Gate
5, 7, 9 & 11 Clarendon Avenue
Toronto, ONT

8 Suites
416-923-3000

Location: Downtown: 15 min.
Airport: 30 minutes
Near: Forest Hill
Walking Distance To: St. Clair Avenue

Price Range & Credit Cards: 1 Bedroom Suite $$$$, 2 Bedrooms $$$$, AmEx/MC/ Visa/Other CC, Children Free, TAC 10%

Hotel Amenities: Laundry, Parking, Pets Allowed

Comps: Limousine Service

Room Amenities: TV, Phones in Rm. (2), Cable TV, Radio, Kitchen, Ind. Heat Ctl., Ind. AC Ctl.

Clarendon Gate is located on a quiet residential street in exclusive Forest Hill, a few minutes walk from St. Clair Avenue. Each suite has a fully-equipped kitchen with dishwasher and microwave; complimentary laundry facilites, and fireplace. Your elegant "Home Away From Home" is only a few minutes drive from downtown Toronto at the Clarendon Gate.

————————————— TORONTO —————————————

Lowther Place
88 Lowther Avenue
Toronto, ONT

5 Suites
416-923-3000

Location: Annex; Downtown: 6 min.
Airport: 25-30 minutes
Near: Bloor and Spadina Intersection, Downtown Toronto
Walking Distance To: Village of Yorkville, Subway
Area Attractions: Univ. of Toronto, Restaurants, Shops, Entertainment

Price Range & Credit Cards: 1 Bedroom Suite $$$, 2 Bedrooms $$$, AmEx/MC/ Visa/Other CC, Children Free, TAC 10%

Hotel Amenities: Laundry, Pets Allowed

Room Amenities: TV, Phones in Rm. (2), Cable TV, Radio, Kitchen, Ind. Heat Ctl., Ind. AC Ctl.

The Lowther Place is located in the fashionable Annex area of Downtown Toronto. This beautifully refurbished, stately residence is only a few minutes' walk from University of Toronto, Village of Yorkville, restaurants, shopping and entertainment. Each elegant suite has high ceiling with classic mouldings, beautiful hardwood floor and a fireplace.

---- TORONTO ----

The Bay—Bloor
1101 Bay Street
Toronto, ONT

57 Suites
416-923-3000

Location: Downtown
Airport: 25-30 minutes
Near: Restaurants, Movie Theatres, Shopping, 24-Hour Grocers, Entertainment
Walking Distance To: Central Business Area
Area Attractions: Fashionable Village of Yorkville

Price Range & Credit Cards: 1 Bedroom Suite $$, 2 Bedrooms $$, Junior $, AmEx/MC/Visa/Other CC, Children Free, TAC 10%

Hotel Amenities: Laundry, Parking

Business Facilities: Banquet Fac.

Recreational Facilities: Pool, Sauna, Fitn. Ctr.

Room Amenities: TV, Phones in Rm. (2), Cable TV, Radio, Kitchen, Ind. Heat Ctl., Ind. AC Ctl.

Bay/Bloor features comfortably furnished suites in a private apartment property. All suites have a fully-equipped kitchen and offer separate living and dining areas. Each suite has been designed to make maximum use of space. The attractive furnishings will make your stay a pleasant one. Restaurants, shopping, entertainment, subway and buses are nearby.

---- TORONTO ----

The Roxborough
66 Roxborough Street, East
Toronto, ONT

10 Suites
416-923-3000

Location: Rosedale; Downtown: 10 min.
Airport: 40 minutes
Near: Village of Rosedale
Walking Distance To: Yonge & St. Clair intersection
Area Attractions: Uptown, Restaurants, Specialty Grocers, Retail Stores

Price Range & Credit Cards: 1 Bedroom Suite $$$, 2 Bedrooms $$$, AmEx/MC/Visa/Other CC, Children Free, TAC 10%

Hotel Amenities: Laundry, Parking, Pets Allowed

Recreational Facilities: Sauna

Room Amenities: Free Paper, TV, Phones in Rm. (2), Cable TV, Radio, Kitchen, Ind. Heat Ctl., Ind. AC Ctl.

The Roxborough is located in prestigious Rosedale, a tranquil residential neighborhood in the heart of the city. All two bedrooms have two bathrooms, a spacious balcony and fireplace. Restaurants, specialty grocers and retail stores are just two blocks away, as is the subway. The Roxborough, a fine, superbly located property, for quiet living.

─────────────── TORONTO ───────────────

The Summit
701, 705, 725 King St., West
Toronto, ONT

40 Suites
416-923-3000

Location: Downtown: 10 min.
Airport: 20 minutes
Near: Fashion District, Downtown Toronto, Restaurants
Walking Distance To: Public Transportation

Price Range & Credit Cards: 1 Bedroom Suite $$, 2 Bedrooms $$, Junior $, AmEx/ MC/Visa/Other CC, Children Free, TAC 10%

Hotel Amenities: Laundry, Parking

Recreational Facilities: Pool, Sauna, Whirlpool, Fitn. Ctr., Squash

Room Amenities: TV, Phones in Rm. (2), Cable TV, Radio, Kitchen, Ind. Heat Ctl., Ind. AC Ctl.

The Summit is a high-rise contemporary apartment complex, conveniently located on King Street West, minutes away from downtown Toronto. This newly developed private apartment contains many facilities. Every unit has a fully-equipped kitchen with dishwasher and enclosed balconies that can be used as a lounge or dining area. Many conveniences nearby.

─────────────── TORONTO ───────────────

The Wellesley
25 Wellesley Street, East
Toronto, ONT

28 Suites
416-923-3000

Location: Downtown
Airport: 25-30 minutes
Near: Government of Ontario, Parliament Buildings, Subway Line
Area Attractions: Fashionable Village of Yorkville, Eaton's Yonge St. Center

Price Range & Credit Cards: 1 Bedroom Suite $$, 2 Bedrooms $$, Junior $, AmEx/ MC/Visa/Other CC, Children Free, TAC 10%

Hotel Amenities: Laundry, Parking

Room Amenities: TV, Phones in Rm. (2), Cable TV, Radio, Kitchen, Ind. Heat Ctl., Ind. AC Ctl.

The Wellesley is a lovely apartment property ideally located on the subway line in downtown Toronto. One and two bedroom suites offer separate living and dining areas. All suites have a washer/dryer and a large balcony.

―――――――――――――― TORONTO ――――――――――――――

The Whitehall
49 St. Clair Avenue, West
Toronto, ONT

Location: Mid-Town; Downtown: 5 min.
Airport: 30 minutes
Walking Distance To: Yonge Street Subway

20 Suites
416-923-3000

Price Range & Credit Cards: 1 Bedroom Suite $$, 2 Bedrooms $$$, AmEx/MC/ Visa/Other CC, Children Free, TAC 10%

Hotel Amenities: Laundry, Pets Allowed

Room Amenities: TV, Phones in Rm. (2), Cable TV, Radio, Kitchen, Ind. Heat Ctl., Ind. AC Ctl.

The Whitehall is a superb midtown furnished residence, just a few minutes' walk from Yonge Street subway. This seven story private apartment property offers large one and two bedroom suites. Each unit has a separate fully-equipped kitchen with dishwasher and large living and dining area.

―――――――――――――― TORONTO ――――――――――――――

Town Inn Hotel
620 Church Street
Toronto, M4Y 2G2, ONT

Location: Yonge-Bloor; Central
Near: Shops, Theatres, Restaurants
Area Attractions: Sightseeing in downtown Toronto

200 Suites
416-964-3311   800-223-1900

Price Range & Credit Cards: 1 Bedroom Suite $$$, 2 Bedrooms $$$$, AmEx/MC/ Visa/Other CC

Hotel Amenities: Parking, Valet Laundry

Recreational Facilities: Pool, Sauna, Sundeck, Tennis

Room Amenities: TV, Phone in Rm., Kitchen, Ind. Heat Ctl., Ind. AC Ctl.

The Town Inn Hotel with its central location is well-suited for theatre groups and business seminars. The staff is eager to assist you with arrangements. Travellers appreciate the spacious suites with kitchens and many recreational facilities. Enjoy the convenience of shopping and outstanding restaurants nearby.

---------------------------------- VANCOUVER ----------------------------------

The Rosellen Suites
2030 Barclay Street
Vancouver, V6G 1L5, BC

32 Suites
604-689-4807

Location: Central; Downtown: 5 min.
Airport: 30 minutes
Near: Stanley Park
Walking Distance To: Stanley Park, Shopping, Dining

Price Range & Credit Cards: 1 Bedroom Suite $$$, 2 Bedrooms $$$$, AmEx/MC/Visa/Other CC

Hotel Amenities: Laundry, Parking, Pets Allowed

Business Facilities: Sec. Serv., Copier, FAX, Telex, Bus. Ctr.

Recreational Facilities: Club privileges; Beach, Tennis, Golf

Room Amenities: TV, Phones in Rm. (2), VCR, Radio, Kitchen, Ind. Heat Ctl., Ind. AC Ctl.

Rosellen Suites offers travellers all the comforts of home. Situated in a quiet residential neighborhood on the edge of beautiful Stanley Park, you can stroll to many restaurants and shops, or prepare quiet meals in your suite's well-equipped kitchens. Work out in the nearby fitness club and pool or explore the beach and marina. Extended stay discounts.

---------------------------------- VANCOUVER ----------------------------------

The Century Plaza Hotel
1015 Burrard Street
Vancouver, V6Z 1Y5, BC

250 Suites
604-687-0575 800-663-1818

Location: Downtown
Airport: 20 minutes
Near: St. Paul's Hospital, Convention Center, Financial District
Walking Distance To: Two Shopping Centers
Area Attractions: Stanley Park, Beach, Expo Site

Price Range & Credit Cards: 1 Bedroom Suite $$$, 2 Bedrooms $$$$

Hotel Amenities: Parking

Business Facilities: Conf. Rm. Cap. 300, Banquet Fac.

Recreational Facilities: Pool, Sauna; Skiing & Health Club

Restaurant/Bar: Roy's Seafood Restaurant/Rum Runners Lounge, Cabaret & Dancing

Room Amenities: Room Service, TV, Phone in Rm., Cable TV, Wet Bar, Kitchen, Ind. Heat Ctl., Ind. AC Ctl.

The Century Plaza Hotel is located downtown, convenient for business or pleasure travellers. Many suites feature beautiful views of mountains and ocean. All have full kitchen facilities. Fine dining and entertainment are available in Roy's Seafood Restaurant, The Cafe Plaza, and Club Mardi Gras.

 **Australia**

Gordon Place
24-38 Little Bourke St.
Melbourne, VC 3000

60 Suites
03-663-5355

Location: Central; Downtown
Near: Theatre District (Princess, Her Majesty's, and The Comedy Theatres)
Area Attractions: Treasury Gardens, Chinatown, Parliament House

Price Range & Credit Cards: 1 Bedroom Suite $$$, 2 Bedrooms $$$$, Junior $$

Hotel Amenities: Gift Shop, Gourmet Deli, Barber Shop, Beauty Parlor

Business Facilities: Telex

Recreational Facilities: Pool, Sauna, Whirlpool, Fitn. Ctr.

Restaurant/Bar: Gordon's Garden Restaurant/The Brasserie/Bar

Room Amenities: TV, Phone in Rm., Kitchen, Ind. AC Ctl.

Gordon Place was built in 1884 and completely restored in 1981. Its old-time charm is complimented within by luxurious, full-service accommodations. Enjoy superb cuisine in the beautiful courtyard restaurant. You'll find your kitchen convenient for breakfast, late night snacks, with the added comfort of valet grocery shopping.

Margeaux Terrace
19-27 Argo St., South Yarra
Melbourne, VC

20 Suites
03-267-8066 008-33-8111

Location: South Yarra; Downtown: 4 min.
Near: Minutes to Central Business District
Walking Distance To: Chapel St. & Toorak Road Shops
Area Attractions: Faulkner Park, Royal Botanical Gardens

Price Range & Credit Cards: 1 Bedroom Suite $$$, 2 Bedrooms $$$$, AmEx/MC/Visa/Other CC

Hotel Amenities: Parking

Business Facilities: Sec. Serv., Telex

Recreational Facilities: Pool, Whirlpool, Tennis, Barbeque Areas

Comps: Breakfast

Room Amenities: Room Service, TV, Phone in Rm., Kitchen

Margeaux Terrace occcupies a pretty landscaped courtyard with a tennis court and a heated pool for relaxation after a busy day. Arrange your own barbeque through the valet grocery shopping, or utilize the dine-in restaurant service. One-, two-, and three-bedroom accommodations feature dining areas, fully-equipped kitchens and homelike comfort.

England

BATH

Fountain House
9/11 Fountain Bldg., Lansdowne Rd.
Bath, BA1 5DV,

14 Suites
(0225) 338622

Location: Central; Downtown
Airport: Heathrow-2 hours
Near: Gatwick Airport-2.5 hours, Historic Houses, Restaurants
Walking Distance To: Galleries, Museums, Shops
Area Attractions: Roman Baths, Unique Georgian City, Music & Art Festival

Price Range & Credit Cards: 1 Bedroom Suite $$$$, 2 Bedrooms $$$$, AmEx/MC/Visa/Other CC, TAC 10%

Hotel Amenities: Laundry, Parking, Car Hire, Pets Allowed

Business Facilities: Mess. Ctr., Sec. Serv., Copier, Telex

Recreational Facilities: Golf and Tennis nearby

Restaurant/Bar: The Hole In The Wall

Comps: Continental Plus Breakfast

Room Amenities: Free Paper, TV, Phone in Rm., Radio, Kitchen, Ind. Heat Ctl.

Fountain House is the first all-suite hotel outside London in the unique Georgian city of Bath. It is a must for all visitors to England, perfect center for exploring the West country and only one hour away from London. Fountain House is a tastefully refurbished Georgian mansion featuring elegant one and two bed suites.

LONDON

John Howard Hotel & Apts.
4 Queen's Gate, Kensington
London, SW7 5EH,

01-581-3011

Location: Central
Near: Kensington Palace and Gardens

Price Range & Credit Cards: 1 Bedroom Suite $$$$+, 2 Bedrooms $$$$+, Junior $$$$

Business Facilities: Conf. Rm. Cap. 25, Sec. Serv., Copier, Telex

Restaurant/Bar: Le Bouquet

Room Amenities: Room Service, TV, Phone in Rm., Radio, Wet Bar, Kitchen, Hair Dryer

The John Howard Hotel in Kensington offers the comfort of your own suite with fully-equipped kitchens, or the convenience of room service and restaurant facilities. This fine historic protected building has been lavishly restored and decorated to offer business or vacation travellers every convenience. There is a 22 days minimum stay.

 France

---
PARIS

La Residence du Roy
8, rue Francois Ier
Paris, 75008

36 Suites
(1)42-89-59-59 800-366-1510

Location: Central
Near: Between Avenue George 5th. and Avenue Montaigne
Area Attractions: Fashion Boutiques, Champs Elysees

Price Range & Credit Cards: 1 Bedroom Suite $$$$, 2 Bedrooms $$$$+, Junior $$$$, AmEx/MC/Visa/Other CC

Hotel Amenities: Laundry, Parking, Car Hire

Business Facilities: Banquet Fac., Mess. Ctr.

Room Amenities: TV, Phone in Rm., Wet Bar, Kitchen

The Residence du Roy is a residence hotel offering all the services of a luxury hotel. Attractively decorated with contemporary furnishings, your suite offers the convenience of a kitchenette for casual meals. Room service will provide breakfast if you prefer.

 **Italy**

Hotel Duca di Milano
Piazza della Repubblica, 13
Milan, 20124

02-6284

Location: Business
Airport: Malpensa-60 min.
Near: Linate Airport-20 min., Public Gardens
Walking Distance To: Finest Shopping
Area Attractions: The Duomo, Brera Art Gallery, Castello Sforzesco, the Lakes

Price Range & Credit Cards: 1 Bedroom Suite $$$

Hotel Amenities: Laundry, Parking, Concierge

Business Facilities: Conf. Rm. Cap. 60, Sec. Serv., Copier, Telex

Recreational Facilities: Monza Golf Club-30 min.

Restaurant/Bar: Il Piccolo

Room Amenities: Room Service, TV, Phone in Rm., Radio, Wet Bar, Ind. Heat Ctl., Ind. AC Ctl.

Situated in a quiet elegant corner of the business center, the Hotel Duca di Milano is the ideal location for business and pleasure travellers. Vacationing visitors will appreciate its convenience to historic monuments and fine shops. Businessmen will be pleased by the conference and business facilities. Comfortable accommodations at affordable prices.

Fountain House, Bath, England

---------------------------------- VENICE ----------------------------------

Palazzo del Giglio
Campo S.M. Giglio 2462
Venezia, 30124

Location: Residential

16 Suites
041-705166/5205166

Price Range & Credit Cards: 1 Bedroom Suite $$$

Hotel Amenities: Barber Shop, Beauty Parlor

Restaurant/Bar: Club del Doge

Comps: Ciga Hotel Launches

Room Amenities: TV, Phone in Rm., Radio, Wet Bar, Kitchen, Ind. AC Ctl.

Palazzo del Giglio is located next to the Gritti Palace Hotel, forming the annex, in the quiet picturesque Campo di Santa Maria del Giglio. There is access to the services of the Gritti Palace Hotel, including the beautiful Club del Doge restaurant. For light meals, the Palazzo offers the convenience of your own kitchenette.

---------------------------------- VENICE ----------------------------------

Residence Excelsior
Lungomare Marconi, 52
Venezia Lido, 30126

Location: Downtown: 12 min.
Airport: 12 minutes
Area Attractions: Historic and Cultural Sightseeing

11 Suites
041-5260201

Price Range & Credit Cards: 1 Bedroom Suite $$$

Hotel Amenities: Parking, Barber Shop, Beauty Parlor

Business Facilities: Telex

Recreational Facilities: Pool, Tennis, Private Beach; Golf & Horseriding near

Comps: Ciga Hotel Launches

Room Amenities: TV, Phone in Rm., Kitchen, Ind. Heat Ctl., Ind. AC Ctl.

The Residence Excelsior offers a quiet location facing the sea with the convenience of the Hotel Excelsior nearby for special services. Each modernly furnished apartment has a kitchenette for snacks and light meals. The restaurant and bar are at the hotel.

# Thailand

---

Royal Wing / Royal Cliff Resort
Pattaya City

86 Suites
038-421421- 30

Location: Top Of Hill; Pattaya: 5 min.
Airport: 2 hours
Near: Orchid Farms, Temples, Sapphire Mines, Coral Island
Area Attractions: Thai Boxing, Motor Racing, Elephant Kraal, Horse Farm

Price Range & Credit Cards: 1 Bedroom Suite $$$$+, 2 Bedrooms $$$$+, AmEx/MC/Visa/Other CC, TAC 10%

Hotel Amenities: Laundry, Library, Parking, Car Hire, TV Lounge, Beauty Parlor, Handicap (86)

Business Facilities: Conf. Rm. Cap. 500, Banquet Fac., Mess. Ctr., Sec. Serv., Copier, Aud/Vis., Telex, Comp. Hook-up, Bus. Ctr.

Recreational Facilities: Pool, Whirlpool, Tennis, Waterski, Windsurf, Jogging Track; Golf nearby

Restaurant / Bar: The Benjarong/Marble Lobby Lounge, Music & Dancing

Comps: Toiletries, Refreshments, Hors d'oeuvres

Room Amenities: Room Service, Free Paper, TV, Phones in Rm. (3), VCR, Radio, Wet Bar, Ind. AC Ctl.

Featuring luxurious executive suites and 2 presidential suites (3 bedrooms, diningroom, lounge or board room, pantry, 2 balconies). The Royal Wing has been designed for discerning travellers who demand the highest level of service, comfort & privacy. Live life like the rich & famous—pampered by your own butler who will serve you breakfast on your balcony.

More All-Suite Hotels

———————————————— Alabama ————————————————

Rime Garden Inn 5320 Beacon Dr., Birmingham, AL 35201 205-951-1200
Federal Square Suites 8777 HWY 20 W, Madison, AL 35758 205-772-8470
Best Western Bradbury Suites 180 So. Beltline Hwy., Mobile, AL 36608 205-343-9345

———————————————— Alaska ————————————————

Inlet Towers Hotel 1200 "L" St., Anchorage, AK 99501 907-276-0110
Park Plaza 201 E. 16th Ave., Anchorage, AK 99501 907-279-2725
Uptown Condos 234 E. 2nd St., Anchorage, AK 99501 907-279-4232
Sophie Station Hotel 1717 University Ave., Fairbanks, AK 99709 907-479-3650
Wedgewood Manor 212 Wedgewood Dr., Fairbanks, AK 99701 907-452-1442
Waterfall Resort P. O. Box 6440, Ketchikan, AK 99901 907-225-9461 800-544-5125

———————————————— Arizona ————————————————

The Boulders 34631 N. Tom Darlington Rd., Carefree, AZ 85377 602-488-9009
Nogales InnSuites Int'l. 700 Mariposa @ I-19 Exit, Nogales, AZ 85621 602-281-2242
Doubletree Suite Hotel 320 No. 44th St., Phoenix, AZ 85008 602-225-0500
Embassy Suites-Phoenix 2333 E. Thomas Rd., Phoenix, AZ 85016 602-9-57-1910
Fountains Suite Hotel 2577 W. Greenway Rd., Phoenix, AZ 85023 602-357-1777
Phoenix Airport InnSuites 1651 W.Baseline Rd. @ I-10, Phoenix, AZ 85283 602-897-7900
Phoenix Central InnSuites 3101 No. 32nd. St., Phoenix, AZ 85018 602-956-4900
Phoenix Northern InnSuites 1615 E. Northern Ave., Phoenix, AZ 85020 602-997-6285
The Pointe @ Squaw Peak 7677 N. 16th St., Phoenix, AZ 85020 602-997-2626
The Pointe @ Tapatio Cliffs 11111 N. 7th St., Phoenix, AZ 85020 602-866-7500
The Pointe at So. Mountain 7777 S. Pointe Pkwy., Phoenix, AZ 85044 800-528-0428
Woolley's Petite Suites 3211 E. Pinchot, Phoenix, AZ 85018 602-957-1350
Sheraton Resort & Conv. Center 1500 Hwy. 69, Prescott, AZ 86301 802-776-1666
Best Western Thunderbird Inn 7515 East Butherus Dr., Scottsdale, AZ 85260 602-951-4000
InnSuites at Eldorado Park 1400 N.77th.St.@ McDowell Rd., Scottsdale, AZ 85257 602-941-1202
Resort Suites of Scottsdale 7677 E. Princess Blvd., Scottsdale, AZ 85255 602-585-4575
Shangrila Resort 6237 No. 59th Pl., Scottsdale, AZ 85253 602-948-5930
Windmill Inn-Sun City West 12545 W. Bell Rd., Surprise, AZ 85374 602-247-2333
Woolley's Petite Suites 1635 N. Scottsdale Rd., Tempe, AZ 85281 602-947-3711
Radisson Suite Hotel Tucson 6555 E. Speedway Blvd., Tucson, AZ 8571-0 602-721-7100
Tucson InnSuites Int'l 6201 N. Oracle Rd., Tucson, AZ 85704 602-297-8111
Viscount Suite Hotel 4855 Broadway, Tucson, AZ 85711 602-745-6500
Yuma InnSuites Int'l I-8 @ 16th St. Exit, Yuma, AZ 85364 6-02-783-8341 800-842-4242

———————————————— California ————————————————

Embassy Suites Hotel 3100 East Frontera, Anaheim, CA 714-632-1221
Granada Inn 2375 West Lincoln Ave., Anaheim, CA 92801 714-774-7370
Beverly Hills Comstock Hotel 10300 Wilshire Blvd., Beverly Hills, CA 90024
The Clark Plaza 141 So. Clark Dr. @ 3rd, Beverly Hills, CA 213-278-9310
Woodfin Suites Hotel & Bus.Ctr 3100 East Imperial Hwy., Brea, CA 92621 714-579-3200

The Residence Inn by Marriott 2761 So. Bascom Ave., Campbell, CA 95008 408-559-1551

Lexington Hotel Suites 69-151 E. Palm Canyon Dr., Cathedral City, CA 92234 619-324-5939

Marriott Suites Costa Mesa Anton Blvd. @ Sakioka Way, Costa Mesa, CA 92626 301-897-1197

Friendship Inn Cypress Suites 6262 West Lincoln Ave., Cypress, CA 90630 714-220-0900

Hotel Alternative 1125 E. Hillsdale Blvd. #105, Foster City, CA 944-04 415-578-1366

The Residence Inn by Marriott 5400 Farwell Pl., Fremont, CA 94536 415-794-5900

The San Joaquin 1309 West Shaw Ave., Fresno, CA 93726 209-225-1309

Chateau Marmont Hotel 8221 Sunset Blvd., Hollywood, CA 90046 213-656-1010

Orchid Suites Hotel 1753 Orchid Ave., Hollywood, CA 90028 213-874-9678

Comfort Suites 16301 Beach Blvd., Huntington Beach, CA 92647 714-841-1812

Trade Winds Airport Hotel 4200 W. Century Blvd., Inglewood, CA 90304 213-419-0999

The Residence Inn by Marriott 4111 E. Willow St., Long Beach, CA 90815 213-595-0909

Marina View Hotel Suites 405 Culver Blvd., Los Angeles, CA 90293 213-305-7000

Plaza Suites Franklin 7230 Franklin Ave., Los Angeles, CA 90046

The Regency 7940 Hollywood Blvd., Los Angeles CA 90046 213-656-4555

Sunset Marquis Hotel 1200 No. Altaloma Rd., Los Angeles, CA 90069

Wilshire Tower Suites 3460 West 7th St., Los Angeles, CA 90005 213-385-7281

Los Olivos Grand Hotel 2860 Grand Ave.,P.O.Box 526, Los Olivos, CA 93441 805-688-7788

Marina City Club Resort Hotel 4333 Admiralty Way, Marina Del Rey, CA 90292

Beverly Heritage 1820 Barber Lane, Milpitas, CA 95035 408- 943-9080

Hotel Pacific 300 Pacific St., Monterey, CA 93940 408-373-5700

The Residence Inn by Marriott 1854 El Camino Real West, Mountain View, CA 94040 415-940-1300

Villa Marina Resort Motel 2008 Harbor Dr. No., Oceanside, CA 92054 619- 722-1561

Squaw Valley Lodge P. O. Box 2364, Olympic Valley, CA 95730 800-922-9920

Lexington Hotel Suites 231 No. Vineyard, Ontario, CA 91764 714-983-8484

The Residence Inn by Marriott 2025 East D St., Ontario, CA 91764- 714-983-6788

Woodfin Suites Hotel & Bus.Ctr 720 The City Dr. So., Orange, CA 92668 414-740-2700

The Executive Lodge 600 Dennett Ave., Pacific Grove, CA 93950 408-373-8777

La Mancha Villas & Court Club 444 Avenida Caballeros, Palm Desert, CA 92260 619-323-1773

Shadow Mountain Resort 45750 San Luis Rey, Palm Desert, CA 92260

La Siesta Villas 247 West Stevens Rd., Palm Springs, CA 92262 619-352-2269

Sundance Resort 2901 Avenida Caballeros, Palm Springs, CA 92262 619-320-6007

Sundance Villas 378 Cabrillo Rd., Palm Springs, CA 92262 619-325-3888

Marina View Hotel Suites 405 Culver Blvd., Playa Del Rey, CA 90293

The Residence Inn by Marriott 1530 Howe Ave., Sacramento, CA 95825 916-920-9111

Best Western Hacienda Hotel 4041 Harney St., San Diego, CA 92110 619-298-4707

Comfort Suites 12979 Rancho Penasquitos Blvd., San Diego, CA 92129 619-484-3300

Comfort Suites-Mission Valley 631 Camino del Rio S., San Diego, CA 92108 800-221-2222

Park Manor Hotel 525 Spruce St., San Diego, CA 92103 619-298-2181

Quality Suites 9880 Mira Mesa Blvd., San Diego, CA 92126 619-530-2-000

Comfort Suites Eucla & Bonita, San Dimas, CA 91773 800-221-2222

Argyle Suite Hotel 146 McAllister, San Francisco, CA 94102 415-552-7076

Airport Plaza Inn Mini Suites 2118 The Alameda, San Jose, CA 95126 408-243-2400

The Residence Inn by Marriott 2000 Windward Way, San Mateo, CA 94404 415-574-4700

El Encanto Hotel 1900 Lasuen Rd., Santa Barbara, CA 93103 805-687-5000

El Escorial 625 Por La Mar Circle, Santa Barbara, CA 93103 805-963-9302

Raffles Inn 2050 N. Preisker Lane, Santa Maria, CA 93454 805-928-6800

Shangri-La Hotel 1301 Ocean Ave., Santa Monica, CA 90401 213-394-2791

Comfort Suites 121 East Grand Ave., So. San Francisco, CA 94003 415- 589-7766

Embassy Suites Hotel 250 Gateway Blvd., So. San Francisco, CA 94083 415-952-6400

Aliso Creek Inn & Golf Course 31106 So. Coast Hwy., South Laguna, CA 92677 714-499-2271

Tahoe Seasons Resort 3901 Saddle Rd., So. Lake Tahoe, CA 95729 -916-541-6700

Olympic Village Inn-Squaw Vall P.O. Box 2648, Squaw Valley, CA 95730 916-581-6000

The Residence Inn by Marriott 3701 Torrance Blvd., Torrance, CA 90503 213-543-4566

Le Dufy 1000 Westmont Dr., West Hollywood, CA 90069 213-657-7400

Le Parc 733 No. West Knoll, West Hollywood, CA 90069 213-858-8888

Le Reve 8822 Cynthia St., West Hollywood, CA 90069 213-854-1114

Le Valadon 900 Hammond St., West Hollywood, CA 90069 213-855-1115

Le Coldion 1020 No. Vicente Blvd., West Los Angeles, CA 90069

——————————————— Colorado ———————————————

The Gant 610 West End Ave., Aspen, CO 81611 303-925- 5000

The Christie Lodge Box 1196, 47 E. Beaver Creek, Avon, CO 81620 303-232-0106

Alikar Gardens 1123 Verde Dr., Colorado Springs, CO 80910 719-475-2564

Best Western Raintree Inn 1645 Newport Dr., Colorado Springs, CO 80916 303-597-7000

Accomodations Plus 4155 East Jewell Ave., Denver, CO 80222 303-759-8577

Many Mansions 1313 Steele St., Denver, CO 80206 303-355-1313

The Residence Inn by Marriott 2777 No. Zuni St., Denver, CO 80211 303-458-5318

Ranch at Steamboat 1 Ranch Rd., Steamboat Springs, CO 80487 303-879-3000

Enzian Lodge 705 Lionshead Circle, Vail, CO 81657 303-476-2050

Lion Square Lodge 660 W. Lionshead Pl., Vail, CO 81657 303-476-2281

——————————————— Connecticut ———————————————

Club Getaway 5 Kent Rd., Kent, CT 06757 203-927-3664

Executive Inn 969 Hopmeadow St., Simsbury, CT 06070 203-658- 2216

——————————————— Florida ———————————————

Park Suite Hotel 225 E. Altamonte Dr., Altamonte Springs, FL 32701 407-834-2400

Four Ambassadors Hotel 801 S. Bayshore Dr., Biscayne Bay, FL 33131

The Residence Inn by Marriott 5050 Ulmerton Rd., Clearwater, FL 34620 813-573-4444

The Inntowne Apts. Inc. 3111 University Dr.,Suite 533, Coral Springs, FL 33065 305-752-1144

Int'l Tennis Resort 651 Egret Circle, Delray Beach, FL 33444 305-272-4126

Sandestin Beach Hilton 5540 Hwy. 98 E., Destin, FL 32541 904-267-9500

Seascape Resort 100 Seascape Dr., Destin, FL 32541 904-837-9181

Galt Ocean Club 3800 Galt Ocean Dr., Fort Lauderdale, FL 33308

The Breakers of Ft. Lauderdale 909 Breakers Ave., Fort Lauderdale, FL 33304 305-566-8800

Comfort Suites 20091 Summerlin Rd., Fort Myers, FL 33908 813-466-1200

Boathouse Beach Resort 7630 Estero Blvd., Fort Myers Beach, FL 33931 813-463-8787

Seawatch on the Beach 6550 Estero Blvd., Fort Myers Beach, FL 33931- 813-463-4469

Sonesta Sanibel Harbour Resort 15610 McGregor Blvd., Fort Myers, FL 33908 813-466-4000

Plantation Beach Club 329 N.E. Tradewind Lane, Hutchinson Isl., FL 33494 305-225-0074

Quality Suites Melbourne 1665 N. State Rt. A1A, Indialantic, FL 3-2903 305-723-4222

Best Western Bradbury Suites 8277 Western Way Circle, Jacksonville, FL 32216 904-737-4477

Marina Del Mar Resort & Marina 527 Caribbean Dr. P.O.Box 1050, Key Largo, FL 33037 305-451-4107

The Suites At Key Largo 201 Ocean Dr., Key Largo, FL 33037 305-451-5081

Ocean Key House O Duval St., Key West, FL 33040 305-296- 7701

Days Lodge/East of EPCOT 5820 Spacecoast Pkwy., Kissimmee, FL 32741 305-396-7900

Lifetime of Vacations Resort 7770 W. Spacecoast Pkway, Kissimmee, FL 32741 305-396-3000

Orange Lake Country Club 8505 West Spacecoast Pkwy, Kissimmee, FL 32741

Fantasy World Club Villas Box 22193, Lake Buena Vista, FL 32741 305-396-1808

Vistana Resort P.O. Box 22051, Lake Buena Vista, FL 32830 305-239-3100

Villas-by-the-Sea 4500 N. Ocean Dr., Lauderdale-by-the-Sea, FL 33308 305-772-3550

Colony Beach Resort 1620 Gulf of Mexico Dr., Longboat Key, FL 33548 813-383-6464

Longboat Key Club 301 Gulf of Mexico Dr., Longboat Key, FL 33548 813-394-8860

Beach Club Of Marco Isl. 901 So. Collier Blvd., Marco Isl., FL 33937

Charter Club of Marco Isl. 700 S. Collier Blvd., Marco Isl., FL 33937 813-394-4192

Eagle's Nest Beach Resort 410 S. Collier Blvd., Marco Isl., FL 33937 813-394-5157

The Alexander 5225 Collins Ave., Miami Beach, FL 33140 305-865- 6500

Golden Strand Ocean Villas 17901 Collins Ave., Miami Beach, FL 33160 305-931-7000

The Roney Plaza 2301 Collins Ave., Miami Beach, FL 33139 305-531-8811

Embassy Suites Hotel 3974 N.W. S. River Rd., Miami Springs, FL 33142- 305-634-5000

The Ritz 1205 E. Silver Springs Blvd., Ocala, FL 32670 904-867-7700

Embassy Suites Hotel 8250 Jamaican Court, Orlando, FL 32819 305-345-8250

Grand Cypress Village One No. Jacaranda, Orlando, FL 32819

Pickett Suite Inn 7550 Augusta National Dr., Orlando, FL 32822 407-240-0555

Quality Inn Executive Suites 4855 S. Orange Blossom Trail, Orlando, FL 32809

Palm Beach Ocean Hotel 2770 & 2830 So. Ocean Blvd., Palm Beach, FL 33480

Best Western Village Inn 8240 No. Davis Hwy., Pensacola, FL 32514 904-479-1099

The Residence Inn by Marriott 7230 Plantation Rd., Pensacola, FL 32504 904-479-1000

Best Western Port St. Lucie 7900 So. US 1, Port St. Lucie, FL 3-4952 305-878-7600

Sandpiper Bay Resort 3500 SE Morningside Blvd., Port St. Lucie, FL 33452

Casa Ybel Resort 2255 W. Gulf Dr., Sanibel Isl., FL 33957 813-472-3145

Sanibel Cottages 2341 W. Gulf Dr., Sanibel Isl., FL 33957 800-237-8906

Song of the Sea 863 E. Gulf Dr., Sanibel Isl., FL 33957 813-472-2220

Tortuga Beach Club Resort 959 E. Gulf Dr., Sanibel Isl., FL 33957 813-481-3636

Benchmarks Inn Inc. 7085 S. Tamiami Trail, Suite B, Sarasota, FL -33581 813-923-7582

Beacher's Lodge 6970 A1A S., St. Augustine, FL 32086 904-471-8849

St. Augustine Beach Resort 1981 Rt. A1AS, St. Augustine, FL 32084 904- 471-9111

Gulf Winds Resort 6800 Sunset Way, St. Petersburg Beach, FL 33706 813-367-2131

Beekman Towers 9499 Collins Ave., Surfside, FL 33154 305-861-4801

Pickett Suite Hotel 3050 N. Rocky Point Dr. W., Tampa, FL 33607 813-888-8800

The Residence Inn by Marriott 3057 N. Rocky Point Dr. E., Tampa, FL 33607 813-887-5576

Innisbrook Resort P. O. Drawer 1088, Tarpon Springs, FL 34286 813-937-3124

Palm Beach Polo & Country Club 13198 Forest Hill Blvd., West Palm Beach, FL 33414 305-798-7000

Royce Hotel 1601 Belvedere, West Palm Beach, FL 33406 305-689-6400

Days Inn—Wildwood I-75 & FLA 44 Rte 2, Box 65E, Wildwood, FL 32785 904-748-2000

──────────── Georgia ────────────

Best Western Bradbury Suites 4500 Circle 75 Parkway, Atlanta, GA 30339 404-956-9919

Embassy Suites Hotel 3285 Peachtree Rd. N.E., Atlanta, GA 404-261-7733

French Quarter Suites 2780 Whitley Rd. NW, Atlanta, GA 30339 404-980-1900

Marriott Suites Atlanta Midtown 35 14th St., Atlanta, GA 30309 301-897-1197

The Residence Inn by Marriott 6096 Barfield Rd., Atlanta, GA 30328 404-252-5066

The Residence Inn by Marriott 2960 Piedmont Rd. N.E., Atlanta, GA 30305 404-239-0677

The Residence Inn by Marriott 1041 West Peachtree St., Atlanta, GA 30309 404-872-8885

Terrace Gardens Inn Suites 1500 Parkwood Circle, Atlanta, GA 30339 404-952-9595

Best Western All-Suite 200 Six Flags Rd., Austell, GA 30001 404-941-2255

Days Inn—Cartersville P.O. Box 1088, Cartersville, GA 30120 404-386-0350

Lodge on Shallowford 2792 Shallowford Rd., Chamblee, GA 30341 404-458-8821

The Residence Inn by Marriott 1901 Savoy Dr., Chamblee, GA 30341 404-455-4446

Comfort Inn Island Suites 711 Beachview Dr., Jekyll Isl., GA 31520 912-635-2261

The Residence Inn by Marriott 2771 Hardgrove Rd., Smyrna, GA 30080 404-433-8877

Sea Palms Golf/Tennis Resort 5445 Frederica Rd., St. Simons Isl., GA 31522 912-638-3351

──────────── Hawaii ────────────

Hanalei Colony Resort P.O. Box 206, Hanalei, Kauai, HI 96714 800-367-8047

2121 Ala Wai 2121 Ala Wai Blvd., Honolulu, HI 96815 808-922-8662

Coral Reef Hotel 2299 Kuhio Ave., Honolulu, HI 96815 808-922-1262

Outrigger Seaside Suite Hotel 440 Seaside Ave., Honolulu, HI 800-367-5170

Pacific Monarch 142 Uluniu Ave., Honolulu, HI 96815 808-923-9805

Waikiki Banyan 201 Ohua Ave., Honolulu, HI 96815

Waikiki Beach Tower 2470 Kalakaua Ave., Honolulu, HI 96815 808-926-6400

Waikiki Lanais 2452 Tusitala St., Honolulu, HI 96815 808-923-0994

Waikiki Sunset 229 Paoakalani Ave., Honolulu, HI 96815 808-922-0511

Ilima Hotel 445 Nohonani St., Honolulu, Oahu, HI 96815 808-923-1877

Imperial Hawaiian Resort 205 Lewers St., Honolulu, Oahu, HI 9681-5 808-923-1827

Island Colony Hotel 445 Seaside Ave., Honolulu, Oahu, HI 96815 808-923-2345

The Whaler 2481 Kaanapali Parkway, Kaanapali Beach-,Maui, HI 96761 808-531-5323

Royal Seacliff Resort 75-6040 Alii Dr., Kailua, Kona, HI 96740 808-329-8021

Kona By The Sea 75-6106 Alii Dr., Kailua, Kona, HI 96740 808-329-0200

Plantation Hale 484 Kuhio Hwy., Kapaa, Kauai, HI 96746 808-822-4-941

Pono Kai Resort 1250 Kuhio Hwy., Kapaa, Kauai, HI 96746 808-822-9831

Kihei Beach Resort 36 So. Kihei Rd., Kihei, Maui, HI 96753 808-879-2744

Kihei Resort 777 So. Kihei Rd., Kihei, Maui, HI 96753 808-946-6305

Royal Mauian Resort 2430 So. Kihei Rd., Kihei, Maui, HI 96753 808-879-1263

Kiahuna Hawaiiana Resort P. O. Box 369, Koloa, Kauai, HI 96756 808-742-7262

Lawai Beach 5017 Lawai Beach, Koloa, Kauai, HI 96756 808-742-9581

Poipu at Makahuena 1661 Pee Rd., Koloa, Kauai, HI 96756 808-742-9555

Kona Reef 75-5888 Alii Dr., Kona, HI 96740 808-329-4780

Mahana at Kaanapali 110 Kaanapali Shores Pl., Lahaina, Maui, HI 96761 808-661-8751

Napili Point Resort 5295 Honoapiilani Hwy., Lahaina, Maui, HI 96761 808-669-9222

Paki Maui 3615 Lower Honoapiilani Hwy., Lahaina, Maui, HI 96761 808-669-8235

Aston Kaanapali Shores 100 Kaanapali Shores Pl., Lahaina,Maui, HI 96761 808-667-2211

Aston Sands of Kahana 4299 Honoapiilani Hwy., Lahaina,Maui, HI 96761 808-669-0400

Kahana Villa 4242 Lower Honoapiilani Hwy., Lahaina,Maui, HI 96761 -808-669-5613

Kauai Hilton Beach Villas 4331 Kauai Beach Dr., Lihue, Kauai, HI 96766 808-245-1955
Manualoha at Poipu 4480 Ahukini #2 P.O.Box 173, Lihue, HI 96766 800-367-8020
Kaha Lani 4460 Nehe Rd., Lihue,Kauai, HI 96766 808-822-9331
Maalaea Banyans Hanoli St., Maalaea Village, Maui, HI 96761 800-367-5234
Valley Isle Resort 4327 Honoapiilani, Kaanapali, Maui, HI 96761 808-667-7858
Wavecrest Star Rt., Molokai, HI 96748 808-558-8101
Coconut Inn P.O. Box 10517, Napili Beach, Maui, HI 96761 800-367-8006
Suite Paradise-Makahuena 4480 Ahukini Rd.#2, Lihue, Kauai, HI 96766 800-367-8020
Suite Paradise-Poipu Crater 4480 Ahukini Rd.#2, Lihue, Kauai, HI 96766 800-367-8020
Suite Paradise-Poipu Kai 4480 Aukini Rd.#2, Lihue, Kauai, HI 96766 800-367-8020
The Shores at Waikoloa Star Rt. 5200, Waikoloa, HI 96743 808-885- 5001

―――――――――――――――――― Illinois ――――――――――――――――――

Executive Suites of 12 Oaks 1126 So. New Wilke Rd., Arlington Heights, IL 60005
312-394-3443
Ambasador West 1300 N. State Pkway, Chicago, IL 60610 312-787-7900
Delaware Towers 25 E. Delaware Pl., Chicago, IL 60611 312- 943-0161
Manilow Executive Suites 1030 N. State St., Chicago, IL 60610 312-787-6000
Marriott Suites Finley Rd. @ Butterfield Rd., Downers' Grove, IL 61515 301-897-1197
Radisson Suite Hotel 1400 Milwaukee Ave., Glenview, IL 60025 312- 803-9800
Radisson Suite Hotel 5500 N. River Rd., Rosemont, IL 60018 312-678-4000
Executive Suites Hotel 9450 W. Lawrence Ave., Schiller Park, IL 60176 312-678-2210
The Residence Inn by Marriott 9450 West Lawrence Ave., Schiller Park, IL
60176 312-678-2210

―――――――――――――――――― Indiana ――――――――――――――――――

The Residence Inn by Marriott 3553 Founders Rd., Indianapolis, IN 46268 317-872-0462
Howard Johnson's Best Western Jct. I-65 & U.S. 231, Remington, IN 47977 219-261-2181

―――――――――――――――――― Kansas ――――――――――――――――――

The Residence Inn by Marriott 6300 W. 110th St., Overland Park, KS 66211 913-491-3333
Lagniappe Inn 630 Westdale, Wichita, KS 67209
The Residence Inn by Marriott 120 W. Orme, Wichita, KS 67213 316-263-1061
The Residence Inn by Marriott 411 S. Webb Rd., Wichita, KS 67207 36-686-7331

―――――――――――――――――― Kentucky ――――――――――――――――――

The Residence Inn by Marriott 120 No. Hurstbourne Lane, Louisville, KY 40222
502-425-1821

―――――――――――――――――― Louisiana ――――――――――――――――――

Lagniappe Inn 710 No. Lobdell Ave., Baton Rouge, LA 70806 504-927-6700
The Residence Inn by Marriott 5522 Corporate Blvd., Baton Rouge, LA 70808
504-927-5630
The Residence Inn by Marriott 1001 Gould Dr., Bossier City, LA 7111-1 318-747-6220
Windsor Court Hotel 300 Gravier St., New Orleans, LA 70140 504-523- 6000

―――――――――――――――――― Maine ――――――――――――――――――

Ville Sur Mer Rt. T, P.O. Box 1330, Wells, ME 04090 207-646-7677

―――――――――――――――――― Maryland ――――――――――――――――――

Brookshire Hotel 120 E. Lombard St., Baltimore, MD 21202 301-625-1300
The Tremont Plaza 222 St. Paul Pl., Baltimore, MD 21202 301-727-2222

Marriott Suites Democracy Blvd. & Fernwood Rd., Bethesda, MD 20817 301-897-1197
Harbor Inn & Marina 101 N. Harbor Rd., St. Michaels, MD 21663 301-745-9001

─────────────────────── Massachusetts ───────────────────────

Island Country Club Inn Beach Rd., P.O. Box 1585, Martha's Vineyard, MA 02557
617-693-2002
Watermark Inn 603 Commercial St., Provincetown, MA 02657 617-487-2506

─────────────────────── Michigan ───────────────────────

Radisson Suite Hotel 37529 Grand River Ave., Farmington Hills, MI 313-477-7800
The Residence Inn by Marriott 2701 E. Beltline S.E., Grand Rapids, MI 49506
616-957-8111
Quality Suites 901 Delta Commerce Dr., Lansing, MI 48917 800-221-2222
The Residence Inn by Marriott 32650 Stephenson Hwy., Madison Heights, MI 48071
313-583-4322
The Residence Inn by Marriott 2600 Livernois Rd., Troy, MI 48083 313-689-6856

─────────────────────── Missouri ───────────────────────

Quality Suites-St.Louis 9075 Dunn Rd., Hazelwood, MO 63042 800-221-2222
Embassy Suites Hotel 220 W. 43rd St., Kansas City, MO 64111 816-756-1720
Raphael Hotel 325 Ward Parkway, Kansas City, MO 64112 816-756-3800
The Phillips House 106 W. 12th St., Kansas City, MO 64105 816-221-7000
The Residence Inn by Marriott 9900 NW Prairie View Rd., Kansas City, MO
64190 816-891-9009
Four Seasons Lodge P.O.Box 215, Lake Ozark, MO 65049 800-843-3010
The Residence Inn by Marriott 1550 East Raynell Pl., Springfield, MO 65804
417-883-7300
Northwest Inn 3570 N. Lindbergh Blvd., St. Ann, MO 63074 314-291-4940
The Mayfair 806 Mayfair Plaza, St. Louis, MO 63101

─────────────────────── Nebraska ───────────────────────

The Residence Inn by Marriott 200 S. 68th Pl., Lincoln, NE 68510 402-483-4900

─────────────────────── Nevada ───────────────────────

The Ridge Tahoe 400 Ridge Club Dr., Stateline, NV 89449 702-588-3553 800-648-3391

─────────────────────── New Hampshire ───────────────────────

Black Bear Lodge P. O. Box 357, Waterville Valley, NH 03223

─────────────────────── New Jersey ───────────────────────

The Atlantic Palace 1507 Boardwalk, Atlantic City, NJ 08401 609-344-1200
Sea Gull Motel 2nd St. N On The Ocean, Brigantine Beach, NJ 0820-3 609-266-7459
High Country Motor Inn Rt. 10 & US 202, Morris Plains, NJ 07950 201-539-7750
Quality Suites Fellowship Rd., Mt. Laurel, NJ 08054 800-221-2222
Betsy Ross 7999 Rt. 130 No., Pennsauken, NJ 08110 609-665- 7750
The Residence Inn by Marriott 900 Mays Landing Rd., Somers Point, NJ 08244
609-927-6400

─────────────────────── New Mexico ───────────────────────

Suite Simpatica 2530 Bloomfield Hwy., Farmington, NM 87401 505-327-4433
Village Lodge At Innsbrook 145 Innsbrook Rd., Ruidoso, NM 88345 505-258-5111
Triple Crowns Condominiums P. O. Box 306, Ruidoso Crowns, NM 88346 505-378-8080
The Residence Inn by Marriott 1698 Galisteo St., Santa Fe, NM 87501 505-988-7300

Quail Ridge Inn Taos Ski Valley Rd.,Box 707, Taos, NM 87571 505-776-2211

―――――――――――――――――― New York ――――――――――――――――――

The Beverly 50th & Lexington Ave., New York, NY 10022
The Lombardy 111 E. 56th St., New York, NY 10022 212-753-8600
The Lowell 28 E. 63rd St., New York, NY 10021 212-838-1400
Royal Concordia 150 W. 54th St., New York, NY 10022 212-838-1185
La Reserve Hotel 5 Barker Ave., White Plains, NY 10601 914-761-7700

―――――――――――――――――― North Carolina ―――――――――――――――――――

Best Western Airport Ex Suites I-85 at Tuckaseegee Rd., Charlotte, NC 28208
  704-399-1600
The Residence Inn by Marriott 5800 West Park Dr., Charlotte, NC 28210 704-527-8110
The Residence Inn by Marriott 9025 N. Tryon St., Charlotte, NC 2820-8 704-547-1122
Pickett Suite Hotel 2515 Meridian Parkway, Durham, NC 27709 919-361-4660
The Residence Inn by Marriott 2000 Veasley St., Greensboro, NC 2740-7 919-294-8600
Best Western Ocean Reef Suites US 158 Bus. Beach Rd, Box 1440, Kill Devil Hills, NC
  27948 919-441-1611
Fearington House Fearington Village Center, Pittsboro, NC 27312
Meredith Guest House 2603 The Village Court, Raleigh, NC 27607 919-787-2800
Quality Suites 4400 North Blvd., Raleigh, NC 27604 800-221-2222
The Residence Inn by Marriott 1000 Navaho Dr., Raleigh, NC 27609 919-878-6100
Shell Island 2700 No. Lumina Ave., Wrightsville Beach, NC 28480 919-256-5050

―――――――――――――――――― Ohio ――――――――――――――――――

Comfort Suites 11349 Reed Hartman Hwy., Cincinnati, OH 45241 513-530-5999
Pickett Suite Inn 300 Prestige Pl., Dayton, OH 513-436-2400
The Residence Inn by Marriott 7070 Poe Ave., Dayton, OH 45414 513-898-7764
The Residence Inn by Marriott 155 Prestige Pl., Miamisburg, OH 45342 513-434-7881
The Residence Inn by Marriott 6101 Trust Dr., Toledo, OH 43528 419-867-9555

―――――――――――――――――― Oklahoma ――――――――――――――――――

The Residence Inn by Marriott 2681 Jefferson St., Norman, OK 730-69 405-366-0900
Lexington Hotel Suites 1200 S. Meridian, Oklahoma City, OK 73108 405-943-7800
The Residence Inn by Marriott 4361 W. Reno Ave., Oklahoma City, OK 73107
  405-942-4500
Governors Inn of Tulsa 8338 E. 61st St. So., Tulsa, OK 74133 918-254-1404
Hawthorn Suites Tulsa 3501 S. 79th East Ave., Tulsa, OK 74145 918-663-3900
The Residence Inn by Marriott 8181 E. 41st. St. S., Tulsa, OK 74145 918-664-7241

―――――――――――――――――― Oregon ――――――――――――――――――

Embarcadero Resort Hotel 1000 S.E. Bay Blvd., Newport, OR 97365 503-265-8521

―――――――――――――――――― Pennsylvania ――――――――――――――――――

The Residence Inn by Marriott 600 W. Swedesford Rd., Berwyn, PA 19312 215-640-9494
Cove Haven Resort Rt. 590, Lakeville, PA 18438 717-226-2101
Pocono Palace Resort Rt. 209, Marshalls Creek, PA 18434 717-226-2101
Paradise Stream P. O. Box 940, Mount Pocono, PA 18438 717-226-2101
Quality Inn Chinatown Suites 1010 Race St., Philadelphia, PA 19107 215-922-1730
The Palace Hotel 18th. & Benjamin Franklin Pky., Philadelphia, PA 19103 215-963-2222
The Residence Inn by Marriott 700 Mansfield Ave., Pittsburgh, PA 15205 412-279-6300
Guest Quarters Suite Hotel 640 W. Germantown Pike, Plymouth Meeting, PA 19462
  215-834-8300

Caesars Brookdale Brookdale Rd., Scotrun, PA 18355 717-839-8843
Snow Ridge Village Star Rt. Box 37, White Haven, PA 18661 717-443-8428

──────────────── Rhode Island ────────────────

Inn on the Harbor 359 Thames St., Newport, RI 02840 401-849-3171

──────────────── South Carolina ────────────────

Wild Dunes 50 Marina Pl., Charleston, SC 29402 803-886-6000
The Residence Inn by Marriott 150 Stoneridge Dr., Columbia, SC 2922-1 800-779-7000
The Whitney Hotel 700 Woodrow St., Columbia, SC 29205 803-252-0845
The Residence Inn by Marriott 48 McPrice Court, Greenville, SC 2961-5 803-297-0099
Radisson Suites Hotel 12 Park Lane, Hilton Head Isl., SC 29928 803-686-5700
The Cottages Resort & Conf Ctr P.O. Box 7528, Hilton Head Isl., SC 22938 803-686-4424
Quality Suites 20 Patriots Point Rd., Mt. Pleasant, SC 29464 803-884-6402
Ocean Forest Villa 5601 No. Ocean Blvd., Myrtle Beach, SC 29577 803-449-9661
Radisson Resort at Kingston Plantation 9770 Kings Rd., Myrtle Beach, SC 29577
   803-449-0006
Ramada Inn Resort 5523 No. Ocean Blvd., Myrtle Beach, SC 29577 803-497-0044
The Residence Inn by Marriott 9011 Fairforest Rd., Spartanburg, SC 29305 803-576-3333

──────────────── Tennessee ────────────────

French Quarters Inn 2144 Madison Ave., Memphis, TN 38104 901-728-4000
The Residence Inn by Marriott 6141 Poplar Pike, Memphis, TN 38119 901-685-9595
Spence Manor Executive Hotel 11 Music Square East, Nashville, TN 37203 615-259-4400

──────────────── Texas ────────────────

AmeriSuites 6800 I-40 West, Amarillo, TX 79106 806-358-7943
Amberley Suites 1607 N. Watson Rd., Arlington, TX 76011 817-640-4444
Hawthorn Suites Arlington 2401 Brookhollow Plaza Dr., Arlington, TX 76006
   817-640-1188
The Residence Inn by Marriott 4020 IH 35 So., Austin, TX 78704 512-440-7722
Wyndham Hotel 6633 Travis St., Austin, TX 77030 713-534-6633
Dallas Plaza Hotel 1933 Main St., Dallas, TX 75201 214-741-7700
Hawthorne Suites-Mockingbird 7900 Brookriver Dr., Dallas, TX 75247 214-688-1010
AmeriSuites 8250 Gateway East, El Paso, TX 79907 915-591-9600
Lexington Hotel Suites 8401 West I-30, Fort Worth, TX 76116 817-560-0060
Casa Del Mar Hotel 6102 Seawall Blvd., Galveston, TX 77551 409-740-2431
Seaside Pointe 7820 Seawall Blvd., Galveston, TX 77551 409-744-6200
La Colombe d'Or 3410 Montrose Blvd., Houston, TX 77006 713-524-7999
AmeriSuites 3950 W. Airport Freeway, Irving, TX 75062 214-790-1950
Lexington Hotel Suites 1701 W. Airport Freeway, Irving, TX 75062 214-258-6226
Barcelona Court 5215 S. Loop 289, Lubbock, TX 79424 806-794-5353
The Residence Inn by Marriott 2551 S. Loop 289, Lubbock, TX 79423 806-745-1963
Casa Del Lago 600 Del Lago Blvd., Montgomery, TX 77356 409-582-6100 800-558-1317
Hawthorn Suites Hotel 250 Municipal Dr., Richardson, TX 75080 214-669-1000
AmeriSuites Hotel-No. 10950 Laureate Dr., San Antonio, TX 78249 512-691-1103
Amerisuites Hotel (Airport) 11221 San Pedro Ave., San Antonio, TX 78216 512-342-4800
The Residence Inn by Marriott 3303 Troup Hiway, Tyler, TX 75701 214-595-5188

──────────────── Utah ────────────────

Grand Hotel Galleria P.O.Box 680128, Park City, UT 84068 801-649-9598
Stein-Eriksen Lodge P.O.Box 3779, Park City, UT 84060 801-649-3700
Sun Creek Inn P.O. Box 3803, Park City, UT 84060 801-649-2687

──────────────── Virginia ────────────────

Guest Quarters 100 So. Reynolds St., Alexandria, VA 22304 703-370--9600
Marriott Suites Madison & St. Asaph St., Alexandria, VA 22314 301-897-1197
Presidential Gardens Hotel 3902 Executive Ave., Alexandria, VA 22305 703-836-4400
The Virginian 1500 Arlington Blvd., Arlington, VA 22204
Marriott Suites Washington/Dulles, Herndon, VA 22070 301-897-1197
The Residence Inn by Marriott 315 Elden St., Herndon, VA 22071
Comfort Suites 8710 Midlothian Tpke (I-60), Richmond, VA 23235 804-320-8900
The Residence Inn by Marriott 2121 Dickens Rd., Richmond, VA 23230 804-285-8200
Barclay Towers 809 Atlantic Ave., Virginia Beach, VA 23451 804-491-2700
Captain's Quarters Resort 304 28th St., Virginia Beach, VA 23451 804-491-1700
Virginia Beach Resort & Conf 2800 Shore Dr., Virginia Beach, VA 23451 804-481-9000
Quality Suites 152 Kingsgate Pkwy., Williamsburg, VA 23185 804-229-6800

──────────────── Washington ────────────────

The Residence Inn by Marriott 18200 Alderwood Mall Blvd., Lynnwood, WA 98037
206-771-1100
All Suite Inns-Birchwood 3445 So. 160th, Seattle, WA 98188 206-246- 8550
All Suite Inns-Innsbruck 3223 160th St., Seattle, WA 98188 206-241-2022
The Residence Inn by Marriott 16201 West Valley Hiway, Seattle, WA 98188
206-226-5500
Lee St. Manor 348 W. Lee St., Tumwater, WA 98501 206-943-8391
The Residence Inn by Marriott 8005 N.E. Parkway Dr., Vancouver, WA 98662
206-253-4800

──────────────── Washington D.C. ────────────────

Anthony Hotel 1823 "L" St., N.W., Washington, DC 20036 202-223-4320
Guest Quarters 801 New Hampshire Ave., N.W., Washington, DC 20037 202-785-2000
Guest Quarters 2500 Pennsylvania Ave., N.W., Washington, DC 20037 202-333-8060
Highland Hotel 1914 Connecticut Ave., N.W., Washington, DC 20009 202-797-2000
New Hampshire Suites 1121 New Hampshire Ave. NW, Washington, DC 20037
202-457-0565
Omni Georgetown 2121 "P" St., N.W., Washington, DC 20037 202-293-3100
Quality Inn Downtown 1315 16th St., N.W., Washington, DC 20036 202-232-8000
State Plaza Hotel 2117 "E" St., N.W., Washington, DC 20037 202-861-8200
The Capitol Hill 200 "C" St., S.E., Washington, DC 20003 202-543-6000
The Georgetown Dutch Inn 1075 Thomas Jefferson St. N.W., Washington, DC 20007
202-337-0900
The River Inn 924 25th St., N.W., Washington, DC 20037 202-337-7600

──────────────── Wisconsin ────────────────

The Residence Inn by Marriott 7275 N. Port Washington Rd., Glendale, WI 53217
608-833-8333
Quality Inn 650 Grand Canyon Dr., Madison, WI 53719 608-833-4200
The Residence Inn by Marriott 501 D'Onofrio Dr., Madison, WI 53719 603-833-8333

──────────────── Virgin Islands ────────────────

Queen's Quarter Box 770, Christiansted, St. Croix, VI 00820 809-778-3784
Gallows Point Box 58, St. John, VI 00830 809-776-6434
Secret Harbor Beach Box 7576 Charlotte Amalie, St. Thomas, VI 00801 809-775-6550

———————————————— Canada ————————————————

Obelisk I , Mississauga, ON
Pl. Royale , Mississauga, ON
L'Appartement Sherbrooke St., Montreal, PQ
Le Nouvel Hotel 1740 Dorchester West, Montreal, H3H 1R3, PQ 514-931-8841
The Thirty , Toronto, ON

———————————————— England ————————————————

Basil St. Apartments 15 Basil St., Knightsbridge, London, SW3 01-723-7252
Clifton Lodge 45 Egerton Grdn, Knightsbridge, London, SW3 01-584-0099
Knightsbridge Service Flats 45 Ennismore Gdn, Knightsbridge, London, SW3 2DF
 01-589-6297
Draycott House 10 Draycott Ave., London, SW3 2SA 01-584-4659
The Apartments 41 Draycott Pl., London, SW3 2SH 01-891-1042
Nell Gwynn House Sloane Ave., Chelsea, London, SW3 3AX 01-584-8317
Huntingdon House 200-222 Cromwell Rd., London, SW5 0SW 01-373-4525
Normandie Suites 165 Knightsbridge, London, SW7 01-589-2900
Ashburn Garden Apartments 3 & 4 Ashburn Garden, London, SW7 4DG 01-370-2663
Queen's Gate Apartments 26 Queen's Gate So., London, SW7 5JE 01-581-3424
Chancewell London 23 Greengarden House, London, W1M 5HD 01-935-9191
Eurodeals House 10 Westbourne Terrace, London, W2 3UW 01-402-13-38 01-606-2002
Garden House Suites 86-92 Kensington Gardens Sq., London, W2 4BB 01-727-0021
Clearlake Hotel 19 Prince of Wales Terrace, London, W8 5PQ 01-937-3274
Alexander Lodge 7-11 Beach House Rd., Croydon, Surrey, CR0 1JQ 01-681-1061
 01-681-1926

———————————————— French Polynesia ————————————————

Hotel Moana Beach Bora Bora, P.O. Box 156, Bora Bora

———————————————— Italy ————————————————

Residence Firenze Nova Via Panciatichi, 51, Firenze 477851
Residence J&J Via di Mezzo, 20, Firenze 240951
Residence La Fonte Via S. Felice a Ema, 29, Firenze 224421
Residence Miniresidence Via G. Caccini, 20, Firenze 410876
Residence Palazzo Ricasoli Via delle Mantellate, 2/6, Firenze 4-95001
Residence Porta Al Prato Via Ponte alle Mosse, 16, Firenze 50144- 055-354951
Residence Ricasoli Via Ricasoli, 8, Firenze 215267

———————————————— Mexico ————————————————

Fiesta Americana Plaza K.M. 11 Boulevard Kukulcan, Cancun, Yucatan 77500
 800-223-2332
Las Hadas P.O. Box 158, Manzanillo, Colima 52-333 800-228-3000
Coral Grande Hotel K.M. 8.5 Carr Barra de Navidad, Puerto Vallarta 800-527-5315

———————————————— Singapore ————————————————

Goodwood Park Hotel 22 Scotts Rd., Singapore 0922 800-877-2227

———————————————— West Germany ————————————————

Hotel Apparte Dusseldorf In der Donk 6, Dusseldorf-Reisholz 400 -0211-748-480

Office Suites

The following is a list of office suites, most of which offer office space, facilities and services for rent on a daily or short term basis. Call or write to inquire into the availability of those services you require. If you know of an office suite we don't list, kindly send us their name and address on the form in the back of the book.

Alabama

EBC Riverchase Galleria 3000 Riverchase Galleria, S800, Birmingham, AL 35244 205-985-3180

Proshare Executive Center, Inc. 130 Vulcan Rd., Suite 200, Birmingham, AL 35209 205-942-1158

Business Services Network 118 East Mobile St., Florence, AL 35630 205-767-7986

Arizona

CFN Corporate Quarters 7500 N. Dreamy Draw Dr # 200, Phoenix, AZ 85020 800-356-5265

Patrick Properties 4250 E. Camelback Rd, Ste.410K, Phoenix, AZ 85018 602-840-4350

Hemcor Development Co. 8283 N. Hayden Rd., Ste. 250, Scottsdale, AZ 85258 602-951-4500

Rio Salado Executive Suites 2121 S. Mill Ave., Suite 206, Tempe, AZ 85282 602-967-0019

California

HQ Alameda 1001 Marina Village Pkwy, #100, Alameda, CA 94501 415-748-8400

Gem Executive Suites 2105 S. Bascom Ave., Suite 350, Campbell, CA 95008 408-879-1300

HQ San Diego (Carlsbad) 701 Palomar Airport Rd, 3rd Fl, Carlsbad, CA 92009 619-931-9889

Execu-Quarters of Concord 1485 Enea Court, Ste 1330, Concord, CA 94520 415-798-1334

Metro Executive Offices 575 Anton Blvd., 3rd floor, Costa Mesa, CA 92626 714-432-6400

American Executive Center 19925 Stevens Creek Blvd., Cupertino, CA 95014 408-725-8885

HQ Emeryville 2000 Powell St., 7th floor, Emeryville, CA 94608 415-655-7511

HQ Fresno 83 East Shaw Ave, Suite 250, Fresno, CA 93710 209-227-1683

HQ Glendale 550 No. Brand, 7th floor, Glendale, CA 92103 818-507-1199

Office Management Services 100 N. Brand Blvd., Suite 200, Glendale, CA 91203 818-507-8119

Execuplan Exec. Office Suites 17100 Gillette Ave., Irvine, CA 92714 714-250-3300

HQ Irvine 1 Park Plaza, Suite 600, Irvine, CA 92714 714-852-4400

HQ San Diego (La Jolla) 8950 Villa La Jolla Dr., #1200, La Jolla, CA 92037 619-455-7490

Regents Executive Suites 4275 Executive Square, Ste 800, La Jolla, CA 92037 619-546-2800

Gateway Executive Suites, Inc. 14241 E Firestone Blvd,Ste.220, La Mirada, CA 90638 213-921-1997

HQ Larkspur (Marin County) 700 Larkspur Landing, Ste. 199, Larkspur, CA 94939 415-461-3500

HQ Long Beach 211 East Ocean Blvd., Long Beach, CA 90802 213-435-2308

HQ Long Beach (Park Tower) 5150 East Pacific Coast Hwy., Long Beach, CA 90804 213-498-0744

HQ Los Angeles (Century City) 1901 Ave. of the Stars, #1774, Los Angeles, CA 90045 213-227-6660

HQ Los Angeles Airport 6033 W. Century Blvd, Ste. 400, Los Angeles, CA 90045 213-645-6655

HQ Los Angeles/Century City II 2121 Ave. of the Stars, 6th fl, Los Angeles, CA 90067 213-551-6666

Gateway Suites 1801 Ave of the Stars, Ste.640, Los Angeles(Century City), CA 90067 213-553-6341

Executive Center at Shoreline 100 Shoreline Hwy, Suite 295B, Mill Valley, CA 94941 415-331-3030

Mountain Bay Business Center 444 Castro St., Suite 400, Mountain View, CA 94041 415-964-1676

HQ Newport Beach 4000 MacArthur Blvd, Ste. 3000, Newport Beach, CA 92660 714-851-6400

Bay Business Center 100 Hegenberger Rd., Ste 210, Oakland, CA 94621 415-568-7373

Executive Center at City Ctr. 505-14th St., Suite 300, Oakland, CA 94612 415-464-8000

HQ Oakland 2101 Webster St., Suite 1700, Oakland, CA 94612 415-446-7700

Headquarters Companies 2101 Webster St., Ste. 1700, Oakland, CA 94612 415-836-4503

Executive Business Centre 5820 Stoneridge Mall Rd, #100, Pleasanton, CA 94566 415-847-2001

HQ San Diego (Del Mar) 5151 Shoreham Pl., 3rd Floor, San Diego, CA 92122 619-546-5000

HQ San Diego (Downtown) 701 "B" St., 13th Floor, San Diego, CA 92101 619-231-0206

HQ San Diego (Rancho Bernardo) 11545 W Bernardo Crt., Ste.100, San Diego, CA 92128 619-451-7771

HQ San Diego/Golden Triang. II 4370 La Jolla Village, 4th Fl., San Diego, CA 92112 619-546-5000

HQ San Diego/Golden Triangle I 4350 La Jolla Village, 3rd Fl., San Diego, CA 92122 619-546-5000

Corporate Center 1 Hallidie Plaza, Ste 701, San Francisco, CA 94102 415-391-8240

HQ San Francisco 44 Montgomery St., 5th Floor, San Francisco, CA 94104 415-781-5000

Custom Executive Suites 2880 Zanker Rd., Suite 203, San Jose, CA 95134 408-432-7200

South Bay Business Center 3031 Tisch Way, Suite 200, San Jose, CA 95128 408-246-4444

HQ San Mateo 100 S. Elisworth Ave., 9th Fl., San Mateo, CA 94401 415-348-9066

HQ San Rafael (Marin County) 100 Smith Ranch Rd., Ste. 301, San Rafael, CA 94903 415-499-0770

HQ Sunnyvale 1250 Oakmead Prkwy, Suite 210, Sunnyvale, CA 94088 408-245-9910

HQ Walnut Creek 1990 N. California, Ste. 830, Walnut Creek, CA 94596 415-932-8600

──────────────── Colorado ────────────────

HQ Denver 999-18th St., Denver, CO 80202 303-298-9000

International Office Centers 1200 17th St, Suite 1950, Denver, CO 80202 303-572-6050

──────────────── Connecticut ────────────────

Corporate Executive Offices 2 Greenwich Plaza, Greenwich, CT 06830 203-622-1300

HQ Hartford One Corporate Center, 15th Fl., Hartford, CT 06103 203-247-1681

HQ Hartford II City Pl., 31st Floor, Hartford, CT 06103 203-275-6500

HQ Stamford Six Landmark Sqaure, 4th Floor, Stamford, CT 06901 203-325-9500

The Executive Suite 700 Canal St., Stamford, CT 06902 203-327-6868

American Executive Centers 191 Post Rd. West, Westport, CT 06880 203-226-2882

--------------------------------- Florida ---------------------------------

Corporate Suites 3511 W. Commercial, Suite 200, Ft. Lauderdale, FL 33309   305-739-3511
EBC Park Centre 4190 Belfort Rd., Suite 200, Jacksonville, FL 32216   904-733-7221
Kenney Executive Center, Inc. 407 Wekiva Springs Rd.,Ste.213, Longwood, FL 32779   407-862-7300
HQ Miami 801 Brickell Ave., 9th Floor, Miami, FL 33131   305-372-0220
World Executive Center, Inc. 1221 Brickell Ave, 9th floor, Miami, FL 33131   305-374-4611
EBC Heritage Court 5020 Tamiami Trail N., Ste 200, Naples, FL 33940   813-649-7377
Corporate Executive Offices 20801 Biscayne Blvd. Suite 400, No. Miami Beach, FL 33180   305-931-1616
HQ Orlando 20 No. Orange Ave, Ste. 1400, Orlando, FL 32801   305-425-5600
Busch Officentre Exec. Suites 9310 No. 16th St., Tampa, FL 33612   813-989-0514

--------------------------------- Georgia ---------------------------------

Crowne Offc Suites @ Perimeter 2344 Perimeter Park, Suite 100, Atlanta, GA 30341   404-455-1003
Crowne Offc Suites At Pavilion 5775 Peachtree Dunwoody,Ste200, Atlanta, GA 30342   404-255-1164
EBC Parkridge 85 No. 3125 Presidential Pkwy, S 200, Atlanta, GA 30340   404-451-1542
EBC Windy Hill Executive Ctr. 2470 Windy Hill Rd. Suite 100, Atlanta, GA 30067   404-956-1010
Executive Office Center 1100 Circle 75 Pkwy., Ste 800, Atlanta, GA 30339   404-892-9951
Executive Suites At Galleria 300 Galleria Prkway, Suite 400, Atlanta, GA 30339   404-956-9041
HQ Atlanta 100 Galleria Prkwy, Suite 400, Atlanta, GA 30339   404-953-7700
Howren Executive Services 1800 Water Pl., Suite 280, Atlanta, GA 30339   404-955-8911
Team Concept 1925 Century Blvd., #4, Atlanta, GA 30083   404-325-9754
Team Concept 3 Dunwoody Park, #103, Atlanta, GA 30338   404-393-0520
Tanner Hall Exec Alternatives 449 Pleasant Hill Rd., St 211, Lilburn, GA 30247   404-925-4065
EBC One Parkway Center 1850 Parkway Pl., Suite 420, Marietta, GA 30064   404-428-2103
Oaklake Executive Suites 5950 Live Oak Pkwy, Suite 130, Norcross, GA 30093   404-448-0087

--------------------------------- Illinois ---------------------------------

HQ Chicago (Loop) 40 West Madison, 14th Floor, Chicago, IL 60602   312-236-2525
HQ Chicago (N. Michigan Ave.) 980 No. Michigan Ave, 14th F, Chicago, IL 60611   312-642-5100
HQ Chicago (O'Hare) 8600 W. Bryn Mawr, Suite 200 N, Chicago, IL 60631   312-693-0444
International Office Centers 3 First National Plaza,Ste1616, Chicago, IL 60602   312-855-0443
Officenter / O'Hare, Inc. 2200 East Devon Ave, Suite 382, Des Plaines, IL 60018   312-297-6730
Suite One Executive Offices 1001 E. Touhy Ave., Suite 245, Des Plaines, IL 60018   312-699-4100
Superior Secretarial Services 6912 Main St., Downers Grove, IL 60516   312-960-2655
Select Office Service, Inc. 3033 Ogden Ave, Ste 203, Lisle, IL 60532   312-420-2300
HQ Chicago (Northbrook) 5 Revere Dr., 2nd Floor, Northbrook, IL 60062   312-564-3488
Execuspace One Northfield Plaza, Ste. 300, Northfield, IL 60093   312-446-0540
International Corporate Office 2021 Midwest Rd., Ste 300, Oak Brook, IL 60521   312-953-1234

HQ Chicago (Oakbrook) Mid America Plaza, Suite 800 S, Oakbrook Terrace, IL 60181 312-574-3666

Officenter/Oakbrook 17W755 Butterfield Rd., Oakbrook Terrace, IL 60181 312-627-1114

Officenter/Palatine 1230 West Northwest Hwy, Paletine, IL 60067 312-934-1550

HQ Chicago (Rolling Meadows) 1600 Golf Rd., 12th Floor, Rolling Meadows, IL 60008 312-364-6222

Sue's Office Service,Inc. 510 E Allen St., Springfield, IL 62702 217-525-0087

──────────────── Indiana ────────────────

May&Steele The Exec. Workplace 11711 N. Meridian St, #200, Carmel, IN 46032 317-843-5500

──────────────── Kansas ────────────────

Corporate Office Concepts 8500 College Blvd., Overland Park, KS 66212 913-451-8338

Executive Services, Inc. 949 S. Glendale, Wichita, KS 67218 316-683-1316

Executive Suites 1117 So. Rock Rd., Wichita, KS 67207 316-681-3333

──────────────── Kentucky ────────────────

Corporex Executive Suites. Inc. 1717 Dixie Hwy, Suite 400, Ft. Wright, KY 41011 606-331-8840

Attache Executive Center 4350 Brownsboro Rd., Suite 110, Louisville, KY 40207 502-893-4500

Professional Suites 233 West Broadway, Suite 1700, Louisville, KY 40202 502-589-5333

──────────────── Louisiana ────────────────

HQ New Orleans Canal Place One, Suite 2300, New Orleans, LA 70130 504-525-1175

──────────────── Maryland ────────────────

Executive Centre 3700 Koppers St. PO Box 2418, Baltimore, MD 21227 301-368-7066

HQ Baltimore 400 East Pratt St., 8th Fl., Baltimore, MD 21202 301-727-5250

InterOffice/Bethesda 3 Bethesda Metro Ctr.,Ste. 700, Bethesda, MD 20814 301-961-1900

InterOffice/Democracy Plaza 6701 Democracy Blvd., Ste. 300, Bethesda, MD 20817 301-571-9300

──────────────── Massachusetts ────────────────

Corporate Office Centers, Inc. 16 Haverhill St., Andover, MA 01810 617-475-0961

Executive Office Centers 303 Congress St., Boston, MA 02210 617-350-3030

Executive Office Centers 50 Staniford St., Boston, MA 02114 617-742-9550

HQ Boston 50 Milk St., 15th Floor, Boston, MA 02109 617-451-6888

International Trade House World Trade Center, Suite 400, Boston, MA 02210 617-439-5300

The Centres At Burlington 67 S. Bedford St., Ste 400W, Burlington, MA 01803 617-272-0541

HQ Cambridge 124 Mt. Auburn St., Cambridge, MA 02138 617-547-0222

The Office At One Kendall Sq. One Kendall Square, Suite 2200, Cambridge, MA 02139 617-577-1200

HQ Framingham 945 Concord St., Framingham, MA 01701 617-620-1790

REG Corporate Ltd. One Speen St., Framingham, MA 01701 617-879-1717

Corporate Office Centers, Inc. 585 Merrimack St., Lowell, MA 01852 617-452-6155

Key Executive Offices, Inc. 33 Boston Post Rd. West, Marlborough, MA 01752 617-481-0522

Office Suites At Jefferson Prk 800 Turnpike St. (Rt. 114), No. Andover, MA 01845 617-685-5440

N. Suburban Business Center 155 John St., Reading, MA 01867 617-944-8383
Cornerstone Executive Suites 800 Hingham St., Rockland, MA 02370 617-749-1933
The Office Center at Stow 132 Great Rd., Ste 200, Stow, MA 01775 617-897-3782
Executive Exchange Complex Inc. 155 W. St., Wilmington, MA 01887 617-270-3700

─────────────────── Michigan ───────────────────

HQ Detroit 400 Renaissance Ctr, Suite 500, Detroit, MI 48243 313-259-5422
AmeriCenters, Inc. 31800 Nortwestern Hwy, Ste 333, Farmington Hills, MI 48018 313-855-8484
Hartland Business Services 11636 Highland Rd., Hartland, MI 48029 313-632-6734
Executive Suites & Services 5955 W Main St., Kalamazoo, MI 49009 616-372-5955
Preferred Executive Offices 19852 Haggerty Rd., Livonia, MI 48152 313-464-2771
Plymouth Executive Service 340 N Main St., Ste 204, Plymouth, MI 48170 313-455-5353

─────────────────── Missouri ───────────────────

Bradlie Business Service 222 S. Bemiston, Clayton, MO 63105 314-726-2496
Hidden Creek Corporate Suites 14440 E 42nd St., Independence, MO 64055 816-373-6966
HQ Kansas City 4500 Main St., Suite 900, Kansas City, MO 64111 816-531-7474
Office at the Point 102 G Compass Point Dr., St. Charles, MO 63301 314-947-9999
Advantage Suites, LTD 12400 Olive Blvd., St. Louis, MO 63141 314-275-4400
HQ St. Louis (Clayton) 231 S. Berniston Ave., Ste.800, St. Louis, MO 63105 314-862-7444
HQ St. Louis (Creve Coeur) 555 N. New Ballas Rd., Ste.310, St. Louis, MO 63141 314-872-9600
HQ St. Louis (Downtown) 906 Olive, Penthouse, St. Louis, MO 63101 314-436-8300

─────────────────── New Hampshire ───────────────────

Northeast Business Centers,Inc. 71 Spitbrook Rd., Nashua, NH 03060 603-883-2255
Gateway Executive Center 18 Pelham Rd., Salem, NH 03079 603-893-5755
The Office 18 Center St., Wolfeboro, NH 03894 603-569-5818

─────────────────── New Jersey ───────────────────

HQ Mountain Lakes Mtn. Lakes Bus. Pk.-Bldg F, 115 Rt. 46, Mtn. Lakes, NJ 07046 201-402-9800
Office Gallery Bridgewater 981 US Hwy 22, Suite 2000, Bridgewater, NJ 08807 201-231-1811
Tarragon Executive Center 811 Church Rd., Cherry Hill, NJ 08002 609-663-5000
Complete Business Offices/Serv One Bridge Plaza, Suite 400, Fort Lee, NJ 07024 201-592-7200
Woodbridge Office Gallery, Inc. 555 US Hwy 1 So., Iselin, NJ 08830 201-750-2610
American Executive Centers One Greentree Centre, Ste. 201, Marlton, NJ 08053 609-596-8337
Office Gallery Princeton 5 Independence Way, Princeton, NJ 08540 609-452-8311
Offices Unlimited, Inc. Park 80 West, Plaza II, Saddle Brook, NJ 07662 201-843-3000
Complete Business Offices/Serv 345 Rt. 17, Upper Saddle River, NJ 07458 201-934-0200

─────────────────── New York ───────────────────

HQ Buffalo 300 Pearl St., 2nd Floor, Buffalo, NY 14202 716-881-6200
Willow Creek Executive Center 3729 Union Rd., Buffalo, NY 14224 716-631-3700
Corporate Executive Offices 599 Lexington Ave, New York, NY 10017 212-836-4888
HQ New York (Fifth Ave.) 730 Fifth Ave., 9th Floor, New York, NY 10019 212-333-8700
HQ New York (Park Ave.) 237 Park Ave., 21st Floor, New York, NY 10017 212-949-0722

The Office Alternative-NY 26 Broadway, Suite 400, New York, NY 10004 212-837-7700
HQ Rye 350 Theodore Fremd Ave., Rye, NY 10580 914-933-2500

——————————————— North Carolina ———————————————

EBC Europa Center 100 Europa Center, Chapel Hill, NC 27514 919-942-0981
Quorum Executive Suites 7506 East Independence Blvd, Charlotte, NC 28212
704-536-3005
EBC Park Forty Plaza 1000 Park Forty Plaza, Durham, NC 27713 919-544-3513
Cornwallis Square Exec. Suites 2100-J West Cornwallis Dr., Greensboro, NC 27408
919-288-9330
Lawndale North Executive Suite 1905-6 Ashwood Court, Greensboro, NC 27408
919-282-1014

————————————————————— Ohio —————————————————————

The Office Place 24200 Chagrin Blvd., Beachwood, OH 44122 216-464-7520
HQ Cincinnati 250 E. Fifth St., Suite 1500, Cincinnati, OH 45202 513-721-0900
HQ Cleveland East (Beachwood) 23200 Chagrin Blvd., 6th Floor, Cleveland, OH
44122 216-831-8220
Statler Executive Suites 1127 Euclid Ave., Cleveland, OH 44115 216-556-8050
HQ Columbus 65 East State St., Suite 1000, Columbus, OH 43215 614-464-1025
Statler Suites 6555 Busch Blvd., Columbus, OH 43229 614-888-4050
Dublin Office Suites, Inc. 4900 Blazer Parkway, Dublin (Columbus), OH 43017
614-766-3600
HQ Cleveland West 25000 Great Northern, 3rd Fl., No. Olmsted, OH 44070
Executive Place on the Parkway 3131 Executive Parkway, S300, Toledo, OH 43606
419-535-1118

——————————————————— Oklahoma ———————————————————

Park Suite on Main 3750 W Main, Suite AA, Norman, OK 73072 405-360-9238

———————————————————— Oregon ————————————————————

HQ Portland 1001 SW Fifth Ave., Suite 1000, Portland, OR 97204 503-221-0617

——————————————————— Pennsylvania ———————————————————

American Executive Centers 2 Bala Plaza, Suite 300, Bala Cynwyd, PA 19004
215-667-2555
American Executive Centers One Sentry Pkwy, Suite 6000, Blue Bell, PA 19422
215-825-6150
American Exec. Suites Headquar 630 Park Ave., King of Prussia, PA 19406
215-337-3707
American Executive Centers 900 East 8th Ave, Suite 300, King of Prussia, PA 19406
215-337-7757
American Executive Centers 1411 Walnut St., Suite 200, Philadelphia, PA 19102
215-569-2649
HQ Philadelphia 1801 Market St, Suite 1000, Philadelphia, PA 19103 215-569-9969

——————————————————— South Carolina ———————————————————

Executive Office Suites 2014 Harrell Square, Charleston, SC 29407 803-766-9900
Executive Suites, Inc. 123 Meeting St., Charleston, SC 29401 803-723-0585
Executive Suites, Inc. 3 Broad St., Charleston, SC 29401 803-723-2197
Executive Suites, Inc. 1517 Gregg St. at Taylor, Columbia, SC 29201 803-799-1419
Executive Suites, Inc. 1728 Main St., Columbia, SC 29201 803-765-2514

Executive Suites Inc. 105 No. Springs St., Greenville, SC 29601 803-242-4401
Executive Suite 200 Professional Building, Hilton Head Island, SC 29928 803-842-3737

─────────────────── Tennessee ───────────────────

Executive Place of the Commons 750 Old Hickory Blvd, Brentwood, TN 37027
615-371-6100
Winston Place Professional Ctr 104 East Park Dr., Bldg 300, Brentwood, TN 37027
615-371-6600
HQ Memphis 6055 Primacy Prkwy, Suite 401, Memphis, TN 38119 901-682-4090
Riverbluff Executive Suites 17 W Pontotoc, Memphis, TN 38103 901-521-1185
Perimeter Park Prof. Ctrl, Inc. 301 S Perimeter Park Dr., S1, Nashville, TN 37211
615-781-4200
The Professional Center, Inc. 162 4th Ave, N 1st Floor, Nashville, TN 37219
615-248-1984

───────────────────── Texas ─────────────────────

Echelon Executive Suites 9430 Research Blvd., Austin, TX 78759 512-345-2994
HQ Austin 701 Brazos St., 5th Floor, Austin, TX 78701 512-320-5820
HQ Corpus Christi 800 N. Shoreline Blvd, 2nd Fl., Corpus Christi, TX 78401 512-880-5700
A-Z Secretarial Service 2995 LBJ Freeway, Suite 200, Dallas, TX 75234 214-484-2823
CFN Corporate Quarters 1350 One Main Pl., Suite 1350, Dallas, TX 75202 214-653-1331
CFN Corporate Quarters 8080 Park Lane, Suite 600, Dallas, TX 75231 214-696-1331
ESP Management Company 2911 Turtle Creek Blvd,Ste.300, Dallas, TX 75219
214-522-1225
ESP Management Company 5430 LBJ Freeway, Suite 1600, Dallas, TX 75240
214-934-9555
ESP Management Company 6060 No. Central, Suite 560, Dallas, TX 75206
214-739-5533
Executive Suites of Dallas 8585 Stemmons Frwy, Ste. 770 S, Dallas, TX 75247
214-638-7230
HQ Dallas (Galleria) 13344 Noel Rd., Suite 500, Dallas, TX 75240 214-458-7391
Premier Place Executive Suites 5910 N Central Expressway, Dallas, TX 75206
214-891-6363
Professional Suites 1501 LBJ Freeway, Suite 550, Dallas, TX 75234 214-620-3100
Professional Suites 1700 Pacific Ave, Suite 1700, Dallas, TX 75201 214-922-9888
The Warwick Executive Suites 8080 N Central Expwy, Suite400, Dallas, TX 75206
214-891-8250
Turtle Creek Executive Service 3811 Turtle Creek Blvd, S 1000, Dallas, TX 75219
214-522-7540
Professional Suites 925 Interfirst Tower, Fort Worth, TX 76102 817-332-6581
Front Office 1700 One Riverway, Houston, TX 77056 713-840-8611
Superior Systms Secrtrl Servs 7007 Gulf Freeway, Suite 133, Houston, TX 77087
713-645-9609
Westheimer Plaza Suites, Inc. 5718 Westheimer, Suite 500, Houston, TX 77057
713-787-1000
ESP Management Company 5215 N O'Conner, 2nd Floor, Irving, TX 75039
214-934-2906
Penthouse Suites, Inc. 800 W. Airport Frwy, Suite 100, Irving, TX 75062 214-554-1936
Waterford Executive Suites 730 Nolana, McAllen, TX 78504 512-630-3800
Round Rock Executive Suites 1106 So. Mays, Round Rock, TX 78664 512-255-5021
HQ San Antonio 700 No. St. Mary's, 14th Fl, San Antonio, TX 78205 512-226-7666

HQ San Antonio (Bexar) 1777 NE Loop 410, Suite 600, San Antonio, TX 78217
512-820-2600
HQ San Antonio North 9901 I-10 West, 8th Floor, San Antonio, TX 78230 512-694-0876

———————————————————— Utah ————————————————————

Office Works 175 East 400 South, Suite 1000, Salt Lake City, UT 84111 801-350-9050

——————————————————— Virginia ———————————————————

Eisenhower Executive Suite 5400 Eisenhower Ave., Alexandria, VA 22304 703-823-6088
South St. Executive Offices 106 South St., Charlottesville, VA 22901 804-979-5007
Business Support Center 10686 Crestwood Dr., Manassas, VA 22110 703-368-4312
Tysons Business Center 8300 Boone Blvd., Suite 500, Vienna, VA 22180 703-848-9290

—————————————————— Washington ——————————————————

Business Service Center 10900 N.E. 8th St., Suite 900, Bellevue, WA 98004 206-454-3077
HQ Bellevue (Campus) 1611-116th N.E., Bellevue, WA 98004 206-646-3020
HQ Bellevue (Tower) 777-108th N.E., 6th Floor, Bellevue, WA 98004 206-646-3000
The Hansell Corporation 11812 N Creek Pkwy, N S 208, Bothell, WA 98011 206-483-4036
Lynnwood Executive Center 3400-188th SW, Suite 324, Lynnwood, WA 98037
206-774-4499
Redmond Executive Suites, Inc. 7981-168th Ave, NE, Redmond, WA 98052
206-882-0332
HQ Seattle 111 Third Ave., 7th Floor, Seattle, WA 98101 206-621-1020

——————————————————— Wisconsin ———————————————————

VIP Executive Center 16800 W Greenfield Ave, Brookfield, WI 53005 414-782-6363
Combined Executive Suites 104 S Main St., Fond du Lac, WI 54935 414-921-7170

————————————————— Quebec, Canada —————————————————

Execu-Centre, Inc. 1200 McGill College Suite 1100, Montreal, Canada, PQ H3B 4G7
514-393-1100
Travelex Business Center, Inc. 1253 McGill College Ave. #195, Montreal, Canada, PQ
H3B 2Y5 514-871-8616

Index

Hotels in bold may be found in the main listings; hotels in light
type are listed in the section titled "More All-Suite Hotels."

We have made every attempt to locate all the All-Suite hotels that are currently open; however, I am sure there are some we may not be aware of. If you know of an All-Suite hotel which is not listed here, please be so kind as to drop us a line at All-Suite Hotel Guide, P.O. Box 20429, Oakland, CA 94620. Thank you for the input.

I would like to (please check one):

_____ Recommend a new All-Suite Hotel   _____ Comment

_____ Critique   _____ Suggest

Name of Hotel _____

Address _____

_____

Phone _____

Comment _____

_____

_____

_____

_____

Please send your entries to:
The All-Suite Hotel Guide
P.O. Box 20429
Oakland, CA 94620

PUBLICATIONS

Available at your local bookstore or directly from John Muir Publications.

22 Days Series $6.95 each, 128 to 144 pp.

These pocket-size itinerary guidebooks are a refreshing departure from ordinary guidebooks. Each author has an in-depth knowledge of the region covered and offers 22 tested daily itineraries through their favorite parts of it. Included are not only "must see" attractions but also little-known villages and hidden "jewels" as well as valuable general information.

22 Days in Alaska by Pamela Lanier (68-0)
22 Days in American Southwest by Richard Harris (88-5)
22 Days in Asia by Roger Rapoport & Burl Willes (17-3) April '89
22 Days in Australia by John Gottberg (03-3)
22 Days in California by Roger Rapoport (93-1)
22 Days in China by Gaylon Duke & Zenia Victor (72-9)
22 Days in Dixie by Richard Polese (18-1) Fall '89
22 Days in Europe by Rick Steves (05-X), 3rd edition
22 Days in France by Rick Steves (07-6) March '89
22 Days in Germany, Austria & Switzerland by Rick Steves (02-5)
22 Days in Great Britain by Rick Steves (67-2)
22 Days in Hawaii by Arnold Schuchter (92-3)
22 Days in India by Anurag Mathur (87-7)
22 Days in Japan by David Old (73-7)
22 Days in Mexico by Steve Rogers & Tina Rosa (64-8)
22 Days in New England by Anne Wright (96-6) March '89
22 Days in New Zealand by Arnold Schuchter (86-9)
22 Days in Norway, Sweden & Denmark by Rick Steves (83-4)
22 Days in Pacific Northwest by Richard Harris (97-4)
22 Days in Spain & Portugal by Rick Steves (06-8)
22 Days in West Indies by Cyndy & Sam Morreale (74-5)

Undiscovered Islands of the Caribbean, Burl Willes $12.95 (80-X) 220 pp.

For the past decade, Burl Willes has been tracking down remote Caribbean getaways—the kind known only to the most adventurous traveler. Here he offers complete information on 32 islands—all you'll need to know for a vacation in an as yet undiscovered Paradise.

The Shopper's Guide to Mexico, Steve Rogers & Tina Rosa $9.95 (90-7) 200 pp.

The only comprehensive handbook for shopping in Mexico, this guide ferrets out little-known towns where the finest handicrafts are made and offers shopping techniques for judging quality, bargaining, and complete information on packaging, mailing and U.S. customs requirements.

People's Guide to Mexico, Carl Franz $14.95 (99-0) 600 pp.

Now in its 13th printing, this classic guide shows the traveler how to handle just about any situation that might arise while in Mexico. ". . .the best 360-degree coverage of traveling and short-term living in Mexico that's going." - *Whole Earth Epilog*

People's Guide to RV and Adventure Camping in Mexico, Carl Franz $13.95 (91-5) 356 pp.

The sequel to *The People's Guide to Mexico,* this revised guide focuses on both the special pleasures and challenges of RV travel in Mexico and on the excitment of non-vehicle adventure camping in Mexico. An unprecedented number of Americans and Canadians has discovered the advantages of RV and adventure travel in reaching remote villages and camping comfortably on beaches.

The On and Off the Road Cookbook, Carl Franz $8.50 (27-3) 272 pp.

Carl Franz, *(The People's Guide to Mexico)* and Lorena Havens offer a multitude of delicious alternatives to the usual campsite meals or roadside cheeseburgers. Over 120 proven recipes.

The Heart of Jerusalem, Arlynn Nellhaus $12.95 (79-6) 312 pp.

Denver Post journalist Arlynn Nellhaus draws on her vast experience in and knowledge of Jerusalem to give travelers a rare inside view and practical guide to the Golden City—from holy sites and religious observances to how to shop for toothpaste and use the telephone.

Buddhist America: Centers, Retreats, Practices, Don Morreale $12.95 (94-X) 356 pp.

The only comprehensive directory of Buddhist centers, this guide includes first-person narratives of individuals' retreat experiences. Invaluable for both newcomers and experienced practitioners who wish to expand their contacts within the American Buddhist Community.

Catholic America: Self-Renewal Centers & Retreats, Patricia Christian-Meyers $12.95 (20-3) 356 pp. April '89

The only comprehensive directory of Catholic self-renewal centers and retreats. Also includes articles by leading Catholic teachers.

A Traveler's Guide to Healing Centers & Retreats, Martine Rudee & Jonathan Blease $12.95 (15-7) 320 pp. April '89

A resource guide for travelers and any person wishing to locate and/or obtain detailed information about healing centers and retreats within North America.

Gypsying After 40, Bob Harris $12.95 (71-0) 312 pp.

Retirees Bob and Megan Harris offer a witty and informative guide to the "gypsying" lifestyle that has enriched their lives and can enrich yours. For 10 of the last 18 years they have traveled throughout the world living out of camper vans and boats. Their message is: "Anyone can do it!!"

Complete Guide to Bed & Breakfasts, Inns & Guest-houses, Pamela Lanier $13.95 (09-2) 520 pp.

Newly revised and the most complete directory, with over 4800 listings in all 50 states, 10 Canadian provinces, Puerto Rico and the U.S. Virgin Islands. This classic provides details on reservation services and indexes identifying inns noted for antiques, decor, conference facilities and gourmet food.

All-Suite Hotel Guide, Pamela Lanier $13.95 (08-4) 396 pp.

Pamela Lanier, author of *The Complete Guide to Bed & Breakfasts, Inns & Guest-houses,* now provides the discerning traveler with a list of over 800 all-suite hotels, both in the U.S. and internationally. Indispensable for families traveling with children or business people requiring an extra meeting room.

Elegant Small Hotels, Pamela Lanier $14.95 (10-6) 224 pp.

This lodging guide for discriminating travelers describes 204 American hotels characterized by exquisite rooms and suites and personal service *par excellence.* Includes small hotels in 39 states and the Caribbean, Mexico and Canada.

Mona Winks: Self-Guided Tours of Europe's Top Museums, Rick Steves $14.95 (85-0) 450 pp.

Here's a guide that will save you time, shoe leather and tired muscles. It's designed for people who want to get the most out of visiting the great museums of Europe. It covers 25 museums in London, Paris, Rome, Venice, Florence, Amsterdam, Munich, Madrid and Vienna.

Europe Through The Back Door, Rick Steves $12.95 (84-2) 404 pp.

Doubleday and Literary Guild Bookclub Selection.

For people who want to enjoy Europe more and spend less money doing it. In this revised edition, Rick shares more of his well-respected insights. He also describes his favorite "back doors"—less-visited destinations throughout Europe that are a wonderful addition to any European vacation.

Europe 101, Rick Steves & Gene Openshaw $12.95 (78-8) 372 pp.

The first and only jaunty history and art book for travelers makes castles, palaces and museums come alive. Both Steves and Openshaw hold degrees in European history, but their real education has come from escorting first-time visitors throughout Europe.

Asia Through The Back Door, Rick Steves & John Gottberg $11.95 (76-1) 336 pp.

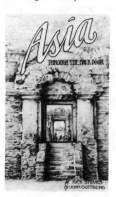

In this detailed guide book are information and advice you won't find elsewhere—including how to overcome culture shock, bargain in marketplaces, observe Buddhist temple etiquette and, possibly most important of all, how to eat noodles with chopsticks!

Traveler's Guide to Asian Culture, Kevin Chambers $12.95 (14-9) 356 pp. Spring '89

Veteran traveler in Asia, Kevin Chambers has written an accurate and enjoyable guide to the history and culture of this diverse continent.

Bus Touring: A Guide to Charter Vacations, USA, Stuart Warren & Douglas Bloch $9.95 (95-8) 192 pp.

For many people, bus touring is the ideal, relaxed and comfortable way to see America. The author has had years of experience as a bus tour conductor and writes in-depth about every aspect of bus touring to help passengers get the most pleasure for their money.

Road & Track's Used Car Classics, edited by Peter Bohr $12.95 (69-9) 272 pp.

Road & Track contributing editor Peter Bohr has compiled this collection of the magazine's "Used Car Classic" articles, updating them to include current market information. Over 70 makes and models of American, British, Italian, West German, Swedish and Japanese enthusiast cars built between 1953 and 1979 are featured.

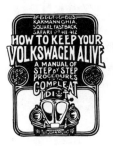

Automotive Repair Manuals

Each JMP automotive manual gives clear step-by-step instructions, together with illustrations that show exactly how each system in the vehicle comes apart and goes back together. They tell everything a novice or experienced mechanic needs to know to perform periodic maintenance, tune-ups, troubleshooting and repair of the brake, fuel and emission control, electrical, cooling, clutch, transmission, driveline, steering and suspension systems, and even rebuild the engine.

How To Keep Your Car Alive: A Basic Sanity Saver $14.95 (19-X) 208 pp. April '89

If you don't know a spark plug from a soup spoon, this book is for you. Gives the basic of how a car works, where things are and what they're called. Demystifies your auto and allows you to drive or talk to your mechanic with confidence. Color illustrations to enhance descriptions.

How To Keep Your VW Alive $17.95 (12-2) 384 pp. (revised)
How To Keep Your VW Rabbit Alive $17.95 (47-8) 440 pp.
How To Keep Your Honda Car Alive $17.95 (55-9) 272 pp.
How To Keep Your Subaru Alive $17.95 (49-4) 464 pp.
How To Keep Your Toyota Pick-Up Alive $17.95 (89-3) 400 pp.
How To Keep Your Datsun/Nissan Alive $22.95 (65-6) 544 pp.
How To Keep Your Honda ATC Alive $14.95 (45-1) 236 pp.
How To Keep Your Golf/Jetta Alive $17.95 (21-1) 200 pp. April '89

ITEM NO.			TITLE	EACH	QUAN.	TOTAL
		·				
		·				
		·				
		·				
		·				
		·				
		·				
		·				
		·				
		·				
		·				

Subtotals _____

Postage & handling (see ordering information)* _____

New Mexicans please add 5.625% tax _____

Total Amount Due _____

METHOD OF PAYMENT (circle one)   MC   VISA   AMEX   CHECK   MONEY ORDER

Credit Card Number   Expiration Date

☐☐☐☐☐☐☐☐☐☐☐☐☐☐☐☐☐☐☐   ☐☐-☐☐

Signature X _____
Required for Credit Card Purchases

Telephone: Office ( ) _____ Home ( ) _____

Name _____

Address _____

City _____ State _____ Zip _____

See reverse side for Ordering Information

ORDERING INFORMATION

Fill in the order blank. Be sure to add up all of the subtotals at the bottom of the order form, and give us the address whither your order will be whisked.

Postage & Handling

Your books will be sent to you via UPS (for U.S. destinations), and you will receive them in approximately 10 days from the time that we receive your order.

Include $2.75 for the first item ordered and add $.50 for each additional item to cover shipping and handling costs. UPS shipments to post office boxes take longer to arrive; if possible, please give us a street address.

For airmail within the U.S., enclose $4.00 per book for shipping and handling.

ALL FOREIGN ORDERS will be shipped surface rate. Please enclose $3.00 for the first item and $1.00 for each additional item. Please inquire for airmail rates.

Method of Payment

Your order may be paid by check, money order or credit card. We cannot be responsible for cash sent through the mail.

All payments must be in U.S. dollars drawn on a U.S. bank. Canadian postal money orders in U.S. dollars also accepted.

For VISA, Mastercard or American Express orders, use the order form or call (505) 982-4078. Books ordered on American Express cards can be shipped only to the billing address of the cardholder.

Sorry, no C.O.D.'s.

Residents of sunny New Mexico add 5.625% to the total.

Backorders

We will backorder all forthcoming and out-of-stock titles unless otherwise requested.

Address all orders and inquiries to:

JOHN MUIR PUBLICATIONS
P.O. Box 613
Santa Fe, NM 87504
(505) 982-4078

All prices subject to change without notice.